# JESUS HUMAN

## PRIMER FOR A COMMON HUMANITY
### SECOND EDITION

## LEONARD SWEET

The Salish Sea Press
Orcas Island
Washington

*Jesus Human: Primer for a Common Humanity*

ISBN softcover 2nd edition: 978-1-63613-027-9

Published by The Salish Sea Press. Box 1492, Absecon, NJ 08201
https://salishsea.press
https://www.facebook.com/thesalishseapress/

The Salish Sea Press is a program of SpiritVenture Ministries.
https://leonardsweet.com/

Copyright © 2023 by Leonard Sweet. All rights reserved.

Designed by Carmen Barber: keepingyouwriting@gmail.com
Cover designed by Sheri DePuy: sheridepuy.com.

Unless otherwise indicated, Scripture quotations are the author's own paraphrase. Other versions are noted in the back matter.

The Salish Sea Press

*To Tia Nicole Sweet*
*My daily mentor, tormentor, and incarnator of
a Jesus Human*

# CONTENTS

PREFACE ..................................................... ix

ACKNOWLEDGEMENTS ................................. xix

INTRODUCTION:
**Who Do You Think You Are?** ........................................... 23

PART ONE:
**Becoming a Jesus Human** ................................................. 39

PART TWO:
**You Need the Divine to Be Human** ................................. 75

PART THREE:
**We Dream, And Some Dreams are Inhumane** ............ 101

    Inhumane Dream #1: Religion ........................ 112

    Inhumane Dream #2: Intellectualism ............... 115

    Inhumane Dream #3: Nostalgia ....................... 122

    Inhumane Dream #4: Economics ................... 125

    Inhumane Dream #5: Politics .......................... 129

    Inhumane Dream #6: Celebrityhood ............... 134

    Inhumane Dream #7: Drugs ........................... 138

    Inhumane Dream #8: Technology ................... 143

    Inhumane Dream #9: Dreamlessness ............... 151

PART FOUR:
**Abecedary of a Global Jesus Humanity**..........155

**Abecedarium of a Jesus Human**..........163

𝔄 is for Adab (Sufi)(Arabic: أدب) Human..........163

𝔄 is for Adiaphora (Greek: Αδιαφόρα) Human ..........172

𝔄 is for Agape (Greek: αγάπη) Human..........183

𝔄 is for Asabiyyah (Arabic: العصابية) Human ..........196

𝔄 is for Ashram (Sanskrit: आश्रम) Human..........201

𝔅 is for Bespoke (British) Human ..........207

ℭ is for Carne (Spanish) Human ..........213

𝔇 is for Dao (Chinese: 道) Human ..........219

𝔈 is for Eucharist (Greek: Ευχαριστία) Human ..........226

𝔉 is for FUBAR (Pop Culture) Human ..........236

𝔊 is for Guanxi (Chinese: 關西) Human ..........243

ℌ is for Hehe (Mandarin: 呵呵) Human ..........246

ℌ is for Humanist (English) Human ..........254

ℑ is for Ikigai (Japanese: 生きがい) Human ..........259

𝔍 is for Jubilee (Hebrew: לבוי) Human ..........265

𝔍 is for Jyuuten or Juut (Japanese: ジュウテン) Human ..........274

𝕶 is for Komorebi (Japanese: こもれび)
Human .................................................................. 280

𝕷 is for Le (Mandarin: 乐) Human ................... 282

𝕷 is for Logos (Greek: Λογότυπα) Human ........ 285

𝕸 is for Mirrorworld (Economics) Human ......... 290

𝕸 is for Mandorla (Italian) Human .................... 296

𝕸 is for Monozukuri (Japanese: ものづくり)
Human .................................................................. 306

𝕹 is for Natsukashii (Japanese: 懐かしい)
Human .................................................................. 307

𝕺 is for Ostranenie (Russian: Остранение)
Human .................................................................. 310

𝕻 is for Paraklesis (Greek: Παράκλησις)
Human .................................................................. 315

𝕻 is for Pax (Latin) Human ............................... 318

𝕻 is for Pentimento (Italian) Human ................ 324

𝕻 is for Pentecostal (Greek: Πεντηκοστιανή)
Human .................................................................. 330

𝕼 is for Qubit (Physics/Scientese) Human ........ 334

𝕽 is for Ressourcement (French Vatican)
Human .................................................................. 338

𝕾 is for Saga (Icelandic) Human ....................... 350

𝕾 is for Satyagraha (Indian) Human ................ 359

- 𝕾 is for Scenius (Urban) Human .................. 370
- 𝕾 is for Sentipensante (Spanish: Sentimientos) Human .................. 371
- 𝕾 is for Shalom (Hebrew: שׁולם) Human .................. 380
- 𝕾 is for Sobremesa/Sobramesa (Spanish) Human .................. 391
- 𝕾 is for Sozo (Greek: σόζο) Human .................. 397
- 𝕿 is for Terroir (French) Human .................. 412
- 𝕿 is for Tong (Korean: 통) Human .................. 416
- 𝖀 is for Ubuntu (Nguni) Human .................. 425
- 𝖁 is for Verboten (German) Human .................. 430
- 𝖂 is for Wateca (Lakota) Human .................. 435
- 𝖃 is for Xenophiliac (Greek: Ξενοφιλικός) Human .................. 438
- 𝖄 is for Yada (Hebrew: עָדַי) Human .................. 441
- 𝖅 is for Zeitgeist (German) Human .................. 449

CONCLUSION:

**Humanly Possible** .................. 453

INTERACTIVES .................. 459

CONNECT WITH LEONARD .................. 479

SCRIPTURE VERSIONS .................. 481

NOTES .................. 483

# PREFACE

*In every hour the human race begins.*
ISRAELI PHILOSOPHER MARTIN BUBER (D. 1965)[1]

*Christianity is an entirely new way of being human.*
MAXIMUS THE CONFESSOR (D. 662)[2]

THE WORLD IS WONKY. People of every location and persuasion testify to this "something's-not-right" sense of a world gone awry and askew. We live in a world that is tearing itself apart, and tearing each other apart. "Is it time to panic yet?" is a natural response to erupting change that ruptures and rips the seams that tie a society together.

The world is losing its senses, because it is losing its sense of what it means to be human. Might the loudly lamented decline in the "value of human life" be partly due to the loss of understanding what it means to be "human" in the first place? The world desperately needs a culture of being human and a renewed understanding of the nature, destiny, and dreams of the human.

The question of "What is human?" is of crisis proportion.

Cambridge historian Richard Rex of Queen's College periodizes three great crises in the history of Christianity. In its early centuries the first crisis revolved around the theological question "What is God?" with all its adjacent questions of how many natures, how many persons, etc. The second crisis was an ecclesiological one, "What is the Church?" and precipitated the Reformation of the sixteenth century and the fragmentation of the Church.

Currently we are in the midst of the third crisis over the identity question of "What is man?" or "What does it mean to be human?"[3] Professor Rex memorably attaches to this anthropological question "an entire alphabet of beliefs and practices: abortion, bisexuality, contraception, divorce, euthanasia, family, gender, homosexuality, infertility treatment,"[4] but that is just the beginning. It goes much deeper than dancing on the hot tin roof of controversial topics. Is the human but a passing phase in the story of intelligent life on planet Earth? Do we join the flashy parade of techno-utopian transhumanism? Or does the human transcend the sun and the stars, the lion and the eagle?

**What's Going On Here?** The COVID lockdown of the human spirit proved more concussive and convulsive than the lockdown of our homes, schools, and businesses. But the ultimate pandemic in the world today is the pandemic of dehumanization which makes the COVID virus look like the sniffles.

# PREFACE

*Bewilderment at the wilderness men make
of what is human and humane.*
SCOTTISH POET LACHLAN MACKINNON, DOVES (2017)[5]

Humans are becoming more humanoid and less humane. We are in an anthropological emergency which *The Trends Journal* has called the "Devolution of Humanity."[6] We no longer know what a human is, either in unity or in diversity. Where once humans made machines, now machines make humans. And the machines humans do make are becoming our most preferred relationships. Few Christians even have an understanding of what it means to be a human in the same way Jesus was (and is). We want Jesus to be like us, rather than us to be like Jesus. We want to leave our humanity behind, when Jesus came to show us how to embrace our humanity fully.

It is our sacred duty to be human. That identity is not who we have become but who we were created to be. Two-stories identity is shaped around: the nature of ultimate reality and human destiny. There is no identity outside of story.[7] And the story of humanity is the story of the First to the Last Adam: the First Adam, a failed human, and the Last Adam, the consummate human—The Human One. Our identity crisis is only a crisis because we have failed to find our identity in Christ and in the storyline of humans created in the image of God.

The human race is a work in progress, or to be more theologically correct, a telic work in providence. In showing us the way to God, Jesus shows us the way to ourselves and the way to be human.

All of human life is here, in one story: The Bible. All that it means to be human is here, in one person: Jesus, the greatest human ever born on this earth. To become a follower of the World's Greatest Human is to live a Jesus humanity capable of driving out the money-changers, rebuking the Pharisees, or seeing in Nicodemus and Zaccheus the sort of persons who deeply yearn for eternity. Every life story has uneven chapters and challenging characters, and thereby hangs a tale.

When Jesus asked the Gerasene demoniac his name, he replied "Legion." He no longer claimed a human identity but admitted he was unworthy of a human name. But Jesus healed him, dispersed his diseases and dependencies, and restored his humanity. Now fully human, the Gerasene wanted to join Jesus with him on the road. But Jesus gave him the harder mission: go home, return to all those dysfunctional patterns and practices that helped make you who you are, and bring wholeness and healing to your habitation.

Learning to be a disciple of Jesus is learning to be a human being in a world that has been humaimed—our true identity has been amputated or disfigured. Archibald MacLeish concludes his "Ars Poetics" (1926) spin on Horace's classic poem with, "A poem should not mean/But be." Even more than true of a poem, a human "should not mean/But be." And in that being, find meaning and mission.

The Jesus story is about "being" human and "human" being—both of which follow from following Jesus. Jesus, the "Life-Giver" and "Author of Life."[8] Or as I put it in an Advent Series on YouTube, The Manual of Life is Emmanuel.[9] What kind of life? Human Life. Jesus gives back to us our full humanity as part of the redemption of all creation, "the restoration of all things."[10] Jesus doesn't help us rise above our humanity but enters our humanity.

*Let Him easter in us.*
JESUIT POET GERARD MANLEY HOPKINS (D. 1899)[11]

Jesus' healing of our human nature brings us, as Paul put it, "newness of life,"[12] and returns us to our original inheritance as true-pure humans: eternal life. By "eternal life" is understood not something that begins after this human life ends, but the eternal presence of the fullness of life in the here and the hereafter.[13]

Don't try to take life for yourself. Take life from Jesus to share with others. His life is the only kind of life that tills and fills, fulfills and thrills.[14] To put Jesus first is to say, I will be human first, and everything else second. Discipleship formation is really human formation.

When the practice of your Christianity leads to the diminishment of someone else's humanity, it's not Jesus Christianity. Christianity is nothing more than the intellectual reflections and institutional embodiments of the Jesus story, and the unfolding history of Jesus followers theologizing and moralizing about Christ's revelation and manifesting these understandings in something called "the Church."

People of God must decide quickly whether Christianity

is to be a religion against some humans and for other humans, or a faith for all humanity. This does not mean anything goes. But it does mean everyone feels invited. The Jesus gospel is a gospel of humanity. "Amazing Grace" is a Hymn to Humanity.

To be human is to have the right to be complicated and "contain multitudes." Humanity is a deeply mixed bag. The human is both humdrum and holy, mundane and macabre. Every human can check the "it's complicated" box. Humorist and writer Mark Twain liked to say that the human race, the only "race" there is, is a race of cowards and that he was "not only marching in the procession but carrying a banner."[15]

Shaun Bythell, a professional bookseller, has compiled a lifetime of stories about his customers into "Confessions of a Bookseller" (2022). He recalls the elderly man on crutches who bought "Advanced Sex: Explicit Positions for Explosive Lovemaking;" the customer who asked if the shop was named a "Bookshop" because it had books in it; and the customer who wanted self-help books, though he didn't know on what subject.

I am tempted to write a companion volume on innkeepers in the hospitality business whose clients asked if the blinking light in the smoke detector could be dimmed because it was keeping them up at night; or the people who complained about how difficult it was to sleep in when the pair of eagles outside their "Eagle's Nest Cottage" woke them up every morning with their cooing; or the people who said they were locked out because the key didn't work but there were two keys on their key chain and they kept using the

PREFACE

wrong one; or the couple that sat out in the rain with their dog waiting for someone to unlock the door when the door was unlocked all the time. Humans are a deeply mixed bag, indeed. Made a little lower than "Elohim," but getting lower ever since. The Russian invasion of Ukraine is living proof that humans cannot underestimate people's capacity for care, or for cruelty.

*Refusing to know God,*
*they soon didn't know how to be human either.*
APOSTLE PAUL[16]

You can't be human without the divine, which makes the process of becoming human, or humanation, part of the Trinity's ongoing incarnation as the Spirit brings Christ to life in each of us. Jesus was the most alive human who ever lived.[17]

There are thunderclouds in the skies over our white steeples and pealing belfries. Do we lean into, or away from, the plasticity of human nature? Do we embrace the adaptive possibilities promised by technology and move from demonizing to democratizing the techno-social revolution? How will we spend the 4000 weeks on average every human is given on Earth?

All humans come from the heart of God. Each of us is a custodian of the humanity of all of us. All of humanity throbs from the same heart. This is revealed early in the Sacred Story when God asks Cain, "Where is your brother?" Some human hearts are hard and closed, others are soft and open, still others are Teflon-hearted or undergoing heart failure. But regardless of the heart condition, we all share the same heartbeat.

Religious faith should not make us less conscious of global developments, but more. People of deep faith, some faith, and no faith must commit themselves to the joint project of protecting the human experience of the transcendent from the fanatics and the superstitious and the loonies and anyone else who would threaten the communality of human pain and guilt.

We are now in the business of simultaneously reconstructing personhood and redefining it after the twentieth century, the bloodiest century in history, introduced a new species of sub-humanity with an estimated minimum of 108 million people killed in its wars.[18]

**Make Mine the Same:** Every human being is made in the image of God—dirt marbled with the divine. The meeting place of the human and the divine is a material place. The uniqueness of our humanity is simple. Our material is made in the image of God, an astounding truth, found virtually nowhere else in ancient thought except among followers of Jesus. The assertion so struck the second-century Greek Bishop Irenaeus in its revolutionary ramifications that he built a whole theology on the incarnational "accustoming" of God to humankind. For humans to be created in the image of God is to carry the DNA of the divine, which is what one scholar argues is the best translation of LOGOS: "Divine DNA."[19] When preachers in the past ascended the spiral staircase to mount the high pulpit, they symbolically proclaimed their role as grafters of the divine and human long before DNA's twisting staircase was discovered.

Jesus did not die on the cross and rise from the dead to save souls. The Holy Spirit does not dematerialize us into a soul, but transfigures us into a new human being—mind, body, spirit. Jesus died to save all of us. Nor did Jesus come to turn us into Christians. Christianity is what we have done to Jesus. The word "Christian" and "human" are fundamentally the same—if by "human" one means "divinely human." God created humans to give voice to creation, and God gave us Jesus to give voice to humanity.

> *Before every person there marches an angel proclaiming, "Behold, the image of God."*
> JEWISH PROVERB

Jesus wasn't crucified for preaching a new and better religion, but for proclaiming the glorious news of the coming jubilee and a new era for humanity. Jesus rehumanized a dehumanized people called homo sapiens ("wise man"), a sentient species that has shown little evidence of living up to its sapient claim. Jesus is the perfect human who shows us a perfected humanity. A Jesus human is one who lives "The Perfect Life"—hospitable to hope, abiding in faith, extravagant in love.

There are other biological candidates for what it means to be distinctly human. Fire, bipedalism, stone tools, culture, teeth–these are all contenders for what stands at the heart of human evolution.[20] But theologically there is only one true candidate for what it means to be distinctly human: Jesus. There is no elixir that, when taken, transforms a person into a true human. But there is the Living Water of Life, Jesus. In a world where people do not know why they exist, Jesus came to show us what do with all of life.

**Dare to Dream:** This book has a simple thesis: Don't strive to be a Christian human being, a Catholic human being, a Protestant human being, or a Pentecostal human being. Desire to be a Jesus human being. A Jesus human. Long to belong and behold a Jesus human being. Dare to dream of a life that is truly human and truly Jesus. A Jesus human learns how to dream in two universal languages, to dream both human and divine dreams. Blue-sky dreaming of the heavens yields a blueprint for humanity.

Can the people of God aim for, pray for, and train for something that is larger than a packed auditorium and a gospel of bullet-points? Can we dare to daredream a new humanity?

# ACKNOWLEDGEMENTS

THERE IS A VERY BIG PRESENCE ON MY SHOULDER as I hand off *Jesus Human* to you. The presence has been pressing down on the two "tells" or ambitions of my life. First, I hope that my life "tells" more about the future than I imagine (which is not the same as being "on the right side of history" since history is not always right). Second, I hope that my life "tells" more about Jesus than I am worthy to speak or imagine possible.

Certain people stood by me when my "tells" weren't telling or were bagatelle brief. Daniel Schwabauer, one of the best writers I have ever mentored, let me know when I would whack the peg but never quite ding the bell. My colleague David McDonald called me on the carpet when I tended to be under-argued and over-exampled (and vice versa) and saved readers from a much longer and byzantine book.

Sometimes my writing can skip a beat. I am prone to rush from one theme or thesis to another, or my mind goes from one thought to three or four thoughts ahead, and then I write the first and fourth down, skipping the second and third. My friend Landrum Leavell III told me when I was skipping beats, and kept the manuscript from multiple arrhythmic seizures. Tim Hunt, who received the Nobel Prize in 2000 for medicine, describes research as "turning over stones and seeing what's underneath." My son Jeremiah Luke helped me turn over a lot of stones, real and research, in the process of writing, and I hope the two of us will do a book together some day.

In the final stages of this book, I used for the first time two wingbots (we used to call them "research assistants") named Bard and ChatGPT. Neither could be trusted, and their mistakes slowed me down tremendously. In fact, ChatGPT could be outright hostile to some of my more Christianese questions. But the laughter their blunders brought to my labor prevented me from firing them. My little AI experiment demonstrated vividly that the role of Artificial Intelligence in the future, as AI becomes more human and more real, is no laughing matter. The ultimate joke may be on us.

My "little brother" Dr. John David Sweet is a Presbyterian minister and Reformed theologian. I challenged him to read this book with a fine-tooth theological comb, making sure his Wesleyan brother, who is known for his slantways semiotic approach to life and the church, was still "contending for the faith once and for all delivered to the saints." Like John, I define "contending for the faith once delivered" to include Maimonides' thirteen articles of the Torah/rabbinical Jewish faith which say that there is only one living and true God (#2), almighty and sovereign (#1), omniscient (#10), infinite and eternal (#4), with only one God worthy of worship (#5), as well as the Nicene Creed's fundamental affirmation of the supremacy of Jesus Christ. My Solid Rock is the

## ACKNOWLEDGEMENTS

universal and eternal validity of the Gospel of the Lord and Savior Jesus Christ, mighty in word and deed, all miracles and titles—Incarnate, Crucified, Ascended, Risen, Rising, Reigning, Returning—the literal interpretation of all twelve articles of the Nicene and Apostles' Creed, a literal virgin Mary, bodily resurrection in the same body in which Christ suffered, a literal Second Coming, the trustworthiness of the Scriptures (though not "inerrant in history and science"), along with belief in the Trinity, Last Judgment, and two eternal destinies. Dr. John Sweet's verdict? In spite of my aggressively aphoristic approach to the topic of Jesus human, my left-brained brother deemed I was still a "contender." His imprimatur is important to me and I thank him for all the time he spent on the manuscript.

My copy editor, Carmen Barber, was superb as always, and my graphic designer Sheri DePuy lived up to all the accolades friend James O. Davis uttered when he recommended her to me. "People who write books take as much punishment as prizefighters," Norman Mailer insisted on television in 1971 in a head-butting argument with fellow-guest Gore Vidal. Without Carmen and Sheri, I would be receiving many more knock-out punishments than I am about to take.

This book was brought to a conclusion while I was teaching some marvelous doctoral students at Northwind Seminary, under the mantling aegis of Duane White from Beyond These Shores Ministries. It has been a high honor for me to study theological semiotics with these perceptive and agile minds: Perrianne Brownback, Paul Brownback, Dave

McGrew, Kris White, Rusty Griffin, Ryan Deaton, Trey Jones, Jody Andrews, Archie Callahan, and Paul Cole. All joined me in eavesdropping at the doors of different disciplines as we explored the semiotic intersections of church and culture, and all were open to being a laboratory for testing out some of the ideas of this book. I learned so much from all of you.

 I live in a modest house that we are making into a wonderland and storybook. When you truly inhabit a house, it becomes a living organism, a living manifesto, a living memorial, to the life you and your family are living. My wife Tia Nicole brings daily marvels and meanings to this wonderland we call "Sanctuary Seaside." Besides being my most trusted advisor, she is my ezer and encourager. Alexander Pope ends his "The Essay on Man" (1733-34) with a hope for "all human race" to be "with boundless beauty blest." I dedicate this book to her, the person who daily showers my life "with boundless beauty blest."

*Father's Day*
*Dolphin Cay, Orcas Island*
*18 June 2023*

# INTRODUCTION:
# WHO DO YOU THINK YOU ARE?

*Jesus is the most spotless being, the most deeply thinking and the most filled with love for humanity of any that ever appeared on earth.*

FATHER OF MODERN HISTORY LEOPOLD VON RANKE (D. 1886)[1]

**Latent Discovery:** POET W. H. AUDEN CALLED HIS free-verse poem "For the Time Being" his "Christmas Oratorio." The poem, which has also been given a musical setting, includes the familiar story of the three "Wise Men."

The first one says, "To discover how to be truthful now, is the reason I follow this star."

The second one says, "To discover how to be living now, is the reason I follow this star."

The third one says, "To discover how to be loving now, is the reason I follow this star."

The moving climax to oratorio when the three speak in unison states this: "To discover how to be human now is the reason we follow this star."[2]

Jesus is Truth. Yes, the truth about God, but also the

truth of what it means to be fully human. Jesus is how we discover how to be human. Jesus is our best shot at being human. Biblical scholar Walter Wink (d. 2012) calls Jesus "the archetype of the Human Being," or "the archetype of humanness."[3] Jesus' favorite phrase for himself was "Son of Man," which more literally translates as "The Human Being" or "The Human One."[4] The saving truth about God and the truth about humans are found in "The Human One," the God-human Jesus Christ whose hypostatic union (fully God, fully human in Nicaean terms) is the lens by which we understand all life, all reality, and the metacontext in which we "live, move, and have our being" in the words Paul quoted of the Athenian poet Epimenides of Crete (sixth to fifth century BCE).[5]

Johann Sebastian Bach celebrated in his *Christmas Oratorio* (1734) the birth of "the most beautiful of all human beings."[6] Why would we not want to share and show that beauty to everyone? Why would we want to hide the beauty under a basket, or keep the music of that beauty silent? The best advertisement for a human being is Jesus the Christ.

Alas, some of the worst advertisements for a human being are other Christians, which is a major reason for the number of people applying for debaptisms, the erasing of their names from church baptismal records.[7] "Inasmuch as you did it to the least of these," Jesus said, "you did it to me."[8] But "did it" does not just refer to positive things we do to help each other, but the negative things we do to hurt and harm each other. Every time we brand, or demonize, or hate another human, we brand, demonize, and hate Jesus as per those words: "the insults of those who insult you have fallen on me."⁹ Jesus is lashed and slashed by our abuse and hatred and stereotyping of each other. Jesus takes things personally. Things we say about each other and do to other humans matter to him.

And to be human means to be truthful now, to be living now, to be loving now.

> *[Jesus followers] do not commit adultery. . . . They do not give false testimony, they do not covet other people's goods, they honor father and mother and love their neighbors, they give just decisions. Whatever they do not want to happen to them, they do not do to another. They appeal to those who treat them unjustly and try to make them their friends. . . . they do not overlook widows and they save orphans; a Christian with possessions shares generously.*
> GREEK ORATOR AELIUS ARISTIDES (D. 181), "APOLOGY"¹⁰

Theologian and bishop John V. Taylor, in his Lambeth Interfaith Lecture of 1977, told two stories that still circulate among Franciscans. Here's the first one:

> St. Francis had a strange meeting with the [Muslim] Sala'din. They had no common language, so little dialogue can have taken place. Yet near the end of the encounter, Sala'din is reported to have said, "If I ever met a second Christian like you I would be willing to be baptized. But that will not happen."

The second story took place almost 300 years later, when a king in Peru said something very similar to a Franciscan friar, yet horribly different.

## JESUS HUMAN

> This friar, accompanying an expedition of the Conquistadores, was offering the vanquished Incas the choice of conversion or death. When their king demurred, his hands were cut off and the appeal was then repeated: "Be baptized and you will go to heaven." "No," said the king. "For if I went to heaven I might meet a second Christian like you."

It is possible to deny our unique vocation as human beings. No one is born a human, only the capacity to become one. A person becomes a human. Humanity is something that must be chosen. Humanity is not simply the sum of things that happen to us or the things we buy or the experiences we have. Humanity is the story which we write by our own choice.

◇

> *Lions do not throw up, shaken to the core, at not being adequately leonine. Elephants do not roll in the mud to vent their desolation at being so grossly elephantine. Whatever else does or does not separate us from animality, the potential to imagine and body forth transfiguration and to acknowledge disfiguration, is what makes us human. Our sense of indignity is the essence of our dignity. Non sum dignus.*
> 
> DOMINICAN FRIAR TIMOTHY RADCLIFFE[11]

Indian missionary theologian D. T. Niles (d. 1970) put it a little differently. "The 'dogness' of the dog is in the dog, but the 'manness' of the man is not in the man. It is in his relation to God. Man is man because he reflects God, and only when he does so."[12]

We are born latent humans, but born with the birthright to be humans. We live out our birthright.

**God Wants Your Body:** For the scientific world there are seven signs that distinguish what is non-living from what is living. If a particular thing has all of these characteristics/signs, it is a living thing. The signs of life are moving, respiration, sensitivity, growth, reproduction, excretion, and nutrition. A non-living object sometimes manifests one or more of these activities but not all of them. All of these activities must be present to turn a non-living object into a living organism.

What turns a living organism into a human is the breath of God. Not just any breath. Divine breath is what turned that first "living creature" into a "human creation." The Tree of Life is what kept the divine breathings pulsating through the garden and kept humans human. You can't be human without the divine, without something beyond yourself. In the Industrial Age, the human body was seen as a well-engineered machine. In the Biological Era, the human body was seen as a gang of cells. For Christians, the human body is the habitation of the divine.

*An artist can never be more or less than they are as a human being.*
MUSIC TEACHER NADIA BOULANGER (D. 1979)[13]

Just as in the garden God breathed into the First Adam the breath of human life; and just as in the garden tomb God breathed into the limp body of the Second Adam the breath of a restored humanity; so the risen Second Adam breathed into his lifeless disciples the rising Spirit ("receive the Holy Spirit")[14] and sent them out ("just as the Father has sent me, so send I you")[15] as rising specimens of a new humanity, ambassadors of a new creation, and priests of the true Temple of God, the body of Christ.

Human beings can't claim to be human if they aren't reaching beyond themselves and their beginnings. To be human is to be always reaching beyond yourself. The reach for the divine, the striving for self-transcendence, is the defining dimension of our humanity. A Jesus humanity is not a method of self-acceptance, but a path of self-transcendence and divine ascendance: "It is no longer I who live, but Christ who lives in me"[16] It is this self-transcendence that enables humans to put others first and eschew self-centered living.

Humanity is something that must be chosen. It is not simply the sum of things that happen to you, or the things you buy, or the experiences you have. Humanity is the story which we write by our own choices but in the context of a relational matrix of other storylines. You have to choose to be human.

> The human being becomes a person not primarily through what he himself does. Rather he is already given to himself with an inalienable dignity and an inalienable level of being. Nonetheless, the person's level of being and dignity consists precisely in the ability to

transcend and to realise himself, and this is in relationship to another.

~German theologian, philosopher and bishop Klaus Hemmerle (d. 1994)[17]

**Who Do You Think You Are?** Everyone's mission in life is to become human—the human God designed them to be from the foundations of the world. "Before I formed you in the womb I knew you, and before you were born I consecrated you."[18] This is the defining dimension of humankind: the quest for humanhood. A human being is not a condition, or a status. A human being is a task, a mission, a formation, an education.

And to be this, you need Jesus.[19] Humans don't "grow" like cabbages. To grow a cabbage, all that is added is water. A cabbage becomes a cabbage. To grow a human being adding water is not enough, although the waters of baptism become the sacraments of humanity.

> *Christ was baptized, that he might plunge the old Adam entirely in the water.*
> ARCHBISHOP OF CONSTANTINOPLE
> GREGORY NAZIANZEN (C. 390)[20]

What if we were to rethink Christianity at its most quotidian and sublime levels? Asked what was most lacking in the world today, Jewish theologian Abraham Heschel gave a one-word answer: "Creatureliness."[21] He may as well have said, "terrestrial humanity" or even, "planetarity."

The question of our age remains: what does it mean to

be human? How can we all participate in the overarching human story?

Or in more Christian-coded language, how can we follow the unconditional call of Jesus while at the same time supporting moral virtues from multiple religious traditions that are compatible with a humane and good society? Cosmopolitanism means "citizens of the cosmos." How can we be Christian and cosmopolitan at the same time? Or more succinctly, how can we be a globally integrated Christian?

*The early Christians did not say in dismay, "look what the world has come to," but in delight, "look what has come into the world."*

E. STANLEY JONES, ABUNDANT LIVING (1942)

We must learn to go where the action is: to walk with those of other faiths and none, to befriend those for whom religion is only a Prozac for the intellectually lazy,[22] to wrestle grimly and gamely with GRAINy (GRAIN is my acronym for Genetic Engineering, Robotics, AI, Infotech, and Nanotechnology) moral issues.[23] Do we lean in, or do we lean away from, the plasticity of our form? Do we embrace the adaptive possibilities promised by technology?[24] Do we reject the homogeneity that dominating forces seek to impose on us?

Christianity's chief concern and apologetic agenda in the twenty-first century may lie more with the flourishing of the defiantly humane, than with what it means to be Christian. The African bishop Saint Augustine (d. 430) was right:

"Make humanity your goal, and you will find your way to God."[25]

*Man is the only creature who refuses to be what he is.*
FRENCH PHILOSOPHER ALBERT CAMUS (1913–1960)[26]

**The Whatifs:** We are the most self-aware, self-actualized, self-preoccupied, self-analyzed, self-esteemized generation that have ever existed. Yet despite all this self-knowledge, we seem incapable of responding to the perils and possibilities confronting this planet. The narratives we consume from streaming services, YouTube, TikTok, Twitter B.E. or A.E. (before or after Elon), and other social media, last about as long as a joke. We need a meta-narrative, an originary dream that can enable people of diverse traditions to thrive in this rapidly changing planetary culture.

Have we lost the connection of our human experience as a Christological experience?

When did we stop seeing that our experience of living the humane and gracious life is actually a demonstration of our Christology?

When did we disconnect our ordinary human experiences with our theology?

Can we make room for one another of whatever stripe while urging the world to make room for Christ? And on a particular level, can we make Christ the heart of every room in our lives?

## JESUS HUMAN

***What if*** we are being called to be who we are, but by serving those who are different?

***What if*** the life of Jesus can point the way to a community of goodness, truth and beauty even for non-Christians?

***What if*** the power of Jesus did not point backward to the overriding of his humanity so much as forward to reveal the overriding potential of what it means to be fully human?

***What if*** Jesus, the fulfilment of the promises of the garden, reveals the garden pedigree and destiny of humanity?

***What if*** in Jesus' revelation of the future of humankind, Jesus is a proleptic human, a prophetic human, a pure human?

---

*Jesus Christ is the power and wisdom of God buried in every child born of a woman.*
ANNE SPERRY CONNORS

---

***What if*** being a Christian included:

* learning what it means to be fellow members of the human race with a disposition to help others,
* learning how to get along with other humans without betraying our common humanity,
* learning a common moral code of concord, of how to treat each other,
* learning universal human rights which are worth having and worth the bother of defending, a new elaboration of natural law in which people of no religious persuasion or diverse beliefs can participate,

* learning to love what God loves (creation, other creatures, etc.),
* learning to live with the risk of being wrong,
* learning to shiver together on the shores of faith,
* learning to start with the world, not with the church.

---

*To treat our neighbor who is in affliction with love is something like baptizing him.*
FRENCH PHILOSOPHER SIMONE WEIL (D. 1943)[27]

**What if** we need to live out of two very different conceptions of the good life: a humanist ethic rooted in ways we're alike (with common views about humanity, nature, and the human condition), and an evangelical ethic rooted in ways we're different (which locates the source of moral value outside the natural realm and finds its hope in the transcendent)? Australian Jesuit academic Gerald O'Collins puts the latter like this: Jesus was "God's human way of being and acting. Jesus was the beautiful, human face of God."[28]

**What if** the future begins with a common humanity? We all spring from the Earth. We all tread the same ground on planet Earth. We all breathe the same air. We all bear the same wounds of broken promises, broken ambitions, broken hearts. We all share a common humanity in need of healing.

**What if** disciples of Jesus are being called to write a new, re-humanized history for the human race featuring the value of every person, the virtue of human interconnectedness, the moral claims of the Stranger, and other planks in a shared Human Manifesto for Planet Earth?

## JESUS HUMAN

*What if* a local/particular, global/universal, and decentralized/hypercentralized world is calling for a new identity to emerge—a Jesus humanist? As a Jesus follower, the meaning of life is Christ. As a humanist, the meaning of life is living together on this planet in ethical, honest, humane ways.[29]

*What if* our humanist universal agenda were to reconcile humans to each other?

*What if* our Jesus particularity were to reconcile humans universally to God?

*What if* our dominant political voices were humanist universal, while our dominant religious voices were Jesus particular?

Have we lost the connection of our human experience as a Christological experience? When did we stop seeing that our experience of living the humane and gracious life is actually a demonstration of our Christology? When did we disconnect our ordinary human experiences with our theology?

Can we make room for one another of whatever stripe while urging the world to make room for Christ? And on a particular level, can we make Christ the heart of every room in our lives?

*What if* we need to develop both a more particular faith and a more universal, humanist, even planetarist spirituality?[30] The former lifts up Christ; the latter lifts up planetary personhood. In fact, it may be more accurate to speak of the particular as a faith religion, and the planetary as a civil religion. Ironically, it's the globalizing forces that make us want to underline our identities, that nurture the need for a punctuated sense of particularity and tribe.

***What if*** Jesus opens up new possibilities for humanity and brings to Earth a cosmic energy called the Holy Spirit that brings Christ to life in every time and place and person?

***What if*** the religions of the world living next door to each other need to learn the side-by-side embrace before they try any face-to-face embrace? What if the doctrine of "equal regard" does not mean equal status or moral equivalence but mutuality of cooperation and reciprocity of partnerships? What if impartiality does not imply neutrality?

***What if*** a whole human being has one side facing God and another side facing other humans?

***What if*** the time has come for Jesus humans to develop a Global Citizens Portfolio?

***What if*** we talked less of discipleship training or spiritual formation than human formation or life formation or even Whole Life formation?

***What if*** the best theology were a lifeology—a life well-played, well-prayed, well-spent, well-served?

***What if*** our communities weren't so much in the Christianity/church business but in the Jesus-human formation business?

***What if*** the body of Christ is the body of a new creation, a new humanity filled with the forerunners of a new human being?

***What if*** the church, the *Ecclesia Mater*, the *Mystici Corporis*, is constantly giving birth (through preaching, sacraments, prayer, and service) to a new humanity in Christ?

***What if*** we were to dream big and wild about the new, pure, and true humanity that history now summons into

## JESUS HUMAN

being, which is shared by all humans of all religious traditions? The unleashing of the human spirit is an agenda all religions can agree on. All religions can recognize as idolatry our human attempt to make ourselves the source of the sacred.

***What if*** a Jesus human is how humans who fall apart can come back together?

---

*If being ordained meant being set apart from them, then I did not want to be ordained anymore. I wanted to be human.*
LEAVING CHURCH (2006) BY BARBARA BROWN TAYLOR[31]

---

***What if*** Jesus is The New Man, The New Adam, the firstborn of the New Creation, the earnest of the New Earth, the image-bearer of a new humanity, the Prototype Adam of a new race of human beings?

***What if*** Pilate got Jesus right as the paradigmatic human when he looked at the man in purple robes and a crown of thorns standing in front of him and said, "Behold the Human?"[32]

***What if*** Jesus is the place and the person where God meets humans and through him this new creation is birthed through the creative power of the Holy Spirt?

***What if*** Jesus transcends in his personhood all that was imagined in all religions before his coming?

***What if*** Jesus is not just in the resurrection of the dead business? As Mexican novelist Carlos Fuentes (c. 2012) liked to put it, "He revives the living. Jesus is the copy editor of human life."[33]

***What if*** the highest human is the "Christ-in-me" human, and the highest humanity is the "Christ-in-us" humanity?

The Wesleyan "grand depositum," the doctrine of "holiness of heart and life" or "Christian perfection" is wrongly formulated and framed in moralistic terms.[34] Sanctification is only properly understood in the context of gracious growth to full humanity.[35] No person is born fully human. You maturate into wholeness. Humans must grow by learnings, listenings, and languages; by deaths and resurrections; by hurts and healings; by growing pains and lurking joys. But most of all, to grow a human being you need Jesus.[36]

I want to be a Jesus human. This is the greatest ambition of my life—to have been, to be, and to become a Jesus human.

## PART ONE:
# BECOMING A JESUS HUMAN

*To be dead is to stop believing in
The masterpieces we will begin tomorrow.*
IRISH POET PATRICK KAVANAGH (D. 1967)[1]

**Hard to Be Human:** IT'S NOT EASY TO BE HUMAN. It may well be the hardest thing you will ever do. It will take as long as you've got, a whole lifetime, to get it right. Becoming human is a slow process. Ludwig Wittgenstein used to say: "The best philosophers go slowest."[2] They take the slow routes to experience and explore the bumps and the bridges as they go across them. The Bible itself presents a variety of views on what it means to be human: some pessimistic (Ecclesiastes), some optimistic (Psalms). All that is wrong in the human heart is not easy to purify. Homo sapiens can become homo stupids very quickly. There is a French phrase *"un travail de benedictin"* which roughly translates as "a Benedictine labor."

Being human is something that takes patient, steady effort to bring to fruition—a Benedictine labor.

## JESUS HUMAN

> *You don't know what you've got till it's gone.*
> *They paved Paradise, put up a parking lot.*
> JONI MITCHELL[3]

Of the three greatest essayists of the late twentieth century (Mailer, Vidal, and Steiner), Gore Vidal sees the human situation with the most penetrating lenses.[4] Here is his pessimism about humanity, as communicated in *Myra Breckenridge*: "we are the constant and compulsive killers of life, the mad dogs of creation, and our triumphant viral progress can only end in a burst of cleansing solar fire."[5]

Homo sapiens are the only bozos on the bus who drive it off the cliffs and enjoy the suicide ride. To be sure, it is amazing to see how much goodness, generosity, and grace there can be in ordinary people—a never-ending miracle! This is especially the case after the modern moral code taught that a "real man" doesn't need others, shouldn't be weak, show emotion, or admit vulnerability—in other words, shouldn't be HUMAN.

But after the horrors of the last century, which should be called the genocide century because of its uberhuman dreams built on mountains of human skulls, we learned that homo sapiens are capable of anything. Human nature is a slippery slope into Hannibal Lecter land, and one that we slide into very quickly.[6]

## BECOMING A JESUS HUMAN

*As often as I have been with men, I have returned less a man.*
LAMENT OF THOMAS À KEMPIS (D. 1471)[7]

The basic imperfections of the human condition are always with us. We may reconcile ourselves to the permanence of human imperfection because imperfection is the shared condition of humanity. But we must never reconcile ourselves to the impermanence of life's highest moments, which are windows into the heart of God. Jesus can change a heart in a heartbeat. But it takes a lifetime of heartbeats for a changed heart to become a Christ heart. We live each day by paying honor and homage to a pure heart full of highest moments.

*Why, he wondered, swerving the car to avoid a dead pye-dog, do I love this place [colonial West Africa] so much? Is it because here human nature hasn't had time to disguise itself? Nobody could ever talk about a heaven on earth. Heaven remained rigidly in its proper place, on the other side of death, and on this side flourished the injustices, the cruelties, the meanness that elsewhere people so cleverly hushed up. Here you could love human beings nearly as God loved them, knowing the worst; you didn't love a pose, a pretty dress, a sentiment artfully assumed.*
NOVELIST GRAHAM GREENE, *HEART OF THE MATTER* (1948)[8]

If humans are not to become a diminishing blot on creation, the need for a new kind of human is greater now than ever. In 1963, the great psychologist Abraham Maslow wrote these words in an essay entitled "The Creative Attitude:"

> It seems to me that we are at a point in history unlike anything that has ever been before. Life moves far more rapidly now than it ever did before. Think, for instance, of the huge acceleration in the rate of growth of facts, of knowledge, of techniques, of inventions, of advances in technology. It seems very obvious to me that this requires a change in our attitude toward the human being, and toward his relationships to the world. To put it bluntly, we need a different kind of human being. . . . We need a different kind of human being to be able to live in a world which changes perpetually, which doesn't stand still. . . . A new kind of human being who is comfortable with change, who enjoys change, who is able to improvise, who is able to face with confidence, strength, and courage a situation of which he has absolutely no forewarning. . . . The society which can turn out such people will survive; the societies that cannot turn out such people will die.[9]

What are the key features of this new kind of human? How can you become a true kind of human? What are the constants of the human spirit that cut across all historical, cultural, geographical, and religious divides? What are the indigenous modes of imagining for the species we call "human?"

Relating to non-Christian, unchurched people as "us and them" is a bad place to begin. Accepting them as one of "us" from the standpoint of our common humanity can build emotional and relational bridges over which they may eventually cross. Enlarging our circle of love is something we must always be doing, but including those who have yet to believe within our circles of relationships is important. We must build the habit of extending acceptance, as Jesus did, and hope for genuine repentance.

**New Kind of Human:** God's dream for the world is a new creation with a new kind of human. God's dream for the world is a human with a new heart, a pure heart, or more precisely, a TRUE kind of human. Jesus is the fulfillment and flowering of God's dream for humanity, the dream of Jubilee. God is in everything God made, especially and including you.[10] Our ancestors were closer to this divine sensibility than we can appreciate; they saw every animal and every plant as a manifestation of some great truth and an inspiration for faith. "Consider the lilies," Jesus said.[11] Consider what it means to be human; learn from the plants and the animals. "Look deep into nature and then you will understand everything better," wrote Albert Einstein.

The veil of the divine is lifted a bit in everything God made, and in everything God created we can see marks of the Creator. The more we see and absorb those markings, the more the glorious image of God we bear and the more we shine the divine light, even in the most grievous of times. "Lead, kindly light, amid the encircling gloom."[12]

JESUS HUMAN

**How Small We Are, How Big God Is:** In its first year, J.B. Phillips' *Your God is Too Small* (1953) sold a million copies. It has become a classic of Christian literature, as well as a popular meme to critique the iron-clad cramps of organized religion, the haltering of the Spirit, and the judging offishness of claimants to Christ.

The world needs someone to write a new book, "Your World Is Too Small." Or even, "Your God is Too Possible."

One of the most popular college religion texts, Phil Zuckermann's *Invitation to the Sociology of Religion* (2003) says that the truth claims of religion are "mind-boggling, implausible," "fantastical," "manifestly unbelievable."[13]

I say: Now you're talking, Dr. Zuckermann. For the very category of "impossible" is God's category. The impossible is the very definition of God. So if you tell me the truth claims of Jesus are "impossible," I say, "Hallelujah!" It's only when you cross the border from the possible to the impossible that you're in God's territory. Faith does NOT stand to reason.

Or to quote Adidas, who stole one of our lines like the T-shirt company "No Fear" stole another one (and owes Christianity massive royalty payments): "Impossible is Nothing."

You tell me the incarnation is "impossible."

I say: Impossible is nothing. For "impossible" is the canon of faith, not the category of logic. It's the "madness of the impossible."

You tell me the resurrection is "impossible."

I say: Impossible is nothing . . . For God specializes in the unexpected and unexplainable, in things thought impossible:

"Got any rivers you think are uncrossable? Got any mountains you can't tunnel through?" It's the "madness of the impossible."

*What you can plan is too small for you to live.*
PACIFIC NORTH WEST POET DAVID WHYTE[14]

You tell me a new kind of human is impossible in an old kind of world.

I say: impossible is nothing. In *Paradise Lost*, the disciples of Jesus settle for nothing less than *Paradise Regained*.

**Morning Has Broken?** Politics may be called the "art of the possible." But religion is the art of the impossible. Jesus humans are people who refuse to conform to the limits of the possible: they practice immoderate, intemperate, odd, double-dare dreams such as love your enemies, overcome evil with good, die to yourself, and forgive seventy times seven times. Walter Benjamin insisted on the inseparability of history and dreams. History, he argued, was not simply a record of the past, but a dream of the future. "Every epoch dreams the one to follow. The awakening to this dream image is the morning of history."[15] For morning to break, history and dreaming must join hands.

One of my favorite biblical expressions is Mary's words of wonderment: "How can this be?"[16] If you aren't hearing or saying these words—"How can these things be?"—it's not God.

You say: Impossible! Jesus says: Impossible is nothing with me!

## JESUS HUMAN

> *O to break loose, like the Chinook*
> *salmon jumping and falling back,*
> *nosing up to the impossible*
> *stone and bone crushing waterfall*
> *raw-jawed, weak fleshed there, stopped by*
> *ten steps of the roaring ladder, and then*
> *to clear the top on the last try,*
> *alive enough to spawn and die.*
>
> POET ROBERT LOWELL (D. 1977)[17]

Not everyone will choose to be a Jesus human. Even on the cross, Jesus himself only convinced 50% to join him. How do we live together in peace and harmony with those who choose different paths? We don't so much live in heathen or godless times, but in realms of skepticism and polytheism. We can either get mad at all the "non-believers" and agnostics around us, or learn to live with them in peace and pleasantry with a loving profession of faith like our ancestors did in medieval Islamic Spain, or under the sixteenth-century Mogul emperor Akbar.

We are all human, wherever and whenever we live. As different and diverse as humans are, a deep commonality exists across space, time and time zones, all of which are increasingly bridged by technology's world-affirming connectedness. It is your (and my) sacred duty to be profoundly human, and to aspire to human greatness.

One phrase, "Jesus human," weds the particular and the universal: Jesus human. The particularity of Jesus yields the universality of human. But the particular comes first. Those who refuse to deign to stoop to particulars end up with everything in general and nothing in particular. The key to a powerful narrative is understanding the particular first, then the universal. Now that we are rooted in the particular, we can move to the grand vision of the universal.

**Faith Religion vs. Civil Religion:** On a global level this will entail the emergence of a new global civil religion (as distinct from a faith religion) built around a global commons and the common good. It will be a pesto of "manyness" from the major faith traditions, as well as seasoning from the heroic stories, civilities, and consciousness of recent all-star humans like Mother Teresa, Nelson Mandela, Muhammad Ali, Mahatma Gandhi, E. Stanley Jones, Martin Luther King, Jr., Howard Thurman, Anne Frank, Rosa Parks, Ellen Johnson Sirleaf, Billy Graham, Winthop Still Hudson, Bono, Dalai Lama, Malala Yousafzai, etc.

After the death of Nelson Mandela (1918–2013), there were those who wondered what more might have been accomplished had he not been imprisoned for those twenty-seven years by his government. If ever anyone in the past one hundred years epitomized civility under fire, it was Nelson Mandela. Yet it was his very experience of imprisonment, his long steeping in suffering, which ultimately enabled him to extend a hand of reconciliation instead of retaliation to those who had imprisoned him and oppressed his nation. What Mandela lived and breathed "when no one was watching" is what made it possible for him to become the world-shaping leader of a nation when everyone was watching. "When no one was watching" is the watchword of every true human, whether a Jesus human or not.

Followers of Jesus must cooperate wholeheartedly with nones, dones, and adherents of other religions in the larger interests of humanity. Many non-Christians have a passion for peace, love, and justice that puts church people to shame. Some of the most "moral" people I know are not religious. They are atheists, agnostics, secular humanists—some of my own family members.

---

*In the basic structure of our being, we are all equal. We are all children of God.*
INDIAN LAWYER MAHATMA GANDHI (D. 1948)[18]

---

The #1 thing behind bigotry and violence, according to the late Rabbi Lord Jonathan Sacks, Chief Rabbi of the United Hebrew Congregations of Great Britain and the Commonwealth from 1991 to 2013:

> One belief, more than any other, is responsible . . . It is the belief that those who do not share my faith or my race or my ideology do not share my humanity. At best they are second-class citizens. At worst, they forfeit the sanctity of life itself. They are the unsaved, the unbelievers, the infidel. . . . From that equation flowed the Crusades, the Inquisition, the jihads, the pogroms.[19]

## BECOMING A JESUS HUMAN

I once had a Hindu limo driver who is about as far apart from me as he could be in his beliefs, but was so totally aligned with me in his values and visions that we spoke the same language. When we talked on our long drives to the various New York City airports about all that was going on in our world, I often thought of Augustine's insistence that the only division that counted among humans was between those who chose good and those who would choose evil.

Jonathan Sacks often reminded the peoples of the world that "our basic humanity precedes our religious differences." He called for side-by-side relationships that formed about common endeavors for human betterment, as well as face-to-face dialogues that probed and pursued deeper understanding of each person's belief system.[20] In a world where we turn our backs to one another, only by walking side-by-side together with "coalitions of the willing,"[21] those who don't think it's too late to build a better world, will we be able to do the harder task of face-to-face. We may not be all on the same Jesus side, but we can be all on the same side for life, love, and the future.

For the best lesson in how to treat people of other religions, we need only go to the Hebrew Scriptures. The Jewish people were careful to include in their story many just and kind Gentiles like Rahab, Ruth, Cyrus, and Uriah. Or go to the New Testament and study how Jesus responded to a Samaritan woman, a Roman centurion, and a Syrophoenician mother. Or remember what Peter (and the whole early church) learned in his experience with Cornelius (Acts 10–11), including a realization that he should be careful about how he talked about people of other religious backgrounds. So should we.

**Prayer In Common, Not Common Prayer:** On 27 October 1986, one of the most impossible events of the twentieth century took place. At Assisi, Italy, John Paul II hosted an assemblage of world religious leaders, not to dialogue about faith but to pray. With St. Francis of Assisi the patron saint of the event, the Dalai Lama gathered with the chief rabbi of Rome, the Archbishop of Canterbury, and leaders from all the major world religions. (Mother Teresa of Calcutta was there, along with John Pretty-on-Top, chief of Crow nation, etc.). "The challenge of peace transcends all religions," John Paul II announced that afternoon, insisting that we had "not come here for an interreligious conference on peace, but rather to invite the world to realize that there exists another dimension of peace and another way to promote it."

---

*No peace among the nations without peace among the religions.*
SWISS THEOLOGIAN HANS KÜNG (D. 2021)[22]

---

Pope John XXIII announced the convening of an ecumenical council, later known as Vatican II, from the Church of St. Paul in the city of Rome on 25 January 1959.[23] On the same day, at the same place, only twenty-seven years later (1986), Pope John Paul II told his audience that he was convening a Global Day of Prayer for Peace. It was his way of responding to the call of the United Nations on its fortieth birthday for a "World Year for Peace." In some ways, the 1986 Global Day of Prayer for Peace introduced more changes than the 1959 Vatican II.

Never before had an eccleastical leader convened the world's religious leaders and journeyed with them. The global peace pilgrimage convened at twelve prayer stations in Assisi where they prayed according to their own traditions. The Pope invited a hundred representatives of various tribes and traditions[24] as well as eleven other faiths: Jews, Native Americans, African Animists, Buddhists, Bahais, Hindus, Jains, Muslims, Shintoists, Sikhs, and Zoroastrians. Represented were Native American chiefs; witch doctors from Kenya, Ghana, and Togo in Africa; Parsees; Jains and Sikhs from India; members of the Rissho-kosei-kai in Japan; Muslims from Asia, Africa, Turkey, Arabia and Italy, etc. In this one place, prayer ascended into the heavens with the Vedas, the Sutras, the Qur'an, the Avesta, the Psalms, and the Gospel. "People prayed with incense, flowers, water, fire, with song and dance, with drum and peace pipe."[25]

"Why We Gather with Other Religions?" was the paper written for the Vatican by British Archbishop Jorge María Mejía, the Argentine vice-president of the Pontifical Commission for Justice and Peace (and later Cardinal), announcing and explaining the reasons for this historic day:

> There is quite a bit to be learned from some of these methods of prayer, as also from the fundamental attitudes, not seldom quite exemplary, when confronting realities that transcend the senses and the imagination.[26]

We can all be "enriched by them. All these prayers . . . as far as they come forth from a pure heart, rejoin one another in the mystery of the unique God."[27]

Non-Christian religions "often reflect a ray of truth which enlightens all men" (*Nostra Aetate*, 2). Christians need an "attentive, respectful and humble openness to these forms of prayer. It is surely possible to learn from them and from those who put them into practice to 'seek the face of God.'" (Psalm 27:8).[28] After all, God "knows those who are his."[29]

While Christians shouldn't "insert ourselves into the prayers of others," nevertheless "it still follows quite clearly that *being present when another prays* or when many come together to pray cannot but enrich our own proper experience of prayer."[30] We live in a world of "too little prayer" and where "we all have a deplorable mutual ignorance of the ways and expressions of the prayers of 'others.'"[31] In the words of John Paul II: "It is a beautiful and salutary thought that, wherever people are praying in the world, there the Holy Spirit is, the living breath of prayer."[32]

In one of his speeches during the Day of Prayer for Peace, Pope John Paul II spoke of "The Challenge and Possibility of Peace:" "For the first time in history, we have come together from everywhere," brought together to affirm "the transcendent quality of peace." While the Pope declared his "humble conviction" that "Peace bears the name of Jesus Christ," he laced his speech with these words: "Either we learn to walk together in peace and harmony, or we drift apart and ruin ourselves and others."[33] By our every action we choose for or against peace.

Peace awaits its prophets. Together we have filled our eyes with visions of people: They release energies for a new language of peace, for new gestures of peace, gestures which will shatter the fatal chains of divisions inherited from history or spawned by modern ideologies.[34]

The pope insisted that the event be one of collegiality and reciprocity: "I shall be at Assisi as a brother among brothers and sisters."[35] But while the Pope called himself "a brother and friend," he also claimed that he was "a believer in Jesus Christ, in the Catholic Church, the first witness of the faith in Him."[36] There was no diminishment of the particularity of Christ, or a demotion of Jesus to the status of other redemption stories, as one finds in Kahlil Gibran's death wish. (Gibran was a Lebanese Christian born in 1883 and taken by his mother to New York in 1895. Gibran asked to be interred in a sanctuary-like room with a Buddha, an Islamic prayer rug, and a crucifix.)

At this Worldwide Day of Peace, there was no least-common-denominator prayers. No theological compromises. No arguments or discussions. No councils on peace or deliberations about people. No striving after terms of consensus. There was only prayer. Each religion prayed in accordance with his or her own tradition. Each religion showed its commitment to peace in religious ways integral to its faith: through spiritual weapons of prayer, silence, pilgrimage, fasting. It was

JESUS HUMAN

global Tong, where each religion prayed together in common, not together prayed a common prayer.

What does it mean for Jesus humans to "live in communion" with other religions of the human family? It doesn't mean praying a common prayer. It does mean praying in common. All religions are responding to the innate "*homo religiosus*" or hungering after the divine which God planted in the human spirit. Prayer is itself an action.

The Pope was savaged for calling this global prayer meeting. Here were some of the slams that came his way:

1. It was all spiritual, with no political elements. Thus, it didn't address those in power.

2. The inter-religious character of the prayers offered was offensive. In one church a Buddha was placed on the altar and prayers were offered to it.

3. Prayers were offered in Catholic churches to Krishna, Vishnu, Allah, and many others.

4. Some of these "religious leaders" were atheists. Wasn't this a mockery of prayer, especially prayer offered to a God they don't believe in?

5. The Pope was accused of having bad theological intentions.

Have we not learned from Plato? From Aristotle? From Elie Wiesel? From Martin Buber? Whyever can't we learn from other religions? We can learn about the mystery of Christ from Buddhists, Muslims, Hindus, Native American religions? The *kenosis* of Jesus models the way for Jesus humans to humble themselves to being hospitable to deepening faith in the Mystery of Christ by learning from the stories of other religions.[37]

> *Start by doing what is necessary, then what is possible, and suddenly you are doing the impossible.*
> ATTRIBUTED TO ST. FRANCIS[38]

We can learn from other religions just as we can learn from the arts, from philosophy, and from music, where God working. In fact, non-Christian religions may have grasped some aspects of God more fully than Christianity has yet; we can learn from them. Each non-Christian religion is a partial truth containing a special value we could learn from. Only the Holy Spirit can lead people to Jesus, but the whole spirit is found wherever there is breath. Faith has more allies than we think. "Master, we saw a man driving out devils in your name, and as he was not one of us, we tried to stop him." Jesus said: "Do not stop him." Disciples of Jesus are not the gatekeepers. Popular jokes aside, St. Peter is not the one who decides who gets invited in or left out. There will be surprises in the kingdom of heaven.

The Jesus gospel is a "Let's Tong" gospel of impossible dreaming and EastWest holism. The highest potential and highest expression of humanity is a Let's Tong virtuosic vision of planet Earth.

Jesus said that God is up to something so great, so vast, so universal, that only those with passionate intensity are able to "lay hold of it." Or in his exact words, "From the days

JESUS HUMAN

of John the Baptist until now, the kingdom of heaven has been forcefully advancing and forceful men lay hold of it."[39] "Be Perfect"[40] is not an instruction to be perfectly divine, but to be perfectly human, as Christ was perfectly human. This term we render "perfect" is τέλειοι (*téleioi*) which means "end." Jesus is summoning us to set as our "end" our highest potential as a human.[41]

The need for "forceful leaders" for a forwardly and frowardly advancing kingdom is another way of talking about the passion for the unimaginable. Humans were made for pursuit of the inconceivable, with an intensity for the impossible, and an indefatigable reach for the highest level of human striving. Higher ground is not the force of armies, governments, or mobs. It is the Satyagraha, Tong force of humble passion—submitted *and* struggling.

> *That was why fictions were born: so that, through living this vicarious transient, precarious but also passionate and fascinating life that fiction transports us to, we can incorporate the impossible into the possible.*[42]
>
> PERUVIAN NOVELIST MARIO VARGAS LLOSA
> SPEAKING ABOUT *LES MISERABLES* (1862)

God's dream for humanity, the Bible says, "is so far beyond what you can even ask or think." Pope Paul VI, reflecting on the meaning of hope, defined it as "hope for something that is not seen, and that one would not dare imagine."[43] God imagines for us what we can't imagine for ourselves. It might be called "the madness of the impossible."[44]

**Original Design:** On each of the first five days of creation, "God saw that it was good."⁴⁵ On the sixth day, with the creation of humanity, God saw that it was "very good."⁴⁶ All of creation is "good," but humans are, in the eyes of God, "very good." The original human design was for us to be the capstone of creation, a "little lower than Elohim."⁴⁷ The first time we meet God in the Bible, in Genesis, God is Elohim. YHWH does not come until later. And Elohim is not a name but an ontological category of being, not one of the "gods" but God. Reflecting on this spiky status, G. K. Chesterton wrote in 1925, "humanly speaking, the world owes God to the Jews."⁴⁸

---

*The one symbol of God is man, every man . . . Human life is holy, holier even than the Scroll of the Torah . . .*
*What is necessary is not to have a symbol but to be a symbol.*
POLISH-AMERICAN RABBI ABRAHAM JOSHUA HESCHEL (D. 1972)⁴⁹

---

Such a high view of the creation of humanity is not a popular thought anymore, and with some justification. God gives us a garden, and we turn it into a sun-blanched desert. God gives us a garden planet floating through space, and we turn it into an asteroid rock hurtling through space. Philosophers like Rice University professor Timothy Bloxam Morton calls such sentiments where humans are the most important beings on the planet "a most stupid thought." We all wonder at times, "are people dupes or dopes?" I've always suspected God signaled something when God put the most humanish animal—with smarts, emotions, likes, sensitivities, family fierce relationships—in the most non-human form: a pig.[50]

For German philosopher Arthur Schopenhauer (d. 1860), existence was little more than inner vanity wrapped in outer delusion. He believed human existence was "a business that does not cover its costs." Schopenhauer was so arrogant that in the 1820s, when he agreed to teach in Berlin, he scheduled his classes for the same hours as the celebrated Georg Wilhelm Friedrich Hegel (d. 1831) was teaching. When forced to choose, the students chose Hegel, so Schopenhauer lectured to the walls, but his confidence was undiminished. Schopenhauer talked about the "death of God" before anyone, even before Nietzsche.[51] But by "God is dead" he meant that the world was emptied of the meaning that Christianity traditionally assigned to it.

But who else is going to solve the problems of our world? Who else is going to address global warming? The chimps? The cicadas? The crows? Where is the real taxonomy of stupid? Maybe Genesis is right: Clay is higher than Silver or Gold when it has been breathed by the divine.

In heaven we will be whole human beings, not asexual, immortal spiritual beings (i.e., angels); not Christians, but pure humans. Jesus did not die on the cross to save our souls (what about our minds, bodies, spirits?) or so that humans could become more spiritual, but that human beings might be restored and reconciled to their authentic humanity.

BECOMING A JESUS HUMAN

*Jesus isn't made simply to forgive or die for our sins. If Christ is preexistent, then everything goes in the other direction. Jesus isn't made for us; we were made for him. We are the ones with whom God wants to share his life. It's not that Jesus is the gift God gives us at Christmas. It's that at Christmas we finally discover that we're the gift God has given to himself.*

METHODIST PASTOR/PODCASTER JASON MICHELI

**Pure-Blooded:** It's time to reclaim that word "pure." Why isn't the highest compliment we can pay anyone or anything to say "That's pure!" We do not have to live as "fallen" people filled with violence, alienation, hatred, and selfishness. Like in so many other things, Leonardo da Vinci was one of the first to prophesy that it might be nature's wish "to extinguish the human race, because it . . . spoils all things."[52] But humans spoil and destroy because we destory our salvation. To destory is to destroy.

But there is hope. We can join the human race again and become fully human through the power of the Spirit who brings to life Jesus, in each one of us together, the human face of God. The dignity and value of the human person is secure within the One-and-Only Incarnation and in the ongoing incarnation. "He re-story-eth my soul," as friend Teri Hyrkas likes to put it.

In the life-story of Jesus, God presents us with the true image of what it is to be human. The Fall from pure humanity has been reversed, as Jesus re-introduced us to our original face and story, the true character of the human spirit. We can be "pure humans" again, a word that belongs to the world of time more than the world of the transcendent. Or in the words of King David, God wants to create in us a "pure heart" and put a "true and right spirit" within us.[53]

> *Lord, prepare me*
> *to be a sanctuary*
> *pure and holy,*
> *tried and true.*
>
> SANCTUARY"[54]

We are saved not for heaven but for the world. Our mission is not in heaven; our mission is on Earth. In the words of the angelic visitors, the "good news" is of "peace on earth, good will toward all." God's dream for humanity is not that we might become "angelic" but that we might flourish as human beings in a place God loved into existence. Human fulfillment and fullness of life entails body, mind, and spirit.

> *Often, we let ourselves off the hook for what we do by saying, 'Ah, I'm only human.' Only human? We're divinity in the form of flesh. Only human? We're spirit as well as a physical body that allows us to manifest thought. That's a gift, not a weakness.*
>
> SINGER-SONGWRITER JEWEL[55]

We overestimate the holiness of humanity and underestimate the humanity of holiness. The apologetic only-human cant of can'ts (as in "I'm only human") does not do justice to humanity as the summit of creation, the crowning glory of

God's creativeness, the pinnacle of soulfulness, the highest and most elevated form of divine creativity, as unfinished as we may be.

**Imago Dei:** John Locke distinguished between "a human being" and "a person," which implied that there were human beings who were "non-persons." We resist any diminishing of the category of "human" to something less than "person." God made us to be human: not to be angels, or humanzees, but humans. "Let us make humanity in our own image." We were created to bear the image of God. Not the identity of God. Not the status of God. But the image of God. For humans to be created in the image of God is to carry the DNA of the divine. That divine DNA is what enables us to be human, not to be divine.

As God's image-bearers, we were created to live in loving relationship with God, not on our terms but on God's terms. When God makes us righteous, God returns us to our true self which is made for relationship with God, ourselves, others, and creation. The real "Lord's Prayer" was for us to have the same relationship with God that Jesus has.[56]

Talk about a huge fuel bill? The brain amounts to 2percent of body mass, but when the body is at rest consumes 15–20 percent of our energy budget. The best brain fuel? Costs nothing but costs everything: relationships. The hard truth is that we are human only in a network of relationships. We are most ourselves—not when we are separate and alone, but when we are actively engaged with and participating in each other. Being is not isolation and separateness

## JESUS HUMAN

but solidarity and communion. Being is not independence and individual agency but transparency and interpersonal dependency.

The life of Jesus is the life of humanity. In His "life is the light of humankind," in the words of Scripture,[57] Jesus ushered in a whole new kind of interpersonal relations based on love: a love without limits, without conditions, without measure, without score-keeping. A life of non-transactional relationships in which sacrificial love is the human norm.

*Religions die when their lights fail.*
GERMAN THEOLOGIAN WOLFHART PANNENBERG (D. 2014)[58]

Only *homo sapiens* were created "in the image of God," even surpassing in some ways the status of the angels. Humans are not just at the top of the mammalian chain, one of 6000 diverse species of mammal life that bring together the African sapiens, the Neanderthals of Europe and the Denisovans of Asia.[59] Humans are the divine masterpiece where all of creation comes to consciousness. A human being is the only being that can question its own existence.

Too often the celebration of the human came at the expense of non-human animals and the environment. More than one million animal and plant species are threatened by human-induced extinction caused in part by a repulsive, brutish and bogus version of anthropocentrism.

But the only thing worse than thinking of oneself more than one ought to think[60] is thinking of oneself less than one ought to think. After the "fall," humans became "a little lower than the angels."⁶¹ The First Human was created little lower than God. The Fall reduced us to lower than the angels. So when Jesus came, he came in that state, but restored us to our original state above the angels.

> But we do see Jesus, who was made lower than the angels for a little while, now crowned with glory and honor because he suffered death, so that by the grace of God he might taste death for everyone. In bringing many sons and daughters to glory, it was fitting that God, for whom and through whom everything exists, should make the pioneer of their salvation perfect through what he suffered.⁶²

The Holy Spirit does not destroy our human nature to make us "partakers of the divine nature," but redeems and restores our human nature and makes it receptive to the divine. It is the very nature of "evil" to oppose what God meant to "live." What makes us to live as "humans" is what evil seeks to reverse and destroy.⁶³

**Creatures or Children?** You can be soulful and not be human. Humans are the only species to point declaratively, though some ape researchers will dispute this and claim self-referentiality for hominids. Humans, however, turn automatically in the direction of a gaze and a pointing finger. No other species does.⁶⁴ In other words, humans are instinctively capable of getting outside themselves. The more an animal

# JESUS HUMAN

is self-referential (the more acute the sense of selfhood), the more soulful it can be said to be.

Psychologists call this the "mark test." A mark is painted on the animal's forehead. When a mirror is stuck in the animal's face, is there any attempt by the animal to wipe the mark off. Dogs, for example, do not recognize themselves in the mirror. There are only five known animals who pass the "mark test:" the chimpanzee, the orangutan, the bottlenose dolphin, the Asian elephant, and us.[65] There are only five "self-recognizers" and there is only one of the Elite Five that is a rational and referential self-recognizer: *homo sapiens*.

Animals are creatures of God. Humans are children of God. Humans are sexed beings, like creatures but with a difference. Sex brings us closest to the animals and at the same time most radically distinguishes us from them. For we are divinely sexed beings, more agapeic than ape-ish. In terms of human sexuality, let's get the monkey off our backs.

---

*You have made them a little lower than God*
*and crowned them with glory and honor.*
PSALM 8:5[66]

---

Birds are not able to know they are surviving dinosaurs, each one a theropod, a class of saurischian dinosaurs that included Tyrannosaurus rex. But humans are capable of knowing they are created in the image of God, the crown of creation that includes in its gene pool Jesus of Nazareth, Christus Rex. This is why humans, unlike animals, eat in social groups. Put food in front of most mammals facing each other, and you'll have a fight. It is peculiar to humans that we share food face to face, smiling and not snarling, even with strangers. This is why it is important to distinguish between individuals and persons. Individuals are faceless humans. A person is a human who has his or her face turned toward God, and toward each other as images of God. In fact, there is no such thing as an individual in the kingdom of God. There are only relationships in the kingdom; we are all relationships in Christ. The government gives you a number. God gives you a name, and the church calls you by nickname.

But this whole mode of reasoning, not "God-of-the-gaps" but "human-of-the-gaps," is suspect to begin with, since such animal cognition and emotion, mind and morality, are NOT threats to the Christianity's doctrine of humanity. Animals can share in what we see as "uniquely human" without any threat to the "image of God." Why? Two reasons:

1. The Bible actually has a high doctrine of animal creation, and the fact that other creatures have features close to ours doesn't impinge on that uniqueness. In fact, animals were the first candidates to "save" (ezer) Adam.

2. Morality and mind—compassion, joy, empathy—are woven throughout the whole tapestry of creation. They are not a one-off, only child gift.[67]

JESUS HUMAN

---

*A lot of our problems in the world could be solved by something that . . . sounds simple when you say it: Be nice. Don't spread poison. Give people the benefit of the doubt.*

DATA SCIENTIST CATHY O'NEIL[68]

---

**Angels and Humans:** The conviction that humans are a higher order of creation than angels is not a universal one. Eminent literary critic Harold Bloom sides with the Gnostics and their Zoroastrian forebears in arguing that humans should see themselves less as part of the creation of the world and more as heavenly beings, or "fallen angels," and he admits to being "increasingly reluctant to distinguish between good and bad angels."[69]

This is exactly the opposite direction this book is going. More in agreement is Edmund Burke's assertion that the significance of defining "man" as a "religious animal" was that it meant that humans were neither angel nor animal. To call someone an "angel" or to speak of "the better angels of our nature" is of limited praise; to call someone a "human" is the highest praise. Humans are superior to and nobler than angels. Angels *are* only spiritual; humans are amphibians, made for two worlds.[70] Humans are not only on the side of the angels, but make the angelic hypnotic.

Only humankind has a missional, relational, incarnational (MRI) life.[71] In spite of Augustine of Hippo's famous observation that humans are "a kind of intermediate being between the beasts and the angels,"[72] when we're participating in God's mission in the world, we are doing something that angels would like to do. The blending of a human being with a spiritual being is called an "incubus," which is supposed to be heavier than angels but lighter than humans. But an "incubus" was seen as a demonic force, not a divine one. The fact that we are able to share the Creator's life is not what makes us godlike—it's what makes us human. The holiness of the union of the spiritual and the material is what it means to be human. "Union with God" doesn't erase our humanity, but enacts our humanity. To be "like Jesus," to be "Christlike," is not to be more divine, but to be more human.

> *Finally, what Christianity gave to its converts was nothing less than their humanity.*
> CLOSING WORDS OF HISTORIAN RODNEY STARK'S (D. 2022)
> *THE RISE OF CHRISTIANITY* (1997)[73]

**In Dreams:** Followers of Jesus especially need a dream worthy of their calling and destiny. At a time in history when dreams are either dead or dread, the world itself desperately needs the vision of a dream society.

> *If you want people to make boats, don't show them how to cut down trees, make timber, plane boards, use pitch. Make them want to be on the other side of the ocean.*
> OLD FRENCH PROVERB

**Dreamseeding:** Every dream begins with a seed, a dreamseed that comes in the form of a metaphor or a hope or a promise. Enacted dreams are the seedlings of the future. "The oak sleeps in the acorn; the bird waits in the egg; and in the highest vision of the soul a waking angel stirs. Dreams are the seedlings of reality."[74]

But the biblical dream for humanity is not that we should want to be an angel, or that we will spend eternity as angels. To trade human beingness for angelic cloudiness is a trade "down," not a trade "up." Humans are not designed to lounge at pearly gates or play harps on clouds. We are created to peer into the mystery of the divine. We are created to be part of the cloud, the great cloud of witnesses and the cloudy mirror of unknowing which offers veiled glimpses into the Story of Everything which lies behind the Theory of Everything (TOE).[75] Where did we get the notion that ethereal emptiness and blissful silence and pure consciousness are trade "ups" rather than trade "downs?" Who wants to be dead from the neck down?

The body of Christ is not a gathering of angels, but a gathering of redeemed, re-dreamed human beings. God's dream for us is a dream that makes us human. When the image of God is married not marred in us, we don't become "like God." That's the serpent's snare and delusion. We become truly human.

**Dream Peacefare:** "In dreams begin responsibilities." Irish poet William Butler Yeats' celebrated epigraph to his 1914 volume of poems, *Responsibilities*, has never been located in his original writings.[76] But it needs highlighting, since thoughts without tasks are toys and toss-aways, not journeys and solutions.

God's love is both creative and re-creative: it brings into existence something new, and it gives new life to what once was but has passed away. God's very creation of humans in the divine image is such a creative and re-creative act. We were initially created for "a way of life," according to the Scriptures.

**Art as "Wakeful Dreams":**[77] And what was that "way of life?" A work of art or a masterpiece of creation in the living language of beauty, truth, goodness. "We are what God has made us," or in a better translation, "We are God's masterpiece," a work of art "created in Christ Jesus for good works, which God created beforehand to be our way of life."[78] A human being is not a human resource but a human gem, a human treasure, a masterpiece of art. You are God's "Master piece," Paul said, a divine artwork. Not a misterpiece. A masterpiece. Each one of us, not a parvum opus. Each one of us, a magnum opus of creation.

---

*The artist, the saint, the lover, the joker. Them and only them the capitalist cannot buy, the nationalist inflame, or the snob deflate.*
WHEN ASKED WHAT HE BELIEVED IN, BRITISH CRITIC CYRIL CONNOLLY (D. 1974) GAVE THIS RESPONSE.[79]

---

All three transcendetals of being are here as living language of one majestic sentence: truth, beauty, goodness. The Last Adam restores the First Adam. Or in the words of another translation, "We are God's masterpiece. God has created us anew in Christ Jesus, so that we can do the good things he planned for us long ago."[80] This is what is behind the importance of the arts in being human. Music, painting, poetry—all are ways of exploring what it means to be human, and to making new out of old, finding originality out of the original.

What joy do you take in your child's creativity? How much more joy must God take in ours?

---

*God made you able to create worlds in your own mind which are more precious to him than those which He created.*

ENGLISH POET THOMAS TRAHERNE (D. 1674)[81]

---

**What Are You Afraid Of?** There is an old saying: "If Michelangelo had been afraid of heights, we'd have the Sistine Floor."

If Jacob had been afraid of heights, we'd have had no "We Are Climbing Jacob's Ladder."

If Adam had been afraid to risk breathing in, we'd have had no "Breathe on Me, Breath of God."

If Abraham had been afraid of risking the unknown, we've have had no "Great Is Thy Faithfulness."

If David had been afraid of risking dark valleys, we'd have had no "Savior Like a Shepherd Lead Us."

If Paul had been afraid to risk being weak, we'd have had no "Make Me a Captive, Lord."

If Peter had been afraid to be risk being wrong, we'd have had no "Rock of Ages."

If Sarah had been afraid of risking laughter, we'd have had no "Shout to the Lord All the Earth, Let Us Sing."

If Samuel had been afraid of a fight, we'd have had no "Come, Thou Fount of Every Blessing."

If Daniel hadn't risked speaking truth to power, we'd have had no "Dare to Be a Daniel."

If two disciples hadn't risked breaking the rules, we'd have had no "All Glory, Laud and Honor."

If Caleb had been afraid to risk going against the majority, we'd have had no "I'm Bound for the Promised Land."

If Gideon had been afraid of looking ridiculous, we'd have had no "Awesome God."

If Mary had been afraid to risk her reputation, we'd have had no "Mary, Did You Know?"

If the innkeeper had been afraid of midnight knocks, we'd have had no "Away in a Manger, No Crib for a Bed."

If shepherds had been afraid to risk the counsel of heavenly visitations, we'd have had no "Hark! The Herald Angels Sing."

If the Magi hadn't wanted to risk saddle sores and other discomforts, we'd have had no "We Would See Jesus."

If Zaccheus had been afraid to risk his financial future, we'd have had no "Amazing Grace."

If Jesus hadn't risked the cross, we'd have had no "Jesus Loves Me This I Know."

Without risk, we'd have no dreams to dream, and dreams are the idiom in which we will seek and reach the future.

JESUS HUMAN

**Permission to Dream:** To fight for a dream is to fight for the future. A dreamless society has no future, so what's to fight for? When you don't have a dream, you don't have a future. Neanderthal people were smarter, stronger, faster, bigger-brained, more organized, and artistic than Homo sapiens. But Neanderthals were timid, halting, risk-averse, with little dreams or ambitions beyond their own communities. Unless a far shore was visible, they never lifted anchor. Homo sapiens were the dreamers, the risk-takers, the adventurers who explored far horizons and unending water.

The New Atheists, the skeptics among us, may win the battle of rationality, of lists of facts on the ground. But their mortal wound is not being able to dream. We live from our dreams: what we dream for our career, our children, our nation, our world, our personal lives. We especially live from our dreams in times of suffering, tragedy, death, and loss. We live most from our dreams when we imagine a better world, and the dream seems real enough that we lace up our shoes and go after it. We are made of our dreams. Without dreams you may have some facts, but you don't have a human being. You don't have life at all.

> *The great turning around . . . which is beyond all '*
> *revaluation of all values,' that turning around in which*
> *beings are not grounded in terms of human being,*
> *but rather being human is grounded from being.*
> GERMAN PHILOSOPHER MARTIN HEIDEGGER (1889–1976)[82]

It's time humans started dreaming again. It's time to start

redeeming the world and humanity through the re-dreaming power of the Holy Spirit. Forget liberal Christianity and conservative Christianity: we need a human Christianity. Conservatives think reality is an illusion. Liberals think illusion is reality. The world needs desperately this Jesus dream of a new kind of human, a true kind of human. It's a dream that can only come true when we tell the truth about The Truth: Jesus is The Way, The Truth, The Life.

Pilate got it right: Pilate was the first postmodern. At first, he stared Jesus in the eye, and asked, "What is truth?"

But Pilate eventually figured it out. At the end. He even put up a billboard. High on a hill, he had something inscribed for all to see, so confident of his answer he had it translated into Greek (the language of trade and commerce), Latin (the lingua franca of the day), and Hebrew. In other words, his answer to the question "What is truth?" was a global answer that applied to the whole earth. It may even be seen as the first Christian sermon.

His answer was this: "Jesus, King of the Jews."

Jesus is the Truth. Not just the truth about God, but more accurately the truth of what it means to be fully human. Only Jesus can tell us what human really is, what we really are, and what we must do to be truly human. Being human is being Jesus.

What's keeping you from sharing this dream of a new kind of human?

What's keeping you from becoming this new kind of human?

## JESUS HUMAN

What's keeping you from this dare dream, this double dream, this sweet dream, this impossible dream?

What's stopping you from being the kind of human whose commitment to Christ translates into a commitment to the world?

What's holding you back from the dying kind of living?

PART TWO:
# YOU NEED THE DIVINE TO BE HUMAN

---

*God has chosen us all in Christ; at the deepest level we
are all called Jesus in the eyes of the Father.*
SWISS THEOLOGIAN KARL BARTH (D. 1968)[1]

---

**What's the Big Idea, the Big Deal?** So, what is human about human life? The divine. You can't be human without it. That doesn't mean that humans get superpowers. Or a celestial credit card. Or a get-out-of-hell-free card. It does mean that God made our story, the human story, God's own story. And as muddied and muddled as that storyline can become—it hasn't helped that we exploded the Bible into fragments of verses and experiences that escape ordinary narrative arcs—it's still God's storyline.

Our problem is not only that we don't know how to be human; our problem is that we don't know what it is like to be human with the presence and power of God living in us. We don't know what it means for the divine to live in the human in the world. Just as Jesus "the human one" had life-changing and world-changing power, so when

JESUS HUMAN

Jesus lives his risen and rising life in each of us, we too have the gift of life-changing and world-changing power. In the words of South African Dominican theologian Albert Nolan (d. 2022), "Jesus' divinity is not something totally different from his humanity, something we have to add to his humanity. Jesus' divinity is the transcendent depths of his humanity. Jesus was immeasurably more human than other human beings, and that is what we value above all other things when we recognize him as divine, when we acknowledge him as our Lord and our God."[2]

The most revolutionary message of a biblical faith is not that we are divine, or that we can become divine, but that there is abiding and abundant possibility of the union of the divine and the human within each of us. In fact, there can be no true human without the divine. You can be a man or a woman without God. But you can't be a real human. All humans are made out of three-plus-one elements. The three are earth, water, wind. The one is fire. The divine is the fire that makes the human whole and four-dimensional.

"Our human hearts are naturally religious" (Cardinal Hume) is no longer a controversial statement among evolutionary biologists. Sir Alister Hardy (d. 1985), a professor of zoology and comparative anatomy at Oxford University, has argued that "the spiritual awareness of the human species has evolved during the process of natural selection as a response to the sacred, and is necessary for our survival." Of course, Christians believe that our relationship with God is much more than that. But in the face of scientific dismissal of religion, this is a huge "scientific" position: spiritual awareness is a human universal, and his self-transcending "consciousness" is what lies behind all religions. If a hunger for the divine is part of what it means to be human, then atheism hurts our humanity.[3]

**Divinely Human:** When we receive the Spirit, the human is divinized and we become new beings, "new creatures in Christ." The gospel is not a new moral code of behavior, or a values-based religion. It is not a revaluation of values but a "transvaluation of values" (as Nietzsche put it—*Umwertung der Werte*).[4] It is not a transformation from the outside in. It is an inside-out transfiguration and transubstantiation of being, a restitution of the original divine design which required the presence of the divine to be fully human. Jesus did not come to take away human society but to sanctify it. Sanctification, or "Christ formation," is the restoration of the divine image in each of us; the restoration of our true humanity is the sanctifying process of grace.

*All lives can shine like transfiguration.*
MARILYNNE ROBINSON, *GILEAD* (2004)[5]

When the divine brings together the mind, body, and spirit, you are not a "soul." You are "human." This is not the time or the place for a big theological debate over this unthinkingly loved quote from Pierre Teilhard de Chardin: "We are not human beings having a spiritual experience; we are spiritual beings having a human experience." As if being human is somehow only accidental to who we are? As if the incarnation, when God made the human condition God's own condition, was not that big a thing? As if our resurrected state does not contain a "new body?" As if the promise of eternal embrace is not one of "a new heaven and a new earth?" As if the whole is not greater than the sum of its parts?

God lures humans in a good and godward direction by getting us to inhabit our humanity—in all its humbleness and hubris, its bent and ascent. In the origins story for humanity, humans find the footing for hubris (divine image) but also the seed of humility (dirt roots). We come from the earth as muddy clumps, and the origin of the word "humility" is "humus" or earth. Humility and hubris are complementary. Humility can turn into hubris very quickly, as we become proud to be so humble (Gandhi came close to this at times). Humility without hubris yields catatonic self-doubt. Hubris without humility yields arrogant over-confidence.[6]

*For those who exalt themselves will be humbled, and those who humble themselves will be exalted.*

JESUS, THE HUMAN ONE[7]

The salvation of the world is not the story of God sharing the divine with us. That's the story of the creation of humankind. The salvation of the world is the story of God sharing our humanity so that humankind could once again be the humans God created us to be, humans who were designed to share the divine image. Pastor/theologian DeVern Fromke (d. 2016) viewed the story of salvation as a "Redemptive Recovery Program" or what Frank Viola calls a "Divine Recovery Program," where Jesus became the "Intervention" to restore us to our original Imago Dei humanity: "Let us create humanity in our image."[8]

To navigate and negotiate life we need fewer "grid-maps" and more "story-maps." We were made to journey by means of stories, not through artificially constructed streets that shut out the natural world. The oldest story in the book is this: Adam meets Eve in Eden. To continue the story, humans lay the ground, but God directs the path and plot.

God speaks to us in a language we can all understand, the language of a human life with all of its dramas and dreams. It is this Adam and Eve story, our origins story, our birth story as humans, that we use to navigate our way forward in this high-tech, GRAINy future. Systems of morality stem from an origins story, and the moral decisions we will make in the next two decades are unprecedented in human history. Technological advancement is not the same as moral advancement.

---

*There's nothing in the world more powerful than a good story. Nothing can stop it. No enemy can defeat it.*

LORD TYRION LANNISTER, IN FINAL EPISODE
OF THE TV SERIES *GAME OF THRONES*[9]

---

Whenever Adam is mentioned in the New Testament, he is spoken of as a real person. Adam is always spoken of as a picture of Christ, a prototypical human, a picture of Jesus who would be. This LAST ADAM (NOT Second Adam) is Humanity 2.0. He is humanity rebooted.[10] The New Adam frees humanity from its mortal coil in which the Old Adam's waywardness had wrapped, trapped, and tyrannized us. Followers of Jesus are invited not into a disembodied life, but into a life more fully human. We are invited to experience the life the First Adam lost—the life the Last Adam revived. The First Adam chose knowledge over relationship. The Last Adam invites us back into relationship. We were protected and prohibited from the Tree of Life after becoming aware of Good and Evil. Through relationship with the Last Adam, we're invited to eat of the Tree of Life again and experience "eternal life."

**Birth Story:** The birth story and death story of the Last Adam rehearse and reflect the birth story and death story of the First Adam. The 184 verses in the birth narratives of the Second Testament repeat or rehearse words from 170 verses from eighteen different books of the First Testament. Biblical scholar Andy Johnson connects the dots of Jesus' death in skillful semiotic fashion:

> Crucifixion did not take place inside the garden itself. Instead, Jesus dies outside the garden, as did the First Adam. But in a reversal of the First Adam's exit from the garden, this Second Adam's lifeless body is brought into the garden (Genesis 19:41) to receive the "eternal life" forfeited by the First Adam in the original garden (Genesis 2:17; 3:19, 22–24). Like the latter's lifeless, dusty body (Genesis 2:7), this second Adam awaits God's life-giving breath/Spirit who, according to John, "makes

alive" (Genesis 6:63). The first day of the old creation begins in darkness . . . here in the garden tomb the first day of a new creation is beginning: indeed, the Second Adam is being brought to life and, hence, a new humanity is being inaugurated.[11]

A lost paradise can be regained. The resurrection promises a risen humanity and a risen world that issues from a rising humanity and rising world. In the life of a Jesus human, there is a daily resonance, rhythm, and rapture of resurrection, as symbolized in the eighth day and the first day of the New Creation. Or in Paul's language, Christ's death and resurrection ushered in a "new man" and a "new creation" in place of the "old man" and "old creation." For both Paul and John, Jesus is the Last Adam, the father of a whole new, true, and pure line of humanity.

These are the words of Fr. Denis Minns, Oxford theologian and former Prior of Blackfriars, Oxford:

> When St. Paul says that to be in Christ is to be a new creation, he cannot mean that God the Creator has looked at the work of his hands, judged that he had made a botched job of it, and decided to start all over again. The work God does in Christ is not a setting aside of our original creation in the image and likeness of God, so that another, better creation might take its place. It is exactly the

same creation, but now the fullness of God's purpose is revealed in it.

It is not God who has botched his work of creating us in his own image and likeness; it is we ourselves who have done this, by our unwillingness to be created in that image and likeness. But, no matter what kind of a mess we have made of God's creative goodness to us, in Christ we can be as God always intended we should be, made in his own image and likeness. That is the new creation now offered to us.[12]

> *Come, Desire of nations, come,*
> *Fix in us Thy humble home;*
> *Rise, the woman's conqu'ring Seed,*
> *Bruise in us the serpent's head.*
>
> *Adam's likeness, Lord, efface:*
> *Stamp Thine image in its place;*
> *Second Adam from above,*
> *Reinstate us in Thy love. Refrain.*
>
> RARELY SUNG LAST TWO STANZAS OF CHARLES WESLEY'S
> "HARK! THE HERALD ANGELS SING"[13]

**<u>Know Your Place</u>:** Jesus does not show us the way to God so that we can be more like God. God does not want us to be more like God. That is what got us into trouble in the first place: wanting to be "like God." We didn't know our place, and respect the place where God put us, a "human" place. Jesus shows us our place, the way to ourselves, to our humanity, to the authentic human ways God designed us to live and love, forbear and forgive, suffer and die. To want to be "like God" is to want to not need God. It is the desire to ditch our "neediness" so that we can create a life for ourselves without dependence on anyone. But as someone once said, "Our needs are angels,"[14] apertures for divine access; they keep us human. To be "like Christ" is not to be "like God." Rather, it is live in communion with God as Christ did.

But there is another specific tree named in Eden. It was positioned alongside the other more famous one in the "midst" of the Garden where Adam and Eve could not miss either of them. Daily a choice between the two trees had to be made. This tree, the "Tree of Life," was the first of the two specific trees mentioned in our origins story, although you'd never know it from the rest of the story. It was the tree we were commanded to "Eat Freely" and partake of along with all the other trees. God gave us a thousand "Yes's!" a thousand "Eat Freelys," and only one "No!" One "Don't Go There!" Life's "Yes's" far outnumber life's "Nos." But you'd never know that from the rest of the story, where we chose the life of the one "No!" over the life of the thousand "Yes's!"

**Jesus Is God's YES!** Despite having one of the highest rejection rates (82.5%), the London headquarters of Oxford University Press is named the "Amen House." Jesus is God's "YES," God's "AMEN" to the world. In fact, "No" can be "Yes," "an Affirmative No," when it's a choice FOR not

AGAINST. Sometimes you say NO to something, so you can say YES to something else.

"Don't let evil conquer you," Paul admonished the Romans, "but conquer evil by doing good."[15] To "overcome evil with good" means to fight FOR things even harder than we fight AGAINST things. This goes against the human grain where we naturally fight against things harder than we fight for things. We are FOR more than we are against.

But Jesus is God's "Yes," not "NO!"[16] Earlier in the letter to the Romans, Paul says that if we don't fight FOR, we will be subsumed into an AGAINST world. We either allow the Spirit to change us by actively working with the Spirit, or we become conformed into the image of the world we're fighting against.

Some think saying "Yes" to Jesus is saying "No" to pleasure and joy and delight and play. This is an insult to everything that is human. Joy is integral to the essence of being human.[17] The Son IS "God's Yes!" Paul insists,[18] "the "Divine Yes," as E. Stanley Jones puts it.[19] But to say yes to "Yes!" is also to say yes to the surrender and sacrifice, pain and renunciation that come with life lived to the fullest.

---

*Yes I said yes I will Yes.*
ENDING OF JAMES JOYCE'S *ULYSSES* (1920)

## YOU NEED THE DIVINE TO BE HUMAN

**Breathings from the Tree of Life:** What was the life of the "Yes!" that God commanded Adam and Eve to enjoy? The precise content of the life of the "Tree of Life" is made explicit in the context of the story. The same Hebrew word for "life" as in "Tree of Life" is used in the "breath of life" a few sentences earlier.[20] God "breathed into Adam the breath of life, and Adam became a living soul." The word for "breath" (*n'shamah*) is translated in Proverbs as "the spirit of man is the lamp of the Lord."[21] It was the Tree of Life that kept the breath of life flowing into man. It was the divine breath, the life of the divine, that made this human creature a true human. You can't be human, truly and fully human, without the divine. God's presiding presence is everywhere in the Garden. Jesus is there in the garden, in the Tree of Life, and in the Breath of Life.

That divine life in the human is not something that has to be worked at. It comes naturally, but only after it is chosen. It is constitutive of the human being, but not constitutional to the human being. It is like the process of breathing itself. When you breathe, you don't suck in air. You don't work to breathe. But you do have to choose to let the air in. Your diaphragm must empty out the air inside. But in exhaling all the toxins and carbon dioxide, a vacuum is created. Your lungs become an empty sack, and the air flows in by itself. So you exhale the bad; the good comes in naturally. Wind abhors a vacuum. Choose to stop holding your breath and empty yourself, and the life of the divine will come rushing in of itself. The human was made for the life of the divine, but the in-breathed life of God is not forced upon the human. The choice of the two trees is daily before us.

This is the backdrop to the assertion that we "bear God's image" or the promise that we are capable of being united with "all the fullness of God"[22] or that we can share "in the inheritance of the saints in the light"[23] or that Christ calls humans to be "participants in the divine nature."[24] This is not something we achieve from our effort, but as a gift from God.

Humans are designed for the divine, and seek in vain elsewhere for fulfilling storylines and soundtracks.

This human-needs-divine-to-be-human thread draws tight the biblical tapestry. It is often hidden in back-stories, missed themes, and mistranslations. Daniel 10:19 is a case in point:

> And he said, "You must not fear, *O* beloved man. *Peace be to you*; be strong and be **courage**ous!" And *when he spoke* with me, I was strengthened and I said, "Let my lord speak, for you have strengthened me.[25]

The problem is that the word courage is **not** in the original. It has to be deduced from and nuanced against "strong" to be included. However, this changes the meaning of the passage. The NIV has it right: "'Do not be afraid, you who are highly esteemed,' he said. 'Peace! Be strong now; be strong.' When he spoke to me, I was strengthened and said, 'Speak, my lord, since you have given me strength.'"

When the red-herring of "courage" is removed and replaced by the original translation, a double strengthening suddenly appears. First, there is a divine strengthening of the human. Second, the human embracing of that divine strengthening leads to a double empowerment whereby the human can be all it was made to be through divine fortification.[26]

**The Vessel:** At the Council of Chalcedon in 451 the "two natures" of Jesus were established after widespread worries over how to make sure that Jesus was seen as a fully human being and not just a divine being who only appeared to be human. The Council never told us how this inseparable union of the divine and the human was possible. Just that it is true, and that what is true of him can be true of us. We, though human, can also share parts of the divine life through Jesus by the implantation of the Holy Spirit.[27] Incarnation means that humanity is the "vessel," the vehicle of divinity. The Incarnation is not a first union and communion between Creator and creation. The Incarnation is a new level of union and communion between Creator and creation. Creation is not an obstacle to grace and holiness. It is a means to grace, a sweetening of holiness.

It takes your breath away: The Creator chose to enter creation, the Infinite became finite, to participate in life as one of us (Emmanuel—"God with us"), with a birth story, life story, and death story. It's called "incarnation" from Latin "in" (into) and "cara/carnis" (flesh). God "in-the-flesh. Are you winded yet?

The stupefying promise that to be human is to be "partakers of the divine nature"[28] is what changed the life of

John Wesley, and changed the world with the Methodist Revolution. It was this exact passage of Scripture to which Wesley opened his New Testament at five o'clock on the morning of 24 May 1738:

> About a quarter before nine, while he was describing the change which God works in the heart through faith in Christ, I felt my heart strangely warmed. I felt I did trust in Christ, Christ alone, for salvation; and an assurance was given me that He had taken away my sins, even mine, and saved me from the law of sin and death.[29]

**Humanation:** To be human is by definition to be "partakers" and partners in the divine. The "human" by definition is a supra-natural being. We lost the supra-natural with the separation from the Tree of Life, but Jesus brought that Tree of Life back to life by his death on the tree. So, to be human is to be supra-natural, to be able to rise beyond the natural, beyond animus and anima, and to live in the "fullness of God" by the in-breathing of the divine. The Jesus human doesn't obsess with how to be a better human. The Jesus human dreams of what its full participation in this new reality of the "fullness of God" and this "new creation"[30] can be.

And God raised us up with Christ and seated us with him in the heavenly realms in Christ Jesus.[31]

We humans have a seat at the heavenly table. But we are not peers of the heavenly hosts: Father-Son-Spirit. We are not gods, but we are godly through the grace of Jesus as we participate in the divine tablelife of Father-Son-Spirit. To be human IS to be holy. To be holy means to be human. We don't need God's power to be divine, we need God's power to be human. We can't be human by ourselves. We become more godly and god-like by becoming more human. In words attributed to St. Augustine: "Make humanity your way and you shall arrive at God."[32]

In Eastern orthodoxy and its doctrine of "theosis," the "energies" of God are at work in us. But what is not understood about Eastern orthodoxy is that our humanation is our divination. In other words, the more human you become the more your human being becomes a divine being. A saint is someone who is fully human, not superhuman, or uberhuman. Jesus is in the humanation business. Jesus is our best shot at being the original, authentic human being God made us. We can't be human without the divine.

⸻ ◇ ⸻

*No question plagues the contemporary spirit so much as the question of the human telos—the "chief end of Man."*
CANADIAN THEOLOGIAN DOUGLAS JOHN HALL[33]

**Full of God, Full of Self?** One of the most misunderstood quotes in the history of Christianity is this fourth century retort to the Arians from St. Athanasius of Alexandria, which has been used umpteen times to explain the doctrine of theosis: "The Son of God became man, that we might become God."[34] Actually, Athanasius was repeating the Greek bishop

Irenaeus of Lyons' (b. 130) famous phrase: "God became man so that man might become God."[35]

When "theopoiesis" (as Justin Martyr first called this) is taken out of context, any number of the early church abbas and ammas of Egypt, Syria, and Palestine can be heard to say the same thing.

> Irenaeus said the Word of God "became what we are in order to make us what He is Himself."[36]
>
> Augustine called attention to the reciprocity of "In order to make gods of those who were merely human . . . One who was God made himself human."
>
> In the seventh century, Maximus the Confessor writes, "We lay hold of the divine to the same degree as the Logos of God . . . became truly human."[37]
>
> Thomas Aquinas writes in the thirteenth century, "The only-begotten Son of God, wanting to make us sharers in his divinity, assumed our nature, so that he, made man, might make men gods."[38]
>
> In his commentary on John's gospel, Aquinas startles us with "We are gods by participation under the effect of grace."[39]

## YOU NEED THE DIVINE TO BE HUMAN

> For Teresa of Avila, the end of contemplation is divinization, when "the soul, or rather the spirit of the soul, is made one with God."[40]

John of the Cross could breathlessly declare "Everything can be expressed in this statement: the soul becomes God from God through participation in him and in his attributes"[41] while at the same time claiming, of course, "it is true that its natural being, though thus transformed, is as distinct from the Being of God as it was before."[42]

Athanasius and all those quoted above did not mean that it is possible for created beings to become God, or even part of God. The Russian philosopher Vladimir Solovyov (1853–1900) understood the deification of humanity and the humanization of divinity, as flip sides of same coin. A new kind of human may turn out to be a hybrid of God and human, or what Solovyov called "the divinehumanity" or "Godmanhood."

What Athanasius and the others meant was not this. Through the power of the Holy Spirit breathing in us, we can know what it means to be fully human and inhabit our creaturely status as the created image of God. Or in the words of Canadian theologian Aaron Riches, "God became man that man might become truly human."[43]

JESUS HUMAN

---

*So, if I am asked, "Do you believe in the divinity of Christ?"
I answer: "Yes, otherwise how could he have been so
wonderfully human?" And if I am asked, "Do you believe
in the humanity of Christ?" I answer, "Yes, otherwise
how could he have been so profoundly oriented toward God?"*

CANADIAN THEOLOGIAN DOUGLAS JOHN HALL[44]

---

Theologian Michael Christensen reminds us that "*theosis*" is not "essence" or "being" language, but relational and participatory language.[45] In other words, "theosis" is not our deification but our humanation.[46] Christiansen points us to the Orthodox Study Bible, which provides a theological clarification to the doctrine of "deification:"

> *What deification is not:* When the Church calls us to pursue godliness, to be more like God, this does not mean that human beings then become divine. We do not become like God in His nature. That would not only be heresy, it would be impossible. For we are human, always have been human, and always will be human. We cannot take on the nature of God.[47]

"Theosis" means humans get to participate in the life and love of God, not ontologically but relationally. Humans are not just given ringside seats. Humans are invited to join God in the rings themselves and become ringmasters.

**Relationality Is Reciprocity:** We aren't mimicking what Jesus did, but actually living his resurrection life with him. Human beings are creatures who share the Creator's life. This is what it means to "become god" for Eastern orthodoxy, or what it means to "be made perfect" for holiness theology. Jesus is the perfection of humanity.

Take the Psalm which Jesus quotes: "I said, 'You are "gods"; you are all sons of the Most High.'"[48] But the context makes it clear that our "godness" is our status as children of God, human beings created in the image of God (*imago Dei*) to do what God would have us do—"rescue the weak and needy; deliver them from the hand of the wicked."[49] Human beings are *imago Dei* creatures given "dominion" to be the Creator's agents and continue God's creativity—you "crowned them with glory and honor. You have given them dominion over the works of your hand."[50] But we are not a sub-category of godedness; we aren't "one" with God in substance or essence, in body or nature. We always remain the creature, and God the Creator.

> *We are not God. We are simply the image of God. . . . Our task is gradually to discover that image and set it free.*
> FRENCH THEOLOGIAN MICHEL QUOIST (D. 1997)[51]

The story of the Scriptures is that of the descent of God, not of the ascent of man.[52] God's dream for humanity is for us to become a true kind of human, the pure kind of human the "Son of Man" or "Son of Humankind" or the "Human One" descended to show us how to be. Jesus' preferred way

## JESUS HUMAN

of referring to himself, "*ho huios tou anthropou*" is almost always translated "Son of Man." The exception is the Scholars Version, which renders the Greek "the Human one." A literal translation of the Greek is "Humanity's Son" or "Son of Humankind," which may actually be the best translation.

God's dream for humanity is for us to become a true kind of human. This is not a heavenly dream; it's an earthly dream, a dream of "thy kingdom come, thy will be done **on earth**." There is a parallel universe out there, an alternative dimension to this one. We call it "eternity." We pray the dream of "thy kingdom come, thy will be done on earth" as it is already being done in this parallel universe. As that *earthly* will is done, we find that it is becoming (through no efforts of our own) "as it is in Heaven."[53] The church is not the end in itself. The church is a means to the reign of God. The reign of God is NOT a religion. It is an experience of God built around Jesus, King of the kingdom, or as John of Patmos and later Handel of "Messiah" put it, "King of kings and Lord of lords."[54]

Jesus never defines the kingdom, or philosophizes about the kingdom. He lives the kingdom, and shows in his life how the kingdom lives. The kingdom is a fancy word for life as God designed it to be lived. We don't build the kingdom as a bird builds a nest. We enter and receive the kingdom as parents gift their child with good things.

Jesus came to give us our life back. Jesus came to show us how to be human, not how to be divine. Jesus came to humanize the world, not to divinize the world. Jesus came to humanize us, not divinize us. Jesus showed us how to be divinely human, not humanly divine. It's not the spark of divinity we have inside each of us, it's the spark of humanity we have inside of us that Jesus came to bring to flame through the breathings of the divine.[55] Our humanity is found in the divine, not in our divinity. Too many are trying to find their humanity in their divinity. Coming to full humanity means receiving divine gifts and reflecting the divine. These distinctions may have a scholastic air, but they are not subtle or snuffy distinctions but substantial ones.

When the divine pervades every strand and fiber of our being, then we are most human, not most divine.

**New Humanity:** Jesus' humanity does not conceal the divine; it reveals and releases the divinity enmeshed in our humanity. Christians are people who show what it means to be true human beings, and our gatherings are places which show what it means to be a new humanity,[56] a "new heaven and a new earth." The kingdom of God proclaims the possibility of a new person, a new human being. "Put on the new man," Paul writes.[57]

Jesus is always about a "new humanity." That's the essence of his message: a new humanity. That's the essence of the incarnation, too: God sanctified humanity by becoming one of us.

When Jesus took on the human condition first-hand, he asked for no special treatment. He not only expressed human characteristics, but was "in every way as we are."[58] Including our limitations and our limits, including the final limit of death.

## JESUS HUMAN

Jesus was:

>so exhausted he slept through a storm;[59]
>
>unafraid of his feelings and willing to show a full range of emotions;
>
>sometimes "agitated" and "distressed;"[60]
>
>compassionate towards lepers and outcasts;
>
>sometimes hungry and thirsty;[61]
>
>so distressed about a place (Jerusalem)[62] and a person (Lazarus)[63] that he wept uncontrollably over them;
>
>openly enraged at legalists and hypocrites;
>
>transparent about his anxiety regarding his crucifixion;
>
>deeply broken over the forgotten and forlorn: "His heart went out to her,"[64] "his heart went out to them;"[65]
>
>able to make his disciples laugh.

What's more "humanist" than God becoming human? This is a major bone of contention with Christianity's #1 conversation partner in the future, Islam. In Islam, God is Muslim. In Christianity, God is God. In Islam, humans are made Muslim.[66] In Christianity, humans are made human. There will be no Christians in heaven. God has no religion. God has a people. "If my people, which are called by my name."[67]

Islam considers the Qur'an the infallible and final vessel

of God's revelation, while at the same time lauding both Judaism and Christianity for containing significant elements of the truth.[68] We can say that other religions often land on the tarmac of truth but are not The Truth. Christianity itself as a religion contains truth but is not The Truth. The Truth is a person who doesn't reveal truth but is Truth revealed.

---

*What the world needs today are ministers of the Gospel who are experts in humanity, who have a profound awareness of the heart of present-day men and women, participating in their joys and hopes, anguish and sadness, and who are at the same time contemplatives who have fallen in love with God. For this we need new saints.*

POPE JOHN PAUL II (D. 2005)[69]

---

The divinity of Jesus and the humanity of Jesus were not competing realities, but harmonious inseparables. But the power of the gospel resides in the humanity of Jesus, not in his divinity. The humanity of Jesus is what attracted people to him and what appalled the religious establishment. What scandalized the culture of Jesus' day was less the showcasing of his divinity (forgiving sins, receiving worship, announcing the "I Ams"), than his showcasing his humanity: here was an eating-and-drinking messiah, one they called a glutton and a drunkard; here was an emotionally transparent messiah, not a Stoic who never showed anger or despair but one who cried in sorrow and cried out in anger or what Thomas Aquinas called "just wrath;" here was a learning messiah, one that "grew in wisdom" and grace, not one that came pre-packaged in perfection; here was a suffering messiah, one that was like

## JESUS HUMAN

us "in every way." Jesus' humanity is more intriguing than his divinity—both now and then.

When the Scriptures say Jesus was "too much for them," it is saying that his virtuosity at being human was fatiguing and frustrating.

The key mark of "sainthood" is not divinity, but humanity: love, joy, peace, forbearance, kindness, goodness, faithfulness.[70] We were meant to live "life according to the Spirit," which is what it means to be human. To "live according to the flesh" is what it means to be sub-human or inhuman.

Each of us bears the birthmarks of a child of God. In a tribute to his mother, a poet wrote, "I am no man until I am your son." Or, "I am no woman until I am your daughter." We are not truly and fully human until we become sons and daughters of Almighty God, "All Creatures of Our God and King."

---

*In times past it was said that man was made in God's image, but this was not made evident. For the Word, after whose image man was made, was still unseen. And this was why he so easily lost the likeness. But when the Word of God was made flesh he established both the one and the other: he displayed the true image by himself becoming what his image was; and he made the likeness secure by uniting manhood to the likeness of the unseen Father by means of the visible Word.*

GREEK BISHOP ST. IRENAEUS OF LYONS (B.130)[71]

---

**The Human One:** In the fullness of time, there was the fullness of revelation: Incarnation. In the incarnation, God

## YOU NEED THE DIVINE TO BE HUMAN

did not claim the divine immunity that came from non-involvement with the human species. In fact, God honored the human by wanting to be known as the Human One, the "Son of Man," part and parcel of the world God created. Divine life participated in human life, so that human life might participate in divine life. Not so humans might become divine. Not to make us gods. But to make humans fully human with all the fullness of life with which we were originally created. Jesus' favorite description of himself was not "Son of God" (which he was) but "son of man," not "The Divine One" but "the human one."

We have lost the sense of oddness that comes with Jesus' favorite self-description as the "The Son of Man" or better yet, "The Human One." This phrase Jesus uses is almost never found in Jewish literature[72] but occurs 81 times in the gospels and over 100 times in the New Testament. Luke's and Mark's gospel quote Jesus using this self-description almost twice the amount of Matthew and John. British priest Joseph O'Hanlon opens a window as to why this might be in Luke: "To meet the Jesus of Luke is to meet one who comes to chat about God's ways, to hear our questions, to engage in our search for love and hope. To meet Luke's Jesus is to meet with one who honors human dignity and respect human freedom. To meet Jesus in Luke is to meet one who shares our common humanity."[73]

Jesus uses "The Human One" in a paradoxical way. For one thing, it signals humility; "I'm one of you," or "I'm a human being just as you are." But it also conveys an opposite, much more exalted sense that is conveyed in the definite article, the: "The" One who looks "like a man" will one day come in glory and wisdom and power.[74] This was not a humblebrag, such as Kenneth Branagh's joke about the great master Sir Ian McKellen: "Isn't it marvelous. This week he's playing Hamlet, and last week he was in something where he just played the footman."

"Oh, really? What was the play called?"

"*The Footman.*"

**Came to Die, or to Live?** Jesus did not come to earth to die. He came to earth to live, and loved in such an uncompromising way that his silencing was certain, his death inevitable. But Jesus did not die solely for our sins. He died at the hands of our sins. Christ's love for us both reveals and mediates God's love for us. It's the same love by which Christ loves us that the Father loves his Son and that Jesus loves his Father: "as the Father has loved me, so have I loved you;"[75] "as the Father has sent me, so I send you."[76] Humanity is realized in God's image, not by the imitation OF God's love but by the participation IN God's love. We live in Christ's life not through his life. Only by the power and presence of the Holy Spirit we can live IN Christ without seeing Christ. The human spirit is where the Holy Spirit lives.

## PART THREE:
# WE DREAM, AND SOME DREAMS ARE INHUMANE

---

*There's a new way to be human*
*It's nothing we've ever been. . . .*

*There's a new way to be human*
*Where divinity blends*
*With a new way to be human.*

SWITCHFOOT'S *"NEW WAY TO BE HUMAN"* (1999)[1]

---

WE ARE ALL LIVING IN SOME KIND OF DREAM, but too often it's the wrong dream, a bad dream, a scream dream, a schizophrenic fueled-by-fear dream. These are dreams gone wild. A dream gone wild, which mistake the primeval past for a primal future. Feral dreams keep us mired in a slow-motion past instead of releasing us to a high-flying future.

A community of faith that is on the move and in mission is less focused on restoring yesterday than on restarting tomorrow. You can't restore the past. You can restart the future by reclaiming and rediscovering and revitalizing the past.

Take the contrition chic of the last three decades. The

first-ever apology by a Pope happened under John Paul II in 1992, when he apologized to Galileo. Then came apologies by John Paul II and Francis for the church's role in the African slave trade (1993), inaction during the Holocaust (1998), the Inquisition (2000), sexual abuse by clergy (2001, 2010, 2015, 2018, 2021), colonialism and mistreatment of indigenous people (2015), refugees (2016, 2017), the LGBTQ+ community (2016), and for the genocide in Rwanda (2017). Australia declared a "National Sorry Day" for the mistreatment of Aborigines and all else it did wrong. To apologize retrospectively for an abhorrent trade that ended 200 years ago, the group Lifeline toured the globe in chains, wearing T-shirts and carrying signs that said "So sorry." They have even apologized to a descendant of Kunta Kinte, the slave made famous in the Alex Haley epic *Roots*.[2] Bill Clinton personally apologized for slavery; Tony Blair apologized for the Irish Famine; Japan's Prime Minister apologized for sex slaves during WWII; and Barack Obama went on what his detractors called an "apology tour." We have gone from striving for an idealized future to repairing past wrongs. Yes, we owe a debt to the past;[3] but we harbor an even greater responsibility to the future. Yes, we should repent of our past sins, but lip service only is an *insult*, **placation** not palliation.

◇

*Anamnesis is the antidote to the amnesia that comes with ingratitude, self-absorption, indifference, and greed.*
PHILOSOPHER DANIEL J. MILLER[4]

## WE DREAM, AND SOME DREAMS ARE INHUMANE

The memory meal for Jews, the Passover Seder, ends with a dream for the future: "Next Year in Jerusalem." That image "Jerusalem" stands for something greater than a physical city. It stands for a better tomorrow. The meal of memory serves up the sweetest dessert of all: the promise of a dream.

**Never in My Wildest Dreams:** A world of dreams gone wild needs a new dream, a God Dream, a transcendent dream, a dream of The True, a dream of The Good, a dream of The Beautiful—an effervescent dream that bubbles and fizzes through our earthbound lives, flavoring everything we do and experience. What about God's Dream for a world God loved so much God sent Jesus, the true Son and pure image of God, to show us the "measureless and pure" love of God? What happened to God's dream for the world that was manifested on the cross, a dream of the love of God, "greater far than any tongue or pen can tell?"

When you peel away the layers from every "Dream Gone Wild" in the West, the dream is wild about one thing: ME. The one common denominator in every dreamscape is this: MINE IS THE KINGDOM, MINE IS THE POWER, MINE IS THE GLORY. It's only a ME DREAM, a misbegotten dream of divinity by a culture of utter self-absorption. You've seen it on TV: "Get me drunk on my indulgence & I'll flash my hedonism for the cameras!" These so-called Dreamers are still waiting for a Spring Break that never comes.

## JESUS HUMAN

> *The horse who knows he is a horse, is not.*
> *Man's major task is to learn that he is not a horse.*
>
> ELIE WIESEL QUOTING THE MAGGID OF MEZRITCH[5]

**Life in the Youniverse:** You want evidence of how bad our "meism" has gotten? When people sneeze, we don't even bother with the charade of "God Bless you." It's enough to say "Bless you." We know who's God and our blessing is enough. That's provided you can get away with giving someone a blessing without them snapping at you, "You some kind of holy person, or something?"

In fact, you can now put on your resume, "Person of the Year." The benchmark of "meism" occurred in the 25 December 2006 issue of *Time* magazine. Who did *Time* magazine select as the 2006 "Person of the Year"? YOU.[6]

Such a culture where everyone is trained to think of themselves as a god, where we are now living like our ancestors could only conceive of gods living, where every commercial and self-help book (e.g., *The Secret*[7]) shouts, "you're #1," "it's all about you," and "you are a god." Such a culture doesn't need to be told that following God's Dream, the Jesus dream, will make us more divine, more god-like, even more "godly."

Let's be honest: people today aren't groping for the "god-ness" of God. People are groping for the "god-ness" of "ME." Our "god-ness" is part of our problem. New York Rapper Nas calls himself "God's Son," and Jay-Z's favorite pseudonym is "J-Hova."

What if the #MeToo generation were less #MeMe and more the #MeWe? Perhaps it could be the #WeToo generation?

This culture has mistaken the search for self, the search for personal fulfillment, with the search for God. We don't need a "god dream." We don't need to dream "what would it be like to be god." We need to dream about what would it be like to be human. Just when GRAIN is ending the human era and ushering us into a post-human future, introducing the "metaman,"[8] the "metahuman," and the "hyperhuman," our understanding of what it means to be human in the first place is as thin as it has ever been. GRAIN supercharges evil, and GRAIN technologies are already proving to be dark temptations to despots and dictators and would-be superpowers.

A culture of jaundiced views of the world needs a Jesus view of the world. What Jesus came to show us was not so much how to be a new kind of Christian (or, rather, a new kind of *Jew*), but how to be a new kind of human. Long before there were Christians there were humans. The church would have been a better place over the past 2,000 years if more people had made sure they were a Jesus kind of human before setting out to be Christian.

Christianity is not a generic mode of existence, but what theologian John Stackhouse calls an "emergency situation." We've been hearing emergency instructions for 2,000 years, and have been busy with dinghy maneuvering when we should be sailing in freedom. Christianity is a means, not an end: You worship God, not your religion.

---

*My religion is simple. My religion is kindness.*
14TH DALAI LAMA (GYALWA RINPOCHE)

---

God's Dream for us is a Human Dream, NOT a Divine Dream or even a Christian Dream. A divine dream is for the angels. God's Dream for us is not super-spiritual but grounded in our earthiness. It is an antidote to a dehumanized, inhumane, and utterly unhuman world. Jesus criticized the oral law because it opposed human decency and kindness,[9] but he also criticized the written law because it didn't side with life and love.[10]

The problem is not that the church is all-too-human. The problem is that the church is not human enough. There is a vast difference between the natural and the humane. New Ageism and the new paganism are natural spiritualities. Christianity is a humane spirituality that shows people less how to be natural, or how to be Christian, than how to be and do human. We live in a world where kindness is the new forbidden pleasure (not sex, money, or death).[11] A Jesus human ought to live life kindly, as well as manifest the other fruits of the Spirit.[12] The chinks in our armor should be where the milk of human kindness gushes forth.

## WE DREAM, AND SOME DREAMS ARE INHUMANE

*Of each other, we should be kind,*
*While there is still time.*
POET PHILIP LARKIN, "THE MOWER"[13]

**Dream Warfare:** Most of the books being written for the Church are attempting to wake it up before it careens off the cliff. I have contributed my share of books about the deep, deep sleep of Christianity from which I sometimes fear we shall never wake.

People need to dream. As we have seen, there are good dreams and bad dreams. Jeremiah had a few choice words about the deceitful dreams of false prophets, especially those who were posing self-serving dreams as God dreams.

Jesus humans especially need a dream worthy of their calling and destiny. At a time in history when dreams are either dead or dread, the world itself desperately needs the vision of a dream society.[14]

*How long will this continue in the hearts of these lying prophets, who prophesy the delusions of their own minds? They think the dreams they tell one another will make my people forget my name, just as their ancestors forgot my name through Baal worship. Let the prophet who has a dream recount the dream, but let the one who has my word speak it faithfully. For what has straw to do with grain?" declares the Lord.*
*"Is not my word like fire," declares the Lord,*
*"and like a hammer that breaks a rock in pieces?*

## JESUS HUMAN

*"Therefore," declares the Lord, "I am against the prophets who steal from one another words supposedly from me. Yes," declares the Lord, "I am against the prophets who wag their own tongues and yet declare, 'The Lord declares.' Indeed, I am against those who prophesy false dreams," declares the Lord. "They tell them and lead my people astray with their reckless lies, yet I did not send or appoint them. They do not benefit these people in the least," declares the Lord.*

SEVENTH CENTURY (D. 570 BCE) PROPHET JEREMIAH[15]

---

To see Jesus' main enemies as Pharisees, Sadducees and Roman oppressors is to miss the deeper story. Jesus' real enemies are Satan, Sin, and Death. This is why Jesus says about other humans "love your enemies." People are not real enemies. People are prisoners of war being captured by the true enemies of Sin, Death, and Satan, that fallen angel whom Saint Ignatius Loyola named "the enemy of our human nature." The ultimate warfare is between good dreams and evil dreams, Edenic daydreams of a new humanity or Nietzschean nightmares of the Übermensch.

**Happy Appy:** When it comes to making good dreams come true, the church has more "how-to" appliances than any person could apply in a lifetime. Everywhere you look some scolding list of must-haves, ought-tos, and never-agains lectures the faithful on right living and dream-making. This frenzied search for the perfect application to plug into your life can be a ploy to keep us from thinking. Worse, it has left many disciples of Jesus with no idea how to simply enjoy the

## WE DREAM, AND SOME DREAMS ARE INHUMANE

gift of life, or to prevent our memories from getting bigger than our dreams.

Humans are now living through the Fourth Information Revolution: speech, writing, the printing press, and now the digital age. In this world of iPhones; digital streaming; AI systems like ChatGPT, Bard, Watson; and imagers like MidJourney, Stability.ai, Dall-E—not to mention demanding work hours—the ancient art of being human has few practitioners. Living "humanly" today is like the vex of sex in junior high school: it's talked about constantly, dreamed of in the twilight hours, but rarely engaged in. Patricia Lockwood's novel, *No One Is Talking About This* (2021), describes what a web-addicted existence comes to feel like. In front of the screen, "pressing closer and closer, the spiderweb of human connection grown so thick it was almost a shimmering and solid silk." The only question is whether that "solid silk" becomes a sail in real life, or a strangulation. A silk cocoon suffocates. A sail unfurled sets free.

Barnes & Noble may introduce us to the realities of self-help authors, but the pursuit of true humanity is the call to live in a reality that matters. In a world where everything is marketed and wired and consumed, what the world needs is a reminder that humans actually live here. Our bodies are not machines. Our personalities are not tools for social media. Our dreams are not given for corporate success. In a world that specializes in soundbites and screenshots, snapchats and Instagrams, are we losing the ability to think the long thought and dream the impossible dream?

The greatest need and most neglected activity of the

people of God is becoming fully human. Running to catch up to the 1980s, we pat ourselves on the back for running churches like the local Target, or entering the political fray like Ronald Reagan with all his witty aphorisms. But our calling is to be real, relational, flawed, imperfect humans who seek relationship with the divine. From that relationship will flow a new reality born of revelation.

No one "gives" to God. We only "give back" to God. "ALL things come from you, and of your own have we given you."[16] The ultimate "give back," the offering that honors and thanks God the most, is the give back of being the fullest version of ourselves, the best rendition of the human God created and gifted us to be.

Faith is the domain of dreams. The biggest battle going on in our world today is not one you will read about in the newspaper or watch on the evening news. It is not a battle between nations, or religions, or even disgruntled celebrities. The biggest battle in the world today is a battle of dreams, a conflict of dreamscapes—each one competing for our soul. Our problem is not that "good men do nothing." Today, good men and good women are working hard and dreaming hard. Our problem is that good men and good women are not playing at the right dream. We are working hard at delusional and dysfunctional dreams. We're dreaming devil dreams, not God Dreams.

**Where Do You Think You're Going?** We live in a world of dashed dreams and dehumanized dreams, a world where no dream, or meta-narrative is sufficient to stitch together the

## WE DREAM, AND SOME DREAMS ARE INHUMANE

centrifugal forces of the future confronting us: an environmental time-bomb, crumbling civilizations, massive globalization, dehumanizing technological advances, a tug of war between de-centralization and hyper-centralization, and on and on.

Unsettling philosopher Timothy Morton names "hyper-objects" those threatening realities like climate collapse that are too dismal and abysmal to be fully comprehended in our Anthropocene geological epoch. PTSD is the new common cold when you are poised on the brink of dissolution, when you are faced with "calamitous climate change, haywire politic, global pandemic . . . a world hurtling towards a profoundly uncertain future at unimaginable speed careening into the unknown, almost incapable of glancing back."[17] The most familiar of the inhumane dreams are the apocalyptic "Grey Goo" scenarios of nano-technology running out of control and consuming the Earth's biomass.[18] The horror genre in film and literature has never been more popular.[19] The more anxious and worried people become, the more horror they consume.

Susan Sontag famously argued against illness as a metaphor for life, while using it herself: "Everyone who is born holds dual citizenship, in the kingdom of the well and in the kingdom of the sick."[20] What follows are some sick, inhumane dreams that herald thunderclouds of exploding afflictions on the horizon. But the worst treachery—the most malicious thievery—is that which robs us of our hopes and dreams.

JESUS HUMAN

## **Inhumane Dream #1: Religion**

*The answer to religion is not no religion, but another way of thinking of it. Another way of being in it.*
INDIAN-BORN BRITISH-AMERICAN NOVELIST SALMAN RUSHDIE[21]

You can't escape a religious sensibility. As Ludwig Wittgenstein said to his former student and longtime friend, Maurice O'Connor Drury (d. 1976), "I am not a religious man, but I can't help seeing everything from a religious point of view."[22] Religion is everywhere, and there are lots of substitutes for it. Science, for instance, provides deep meaning from a comprehensive story. This is the sort of meaning religion used to provide before trust in the divine eroded. The truth is, science is the study of God's imagination, while theology is the study not of God but of faith in God.

*If God existed, and if he cared for humankind, he would never have given us religion.*
BRITISH NOVELIST AND ESSAYIST MARTIN AMIS (D. 2023)
CRITIQUED BY HIS MORE FAMOUS NOVELIST FATHER KINGSLEY AMIS (D. 1995)
FOR HIS "TERRIBLE COMPULSIVE VIVIDNESS"[23]

**Bad Ol' Days:** As our world becomes smaller, more generic, and more global, a plethora of self-proclaimed prophets want to call us back to the good ole' days of religious belief. These ecclesiastical throwbacks believe we would live meaningful

## WE DREAM, AND SOME DREAMS ARE INHUMANE

lives, have healthy families, and find our souls if we could simply embrace once again the "old-time religion."

But that "good ole' old-time religion" was never really "good" or "old" to begin with. As learning and technology and information have rolled down from the mountains, many self-respecting people have found it best to leave religion. They view religion like an overweight middle-aged bather who still thinks she/he is svelte and skinny. When asked to put on a cover over the swim-wear, the bather feels the snub and goes away only to come back wearing a thong.

---

*Nothing so masks the face of God as religion.*
JEWISH PHILOSOPHER MARTIN BUBER (D. 1965)[24]

---

Whether it is Islamic or Christian or Jewish fundamentalism, religion seeks to make its adherents less human and its followers inoculated from ever tasting the "real thing." While religion is accelerating the rate of what scholars call "secularization," but is really sacralization,[25] the world needs a Jesus-led humanization.

Political campaigns, charged rhetoric, Mosaic, Pauline and Sharia laws, and culture wars have become the domain of the Evil One. Their adherents, convinced in the purity of their Jihad in Muslim or Christian forms, are becoming less than human. They are in danger of being made in the image of the spirits they follow. Yes, these principalities are more interesting than all things manufactured, and they are immortal souls. Yet their tracks and tenets lead to the depths not the heights. Ironically, secular people see these religious attempts for what they are: spiritual sirens that quote Scripture and pray fervently—all the while luring their fold not to heaven, or even earth, but under the earth.

In the Robin Wright film "Land" (2021), the character she plays asks a stranger, "Why are you helping me?" The stranger replies, "You are in my path." You can't help everyone. But we can help those in our path. And if everyone helped those in their path, what a different world this would be. In Spanish the "neighbor" we're mandated to love is el projimo—the one nearest to you, the "proximate."

Christianity represents a sea change in human sensibility about what it means to be "humane," where people are more attuned to each other's needs, where the view (and worldview) of those in the back seats and skid rows are as important as those in the box seats or front rows, and where, in the deep words of Lutheran colleague Jim Mueller, "Do for one which you wish you could do for all."[26]

With ChatGPT and Bard, the AI pastor has arrived. Type in your spiritual state or theological perplexity, and ChatKJV will deliver an answer from the Scripture.[27] The problem is ChatKJV elevates the Bible as solution giver instead of promoter of a relationship with God, Jesus, each other, and creation. In other words, the antihumanization of religion has arrived, if not the creation of a whole new religion itself.

WE DREAM, AND SOME DREAMS ARE INHUMANE

## **Inhumane Dream #2: Intellectualism**

The most precious things in life can't be rationalized, intellectualized, audited, or measured. But for human elevation to take place, the world needs more rationality and intellect, not less. Cognitive psychologist Steven Pinker talks about a public sphere that has abandoned rationality, a public square "infested with fake news, quack cures, conspiracy theories, and post-truth rhetoric."[28]

> *Truth is whatever your contemporaries let you get away with saying.*
> PRAGMATIST PHILOSOPHER RICHARD RORTY (D. 2007),[29]
> GRANDSON OF WALTER RAUSCHENBUSCH

But human beings are more than human brains, no matter what neuromaniacs say.[30] The current fashions and forms of rationality cultivate crusaders more than critics—the intellectual dimness of a plodding, bureaucratic rationality; a politicized, propagandistic reasoning contaminated by "noble lies" and "righteous anger;" or a detached, anti-historical intellectualism. Every artist and author knows that creativity hangs on an intelligence deeper than rational thought.

**Mere Academia:** Education is in crisis, not just in the US but around the world.[31] The halo of education's sacred mission has been burnished, banished, or betrayed. To take but one example, whether US higher education has become more of an obstacle than a path to upward mobility is a hotly debated one. The creation of a new model of academe that incorporates both hemispheres of the brain, which is the only model that can birth the new renaissance human, is one of the great intellectual endeavors of the twenty-first century.[32]

Dostoevsky said that the triumph of any "*ism*" (a word he himself italicized) would be "the furthest point of removal from the Kingdom of Heaven."[33] And intellectualism has turned dreams into nightmares almost faster than anything. Each "ism" harbors a profound partial-truth, but when that part is made into a whole, there is falsehood. The Romantics countered the Cartesian *cogito ergo sum* ("I think therefore I am") with *volo ergo sum* ("I desire therefore I am"). Fyodor Dostoevsky's novella *Notes from the Underground* (1864) has the Underground man state this explicitly: "Reason, gentlemen, is incontrovertibly a good thing, but reason is no more than reason—while desires are an expression of the whole of life."[34]

---

*Nine-tenths of tactics were certain enough to be teachable in schools; but the irrational tenth was like the kingfisher flashing across the pool and in it lay the test of generals.*
T. E. LAWRENCE (A.K.A. LAWRENCE OF ARABIA)[35]

---

Humanization is not coincident with bigger brain encephalization. Human intelligence is in short supply today, even in places where you might imagine it would flourish, such as the CIA.

The conception of a new model of academe is one of the great intellectual endeavors of the twenty-first century.

As a bastion of defense against the sin of religion (yes,

## WE DREAM, AND SOME DREAMS ARE INHUMANE

Religion can be a sin), and its "mindless" praying hordes, some want to lead the world into cool, rational sensibility. Descartes, Locke, and a myriad of neuro-biologists have become the celebrated master humans, the ones to study, the ones from whom the movers and shakers seek counsel. Though this heady pursuit seems safer than traditional aspects of the religion option, its year-end dividends are just as poisonous. Academics can be some of the biggest bigots and bores in their high-brow hostility against the uneducated, their haughtiness about the hoi polloi, their arrogance in endowed know-it-all-ness.

Nothing is more bloody than the corridors of academe, where reputations have been slaughtered mercilessly over the slightest of disputes and where entire careers are consumed with protecting fiefdoms and filtering out anyone who might burst one's bubble of like-minded academics. Freud diagnosed the characteristic trait of intellectualism "the narcissism of small differences." Bloody encounters between competing schools of thought and the inconsequential precision of academic scholarship have precipitated a decline in academic reach; today the typical scholarly monograph is lucky to sell 500 non-library copies. The old "wisdom" that the average academic article has "about 10 readers" and that 50% are never read at all is surely overstated, and has never been documented. But the fact that 80 percent of those who cite an academic paper ("citers") never read what they are citing has been documented, and leaves as bad an aftertaste.

Nevertheless, our pursuits of science and learning are not activities to be abandoned. Neither is our pursuit of theology.

But the purpose of theological study is not to create more theologians; it is to create whole and complete human beings.

Education as an attempt to "save us" will do little more than jump-start Frankenstein's monster. People can be more educated, more knowledgeable, more practical, more successful, and more healthy, and still be less human. If we are not careful, we will do nothing more than realize the science fiction of *Terminator* movies. What makes life real life are the aspects of who we are and who we are made to be—aspects that are not the result of pure knowledge and a vain attempt to be like the Creator.

*Truth has perished; it has vanished from their lips.*
JEREMIAH 7:28B NIV

I am a nomadic predator of truth in a world of entrenched intellectual allegiances and barbed-wire disciplines, unimpressed by reputations and prone to rescue the obscure or take seriously the neglected, dismissed and suppressed. I have spent a lifetime in academe, but my home has never been the academy. Nature and human nature are my habitats.

Much of Western Christianity has been bound in the shackles of intellectualism for too long, as the spirit of academia (or academentia) has taken pride of place over the mind of Christ. Jacketed in the garb of academia rather than the robes of ecclesia, theologians of the church fantasize about a life of academic glory over the glory of contributing to the body of Christ. The paths to theological glory in the academy are paved with declarations that God is dead or dormant or

## WE DREAM, AND SOME DREAMS ARE INHUMANE

the pious posture of academic uncommittedness. Survival in some theological circles is a maze of mayhem and a game of lethal hopscotch with mysterious lines that are fatal to cross.

When skeptics accuse followers of Jesus of "not being rational," they are exactly right. The biblical definition of faith is the "substance of things hoped for, the evidence of things not seen."[36] Faith is all about the up-in-the-air, the pending and the invisible, neither of which is subject to rational scrutiny. To say that "faith is the possibility of the impossible" is to say something that is not just non-academic, but anti-academic.

Faith is the domain of dreams. The realm of what can be not simply what is. The most important things in life are beyond rational thinking. The life of faith means a scholar who is a Christian will always hover on the margins of academic respectability.

*Reasoning will never make a man correct an ill opinion which by reasoning he never acquired.*
JONATHAN SWIFT IN A 1721 LETTER TO CHARLES FORD[37]

Academics advocate openness. We want an "open society," with open borders and open habits of mind. In fact, universities are supposed to be open corridors to conversation and discussion. Instead, they have become closed circles, bastions of "safe spaces" and "no platforming." They are as closed as those we are argued against, closed to the minds of ordinary people, and closed-minded to uneducated people. We're even closed to open markets.

**Pull Up the Drawbridge:** Universities are not meant to be protection rackets for progressivism and liberalism, each a closed shop of ideological correctness.

Yet no one reproduces privilege more than universities. And no institution is more cookie cutter than a college. Princeton is located just 15 minutes by car from Trenton, NJ, which may be the poorest place in the state. How many of those Princetonians have ever driven there, or if they've driven through, have gotten out of the car and talked to anyone?

But of all the thought-crimes of the academy, perhaps the worst is its condescension. Who says the best ideas have to come out of universities? My mountain Gramma had some very wise things to say and wise aphorisms to remember. She was a literal homo sapiens, a "wise human." We equate literacy with intelligence, forgetting how much wisdom and learning pre-literate people carried, much of it lost in the transitions of time.

Toward the end of his life, German Jesuit Karl Rahner, one of the most influential theologians of the twentieth century, was asked: "What constitutes the *mysterium* of human life?" He responded with the erudition of a lifetime: "That is difficult to answer. Perhaps it could be put briefly this way: ultimately, for me, the mystery consists in being able to grasp rationally that the incomprehensible really exists. This is the highest act of human understanding."[38]

The highest act of human reason is the rational acknowledgment that mystery exists, a mystery that is alive and active. That mystery has a name: "the mystery that has been

## WE DREAM, AND SOME DREAMS ARE INHUMANE

kept hidden has now been revealed—Christ in you, the hope of glory."[39] The most influential philosopher of the twentieth century, Martin Heidegger, was more right than he knew when he admitted that the biblical idea of having life in Christ was a crucial resource in the philosophical quest to understand authentic human existence and to get beyond a tired rationalism and arid intellectualism.[40]

## **Inhumane Dream #3: Nostalgia**

The human appetite for fantasia is only exceeded by the human appetite for nostalgia. Nostalgia is a permanent resident in every human heart. Nostalgia can be seen in the human hankering after an idyllic past, or a more fabled future. But nostalgia causes us to stall when we should soar. Not to mention that, as someone observed, "nostalgia ain't what it used to be."

Who cannot identify with Lot's wife? She was able to go forward only by not looking back. The way forward is not by way of the rear-view mirror. Yet she didn't want to forget. She wanted the world to remember what she'd been through and what she left behind. The tears she shed for the past drowned out her future in a teary tsunami of salt. We may not cry ourselves to death, but we season all our statements about the future with great big pillars of salt.

Some people are hot-tubbing it in dreamy nostalgia—dreaming for the good old days of home-bound mothers and work-bound fathers, when men were men and women were women, when stewardesses smiled, when the center held, when the best *man* won, and when church meant one-hour of congregational worship on a Sunday morning. Rather than being tinctured by the tradition, nostalgia tapeworms us in the tradition.

Nostalgic yearnings are evident in what the late Polish sociologist Zygmunt Bauman liked to call a "Retrotopia" or what British cultural theorist Mark Fisher (aka "k-punk")

## WE DREAM, AND SOME DREAMS ARE INHUMANE

calls a "retromania." Today you can even buy "self-cracking" paint.

Even when communities of faith want to move beyond survival to revival, our "revival" dreams are more "give me that old-time religion" than a call to go forward into a new and higher life. At best the transition dreams are what the Germans call *Fernweh*, or a longing for faraway places. To "live by faith"[41] means to come fully to human life—which only comes by living in faith and from faith.

"You must be born again," Jesus said. You must die to the past to be born to the future. Dying to the past doesn't mean you don't take the past with you, but it does mean you die to its power over you. Just as the children of Israel took the bones of their ancestor with them,[42] so we are guided by the past and preserve its memory. A Jesus human is inspired by the future, but instructed by the past. As architect Maya Lin indelibly etched in her basalt wall, you can't separate the living from the dead, just as the reflection of your face overlaps the names of the fallen in the Vietnam Veterans Memorial.

Jason Rutledge, of Holmes County, Ohio, exclusively uses heavy horses for his farming needs. But he's doing so not out of any anti-technological or pro-Luddite sensibilities, or because almost 50% of the county is Amish. It's much deeper than that. "It's disrespectful to throw away thousands of years of expertise for seventy-five years of fossil fuel," Rutledge says. "I don't work with horses because I want to go back to the past. I'm doing it because we must preserve this as a valid tool in the toolbox of humanity for the future."[43] Small communities throughout the US and Europe are committed to a sustainable, organic, and solar-powered future in which real horse power has a permanent and vital role alongside the most frontier-level technologies.

The Jesus human life is not linear but organic; it evolves through choices or reactions to one's environment as one moves into the future. Some people think they're "rooted" when they're really stuck. There is a big difference between the two: rooted and stuck. The more your roots reach down, the less stuck you are and the more stretch and strength you have.

Humans are best seen as the recipients of God's love and desire, not the objects of God's decrees and commands. A Jesus human is not someone who survives but abides and attends—not someone who is merely tutored in survival skills like knowing how to start a fire, but someone who has learned abidance and attendance skills like knowing how to keep a fire going in the midst of hailstorms and hurricanes. "If you abide in me," Jesus said, "and I abide in you, ask what you desire, and God will give you the desires of your heart."[44] Abidance issues in abundance, not nostalgic belongings and yearnings.

WE DREAM, AND SOME DREAMS ARE INHUMANE

## **Inhumane Dream #4: Economics**

Some dictatorships are not political. It could even be argued that most live in economic dictatorships.

The world will not be saved by economics, by politics, or even by religion. Only Jesus can save the world. Still, these things may enable us to not just tell a better story, but to tell ***the*** Story better.

The problem is that we tend to maximize productivity at the expense of humanity. Out of the top 100 economies in the world, most are not nation states but corporate states. The 500 most powerful companies alone represent 70 percent of world commerce.[45]

In the words of Johan Verstraeten, a theologian and ethicist at KU Leuven, a research university in the Flemish-speaking city of Leuven in Flanders, Belgium, "The good life of an individual is always realized in community with others. There can be no common good without the basic condition for human flourishing or, in classical terms, the fully human development of the whole person and of all citizens. A society that does not provide its citizens with the conditions for full integration as participants cannot be a good society."[46]

---

*True union, the union of heart and spirit, does not enslave, nor does it neutralize the individuals which it brings together, it super-personalizes them.*
FRENCH PRIEST PIERRE TEILHARD DE CHARDIN (D. 1955)[47]

---

Two friends, Cuba's Fidel Castro and Argentina's Che

JESUS HUMAN

Guevera, conspired to conduct a revolution. Their revolution was all about engendering a "New Man," a new human who would live in this world primarily not out of response to material prospects but only motivated by moral incentives. They drew from Christianity its "social vision," as Castor called it, but wanted nothing to do with the moorings of that "social vision" in Christianity.

Crush-and-burn communism and slash-and-burn capitalism end at the same dead-end: hyper-centralized control (whether online businesses or government bureaucracy). We don't need more or bigger bureaucracies where it is always the mallet, never the scalpel.[48] We need personalized, localized face-to-face economics.

A flourishing economy needs Catholic Social Teaching (CST), as outlined in Pope Leo XIII's 1891 encyclical letter *Rerum Novarum* and the foundation text for its three pillars: not individualism but the common good; not centralized control but subsidiarity; and not a vast wealth gap but solidarity with the needs of others.

In short, a "Jesus human" economy where justice emerges from love should embody the Siamese triplets of ethics: subsidiarity, solidarity, and sustainability.

Subsidiarity: The Oxford English Dictionary defines subsidiarity as the idea that a central authority should have a subsidiary function, performing only those tasks which cannot be performed effectively at a more immediate or local level. In other words, the local is privileged over the universal, the lower agency (family, church, community, private initiative, voluntary sectors) should be privileged

## WE DREAM, AND SOME DREAMS ARE INHUMANE

over the higher agency (state, corporate entity). The most decentralized, lowest, and least entity is the best manager of affairs. We cannot afford to lose what scholars now call "cultural ecosystem services" like those found in conventional barber shops, diners, feed stores, gas stations, burger joints, taverns, etc. in which the wisdom of other generations is passed.

Solidarity: We're all in this together. Humans need a vast web of kindness, tenderness, and mutual obligation that manifest themselves in mannerly interpersonal and ceremonial ways.[49]

Sustainability: This involves social issues as well as environmental. The World Economic Forum has called sustainability the business issue of the millennium.

**Rigged for the Bigs:** The Siamese triplets of ethics makes us concerned about the human spirit—and how much of it we are willing to sacrifice for productivity, efficiency, quarterly reports, and the "selfish gene." True genetics is not "eat what you kill" (Economic Man) but "share what you kill" (Jesus Human). Fred D'Aguiar's "Ballad of the Throwaway People" has this line:

> We are the throwaway people
> The problem that won't go away people.[50]

## JESUS HUMAN

*If socialism is out, neoliberal technocracy unbearable, and populism unsustainable, what else is possible but to attempt a system in which the powerless and voiceless take some power and voice, and with these their share of responsibility.*

ALICE MARTIN AND ANNIE QUICK[51]

Named after the anthropologist Robin Dunbar, the Dunbar Constant is the theory that humans function best in groups of 150. This is the cognitive limit to the number of people with whom we can maintain social relationships. Any more than 150 issues in the need for hierarchy and weapons and policing.

The Dunbar Constant needs to be expanded for two reasons. First, our networking on social media has vastly increased our potential for human association. Second, it flies in the face of research (ostrich-eggshell bead currency, for example)[52] that shows how our ancestors were parts of social networks of far more than 150 people without the need for monarchs or military.

WE DREAM, AND SOME DREAMS ARE INHUMANE

## **Inhumane Dream #5: Politics**

The kingdom of God is portrayed as the "one pearl of great price."[53]

But when people think of the "kingdom," they immediately think of politics, which is downstream of culture. This is especially the case with Jesus' usage of "kingdom" and his alleged putting the kingdom central in everything he did. I will never forget getting into a burly argument with a couple of proponents of what was then called "the emerging church." They argued that "the US budget is a kingdom document. It's a document of Jesus morality." No, I countered, it's a political document. It's a snapshot of politicians caught in compromising positions, in flagrante budgeto. Georgia pastor/senator Raphael Warnock wisely defines legislation as "a letter to our children."[54] But when all you can think of is "systemic injustice" in political not relational terms, dead letters are what you end up with.

All the temptations of Jesus were about choosing politics: he could be a king, a judge, or a rebel. Jesus himself said clearly that the kingdom is not as lowly as the political but as high as the loftiest dreams we share as humans:

> Once the Pharisees asked Jesus when God's kingdom would come. He replied, "The coming of God's kingdom is not something you can see just by watching for it carefully. People will not say, 'Here it is.' Or, 'There it is.' God's kingdom is among you."[55]

## JESUS HUMAN

There it is. In the words of David Lloyd Dusenbury, it is Jesus' very "resistance to the political that makes his life, unexpectedly redemptive."[56] God's kingdom is best seen in relational not political terms. Jesus insists that his messiahship has total continuity with the Israel's past, and even that he himself is Embodied Torah, defined now relationally not politically or institutionally ("I have come to fulfill the Law"). Jesus shows how this works in his suggested "apps" called the "Beatitudes" to his own Sermon on the Mount.

> Therefore, if you are offering your gift at the altar and there remember that your brother or sister has something against you, leave your gift there in front of the altar. First go and be reconciled to them; then come and offer your gift."[57]

What is more important than keeping "right" the protocols and processes of the religious and political establishments? Keeping "right" the relationships that define life and don't de-form identity. The journal *Genetics* published an article arguing that one's choice of spouse may have a greater impact on lifespan than genetics.[58] The Beatitudes, where "Blessed" is best translated as "Human Flourishing," are the life apps to a Jesus human.

Politics has now become religion; and science has become political science. The whole logic of politics, especially post-truth politics, which is the logic of our day, is that the devil is stronger than God, that one can destroy evil only with evil, even if it is called anti-evil, and that what Machiavelli first

## WE DREAM, AND SOME DREAMS ARE INHUMANE

called the "noble lie"[59] is a legitimate instrument of statesmanship. Winning is not all that matters in life, but it's all that matters in politics. When politics turns into its own form of religion, authoritarianism is not far behind.

Jesus taught his disciples to do what he did: preach, teach, and heal. There will be no healing, and social fabrics will continue to fray, frazzle, and tear, until we stop confusing ends and means. Can we agree to disagree on venues and avenues (means), shared values, and common dreams (ends) without impugning each other's moral character? Physicians of the body are trained not to be caught up in politics. They are in the healing and helping business. Why are physicians of the soul, doctors, and "curates" of the whole body-mind-spirit, not living up to similar standards? Do we only care for and attend to those who agree with us? The body of Christ is a community of faith, not a political caucus.

*If you learn someone shares your faith but not your politics, and you immediately distrust their faith, then your politics might be displacing your religion.*
DAVID A. FRENCH[60]

Comedians were once paid to be funny. Now they're paid to be political. If Jesus followers in the first century spent as much time as we do in the twenty-first century obsessing over the politics, politicians, and policies of the Roman Empire (and the US republic is partly based on Rome's model), there would have been no Christianity to celebrate. After all, Tiberius, Caligula, Claudius, and Nero were not nice people.

JESUS HUMAN

We are called to lift up the good news of a Jubilee Jesus, a realm of reality above, brought below, in the story of Jesus' birth, death, resurrection, ascension, and return.

Russian Orthodox theologian Alexander Schmemann puts it like this:

> How understandable and needful becomes Christ's silence about all the things that so passionately interest us: government, religion, history, even morality. He always talks to me and about me-only that is of interest to Him. But in me, for Him, is the whole world, the whole of life, the whole of history. Therefore He saves me, not Russia, nor the government, nothing else. So that any fight, any 'anti'—always has and carries in it the most awful 'spiritual' defeat. Christ saves the world in me. "All creation rejoices."[61]

Some people are boot-camping it in imperial dreams of a new world order. Some people are Wall-Streeting it in the dream of one-worldism under the rule of a Global Market. Some people are balloting it in the dream of one-worldism under the Empire of Democracy.[62] And some people are praying it in the dream of One World under Sharia Law.

Islam is not just the fastest growing religion in Europe and North America. The Muslim demographic is handwriting on the wall: native populations in the West are aging, fading and enfeebled, while Muslim populations are young, surging and evangelistic. The Bible says, "Where there is no

## WE DREAM, AND SOME DREAMS ARE INHUMANE

vision, the people perish." But it is equally true that "Where there is no people, the visions perish."[63]

Nobody could "figure" Jesus out. Not the religious establishment. Not the political establishment. Not the economic establishment. Not even the disciples could figure Jesus out. He didn't "fit" any of the conventional cubbyholes. That's what made everyone so mad, even why they called him "mad." If you think you've figured Jesus out, or made sense of him, you're pondering the wrong Jesus. Jesus is beyond our figurings and configurings. So too should be his disciples: beyond labels and tags, categories and configurations. The line between good and evil, the divine and the diabolical, runs through every human heart, not around politics and ideologies and cultures.

*I won't mix in politics. . . . I don't involve myself: that's all. If I get stuck in politics, I will stop loving. Because I will have to stand by one, not by all. This is the difference.*
MOTHER TERESA[64]

If "political" means staying engaged with current issues of the day, then we all need to be political. But that would make prayer a political activity. If politics is the art and science of working together to live together in harmonious difference; if politics is creating fertile conditions for human flourishing, then politics is service and a form of mission—a far cry from the debased political culture of our day.

## **Inhumane Dream #6: Celebrityhood**

In his studies into the quest for immortality, University of Toronto professor H. J. Jackson argues that humans desire four things for immortality: celebrity, popularity, critical appeal, and influence.[65] Get all four, and you hit the jackpot. Today all four are encapsulated in that one word: celebrity.

One of the big changes in our culture is the number of people who claim that "being famous" is one of their big goals in life. Fifty years ago, the percentage of under 20s who listed fame as a "goal" in life was in the single digits or teens. Today it often tops the list of life goals and dreams.

One might call this California Dreaming—a fantasy land of fame and fortune and film. Hollywood[66] is a dreamland filled with small people, people smaller than life. The great magnifying glass of the screen makes celebrities godlike. Pop culture is often a revolving carousal of revolting idols and hollow celebrities whose true selves disappear into the spotlight.

Everyone will tell you that there is more to life than having everything. But everything that comes out of Hollywood says the opposite. In the California Dream, "show-me-the-money" aspirations have replaced the "gold-digger" sneers and "anything-for-a-buck" aspersions of our ancestors. The true "American Dream" of going from log cabins to white picket fences and even a White House had more to do with leaving behind a legacy of a good name and good will than bequeathing a Hummer home and mega bucks.

Look how far the happiness needle has moved from a time when "happiness" meant better communities, better

## WE DREAM, AND SOME DREAMS ARE INHUMANE

environments, and better futures for our children; from a time when a "heart of gold" didn't refer to any precious metal.

The term "The American Dream" came from James Truslow Adams' book *Epic of America* (1931), which came out of the early years of the Depression. In other words, the greatest dream suppressor in USAmerican history ("The Great Depression") gave us the most famous dream stimulator in history, "The American Dream."

But what "The American Dream" meant to the person who coined the phrase is different from the Dream Lite it has come to mean today, which is often a "greed is good" creed. The American Dream is not success or fame or fortune, but service and greatness in overcoming obstacles. The American dream was not originally an individual dream, but a community dream where everyone pulled together. For James Truslow Adams the "American dream" was a:

> dream of a land in which life would be better and richer and fuller for everyone, with opportunity for each according to ability or achievement. It is not a dream of motor cars and high wages merely, but a dream of social order in which each man and each woman shall be able to attain to the fullest stature of which they are innately capable, and be recognized by others for what they are, regardless of birth or position.[67]

The key to living the original "American Dream" is not looking at where you are now, but looking at how far you've come from where you began, and measuring that distance in terms of every aspect of life.

---

*I never said it was always wrong to enter fairyland.
I only said it was always dangerous.*

G. K. CHESTERTON'S FATHER BROWN[68]

---

This is a celebrity culture. But humans don't need celebrity idols. We do need icons—models to nourish our ideals, icons to point us to transcendence, magnets to animate our ambitions, navigators to chart scenarios to pursue, Yodas with sayings to memorize, sages with patterns to paste in our playbooks (notebooks, workbooks, sketchpads, etc.), and heroes to inspire us toward greatness. At its roots, celebrity culture reflects a search for transcendence and connection.

A celebrity culture majors in "personality" and minors in "personhood." The Roman Emperor Vespasian (d. 79) quipped on his deathbed, "Oh dear, I think I am becoming a god." Godifying the self is the occupational hazard of every human born into celebrityhood and its consumer ethos that tells us every day from every angle of a mirror or screen "You are a god;" "You are #1;" "Put yourself first;" "You deserve it." Or in the prideful words of the original "top-of-the-heavens" Babel, tower over everyone and "make a name" for yourself.[69] Self-love has reached its logical conclusion in the current trend of sologamy, where more and more women and men are feeling called to marry themselves.

To die to self is hard enough in a celebrityhood culture, but to some degree humans can't escape selfism. The word

## WE DREAM, AND SOME DREAMS ARE INHUMANE

pupil comes from the Latin *pupilla*, "little doll," because when we look in other people's eyes, we see a tiny reflection of our "little-doll" selves.

Celebrity is based on the fantasy of intimacy. When the spell of the fantasy is broken, the celebrant's blood boils and goes on the warpath, out for blood to make the fantasy real one way or another. Since we created these celebrity gods, we claim the right to chew them up and spit them out. Celebrities are brought down to crash and burn as surely as celebrity cultures will crash and burn.

## **Inhumane Dream #7: Drugs**

More USAmericans die yearly of overdose deaths than died in the entire Vietnam War. We designed on purpose addictive algorithms, habit-forming products, and pill-mill therapies as outlined by consumer psychologist Nir Eyal *Hooked: How to Build Habit-Forming Products* (2014). Eyal has now done an about-face about our narcotized life, and written an interventionist book called *Indistractable: How to Control Your Attention and Choose Your Life* (2019).[70]

Some people are walking around in a zombieland of pipedreams—blissed out on Prozac, turned on by love drugs, possessed by Fentanyl, zoned out on cocaine, and zoned in on Ritalin. In San Francisco, one of the wealthier cities in the world, there are 50% more injection drug users than students enrolled in its public school system.[71] An astounding one in six USAmericans are on psychiatric medications. One quarter of women aged 60 and over now take anti-depressants. Yet it seems the more we take depression medicines, the more the depression rates climb, proving the paradoxical meaning of the ancient Greek *pharmakon*, which meant both "cure" and "poison."

Like the devil, drug addiction comes in many disguises. Ask any member of Gamblers Anonymous. As honorific and entitled a status as to be rewarded VIP status in the gambling world, for a casino to designate someone a VIP is shorthand for "loser" and human ATM. But what is Wall Street but a gilded casino in the grip of gambling fever? And what Wall Street is to the rich, lotteries are to the poor. Even Methodism which is known for its hard line against gambling turned

## WE DREAM, AND SOME DREAMS ARE INHUMANE

soft when it came to lotteries: "I never bought a lottery ticket myself, nor ever will," John Wesley boasted to George Whitefield in 1743, "but I blame not those who do."[72]

Nothing can wipe away a certain dismal feeling, induced by the spectacle of so much folly and stupidity, as when a pregnant woman smokes, drinks, does drugs, and generally doesn't take care of herself, thereby turning her womb into a wombat. FAS, SIDS, a tsunami of birth defects, and disabilities flood the culture, leaving long-term consequences in their wake. Could Marx have ever really believed that in a "classless society" there would be no desire for drugs/opium and no need for religion?

Jennifer Clement's troubling novel *Prayers for the Stolen* (2014) is the story of Ladydi Garcia Martínez, a girl growing up in a rural community of Mexico, where to protect their daughters from drug traffickers, parents either had to pass their daughters off as boys, uglify them by, among other things, blackening their teeth, or hide them in holes dug into the ground in cornfields. At one point, Ladydi confesses that "Life is a crazy, out of order, inside out, salt mixed with sugar place where the drowned can be walking on dry land."[73]

We are stimulating ourselves to death in every corner of our existence. Stimulus bills are passed to pump up flagging demand, boost stalled economic activity, and solve our economic woes. We stimulate our digital kids so that they can learn in ways our analog adults feel comfortable teaching. Our houses of worship stimulate their congregations with 40 minutes of a "spiritual high" so that they will sit down, sit still, and listen to 40 minutes of teaching.

A new era of mental health is being heralded in the wake of a psychedelic renaissance. Long outlawed drugs such as LSD, DMT (n-dimethyltryptamine), and especially psilocybin, the psychoactive compound in magic mushrooms, promise healing therapies that can revolutionize the mental health world.[74] Since "psychedelic" carries the whiff of Patchouli-hippiedom, the new phrase for it is "5-HT2A."

Big Pharma has turned many scientists into marketing shills. They manufacture new diseases whose primary function is to necessitate new varieties of psychotropic pills. With an ever-expanding array of problems being added to psychiatry's *Diagnostic and Statistical Manual*, "diseases have all but become commodities and are as subject to fashions as other commodities, with the main determinant of the fashion cycle being the patent life of a drug."[75]

Anger running wild? Take a pill to calm down. What is still a human problem in many parts of the world has now become a medical problem. In the USA, we medicalize everything, blind to the reality that to be human is sometimes a medical condition.

The dream of a chemical solution to every problem creates its own ironies. For instance, it's illegal to take amphetamines to help you stay awake and cram for exams. Such behavior could get you ten years in jail. But the same Class 1 controlled substance is widely prescribed to help you learn better. In the language of the Columbian drug trade, you are offered *plata o plomo:* you can choose *plata* (silver) *or plomo* (lead)—accept a bribe & sell out to the Cartel, or face a bullet between the eyes. Make a killing or be killed. *Plata o*

## WE DREAM, AND SOME DREAMS ARE INHUMANE

*Plomo* is a choice between two epitaphs: he was bought off, or he bought it.

Not until the second half of the twentieth century have "drugs" and "treat and street" medicine begun doing more good than harm, thanks to the introduction of penicillin in 1942. For example, we still don't know whether drugs that reduce fever make the illness better or worse. Fever is vexing to the patient, but it's even more vexing for germs and bacteria, which is its purpose. Is nobody allowed to experience pain anymore? Iatrogenic illness, or diseases induced by medical treatments and drugs, is the third leading cause of death in North America, superseded only by heart disease and cancer. Two-thirds of the increase in white midlife death rate is drug overdosing, the remaining causes are suicide and chronic liver diseases.

We inhabit a fragmenting, dysfunctional, out-of-control world boasting whirlwind joy-rides of purpose and tilt-a-whirls of kaleidoscopic experience, many of them fueled by Big Pharma. But at the end it all comes to nothing.

The answer to the "Drug Dream" is not a renewed War on Drugs, a federal and state offensive which drove the market underground and made it stronger, but instead to inspire a better dream.

---

*A miracle drug is any drug that will do what the label says it will do.*
BEST-SELLING NOVELIST ERIC HODGINS (1899-1971)

---

To mark the Jewish New Year, the then chief Rabbi Lord

Sacks was given a television show on BBC called "What's the Point of Religion?" Sacks included sociologist Robert Putnam, who ended the show on this warning note: "Religion is a powerful medicine. It has powerful effects. But taken in high doses, it can be lethal for a civic community."[76]

Bishop Todd Hunter has an excellent probe of "Finding True Faith in the Bubble of Bad Religion" entitled "What Jesus Intended" (2023). But this notion that religion does more harm than good has been academically reinforced by a series of surveys that argue precisely this. Especially deemed harmful are TV evangelists and faith healers.

This is not true. Not all TV preachers are bunko, huckster, snake-oil quacks. From 1978 until his death in 2023, Charles Stanley's TV "In Touch" ministry charmed and blessed millions and was heard in 127 languages around the world. Besides, Benny Hinn and his ilk are seldom really dangerous. Instead, they activate the Placebo Effect. Drug companies, on the other hand, invent whole categories of disease, such as ADD or "social anxiety disorder" in order to sell their cures. We've even made normal anxieties such as the fear of public speaking, a.k.a. stage fright, a disease requiring medication. Since 1999, stage-fright is listed as a psychiatric disease, with symptoms of blushing, sweating, heart racing, trembling, stammering, etc. Remedy? Prayer, anyone?

Jesus will let us take him for granted, but the loss is ours: we lose the wonder and majesty of his presence. But when Jesus is not just honored but lived, life is constantly affirmed in all its unpredictability, indecipherability, and mysteriousness.

WE DREAM, AND SOME DREAMS ARE INHUMANE

## **<u>Inhumane Dream #8: Technology</u>**

Among science fiction writers there has been a recurring theme of "the dream machine"–the symbiosis of human and machine.[77] We are now on the brink of being there. Are we living the dream? Or are we outliving the nightmare?

What have humans wrought in their journey to "the dream machine?" We now can revive extinct species, modify genes, split atoms, engineer weather patterns, and transplant entire people groups. Even Dr. Faust never imagined such power.

You think this is an exaggeration. There are genomes, and then there are epigenomes. Epigenomes are outside influences which can decide which genomes to flip on and off (food, stress, exercise, etc.). CRISPRoff is a new technology which allows scientists to turn any gene in your genome on or off without making changes to your genes themselves. Once a gene is turned "off," it will stay "off" for generations until they use the CRISPRon tool to turn it back on.

On the one hand, we say: What a huge breakthrough. No more diabetes. The end of gene-based illnesses and birth defects. BUT on the other hand, the "on" and "off" switch brings with it things like the choice of eye-color in fetuses which brings with it "Designer Babies" and aversions to any genetic gambles. Here we are, but do we want to be here where we are? We also know how religious minorities have been targeted with digital persecution. In some African and Asan countries, technological oppression and surveillance are bringing us to an Orwellian existence.

**<u>Blurred Boundaries Between Born and Made:</u>** When things get bad, our only hope seems to be the emergence

## JESUS HUMAN

of a new kind of human. And the quickest ways to birth this new kind of human are all fostered by technology. But this technology can quickly go off the rails. A 2023 *Forbes* article listed the ten scariest technologies where things could go terribly wrong: 1) AI Singularity; 2) Editable Humans through Heritable Human Gene Edition; 3) Merging of Humans and Machines; 4) 3-D Print Anything; 5) Quantum Computing; 6) Autonomous Smart Robots; 7) Killer Drones; 8) Digital Surveillance; 9) Deep Fakes in the Metaverse; 10) Weaponized Nanobots.[78]

> *The Christian concept of the mystical body—all humans as members of the body of Christ—this becomes technologically a fact under electronic conditions.*
> PIERRE TEILHARD DE CHARDIN (D. 1955)[79]

Each of these ten technologies comes with a full canvas of caveats. Can human well-being be placed at the center of technological development in a way that doesn't happen on autopilot? Can we create an AI that loves humans rather than reinvents humans or requires human worship? Are all the "its" of life really better as "bits"? Can we trust technocrats and elites undistinguished by eminence of consciousness to insert that missing consciousness into the machines they create in their image? Are humans endlessly "hackable" without disrupting human society and disbanding the meaning of human life itself?[80] When Microsoft has to lay off employees, who are the first to go? The team responsible for AI ethics.[81]

Welsh poet and Anglican priest, R. S. Thomas, preached to his congregation on the evils of machines such as washing

## WE DREAM, AND SOME DREAMS ARE INHUMANE

machines, refrigerators, etc. And US poet Wendell Berry declaims against technology on his 1956 Model B IBM typewriter. Those who imagine technology as the "fix" to every problem soon find themselves in a "tech-no-fix" culture.

In September 2019, Pope Francis convened a Vatican seminar on "The Common Good in a Digital Age." As a follow-up, the Vatican issued in February 2020 a "Call for an AI Ethics" which invoked the development of a "common language to interpret what is human" in order to create a future in which "digital innovation and technological progress serve human genius and creativity and not their gradual replacement by a claimed artificial superintelligence."[82]

Technology and humanity, or technology and religion, have always been in dialogue. For example, technology and worship have been in exchange in every period of history.[83] The story of the introduction of overhead projector, and the collapse of the hymnbook, is one that any retired pastor can tell.

In short, technology is no longer a separate category. It is now part of what it means to be human. We are all cyborgs now. The main antagonists of "the human race" in the Battlestar Galactica series, the Cylons, raised most sharply the question of what it means to be human.[84] Can a Jesus human be metahuman? Is metahuman less mutation than mutilation?

Some people are dreaming woo-woo dreams of technism—posthuman, metahuman, techno-dreams—where we have nothing to fear because human ingenuity and technological progress will save us. Just send out that avatar or

## JESUS HUMAN

Master Chief (Halo) to meet and defeat the Four Horsemen of the Apocalypse,[85] the Axis of Evil, the "Great Satan," or any other threats galloping our way. Thomas More is alive and well today in the Silicon Valley of technological transcendence.[86] Humans tend to make our tools into totems. An iPhone is a tool, not a totem. The only thing worse than to taboo a tool is to totem a tool. Today we swing from taboo to totem.

Austrian phenomenologist Gunther Anders (d. 1992), a refugee from Nazi Germany, devised a philosophical anthropology for the age of technology. Anders maintained that the advance of technology drives humans to 'become the product of their own produce'; the result is people who 'can no longer live, up to the demands that their own products place on them.' The end point of this trajectory is that, in the words of political philosopher Matthew Crawford, "the world becomes a techno-zoo for defeated people."[87]

An increasingly trans-humanized world demands we contend with the question of what it means to be human. "Transhumanism" or what I prefer to call "metahumanism" is a movement that aims to overcome human limitations and celebrates the "emancipation" that comes from the merging of humans and machines to extend and expand life.[88] You can already go to conferences, like those conducted by the Foresight Nanotech Institute, and attend workshops on "Mind Uploading: How to Really Do It," a step-by-step blueprint for transferring human consciousness onto a laptop. Or you can hear plenary speeches on "The Need to Reengineer the Human Brain." There is a World

# WE DREAM, AND SOME DREAMS ARE INHUMANE

Transhumanist Association, headquartered in Palo Alto, as well as other competitor groups.

**Gutenberg-to-Google-to GRAIN:** Julian Huxley coined the phrase "transhumanism" in 1951 as a way of "man remaining man, but transcending himself; by realizing new possibilities of and for his human nature."[89] Who would not relish some bio-hacking if your skin could be de-aged by thirty years (which became possible in 2022)? To promote transhumanist agendas, however, GRAIN (GRAIN is my acronym for Genetic Engineering, Robotics, AI, Infotech, and Nanotechnology) technologies are increasingly being integrated into the medical and food industries, each application turning tighter the biosecurity-based totalitarian control grid. The answer to every problem, to every crisis from microaggressions,[90] to anthropogenic climate change, to domestic tranquility, to world famine is the same: more surveillance, more intervention, more data gathering, and more behavior modification determined by technocratic "experts."

Is metahumanism a running away from being human, or a running forward to new ways of being human? Francis Fukuyama called "transhumanism" "the world's most dangerous idea."[91] It's not a new idea, though. Only a fancy new word for the old eugenics, the science that brought us the Holocaust[92] and is now bringing us a technocratic transhumanist system that brings together Silicon Vally, Big Pharma, and Big Government.[93]

Others like Bill McKibben warn that tampering with the human body may irreversibly screw up our genetic composition.[94] Just as interesting as thinking about how society will adapt to climate change or to new modes of communication, is how society will react to and evolve with our future abilities to enhance human capabilities through technology. As of 2022, twenty-five million people have indwelling medical devices in the US alone (stents, pacemakers, artificial organs, joints, valves, lenses, neural implants, and this does not begin to address the pharmaceutical body-modifications). Tolkien's assessment of cyborg immortality can be found in his millennia-old Ringwraiths with unliving but undead flesh. Tolkien warned of "the hideous peril of confusing true 'immmortality' with limitless serial longevity."[95]

Our only hope: We need to become a new kind of human. This new kind of human can be fostered and fashioned by technology, but not defined and determined by technology.

*We have lost our way. We have lost our bearings. We have lost our sense of the sacred. We must reinvent the human.*
WENDELL BERRY POEM "A WORK OF MERCY"[96]

Besides, technology is not really about technology. It's about creativity. And this is where faith communities can shine if they understand the divine business is the creativity business. Silicon Valley's success has nothing to do with technology. Its product is technology, but its process of development is social and cultural and relational.

All sorts of places in the world are trying to be the next Silicon Valley, from London to Quatar to Beijing to Seoul to Warsaw.[97] But even Silicon Valley is not in the technology

## WE DREAM, AND SOME DREAMS ARE INHUMANE

business. It is in the imagination, innovation, ideation, and creation business. When people think of Silicon Valley, they think of AI. But what AI can't do is what communities of faith can be greatest in: creativity, empathy, dexterity—the battery charge of genius.

> *I could go on carving for 2000 years and never get tired or ever reach the end of ideas that I have.*
> SCULPTOR BARBARA HEPWORTH[98]

For the church to get in the real "technology" business as well, it must give up the status quo. Jesus humans are hazardous to the status quo, which kills genius and creativity. Every status quo needs to be taken by the lapels and given a good shaking. Faith communities need more people, not less, who ask: "But why must it be that way?" Jesus was a why-must-it-be-that-way person, a "you-have-heard-it-said-but-I-say" Messiah.

If everyone already agrees on something and with what you are saying, then why is saying it again not a waste of time? Why isn't such uniformity a waste of time? Why not say what matters, what changes things, not just point out the obvious? Besides, the status quo has left us in a mess: global financial mayhem, stock and crypto-market bubbles, obscene levels of inequality, volatile capital flows, extreme weather, etc.

We need a new social contract. We would be wise not to rake up the ashes yet again. Returning to business as usual really just means magnifying our current problems. We need to find a new Operating System (OS), maybe even discover the Original OS, which is Missional ("Go into all the world"), Relational ("make disciples"), and Incarnational ("of all cultures").[99]

WE DREAM, AND SOME DREAMS ARE INHUMANE

## Inhumane Dream #9: Dreamlessness

To act on our humanness is to dream. Not to sleepwalk through life. Not to live in a state of "stuckness" where the human spirit that makes humans human, the experimental spirit of freedom and creativity, gets stuck in a sedimented state of inertia and entropy, fear and timidity. There are people who have given up dreaming altogether, who are either tone-deaf and color blind to dreams, or who are *so* busy eking out an existence they are almost forbidden to dream or fearful of dreaming.

We live like kings, while others live like paupers. Half the world has fingers without rings; the other half has rings without fingers. People are dying of diseases for which there are vaccines that cost 12 cents. Two billion people live on less than $2 a day; 1.4 billion people do not have regular access to drinking water. How can we sleep when water is the drink of death for a billion people? Why is anyone on this planet drinking death? Can't we at least agree on that? "Of the 4.4 billion people who live in the 'developing' countries of the world, one-third do not have adequate access to drinking water, one-quarter have no proper housing, and one-fifth do not have access to modern health services."[100]

"To be a parent," as the saying goes, "is to only be as happy as your least happy child."[101] If God is our Parent, then how happy do you think God must be? Maybe one reason why the Bible says we can't look at the face of God and live is not because God's beauty is so blinding, but because

God's face is so contorted and grimaced by the pain of God's children.[102]

In the face of all our human dilemmas, it is easy to stop dreaming. In 1970, the third Secretary General of the United Nations, Burmese diplomat U-Thant (d. 1974), gave it as his judgment that at best we have ten years in which to find new answers to basic human problems. Unless we can find those answers quickly, he said, there is no hope, whatsoever, for the human experiment, no hope for continuing into the future. There are a lot of people today who have given up, refuse to bring children into the world,[103] and wait for—if not worship—Armageddon. It is a fine line between a degrowth and a dehuman agenda.

**In Your Dreams:** When you can't dream anymore, you live your nightmares. This is the definition of schizophrenia: people who can't dream, people whose waking lives become their walking nightmares. Even walking the streets today can be a nightmare. Despite the Hollywood myth of the wild, wild West (Dodge City & Tombstone had very few gun deaths), Stanford University historian Richard White has claimed that the Old West "was a far more civilized, more peaceful and safer place than American society is today."[104]

Just as we have a biological need to dream while sleeping, we have a spiritual need to dream while waking. Like our nocturnal dreams, these day dreams are shaped around the stories, songs, metaphors, and memes that make sense of our lives and are the molds into which our experiences are poured.

## WE DREAM, AND SOME DREAMS ARE INHUMANE

At night you're a novelist.
At day you're a poet at play.

---

*It is in our idleness, in our dreams,*
*that the submerged truth sometimes comes to the top.*
ENGLISH WRITER VIRGINIA WOOLF (D. 1941)[105]

---

PART FOUR:

# ABECEDARY OF A GLOBAL JESUS HUMANITY

---◇---

*Isaiah boldly says, "I was found by those who did not seek me;
I revealed myself to those who did not ask for me."*

APOSTLE PAUL[1]

---

LANGUAGE IS A DEFINING FEATURE OF BEING HUMAN, a biological function and gift of God to Adam when Adam was given the mission of giving names to every living creature. Some scholars now seriously discuss the likelihood of an "Ur Language" at the root of all languages. This notion of a common historical origin behind all languages is based on a computerized cross-comparison of words forming the basic vocabularies of the major world languages. At least twenty roots have been found that are common to all "macro" language groups.

Furthermore, Noam Chomsky's research into how children universally acquire grammar argues that language is a biological function and is innate in every child as an internal structure. Language and grammar are organs that develop in every human just like liver, lungs, kidneys, bladder, brain, and eyes. Others have argued the opposite: that language first began as a form of gesture, and that only later did it migrate from sign to speech. But humans speak languages, we don't just sign them.

**Adam/Eve's Mother Tongue?** What was this language that Adam spoke, the language that the first human spoke until the Tower of Babel, when God made different language groups as a curse so we would not challenge God's supremacy?

No one knows for sure. The Suzuki method is based on the fact that music is the universal language of humans. Did we chant our first words? Is the language of music, the world of song, our native tongue that expresses our universal desire for beauty and grace? For Charles Wesley, the two most important languages of humanity, theology and music, were one and the same. Did Adam "name" the animals by sounding out their essence? Energy and matter are different expressions of the same reality. Form is relationship. Structure is rhythm. Sound creates structure, not the other way around. There is a sound to being human, which is why music is fundamental to being human. "There's no human culture that doesn't have some form of music and dance," contends neuroscientist James Kilner.[2]

So, what inclusive idiom can we speak that articulates the fundamental values by which we want to live as simultaneous citizens of a particular place and a global planet? Elon Musk is devoted to turning humans into a multi-planetary species. But first we must learn to see ourselves as a planetary species. And before multi-planetary species, even as interspecies humans in a dawning Interspecies Age. There are 8.7 million species on the planet, most of which we know nothing about and do not appreciate.[3] We live in an "entangled" world where everything hooks into everything else, and the connections between humans and other-than-humans has yet to be explored.

> *One should be as inclusive as the ocean, which is vast because it admits hundreds of rivers.*
> ANCIENT CHINESE PROVERB[4]

This assumes, of course, that there are universal values that cross religious and cultural divides, values that call out our common humanity, not call each other's humanity into question. Certain books come closer to conveying what "human" means on a universal scale than any "international laws" or "modern laws of nations." Teilhard de Chardin's best-known book *The Human Phenomenon* (1955) and C. S. Lewis' least-known book *The Abolition of Man* (1943) come immediately to mind. Leïla Slimani, the French-Moroccan writer and French diplomat, has repented of her relativistic refutation of universal values in these words:

> For a long time . . . I bowed to the notion that to impose my views on others amounted to a kind of condescension. But now I utterly reject the idea that identity, religion or any historical heritage should dispossess individuals of rights that are universal and inalienable.[5]

## JESUS HUMAN

All the world's faith traditions have past and present shamefulness about how they treat each other. Documentary film producer Selina O'Grady's study of Muslim/Christian interfaces discloses how Christendom was generally less accepting of religious differences than when Islam was in a dominant position of power.[6] Inclusion through dilution leads to disillusion and dissolution. Inclusion through harmonious difference leads to embracing, enveloping symphonic sound, which is what this playful "Global Abecedarium of a Jesus Human" is meant to be.

The need to build genuine solidarity between those divided by religion and culture is a high imperative if the seeds of human destruction are not to be sown and grown. In an interdependent globalized world, the need for all peoples, all religions, all nations to form a cohesive agency against common threats is more pressing than ever. As Earthlings who both are loyal to the land where their ancestors are buried, and love the physical land of Planet Earth, we must build a moral structure that upholds universal values and humanitarian ideals while respecting humanity's enormous diversity and differences in political worldviews, religious beliefs, and economic persuasions. Jesus taught us to see in color, as God created the world and all its inhabitants in color.

**"Collision of Opposites":** Can you imagine a celebration sponsored by journalists that included on the guest list (and showed up) the likes of Jerry Falwell and Louis Farrakhan, Mel Brooks and Jack Kevorkian, Elie Wiesel and Leni Riefenstahl. What is even more shocking than everyone living to tell the story? The anniversary dinner was sponsored by Time-Life, Inc.[7]

It used to be said that it would take something like an impending collision with an asteroid to bring the peoples of this one world together. But we did and do have an impending asteroid collision. One is climate change. The other is the "Season of COVIDtide." How did we respond to a global pandemic and menacing interruption? As citizens of a global planet? As a united international community?

We defaulted into vaccine nationalism and succumbed to the self-interest of global corporations. The "Reign of King COVID" could have been a defining moment for global cooperation in facing a common threat. But the opposite happened. Everyone closed their borders and governments went on their own into vaccine-land.[8] No economic theory or political platform proved to be of any help. The World Health Organization revealed itself to be absolutely worthless to bring the world together to fund and distribute a vaccine, not to mention tell the unvarnished truth about the origin and nature of the threat. The more the world requires collective action, it seems, the harder it is to make collective action happen. Witness the swelling of our seas.

A truly "human" culture is one that we can share with all humanity. In the words of Benedict XVI, there are universal values and virtues which are non-negotiable. "These principles are not truths of faith, even though they receive further light and confirmation from faith; they are inscribed in human nature itself and therefore they are common to all humanity."[9]

JESUS HUMAN

---

*Grant that I may be a blessing to all thy children, of every faith and belief, that together we may discover the ways of gentleness and be led into the paths of peace; through Jesus Christ our Lord. Amen.*[10]

CORONATION PRAYER OF KING CHARLES III (06 MAY 2023)

---

**Magnolia Manifesto:** This Global Abecedary of a Jesus Human is offered in the same spirit as the Magnolia Manifesto, printed at the back of every *Magnolia* magazine. Written by two strong Jesus humans, HGTV reality stars Joanna and Chip Gaines, it demonstrates how a global citizens portfolio can stem from the particularity of the Jesus story.

> We believe in home, that it should restore us from today and ready us for tomorrow.
>
> We believe in friendship, because friends who feel like family are the best kind of friends, and that nothing matters more than family.
>
> We believe in seeking the balance between hustle and rest and learning to find contentment in both.
>
> We believe everyone deserves a seat at the table and everyone has a story worth telling.
>
> We believe in human kindness, knowing we are made better when we all work together.
>
> We believe in courage, in cartwheeling past

our comfort zones and trying something a little bit scary every day.

We believe that failure needn't be a negative thing; rather, we learn from our mistakes and fail smarter next time.

We believe in doing good work that matters and in choosing that, nudging others toward doing the same.

We believe that newer isn't always better and that it's time for the pendulum of trend to swing back to the basics.

We believe in unearthing beauty, however hidden or subtle it might be.

We believe that each day is a gift and that everyday miracles are scattered about if only we have eyes to see.

And of all heroic pursuits large or small,

We believe there may be none greater than a life well loved.

There is light from other lamps.[11] The Book called Ecclesiastes is a Greek translation of the author's Hebrew name Qoheleth, which is a title for someone who is a gatherer (of wisdom sayings) or collector (of pearls, gems, antiques) or assembler (of students, listeners).[12] This abecedary presented here is an ecclesiastes exercise of gathering from a variety of lamps a global alphabet that can lighten our path towards a common humanity without dimming the lamp of the Lamb. It is offered in the belief in the regenerative power of linguistics as a form of rewilding, and in the hope that these metaphors might be some of the building blocks and construction material for a humane world and the restoration of humanity.

The nineteenth-century Russian novelist and playwright Ivan Turgenev (d. 1883) dreamed one day of kneeling in a wooden Orthodox church where slim wax candles guttered in front of icons. A man comes and stands behind him and all at once he senses that this man is Christ:

> a face like every one's, a face like all men's faces.... The hands folded and still. And the clothes on him like every one's. "What sort of Christ is this?" I thought. "Such an ordinary, ordinary man! It can't be!" I turned away. But I had hardly turned my eyes away from this ordinary man when I felt again that it really was none other than Christ standing beside me.... And suddenly my heart sank, and I came to myself. Only then I realized that just such a face—a face like all men's faces—is the face of Christ.[13]

# ABECEDARIUM OF A JESUS HUMAN

 is for Adab (Sufi) (Arabic: أدب) Human

A quote from William Shakespear's play *Julius Caesar* (1599) defined the meaning of "gentleman" for many centuries.

> His life was gentle, and the elements so mix'd
> in him, that nature might stand up and say
> to all the world, 'This was a man!'[1]

***Adab*** is the Arabic word for an expanded understanding of "gentleman." In much of contemporary usage, it means little more than literature, but historically it was a concept in the Eastern Enlightenment which presaged Europe's philosophes. An ***adab*** lifestyle means that you remain human in whatever the situation—even when evil tasers your amygdala with all the wicked lasers it can muster.

The greatest writer of the Arabic ***adab*** was Abu Hayyan Al-Tawhidi, who meant by the word a code of conduct and refined carriage even when living out what Tawhidi claimed was "the queen of all questions:" why bad things happen to good people, why the wicked flourish and the righteous perish, why intrinsic character coincides little with worldly fortune or fame.²

A Jesus human leads an *adab* life, a disciplined lifestyle that is gentle, kind, learned, cultured, refined, and well-rounded in whatever the circumstance, "whatsoever the state"³ one is in.

When the Scripture says "knowledge puffs up but love builds up,"⁴ it is not making a case against knowledge and study, but for an *adab* life where the head is always connected to the heart and hands. We translate the Koine Greek word *mathētes* as "disciple," but it more accurately means "learner" or "student" or "follower of an instructor." I used to be a learned professor. Now I'm a learner. To the learned, it is a question of how much I know. To the learner, it is a question of how much I'm being stretched. The more I know Jesus, the more there is to know, the more I know I don't know, and the deeper the mystery.

Humans learn to keep their humanity, even to the point where it is suggested that "Only out of ignorance can we give an opinion: the more you know or study or experience something, the more confused and useless your point of view becomes."⁵ The *adab* human less waits for the answer or inhabits the question than lives the mystery.

---

*Meaning is that process by which the world to which we belong becomes the world that belongs to us.*
DOMINICAN THEOLOGIAN CORNELIUS ERNST (D. 1977)⁶

---

For our *adab* ancestors, intellectual pursuits had meaning

## ABECEDARIUM OF A JESUS HUMAN

when they were motivated by learning and love. Here is the medieval monk Bernard of Clairvaux (1090–1153) exploring our mixed motives for learning:

> For there are some who long to know for the sole purpose of knowing, and that is shameful curiosity; others who long to know in order to become known, and that is shameful vanity . . . There are others still who long for knowledge in order to sell its fruits for money or honors, and this is shameful profiteering. Others again who long to know in order to be of service, and this is charity. Finally there are those who long to know in order to benefit themselves, and this is wisdom. Of all these categories, only the last two avoid the abuse of knowledge, because they desire to know for the purpose of doing good."[7]

An *adab* human assumes no unmixed motives but trusts God, in all mixing and mix ups, to bring the cream—the wise, the good, the loving—to the top.

*Adab* is untranslatable into English, although it is a key word and cardinal concept in classical Arabic and thus Hebrew literature. Of the three streams that make up the Christian tradition—Greek East, Latin West, Syriac Orient—perhaps *adab* is best interpreted within the hospitalities of the Syriac Orient context, although its themes can be found in the Greek East and Latin West as well. The Roman philosopher and statesman Cicero, who lived from

106–43 BCE, proposed an ***adab*** maxim for life: "*Si horium in bibliotheca habes, nihil deerit*" ("If you have a garden and a library, you have everything you need"). English writer and diarist John Evelyn took this maxim and added a third ingredient to the good life: a friend.[8]

A possible Greek synonym for ***adab*** might be the notion of *Paideia*, a sustained corpus of lifelong learning and serious curriculum of disciplined and cultured instruction. You can only slurp down so much *Chicken Soup for the Soul* without hungering for something more solid. Humanists thought that classical learning helped people to attain moral excellence. We know now that "learning" isn't enough without living the learning in a lifestyle of wisdom, welcome, and wit. The valorization of action over reflection must be valanced.

My mentor in graduate school, the American religious historian Winthrop Still Hudson, was celebrated by colleagues and students alike as a "gentlemen and a scholar" both in the best and worst of times.[9] At one time this phrase was the highest compliment anyone could receive. In Win's eyes, good scholarship required the ***adab*** architecture under which we develop our humanness and in which humanity can flourish and find its home: gentleness, humility, courtesy, kindness, justice and mercy.[10] For Win, you couldn't be a good scholar without helping others become good scholars. You can't be a good human being without helping others become good human beings. Human beings become fully human by helping others become humane.

An ***adab*** world is one where different kinds of people can live together pleasantly and in peace. Increasingly in this culture, you are not allowed to associate with people you disagree with upon penalty of ridicule and recrimination. A militant cancel culture has nullified the academic ideal of the "gentleman and scholar," returning us to Plato's critique of Athen's intelligentsia who he found dangerously closed-minded and "swamped by the flood of popular praise and blame, and carried away with the stream till he finds himself agreeing with popular ideas of what is admirable and disgraceful, behaving like the crowd and becoming one of them."[11] The age of chivalry is dead. The age of civilization is not. ***Adab*** helps insure it's the right kind of civilization.

There is no true civilization without civility. In fact, "civil" is the key to "civilization."[12] By "civil" is meant a well-mannered life of refinement, courtesy, whole-brained personhood,[13] goodness, beauty, truth, respect for the ancestors, and gratitude for the bridges that carried you across. Regardless of what side of the political divide you are on, no "righteous indignation" gives one license to be callous, mean, vindictive, and unforgiving. Too many of us simply have too much acid in our batteries.

Hence the literary product of ***adab*** called the *risala*, an essayistic encomium addressed by its author to a patron, and focused on a particular virtue.[14] A contemporary ***adab***-inspired risala needed today might be a treatise on the ethics of social media.

For example: a) if you share a post, like that post first; b) if you post something on your timeline that someone else alerted you to, give credit to that person; c) post not just to join in a world where everyone says something, but few have something to say: "whatsoever things are true, honest, just, pure, lovely, of good report, virtuous and praise-worthy, post these things."[15] An ***adab*** human exercises mastery of the mute button.

> *None of you will have authentic faith until your hearts are made right, nor will your hearts be made right until your tongues be made right, nor will your tongues be made right until your actions be made right.*
>
> HADITH FROM THE PROPHET MUHAMMAD[16]

The more the culture opens the curtains of transparency, it seems, the more the culture draws the curtains of transcendency. Transparency can be a form of intellectual nudism, quite aggressive in foisting on you things you don't want to see or hear or even know. When combined with the cult of authenticity, the question of identity shifts from society to the individual, and the production of self becomes a permanent activity. Transparency and authenticity thus atomize society.[17] An ***adab*** style of living blanches at the insistent on-demand calls for instant intimacy, flash-it transparency, and prove-it authenticity.

Jesus is One-Of-A-Kind, but he did not intend that he be one-off and one-and-only: "As the father has sent me, so send I you."[18] "As the Father made me missional, so I make you missional," especially in a mission field today that not only does not know Jesus but in its essence is opposed to Jesus. Religious faith is increasingly unintelligible and undesirable, and prejudice against church so strong it is enough to make your stomach not just turn, or growl, but throw a jazz party.

But *adab* commands that we be friends with people who disagree with us, and who might even be called enemies. Not just show them civility and courtesy, but show them hospitality and learn from them. Creativity is the coupling of disparate realities. Nobel Prize winning Israeli-American economist and psychologist Daniel Kahneman champions the idea of "adversarial collaboration" as the best crucible of creativity and the best way to overcome human shortcomings. When studying something, work with people you disagree with.[19] Bring together quarrelsome and garrulous human beings under one roof and at one table.

To be missional for a Jesus human is not to offer anything of self, but only one's sentness with what has been received and revealed as a withness and witness to others. As one "sent" (used forty-one times in John's gospel), Jesus is missional in his very being, as humans are called to be "missional" in our very being.

After reading extensively in the literature of "*adab*," here is an "executive summary" of the human process of *adab* in 10 Commandments form.

## 10 Commandments of an Adab Human

1. Get over yourself: move from self-help to self-discipline. Keep ego under check when it prevents the pursuit of proper *adab*, and the realization that the greatest ally is always love.[20]

2. Humble yourself: be honest with yourself about yourself; act as if everyone else is of a higher station than ourselves; focus on your faults rather than others.

3. Focus yourself: on pleasing God not the applause of others or the praises of the world. Make one's practices more and more inwardly sincere, rather than outwardly apparent.

4. Serve Others: Especially the good of one's brothers and sisters with all one's physical and other resources.

5. Let Go and Live in Trust: Be free of spiritual envy and ambition, including the desires to lead or teach.

6. Show steadfastness, endurance, and a poodle persistence in the face of trouble and turmoil. When others are inconsiderate, don't greet rude with crude. Every time we speak words of calumny and contempt we are partnering with the forces of evil.

7. Go ahead and vent if you must, just make ventings not vexings but valuations that are true, helpful, inspirational, and kind.

8. Accept suggestions and even criticism with gratitude and non-defensiveness. (The proper *adab* response is always "*Eyvallah*"—a devout way of saying "OK" in Arabic that means "All good comes from God").

9. Combine the serious and the humorous: It was customary in medieval *adab* to mingle the comic and the serious ("*al-hazl wa'l jidd*").[21]

10. Heal any wound you may have caused to another, and correct any misunderstanding within three days if possible.

———◇———

*You ask the secret,*
*It has one name: again.*
"ODE TO JOY" BY CZECH POET/BIOCHEMIST MIROSLAV HOLUB[22]

## 𝔄 is for Adiaphora (Greek: Αδιαφόρα) Human

A Jesus human espouses a theology of indifference.

The Greek word *diaphora* means difference. The Greek word ***adiaphora*** means indifference. The basic translation of this Latin translation of a Greek term is "things indifferent." In regards to faith, "***adiaphora***" defines those matters not regarded as essential to faith, but nevertheless permissible for Christians or allowed in church. I am with Paul Tillich's "No truth but the way to truth" until it comes to Jesus, who IS The Way, The Truth, The Life. The Holy Braid of Jesus/Scripture/Spirit is Absolute. The rest is ***Adiaphora***.

◇

*A threefold cord is not easily broken.*
ECCLESIASTES 4:12

In a world where everything and everyone is heavily politicized, ***adiaphora*** depoliticizes doctrine from within the faith and enables us to talk to one another with respect and reciprocity. ***Adiaphora*** is different from "*de minimis*," a Latin term meaning "too small to bother with." ***Adiaphora*** are often large issues that need bothering with and arguing about, but our salvation and health do not depend on them.

George Whitefield traveled thirteen times across the Atlantic to ignite the Great Awakening, which made possible the American Revolution. Even though he was a Calvinist, and held major theological differences with John Wesley, he made sure those disputes did not interfere with either one's preaching of the gospel.

After Wesley died at age 88 in 1791, Whitefield was asked if he thought he would see Wesley in heaven. "No," Whitefield responded. "I fear not, for he will be so near the eternal throne, and we at such a distance, we shall hardly get sight of him."

If only preachers and prophets had such a spirit of **adiaphora** today.

In matters of faith, some things definitely matter. In 1548, two years after Martin Luther's death, Charles V tried to reunite Catholics and Protestant with a declaration called the Augsberg Interim. The document was rejected by Protestant leader Philip Melanchthon because it failed to recognize "justification by faith" as an undisputed point. Later, in 1548, another version of a compromise, the Leipzig Interim, was accepted by Melanchthon. He approved the renewed emphasis on "justification by faith," despite the fact that there were still many, many differences between Catholics and Protestants. Melanchthon called all these other differences on worship, music, and liturgy "***adiaphora***," or "things indifferent to the essence of faith."

Some things are written in pencil. Some things are written in ink. Some things are written in stone. For all of us, it takes a lifetime of faithfulness and learning, compassion and humility, and prayer and meditation to figure out that harmony of pencil, ink and stone. The focus of our faithfulness should be on bringing everyone we can to the table. It is written in stone never to make our own pencils and pens to "cause one of them to fall."

*Images, bells, eucharistic vestments, church ornaments, altar lights, and the like I regard as things indifferent. Anyone who wishes may omit them. Images or pictures taken from the Scriptures and from good histories, however, I consider very useful yet indifferent and optional. I have no sympathy with the iconoclasts.*

PROTESTANT REFORMER MARTIN LUTHER (D. 1546)[23]

We celebrate difference, but **adiaphora** teaches us to celebrate indifference when rites, rituals, and rules are "indifferent to salvation." The rich are not different, someone once wrote; they are indifferent. That is not the indifference of Jesus humans, who learn to make themselves indifferent to some things:

Indifferent to cravings that cause us to consume;

Indifferent to hungers that feed injustice and oppression;

Indifferent to blasé postures about living honestly and godly in a consumerist, celebrity culture.

I affectionately call my Calvinist brother John "Tulip John." John calls his Wesleyan brother (me) "Daisy Len." When he visits me, he sometimes brings a tulip which I proceed to disassemble to the litany of "There goes Total Depravity. There goes Unconditional Election. There goes Limited Atonement. There goes Irresistible Grace. There goes Predestination and Perseverance of the Saints." When I visit my brother, I sometimes bring a daisy, which he proceeds to break apart with the words, "God loves me. God loves me not. God loves me. God loves me not." Two brothers known as the Cappadocian fathers, Basil (330–379), bishop of Caesarea, and younger brother Gregory (335–395), bishop of Nyssa, had big theological disagreements with each other, but "broke ground" for the understanding of the Holy Spirit we share today. Cooperation is not an option for Christians. We must get along with and learn from brothers and sisters in the faith who express and embody our shared faith differently.

> The way of the knowledge of God lies from One Spirit through the One Son to the One Father, and conversely the natural goodness and the inherent holiness and the royal dignity extend from the Father through the only-begotten Son to the Spirit.
>
> ~St. Basil of Caesarea (d. 339), *De Spiritu Sancto*[24]

***Adiaphora means:*** Why can we not let others live their lives and give them a long leash to follow Jesus where he is leading them?

***Adiaphora means:*** Real is not only what happens to you. Real is not only what happens to you physically and personally. Real is what happens to your companions in the faith and connections in the community.

***Adiaphora means:*** "Everything is permissible for me—but not everything is beneficial." (1 Corinthians 6:12 AMP)

"Everything is permissible for me—but not everything is constructive." (1 Corinthians 10:23 AMP)

"Everything is permissible for me . . . but I will not be mastered by anything." (1 Corinthians 6:12 CSB)

***Adiaphora* means:** All "doctrines of the atonement" have something to contribute to an understanding of what happened at Calvary. In fact, the true story of the cross cannot be told without all the doctrines, as a diamond cannot be truly seen without all its facets in view. At the cross, a ransom was paid, a sacrifice offered, a will obeyed, a prophecy fulfilled, a covenant established, a victory won, a love exemplified, a relationship reclaimed. Why isn't the atonement all of these?

***Adiaphora* means:** Theological debate is not a tempest in a teapot. Living faith is not a tea party. But it's not mortal combat either. It's a tourney that takes place on a journey that we're all on together.

***Adiaphora* means:** "We don't have to see eye-to-eye to walk hand-in-hand." (Rick Warren)[25]

Daniel's father died in 2012, and his mother in 2021. His mother wanted blue carnations at the wedding, but the Lutheran pastor, who should have known and shown some ***adiaphora***, said no. Not in church. Blue was not a natural color, so the colors on the altar could not be blue carnations.

But for the rest of their marriage, on anniversaries and birthdays, they celebrated with blue carnations.

Dan, his father, and his mother were looking at all the flower arrangements sent in for the memorial service when they found one made entirely of blue carnations. Dan's mother asked her kids which one of them had sent that arrangement, but they all denied it. Dan still keeps a picture on his iPhone of the hand-written note sent with the flowers. No one knows how his father made this happen, except that he was a consummate planner, but the card read: "For my beautiful bride. I'll see you when you get here."

***Adiaphora means:*** Every person you meet this day is hurting deep inside from something. Go gentle into this good day. Show some ***adiaphora.***

Most importantly, ***adiaphora*** teaches us how to fight fair.

So much of our telling—telling this, telling that, telling the truth, telling it like it is—can hide the barb of telling off. Just watch Sunday morning news "talk" shows. Nobody "argues" anymore. They just spout and shout bullet points. To put forth an argument requires respect, listening, nuance, and logic. To "come to terms" with something is not to make peace with it or to agree with it, but to engage it from within. To be compatible does not mean to comply.

In the late second century, the Greek writer Celsus observed that though Jews and Christians quarreled, they did not quarrel as loudly and as viciously as Christians quarreled with each other. When Christianity becomes a razor-bladed religion, its conversations are meant not to critique, chasten, and correct, but to cut, crusade, and conquer.[26]

It is not just conversations on race that need "rules of engagement." Followers of Jesus need to learn once again to have conversations with each other that are not interrogations, even when they might be interventions. Conversation partners need the freedom to look foolish and say foolish things across the table. Tables breed stories, and relational stories are the healing balm of the world.

For those bearing the monogram of the Messiah in their hearts, there are ten rules of engagement that apply to all honest engagements, whether they are about race, revival, or carpet colors in the sanctuary.

## 11 Rules of Adiaphoric Human Engagement

1. No one has any right to argue with anyone until they can state back at you the case you are making to your satisfaction. In other words, each "side" bears the burden of stating any person's position to the point where they can say, "Yes, that is what I am saying." Without that grounding, any debate is just two people shouting at each other. It is not our job to curse or condemn. We are called to offer new possibilities, new promises, and new relationships.

    If you're going to win an argument, you have to make a better case for the opposing side than they can make for themselves.

2. Never stoop to respond to hate. Give hatred the death dismissal. Haters need conversion, not conversation.[27] The "tip of your tongue" is always the most toxic, and almost never, the most telling. Have any of us ever felt that what we declared in the heat of an argument revealed the best of what we hope for and pray for?

## ABECEDARIUM OF A JESUS HUMAN

*Stand firm in the faith. Be courageous.*
*Be strong. And do everything with love.*
APOSTLE PAUL[28]

3. Say No to Negativity. Jesus is God's "Everlasting Yes!" as Paul liked to say.[29] Cringe from criticizing each other, and complaining about each other. But remember that the right to complain is a "blessing." Martin Luther King, Jr. did not offer an address that declared "I have a complaint," "I have a beef," "I have a kvetch." Martin Luther King declared, "I have a dream." Martin Luther King looked forward, not back. He looked to the message of Jesus, not the nay-saying of the Pharisees. It is easy to break eggs. It is hard to make an omelet.

4. Tweak noses, but no cheap shots or straw men. If differences are not substantial enough to merit debate, don't make them up where they don't exist. Don't play fast and loose with anyone's facts or feelings.

5. Abstain from playing the "reductio ad Hitlerum" card or pushing the button of the nuclear option "that's Naziism." The whole "like Hitler" accusation is a ruse and red herring, and doesn't mean "like Hitler" is Hitlerian. Hitler loved dogs and opera and opposed tobacco and red meat. You are not Hitlerian because you like what Hitler liked. When you declare someone a Hitler, or "like Hitler," you have now polarized

your opponent into sheer evil and ended all constructive conversation.

6. Choose your battles. A full court press cannot be sustained. Learn to say, "I have no dog in that fight" or "That's not my issue" or "I'm not bowling down that alley." Declare a fair catch when needed, and be quick to admit "good point" or "got me on that one."

7. Learn to lose gracefully. You can't win them all. You will lose some fights you deserve to win, and you will win some fights you deserve to lose. Life is not fair.[30] All losses and loose ends find their home in Jesus.

8. "The Battle is Not Yours."[31] These five words about the missional life ("The Mission is Not Yours") rebuke and comfort simultaneously. They rebuke all lordliness about our importance to God's mission. They comfort our sagging shoulders about how we're faring in advancing God's mission in the world, which will be victorious in the future with or without us.

Don't get caught in the rubble of yesterday's defeats and disappointments. Don't live out of the wreckage of the past. Today is a new day. "Our God will fight for us."[32] Or in the words of Isaiah 30:15: "In repentance and rest you shall be saved; in quietness and in trust shall be your strength."

# ABECEDARIUM OF A JESUS HUMAN

*Trust in Allah, but tie up your camel.*
OLD ISLAMIC PROVERB

9. Don't pick a fight. No spoiling for a fight. Win, Lose, or Draw, be humble. Be patient with each other, more commending than condemning. Why? If something is of human construction, it will disappear. But if it comes from God, you cannot possibly defeat them. In fact, you could find yourself fighting against God.

10. Don't worship divisiveness for divisiveness' sake. When you divide the body, you divide yourself from Jesus. When you lop off the source, you might as well throw in the towel. Cleave to Jesus, the only King and Judge. Let there be no clefts in the church, except for one: "Rock of Ages, cleft for me, let me hide myself in Thee."

11. When you're in doubt about how oppositional an opposing position really is, give it the benefit of the doubt. Be more ready to put a good construction on another's argument than to condemn it as false.

Our ancestors in the faith invoked a caveat when they engaged in theological debate. When they arrived at some consensus or conclusion about matters of the divine, they would end the discussion with these four words: "God is always greater."

Give it your best shot. Bring it on. Think as hard as you

can about the ways and whys of God. But remember: "God is always greater." God is "able to do exceedingly abundantly above all that we can ask or think"[33] only because God is always greater than we can "ask or think."

A Jesus human always remembers the four words the church fathers used as a "PS:" "God is always greater."

ABECEDARIUM OF A JESUS HUMAN

##  is for Agape (Greek: αγάπη) Human

*Loving and being loved is God's passion. It is almost—infinite love—as if he is bound to this passion, almost as if it were a weakness on his part; whereas in fact it is his strength, his almighty love, and in that respect his love is subject to no alteration at all.*
DANISH THEOLOGIAN SOREN KIERKEGAARD (D. 1855)[34]

***Agape*** is a big deal in what it means to be a Jesus human, and in the kingdom of God. A Jesus human is a-gape with ***agape*** love.

In the original Inuit cultures and Eskimo–Aleut languages of the Arctic and subarctic regions of Greenland, Labrador, Quebec, the Northwest Territories, and Alaska, there are over twenty different words for snow. This makes it possible for Inuits to define and describe various snow experiences. It also sharpens their readiness for shifts and nuances in the weather, and broadens their understanding of nature's vastness and diversity.

The English language has more words for snow than one thinks (Scots have 421 words for snow). But there is only one English word for love. There are at least seven Greek words for love:

Eros: romantic, passionate love
    Philia/Phileo: intimate, authentic friendship
    Ludus: playful, flirtatious love
    Storge: familial love

Philautia: self-love

Pragma: committed, companionate love

*Agápe*: lay-it-down, sacrificial, suffering, unconditional love.

The word Jesus used for love is the verb form of ***agápē***.[35] He put it in the form of a "new commandment" for humanity that encases and embodies all the other commandments. "A new command I give you: Love one another. As I have loved you, so you must love one another."[36] The pattern of human love is "as I have loved you." In other words, Jesus humans are to be known by our self-giving, sacrificial, unconditional love for one another.

We are so caught up in ourselves and caught up in getting ahead in life and living our "best life" that truth seldom catches up to us and catches fire before we are caught dead. And what is that truth?

The New Testament speaks of one great truth: God loves us "to the end."[37] Jesus underlines the maximal extent of this love: "Greater love than this no one has than that he lay down his life for his friends."[38]

God's first word to us in a straw stable was "I love you."

God's last word to us on a wooden cross was "I love you."

God's first word to us from a stone-blown cave that birthed a new humanity was "I love you."

**Ancient Cry of "Ave Crux Spes Unica!" ("Hail to the Cross, Our Only Hope"):** As the Savior dies on the cross, his last words are, "It is finished." In that one word, *Tetelestai*, the divine project of showing us how to be human and restoring our humanity was completed. In his life and death, he showed us how to live as a true human and how to die as a true human.

There is no greater love than this: "But God shows his love for us, because while we were still sinners Christ died for us."[39] The greatest love, a love greater than all other loves, shines in the deepest darkness.[40] The quest of humankind for the greater is in fact the quest for *this* ever-greater love that is revealed in Jesus. The sacred language of Islam is Arabic; the sacred language of Judaism is Hebrew; the sacred language of Christianity is the church, the body of Christ. The sacred language of God is love. Or in Arabic, Allah Mahaba: God is Love.

The Mystery of Life has a Name: LOVE

The Mystery of Love has a Name: Christ.

God is Lover. Jesus is Loved. Spirit is Loving.

Mystery is Chrystery.

Paul describes in detail what ***agapic*** love looks like, practically speaking. What is the first thing that comes to your mind when you think of ***agapic*** love? For Paul, strangely enough, it was patience. Paul begins his list of what ***agapic*** love is with the word patient.[41] One wonders: Was it just the first word to come to his mind? Or was the selection intentional and strategic, intended to be the lens through which everything which follows is to be understood? Maybe it was intended to tell us something about God's love, a love known for its endurance and steadfastness.

When love is involved, there is no risk management or danger assessment or transactional analysis. There is no scorecarding or bookkeeping. There is only the leap into the unknown and laying one's life on the line. If life were only about certitude, consistency, constancy, and comfort, there would only be mathematics, and we would all be mathematicians.

When Scripture says "knowledge puffs up but love builds up,"[42] it is not making a case against knowledge and study but for a head that is always connected to heart and hands. For our ancestors in the faith, intellectual pursuits had meaning when they were motivated by learning and love.[43] Knowledge without Love yields wastage.[44] Love without Knowledge yields wreckage. But Knowledge with Love yields wisdom and bliss.

*Agapic* love is a lay-down, rise-up, John 3:16 love.

*Agapic* love is a love divine all loves excelling.

*Agapic* love is a love that will not let you go.

*Agapic* love is a love that "bears all things, believes all things, hopes all things, endures all things."

*Agapic* love is a love that "never ends."

The First Adam knew this kind of love, even in his "Fall."[45] Why did Adam choose to join Eve in eating the forbidden fruit even when he could have chosen to take another path? Because of the very nature of *agapic* love itself, the very nature of God's love. Original sin is birthed out of a place of love. At least this is what Augustine thought in his *City of God*:

> [Adam], by the drawing of kindred, yielded to the woman, the husband to the wife, the

one human being to the only other human being. . . . The man could not bear to be severed from his companion, even though it involved a partnership in sin.[46]

John Milton outlines a similar love-story scenario behind the Fall in *Paradise Lost*[47] which contains Adam's reaction to Eve's eating the forbidden fruit, first in a soliloquy to himself, then in a back-and-forth conversation with Eve. Lines 991–993 summarize this internal dialog: "he his love had so ennobled, as of choice to incur Divine displeasure for her sake, or death." *Paradise Lost* doesn't end there, but continues until Book XII with 3,000 more lines of salvation history as explained to Adam by the archangel Michael, the polar opposite of Satan.

The First Adam chose God when choosing Eve even while disobeying God and bringing sin into the world.

The Second Adam chose God when he chose to lay down his divinity, to enter our humanity, and to show us true ***agapic*** love, what God's love means, all without sinning.

This is the meaning of *felix culpa*, or "fortunate fall"[48] which was so important to Christianity's greatest theologians like Ambrose, Augustine, Aquinas, Anselm, and others.[49] We win more in the Last Adam than we lost in the First Adam.

What did Jesus, the Last Adam, come to demonstrate? God's power? God's authority? God's majesty? "No greater love than this .."[50] Jesus came to manifest in his life, death, resurrection, and ascension the true nature of God's love. When the only love you have for someone is the love of

Christ, or loving at ground zero, that's not the worst place to be. Maybe that's the best place to start the ***agapic*** journey. The cross is a compelling sign not only of an inexhaustible love but of a vulnerable love.

The medieval theologian considered to be the apex of the classical tradition sired by Augustine, St. Thomas Aquinas, put it like this: "The cross prompts us to love, and it is by this that we are forgiven." The cross retrieves our original relationship with God. The sign of disgrace and exclusion, the sign of failure, is turned inside out to be a sign of God's freedom to be God whatever we humans do. But it is also a sign of the riskiness, the vulnerability, which such freedom must mean.

As the green-pastures, still-waters, one-talent servant learned the hard way, the ultimate risk is not to risk anything. Anything good entails risk, and imagination, and vulnerability. If the church is to be the body of Christ, it needs a theology of risk. The church is not a place of safety from risks, but a safe place to take risks. The time until Jesus returns is not the time for rocking-chair readiness, or for franchised dreams of rapture, or for risk-averse strategies. A Jesus human is not a "venture capitalist" but a venture disciple called to the greatest adventure in adventing this world will ever know: following Jesus.[51]

---

*To fall in love with God is the greatest romance; to seek Him the greatest adventure; to find him, the greatest human achievement.*

UNIVERSALLY ATTRIBUTED TO ST. AUGUSTINE,
BUT MOST LIKELY FR. RAPHAEL SIMON[52]

## ABECEDARIUM OF A JESUS HUMAN

Jesus does not author your story so you can be bored by it. This is the time to blaze new trails, to find new truths, to explore strange new lands, to dare-dream better worlds in which to live and love and laugh.

No one who loves as Christ loved and loves still cannot live in this world without bringing back a whole world and birthing a whole different world. That means, for the follower of Jesus, stepping on toes is a lifestyle, and trespassing a dance step.

---

*We are the music-makers*
*And we are the dreamers of dreams,*
*Wandering by lone sea-breakers,*
*And sitting by desolate streams;*
*World-losers and world-forsakers*
*On whom the pale moon gleams:*
*Yet we are the movers and shakers*
*Of the world for ever, it seems.*
ARTHUR WILLIAM EDGAR O'SHAUGHNESSY (D. 1881)
ON POETS AND ARTISTS AND SCIENTISTS[53]

---

Many years ago, a newspaper story carried the headline, "Doorstep Baby Abandoned Twice on Birthday."[54] The news story told of a baby born in the city of York, England, whose mother, after giving birth, put the child in a cardboard box and covered him with a ragged woolen coverlet and a worn-out sweater. She attached a letter asking whoever found the little stranger to care for him because she could not in her dire circumstances.

Someone did find the child, but then left him at the

emergency entrance of a hospital with a second note that read, "Did not want to get involved." Who can forget the story of a twice-abandoned baby?

There was once a Christ child left in love on the doorstep of the world in a place called Bethlehem. This is God's way of knocking on our door and asking people to get involved: first Mary and Joseph, Elizabeth and Zechariah, shepherds and magi, then disciples, and ultimately all who follow Jesus. The incarnation calls us to get involved, to take some risks for life and love, to reach our hands across the manger to love one another, to come together, and dare some dreams of peace on earth, good will to all.

Again, our poets and artists get there before we do: Here are the closing lines of storyteller/songwriter Justin McRoberts' song "Safe" (2005): "A thousand times I'd rather fall than be afraid to move at all/And after all, what is this thing that you call grace? Is it safe?"[55] The worst sin towards our fellow creatures is not to hate them, but to be indifferent to them: that's the essence of inhumanity.

> *Thus says the Lord: Fear not, for I have redeemed you. I have called you by name, you are mine. When you pass through the waters, I will be with you; . . . When you walk through fire you shall not be burned. . . . You are precious in my eyes!*
>
> ISAIAH 43:1–4 ESV

The first words of angels to humans were, "Be not afraid."

Well, "Easy for you to say," humans are tempted to respond to angels.

## ABECEDARIUM OF A JESUS HUMAN

Angels don't have an amygdala. Angels don't know fear, and they aren't vulnerable and wounded. They're invincible. You have to be vulnerable to know fear.

Anyone ever ask: how's Your amygdala (pronounced amig'dala)? This little bundle of nerves in mammalian brains is a key component of the limbic system.[56] Amygdala is the almond-shaped mass of gray matter that governs fear and gatekeeps primal emotions. Each one of us has two of these almond-shaped amygdalae (Greek for "almonds") deep inside the temporal lobes, with parts of this nerve-ball in both hemispheres. The amygdala jump-starts the reflex responses of fight, flight, freeze, or fawn. The amygdala also processes smell, the one sense that skips the grand central station of the brain, the thalamus.

People without any amygdala show no fear, of anything or anyone. They eagerly pet poisonous snakes, or reach into the jaws of lions to see what their tongues feel like. Urbach-Wiethe disease is a rare disorder that kills amygdala cells and leaves the brain with "black holes" instead of almonds. Physicians doing autopsies hunt out the deceased's amygdala, because it reveals how people died (and lived). Whether your amygdala is tight, loose, or bound tells whether you lived an uptight, fear-bound, or romantic, fearless life.

But most importantly, the amygdala is a key player in what scientists call the brain's "so what streams" that flag what things in our environment are worth paying attention to. If the amygdala determines that something is worth further scrutiny, it shifts from park to first to high-gear and summons your army of emotions to confront the reality. The amygdala both awakens you to the threat of something to fear, and helps you mount the emotional response that can deal with the fear out there. The human problem is often a hyper-active amygdala that goes postal, or, a sleepy amygdala that fails to post alarm.

When amygdala meets *agape*, you end up with a dare-to-love dream. *Agape* by definition over-rides amygdala and puts the self at risk. Vineyard founder John Wimber is famous for saying that faith is spelled "R-I-S-K." If you live by faith, you live by laying your life on the line.

The word "risk" is derived from the early Italian *risicare*, which means "to dare."[57] To live an *agapic* life is a dare dream. Jesus was always diffusive of himself. An *agapic* human is diffusive of themselves. A Jesus human seeks fulfilment through moving beyond oneself, and finding one's good in the good of others, even the stranger and the enemy. *Agapic* actions precede and conceive apprehensions. Immanent love precedes and conceives eminent wisdom.

Then there is the peril of the pearl—The Pearl of Great Price, the "Greatest Commandment." The Peril of the Two Greatest Commandments–Love God and Love Neighbor—is that the second can elbow out the first, or become the first. The way to escape this danger is to do what Jesus told us to do: see him in the stranger and the neighbor, so that every human being is Christ.

*Agapic* love is one that loves others "as Jesus loved us."

## ABECEDARIUM OF A JESUS HUMAN

In other words, a Jesus human does not love with old human love, no matter how noble and beautiful that love may be. A Jesus human goes beyond the old human love to a Jesus kind of human love—to love not with our love, the love we have to give, but to love with the love of God, a divine love that makes human love truly human. Old human love can be beautiful, but Jesus human love is divine.

---

*We crowned ourselves Homo sapiens, the wise ape,*
*but Homo limbus might have been more apt.*
BEST-SELLING AUTHOR SAM KEAN[58]

---

The more Jesus does good, the more Jesus loves, the more he inspires hatred and prompts opposition. The brighter the light he shines, the stormier the clouds that form. That's why no good deed goes unpunished. But the forces of death and dying are met and conquered by the Author of Life and the forces of love.

Malcolm Muggeridge once interviewed the Soviet dissident Anatole Kusnyetsov and asked him how he could embody such a strong faith amidst the strong persecution and prohibition of Christianity in the Soviet Union.

> He made a remark which is one of the most extraordinary remarks anyone has ever made to me and has echoed in my mind more often than I can say. He said to me this: "That if in this world you are confronted with absolute power, power unmitigated, power unrestrained, extending to every area

of human life—if you are confronted with power in those terms, you are driven to realize that the only possible response to it is not some alternative power arrangement, more humane, more enlightened. The only possible response to absolute power is the absolute love which our Lord brought into the world."[59]

What is most missing from this world? Love. Evil is unlove. Love is the summation and implementation of the good, true, and beautiful.

It used to be said of Athenians, "They would applaud Demostehenes' oratory, and loved his philippics against Philip of Macedonia, but failed to march." We love to talk love, and we talk a good game, but we fail to engage the real roots of evil by overcoming evil with love, by over-riding amygdala with **agape**.

---

*Love is very patient, very kind.*
*Love knows no jealousy;*
*love makes no parade, gives itself no airs,*
*is never rude, never selfish, never irritated, never resentful;*
*love is never glad when others go wrong,*
*love is gladdened by goodness,*
*always slow to expose, always eager to believe the best,*
*always hopeful, always patient.*

APOSTLE PAUL[60]

---

Humans are invited to participate in God's mission in the

world. The Bible is more than a battery of missional energy for life. The Bible is a nuclear power plant that generates the explosive, expulsive power of love. The nuclear fission of the universe comes, not from a plutonium core, but from a nuclear core of love. A particular kind of love called ***Agape*** love.

## 𝔄 is for Asabiyyah (Arabic: العصابية) Human

*Asabiyyah*, an Arabic word from a root meaning to wind, tie, or wrap, is frequently translated as tribal or social solidarity, a form of group feeling. One scholar argues that the adjective closest to **asabiyyah** lexically is asabi, which is what Ibn Khaldun had in mind when he built a philosophy of supreme virtue around "sinewy" or "sinewy strength."[61] *Asabiyyah* indicates a group's capacity for harnessing their collective identity in pursuit of economic, social or political ends.

An *Asabiyyah* human is as nimble in the small scale as coherent in the broad sweep. The world is becoming more tribal and more global, more postal code and more planetary at the same time. We might even coin a new word, "tribplan." We live in a tribplan world.

Tribes are good. But tribalism is bad. Tribal is the Hebrew sense that there are many (i.e., twelve) right ways of being a worshiper of Yahweh, and each tribe has a unique mission and identity. Tribal is the branding of Arabic symbols on camels and other animals to indicate tribal identity and ownership. You had one totemic symbol on yourself and on your camel because it "marked" who you were and to whom you belonged.

Tribalism is the clannishness that says "if you're not part of my tribe, I'll kill you." This is why, in Thomas Aquinas' mind, it is theologically correct to say "the human being exists" but not "the Englishman exists" or "the Viking exists" or "the Arab exists" or even "the Christian exists."

We are humans above all else. But there are many kinship groups to the human family. It's the church's job to brush off that word "family" (both domestic and international) from its filth and dirt and abuse, to fill that word with pleasant memories and happy associations, and to make "human family" what God intended it to be.

There is a French way of being human, a Spanish way of being human, a Russian way of being human, a Chinese way of being human, an Indian way of being human, a Bantu way of being human, an Inuit way of being human.

When a Gentile converts, they are encouraged to choose a tribe with which they have personality traits in common. The characteristics of the tribes are to be found in the portrayals in Genesis 49:3–27 and Deuteronomy 33. A convert should also feel some affinity for the landscape of Israel that was apportioned to the tribe they have chosen. Levi is not included in this list, because one can only be a Priest or Levite by descent, NOT conversion. In the same way the ideal Hebrew is comprised of all the tribes; the ideal human is comprised of all the peoples of the world in a Jacob's coat of many-colored humanity:

> Persian by breeding, African in arts, Iraqi in culture, Hebrew in lore, Western in intellect, Syrian in devotion, Greek in science, Indian in discernment, Chinese in food, Japanese in technology.

JESUS HUMAN

Ibn Khaldun (1332–1406), the Arab Muslim philosopher and one of the greatest minds of the Middle Ages, expanded on what he means by ***asabiyyah*** in his first volume of a planned world history called *Muqaddimah* (1337). He retells the story from the Hebrew Bible (book of Numbers) about God's rescuing the Israelites from slavery in Egypt. Then God leads them to the low-lying desert just beyond the borders of Canaan, which he commands them to overcome and make their own. They refuse. The land is full of terrifying giants they cringe and complain. If God wants them to inhabit the Promised Land, then God should conquer the land on their behalf. God's chosen people's cowardice causes God's curse for them to wander in the desert for forty years. It would take a couple of generations to winnow and wipe this cowardice negativity and grumpiness out of the chosen people's gene pool and restore them to confidence and courage.

Ibn Khaldun contends that the Israelites' refusal to take on the Canaanites directly, expecting God to fight their battles for them, shows their lack of ***asabiyyah***. They lost it, he argues, during their long sojourn in Egypt, where plentiful food undermined their earlier initiative, industry, and group identity. Bound belly-and-brain to a slave mentality, they began relying instead on their Egyptian overlords for sustenance and protection. A couple of generations of hard desert suffering toughened them up so they could get their ***asabiyyah*** back.

Ibn Khaldun's theory of ***asabiyyah***, which causes him to rate the Bedouin so highly, lifts up a tribal identity as

## ABECEDARIUM OF A JESUS HUMAN

something that God puts into the human heart. ***Asabiyyah*** births courage, compassion, selflessness, service. An ***asabiyyah*** dream is an internationalist vision as opposed to a globalist or nationalistic one, but one that is anchored in the local, the tribal, the patriotic. Some of the most anti-binary people can be the most binary in their thinking.

You can be patriotic and anti-racist and, as hard as it is for some people to hear this, as far as we can tell, Jesus was not an American.

You can be tribal and have an internationalist, planetary vision: "For God so loved the cosmos."

You can be courageous and safe at the same time.

You can be confident and humble at the same time.

When I looked back at some of my past and current favorite TV series—*Yellowstone, Mare of Easttown, Mayor of Kingstown, Curse of Oak Island, Blue Bloods, Downton Abbey, Ozark*—it suddenly hit me that all are fixated on particular locales. The more global the world gets, the more enchanting and enthralling the local and the homegrown. The story of Jesus began as a Jewish story and exploded into cosmos story. The way to the universal is through the particular.

How easy it is to fall in love with love; how hard it is to fall in love with people who need love.

> *Whoever saves a life, it shall be as though*
> *he had saved the lives of all mankind.*
> FROM THE ISLAMIC SACRED TEXT QUR'AN[62]

Sometimes you are batting for the whole human race and

planet Earth itself. Every doctor takes this oath: "I solemnly pledge to dedicate my life to the service of humanity" . . . vows derived from the Hippocratic Oath of ancient Greece and reinforced in the 1948 Declaration of Geneva. "I will maintain the utmost respect for human life." In 2017, these words were added: "I will attend to my own health, wellbeing, and abilities in order to provide care of the highest standard."

We see perseverance time and again in Scripture—the "Tried and True." Elijah pressed on through his depression.[63] Jeremiah remained true to his convictions even as he was labeled unpatriotic and heretical.[64] Nehemiah continued to rebuild the wall around Jerusalem even as people around him tried to tear him down.[65] The elderly priest Zechariah and wife Elizabeth, in the midst of her high-risk pregnancy, welcoming into their home a pregnant teenager, a cousin of Elizabeth's named Mary. In taking Mary in, they put their own repute and respect on the line. In spite of the scuttlebutt and tittle-tattle, the whispers and the chin-waggings, they shelter the pregnant virgin Mary from attack and abuse at what must have been great cost to themselves.

A "Tried and True" human means a person took the time and trouble to keep trying no matter how trying or troubled the times.

ABECEDARIUM OF A JESUS HUMAN

#  is for Ashram (Sanskrit: आश्रम) Human

*The Ashram Movement is a living fellowship within a redemptive community in which the whole gospel, for the whole person, for the whole world is preached, taught, shared, and experienced.*
GREATEST MISSIONARY SINCE APOSTLE PAUL: E. STANLEY JONES (D. 1973)[66]

Literally a "hermitage" in Indian Hindu religions, the word ***ashram*** has come to mean any place of religious retreat or withdrawal from the world for group study, prayer and devotion. The word became a movement in the West through the writings and projects of theologian and missionary E. Stanley Jones, who started in India an ***Ashram*** movement contextualized for Christian faith, and then adapted it to the US and Canada, and to other countries around the world. A normal ***Ashram*** would last a week, but "Brother Stanley" introduced "little ***ashrams***" that telescoped the experience into one or two days and could be conducted anywhere, anytime.

A cognate word to ***ashram*** from Zen Buddhism is "sesshin," which comes from two Japanese words, "setsu" and "shin." "Setsu" means "to collect," "to bring together," "to unify." "Shin" means "heart/mind." Thus, sesshin means to unify heart/mind, a unification that can take place on multiple levels, but is most associated with a retreat lasting multiple days (most often seven) called a "sesshin."

Officially the words "***ashram***" and "sesshin" mean "retreat"—a time of repose, repast, and re-enchantment of life. But maybe it's time to mentally translate "retreat" as "advance." Jesus humans advance, not retreat. "He has sounded forth the trumpet that shall never call retreat"[67] is a phrase from the Julia Ward Howe hymn "Mine Eyes Have Seen the Glory of the Coming of the Lord," the very last words of the very last Martin Luther King Jr. speech ("I've Been to The Mountaintop," 03 April 1968) the night before he was assassinated.

Marines are proud to claim they never "retreat;" they "advance forward by another route" or "advance in another direction." Bible expositor Herbert Lockyer (d. 1984) liked to quote Methodist preacher Samuel Chadwick (d. 1932) as saying that there were two people in the history of Christianity who "never knew retreat." Their names were John Wesley and the husband-wife team of William and Catherine Booth.

*Come apart and rest for a while.*
JESUS[68]

Why are advances so important for the human spirit? We come apart so we can come together so we don't come undone. It was said of composer Benjamin Britten (d. 1976): "He had compassion for others; unhappily, he had none for himself."[69] Humans can be Benjamin Brittens, easy on others but hard on themselves. If we do fall apart, we need to come apart to mend again with others, because we can't do it on our own. **Ashrams** and **sesshins** and other forms of retreats/advances are essential to moving forward whether in creeps or leaps. We all need safe places and safe people to run to for recovery and rediscovery.

When the search function on your computer stops working, your best recourse is not to see what is wrong with the search engine, but to turn off the device, give it some rest, and then turn it back on again. Nine times out of ten that's enough to fix your search function. It's the same way with life. It's why God created the Sabbath to begin with. Repairing is what our ancestors called "repairing" as in "after dinner, let us repair to the living room." As we change our position and posture and pace, as we "repair," we enter a new realm where digesting and healing and "repairing" can take place. The first step of preparing is repairing.

Ask any kid or young adult: "Where is your most intense experience of God? Where did you come to Christ?" Most likely they will tell you of some kind of ***Ashram*** experience—either at a summer camp or weekend advance or mission trip or group encampment at some mountain, desert, or water setting (lake/ocean/river). "High mountain" in the Bible doesn't mean "height" but a place where God appeared in special ways to special people at special times. Every human can have "high mountain" moments if we're open to receive these visitations. Where's your "river deep–mountain high?" Where's your "desert island" and "desert moon?" Where's your "sittin' on the dock of the bay?"

## JESUS HUMAN

> *People say you have to travel to see the world. Sometimes I think that if you just stay in one place and keep your eyes open, you are going to see just about all that you can handle.*
> AUGGIE WREN CHARACTER (PLAYED BY HARVEY KEITEL) IN THE 1995 FILM *SMOKE*

Jesus was always seeking **Ashram** time for himself in the mountains, the desert, or the water, and tried to corral his disciples into disciplines of silence and solitude.

> Then, because so many people were coming and going that they did not even have a chance to eat, he said to them, "Come with me by yourselves to a quiet place and get some rest. So they went away by themselves in a boat to a solitary place. But many who saw them leaving recognized them and ran on foot from all the towns and got there ahead of them. When Jesus landed and saw a large crowd, he had compassion on them, because they were like sheep without a shepherd. So he began teaching them many things."[70]

The priest and poet Gerard Manley Hopkins chose to live in an **Ashram**, a place called St. Beuno's Jesuit Retreat Center in rural North Wales, where he could master the art of nesting in the Spirit and awakening to the everyday presence of the "deep, down things."[71] Humans need liminal places and sanctuary spaces like **Ashrams** to explore the "deep, down things." Advances are designed to help people meet God in beauty and silence and conversation so that we can meet the evils of our world with courage and confidence. **Ashrams**, like Sabbaths, are mini-suspensions of the Fall where all that we do is play, not work. The placed presence of awe and wonder and beauty opens one up for healing and hope.[72]

When space and time come together, there is formed something magical called "place." But, according to the science of space called "proxemics," humans need four different types of space for full human placement.[73] First, personal space is where everyday social interactions are conducted. Second, social space is the distance that people maintain in business or professional settings. Third, public space is the arena for crowds and public places. Fourth, intimate space is the hardest space in which relationships can form, because it's the closest and most vulnerable venue reserved for intimate friends, family, and romantic partners. The amount of space that people need varies from culture to culture, of course, but **ashrams** are ideal for cultivating deeper dimensions of personal and intimate space. When we hear God say, "I go to prepare a place for you, that where I am, there you may be also," we are hearing God wanting to spend eternity with us in a holistic place of public, personal, social, and intimate fullness.

There is a fifth space missing in the proxemics formulation of spaces humans need. That fifth space is where humankind and the natural world come together—the wild, wild world of mountains and rivers and deserts. And within that natural world of creation, each of us has a "special place" where we luxuriate in the landscape, a "happy place" where we feel most at home and that summons us to come home.

After the assassination of John F. Kennedy in 1963, Leonard Bernstein unveiled his strategy for dealing with evil: "This will be our reply to violence: to make music more intensely, more beautifully, more devotedly than ever before."[74]

---

*Beauty is God's idea of the creature, of man and of the world . . . The transfiguration of the world is the attainment of beauty.*
NICHOLAS BERDYAEV[75]

---

To "get away from it all" does not mean to get away from oneself. In fact, the ultimate **ashram** "away" is "here" and "within." Deep within ourselves is where the ultimate **ashram** is to be found, a sanctuary of peace and quiet where we can hear the "still small voice" that whispers to us when the Lord passes by.[76] The deeper in we go, the higher up we grow.

##  is for Bespoke (British) Human

***Bespoke*** is a bygone word that has made a comeback. It started as a verb, became an adjective, now Samsung has made it into a noun with a lot of "***Bespoke***" appliances

In Korea, the word is everywhere. When I mentioned this word in LenTalk #124, Colleague Guy Taylor wrote back: "I live literally in the center of Daegu and within a few-minutes' walk is THE place for fashion and such. When I look around there is ***bespoke*** everywhere . . . coffee, restaurants and even pet care." The popularity of ***bespoke*** is an expression of a culture hungry for authenticity and honesty.

---

*I'm trying to be real but it costs too much.*
VIETNAMESE AMERICAN POET OCEAN VUONG[77]

---

We are God's ***bespoke*** beloved, and the Jesus human dream is a ***bespoke*** dream.

The more Jesus fills us, the more we sound like ourselves. The more we are influenced by geniuses, the more we become ourselves. Take the mid-60s Beatles, Beach Boys, and Bob Dylan—they were all feeding off each other and experimenting with the times.

How can we know what is in us if we can't be with ourselves long enough to be surprised? We live in a constant state of "permanent receptivity," waiting to check our devices. In four years, people in the UK went from 12 minutes (2018) to four minutes (2021) between checking cell phones.[78] This culture of inattention does not have attention deficit disorder (ADD). It has a Distraction Disorder (DD) or a Misplaced Attention Disorder (MAD) or Stolen Attention Disorder (SAD).[79] We are attending to things that do not build up or make anything or connect to the living world.[80] Instead we scan the bombardments of moving events, much of it negating and enraging, that shell us hourly on our digital screens and shock us out of those meandering flows and meditative states that are essential to creativeness and sound judgment.

*Love is a phenomenon of attention.*
SPANISH PHILOSOPHER JOSÉ ORTEGA Y GASSET (D. 1955)[81]

Steinway has no blueprint for its masterpieces. Each one is an original design of the maker in partnership with the wood and wire and metal and felt. The master carver feels the timber and texture of the wood and adjusts his stringing of the spring steel accordingly.[82] That's why no two pianos sound alike. It's impossible to make two pianos make the same sound.

Frank Mohr died 28 March 2022 at age 94. He is someone few people ever heard of, but no great concert pianist who played on a Steinway ever traveled without him wearing his black Steinway apron as he tuned the piano. This is why his obituary was written up on the last page of *The Economist*, which boasts the most influential readership of any magazine in the world.[83]

Arthur Rubinstein, Van Cliburn, Glenn Gould,

## ABECEDARIUM OF A JESUS HUMAN

Vladimir Horowitz: where they went, Mohr the master Steinway tuner went. Every maestro had a special way they wanted their piano tuned, and Mohr obliged. Horowitz wanted a petal-light touch that was borderline out-of-control for other pianists. He also liked a raw, nasal quality to the keys. Rubinstein forbade any cleaning of the keyboard because he liked the resistance of the grime and grit. He refused any electric strobes in tuning, because he liked the darker sounds that came from hearing and touch setting the pitch. Gould wanted the hammers to drum when he sped up. No two concert pianists want the same sound from their piano.

Mohr oversaw the piano's disassembly at Steinway, and reassembly in the concert hall. Horowitz was insistent that only Frank Mohr be his tuner, partly because Mohr came to tune Horowitz's spirit as well as his instrument. He would warm up the great pianist's cold hands before a concert. "I admire you with your warm hands," the maestro said once. He also said, "Franz, you are the most important person here." "No, Maestro, you are!" "No, no" came the reply. "If the piano's not right, I'm not going to play."[84]

*Isn't originality the only plagiarism?*
ENGLISH POET RUPERT BROOKE (1887-1915)

*Originality is undetected plagiarism.*
ENGLISH "DEAN" WILLIAM R. INGE (1860-1954)[85]

## JESUS HUMAN

The biggest "ism" in the church today is plagiarism—we flagrantly and on a grand scale plagiarize our lives by copying others and simulating ourselves. **Bespoke** humans don't copycat others but copyright themselves. Why do Jesus followers have to be such Jargonauts, Cliche-pimps, Bromide dispensers, and Platitudinarians? Why are so many Christians the enemy of style? Style is what makes each person **bespoke** and sets them apart as both imitable and inimitable. A **bespoke** human is aware of his or her own uniqueness. A New Englander once told the most influential philosopher of his day William James (d. 1910): "There ain't much difference between one man and another, but what little difference there is, is awfully important."

Each one of us is a **bespoke** creation of God, a genesis gift of creation, an original human with singular tricks, tics, and tropes. A **bespoke** human has the hum of rightness . . . everyone has a right size, right shape, right fit, right stuff. How far have you gone into your own story? Do you know your own "rightness?" You aren't very far if you don't gasp when you grasp just how unique a human you are and unlike anyone else God made. You say: "I'm not an original thinker." I say: But people who are not original thinkers can still think for themselves, which is the very definition of an "original thinker."

◇

*I milk a lot of cows, but I churn my own butter.*
ANONYMOUS MOUNTAIN PREACHER

## ABECEDARIUM OF A JESUS HUMAN

Marcel Proust called Spanish fashion designer Mariano Fortuny's creations "faithfully antique and markedly original." Most followers of Jesus today are neither "faithful" to the past or "markedly original." Rather than play whack-a-mole with any sign of originality or "eccentricity," why can't we honor each other's uniqueness and stylishness without trying to bend each other out of our true shape?

There are four meanings of original:

1. oldest—the thing from which another is reproduced
2. free from imitation
3. the beginning, the genesis, the originary
4. generative of other births and conceptions

Historian Todd Longstaffe-Gowan has exhaustively studied "English Garden Eccentrics" (2022) as an expression of personal autobiography of their owners.[86] He wrote the book partly to challenge other gardeners like himself to "defy dull conventionality" and "to inspire those who feel a spirit of freedom welling up inside them to dare to be eccentric—to pluck up the moral courage and indulge with impunity."[87]

Eccentric literally means "off-center." We are all designed to be "off-center" or "not normal." In fact, Erich Fromm (1900–1980) wrote a whole book on "the pathology of normalcy."[88] A ***bespoke*** human has the "moral courage" to do "abnormal" and to go down what cartographers call "desire lines." These are paths where humans or animals have veered off the established trail and forged their own way forward, a new route to their destination.

What desire lines are we laying down and traveling in?

##  is for Carne (Spanish) Human

To be human is to have a body: to live in your skin. A Jesus human is a ***carne*** human: someone who lives in their skin, and embraces their own incarnation.

The very word "incarnate" is based on the word "***carne***" which gives us in English "carnal." "Carnal" literally means "to put flesh on" or "to put skin on." The word "carnal" has given us carnival, carnivore, chili con ***carne***, carnitas, and carnal. A faith not in the flesh is a false faith.

The primary definition of "carnal" is not derogatory or salacious. It just means material or physical or "fleshed." In Jesus, God became carnal: Jesus the Christ is Creator Con ***Carne***. In the Incarnation God blessed matter, God romanced the material. God chose to be known to us as spirit wrapped in matter, glory wrapped in flesh.

Roman Catholic theologian at Fordham University, Elizabeth Johnson, puts what it means that God became "in the flesh" like this:

> The atoms comprising [Jesus'] body were once part of other creatures. The genetic structure of the cells in his body were kin to the flowers, the fish, the whole community of life, that descended from common ancestors in the ancient seas.[89]

The Incarnation is the fleshing out of God, the fleshing out of the story of God . . . of the divine becoming flesh . . .

of "Emmanuel" or God WITH Us . . . of God taking human flesh. Incarnation and the elevation of matter is a key component of the doctrines of creation, incarnation, resurrection. Plato and his opposition of soul and body, as well as all forms of Gnosticism and its fear of flesh, are totally alien to Christianity. As John of Damascus in the eighth century put it, "It was through matter that my salvation came to pass."[90]

And matter itself is transmigrated in the resurrection story. In the words of theoretical physicist/Anglican priest John Polkinghorne (d. 2021):

> We have seen that two remarkable New Testament passages (Romans 8:18–25; Colossians 1:15–20) do indeed speak of cosmic redemption. Just as we see Jesus' resurrection as the origin and guarantee of human hope, so we can also see it as the origin and guarantee of universal hope. The significance of the empty tomb is that the Lord's risen and glorified body is the transmuted form of his dead body. Thus **matter participates in the resurrection transformation**, enjoying thereby the foretaste of its own redemption from decay. The resurrection of Jesus is the seminal event from which the whole of God's new creation has already begun to grow.[91]

The Incarnation is the Ultimate Paradox, The Supreme Paradox where "Word becomes Flesh," spirit becomes matter, sound becomes sight. Every spiritual vision becomes a material vision or it isn't a true vision. There is no division between spirit and matter. Christianity is a deeply materialistic religion. This is what makes incredulous the French physicist who won the Templeton Prize in 2008, who boasts he is "deeply spiritual" but has "no faith" and does not "practice religion."[92] One of the earliest heresies was Docetism, a branch of Gnosticism that portrayed Jesus as a kind of angel who came to reveal "spiritual truth" but who had no physical body, only a phantasm of a body. There is no purely "spiritual" world or "spiritual" faith. Spiritmatters.

There are two scandals of the Incarnation: imago Dei, imago hominum. First, "And God said, 'Let us make the human in our image, after our likeness.'"[93] God made humans in the divine likeness. But to keep humans in the divine likeness, God sent God to be "made in the likeness of the human."[94] Second, humans were made in divine likeness, and humans keep returning the favor and make the divine in human likeness.

The doctrine of the Incarnation is positioned as the centerpiece of Eastern Orthodoxy. The Western church puts soteriology at the heart of theology. The Eastern Church puts Incarnation at the heart. But you cannot separate creation and incarnation. It is part of God's nature of self-giving love.

The Incarnation is not a Plan B. The Incarnation is part of the original design from the beginning, the design of a God who wants to share the divine life with creation itself.

The first incarnation of God in the world zings all of creation with the presence of God, although it is easier for

## JESUS HUMAN

humans to understand the omnipresence of evil than the omnipresence of good. God's presence itself is a distinguishing mark and characteristic of God. Before the Incarnation of Bethlehem 2000 years ago, when the divine became definitive human, there was the incarnation of The Big Bang ("The Big Bloom") of Creation in Genesis 1 & 2, when Spirit first became matter. "Creation," wrote St. Thomas Aquinas, "is the primary and most perfect revelation of the divine . . . If we do not understand Creation correctly, we cannot hope to understand God correctly." Theologians like Aquinas, John Duns Scotus, Bonaventure, etc. have argued that the whole of creation was requisite preparation for the divine incarnation in Jesus. "The only real fall of humanity," wrote Eastern theologian Alexander Schmemann, "is its non-eucharistic life in a non-eucharistic world."

*The wisdom of the Word was in the human heart long before the birth of Jesus.*
FR. DANIEL O'LEARY[95]

When the Son of God, the Divine One, became the Son of Man, the human one, a nuclear Rubicon was crossed and the coupling of the divine and the human was not for a moment or a lifetime but for all time, an eternal metaphysic, a forever mystery.

Jesus came into this world, not to leave it, but never to leave it by leaving it with God's presence through the Holy Spirit. The Incarnation is not a first union and communion between creator and creation. The Incarnation is a new level

## ABECEDARIUM OF A JESUS HUMAN

of union and communion between Creator and creation. Incarnation does more than zap earth with heaven, or zipline the heavens to earth . . it zips the divine into the human and zings the Earth with the presence of Jesus. Incarnation means that humanity is the "vessel," the vehicle of divinity . . . not divine itself. But the organ of divinity.

What will incarnating the word look like in your heart, in your home, in your church? What kind of unexpected journeys might true faithfulness put you on? Incarnation takes context seriously and honors cultural logics.[96] For example, in Bulgaria, you shake your head sideways when you want to say "yes," and you shake your head up and down when you want to say "no." Somali nomads don't have pillows unless you call carved wooden headrests "pillows."[97] The Maasai people in Kenya greet you with spit, in your hand or on your chest, a sign of respect and honor.

---

*Culture is the name of that whole process in the course of which God does what it takes to make, and to keep, human beings human.*

EXETER THEOLOGIAN TIMOTHY J. GORRINGE, *FURTHERING HUMANITY: A THEOLOGY OF CULTURE* (2004)

---

Some journeys are hard. When Mary affirmed "Let IT be with me according to your word," she could not foresee all that little word "it" would bring to her life. Sometimes "it" is not fragrant or fun.

"It" would be a pregnancy out of wedlock.

"It" would be giving birth far from her home.

"It" would be a night of wonder filled with shepherds and angels and gifts from strangers.

"It" would be a royal threat to the child's very life, and fleeing to Egypt for safety.

"It" would be long years of a seemingly simply, ordinary life.

"It" would be three years of coping with people coming to terms with her son as the Messiah.

"It" would be the horror of the cross, and a mother's heartbreak at the tomb.

"It" would be, finally, the glory of the resurrection.

What is your "it" as a Jesus human? What "it" will bring your faith out of Christmas "cuteness" and into incarnational acuteness of voice, vision, and venture?

##  is for Dao (Chinese: 道) Human

The Chinese word **Dao** (or Tao)[98] means a way or a path, a course or a road. Confucians used the term **Dao** to speak of the way human beings ought to live morally and ethically in the world. But in Daoism (or Taoism), **Dao** means more like the way of the universe, and our need to live in harmony with The Way or **Dao**.

What is important to learn from the concept of **Dao** is that The Way is not just a human way but a way of creation, an infinite way of living in the universe. "For God so loved the cosmos . . ." is the most correct translation of everyone's beloved verse John 3:16. But the universe is not a great machine; it's a great mind.

It is well known that the earliest name for those who followed Jesus was "The people of The Way." Before there were Christians, there were followers of "The Way," starting with the Magi, who took the way of the star to the Christ child, and then went home "by another way."[99]

The key word in Confucianism is "**Dao**" which translates as "the Way."

The key word in Taosim is "Tao" which translates as "the Way."

The key word in Islam is "Sharia" which means "the Way."

In Confucianism, "the Way" is harmony with humanity.

In Taoism, "the Way" is harmony with the universe.

In Islam, "the Way" is harmony with the Law of Five Noble Pillars.

JESUS HUMAN

In Christianity, "the Way" is harmony with a person, a Healer and Savior, who called himself "The Way."

> If any of you wants to be my follower, you must give up your way, live God's way, and follow The Way.[100]

I am writing this in an airport, where I overheard someone on their cell say, "Come back. Come home. You know the way." Do we? Have we forgotten The Way home? Has even the church, waylaid by all sorts of goods and goodies, lost the way to The Way? "This is The Way. Walk in it," Isaiah says.[101]

A ***dao*** human isn't truly on the way unless they're willing to go out-of-the-way and sometimes get in-the-way to follow The Way. The Way is not an end or an event but an adventure in advent, a life of starting where you are and journeying from there with many interruptions and interventions.

◇

*Caminante, no hay camino*
*Se hace camino al andar.*

*Wayfarer, there is no road,*
*you make the road as you go.*
ANTONIO MACHADO

A ***dao*** human knows that the way has a multitude of components:

> ***Dao*** is a way of thinking.
>
> ***Dao*** is a way of living.
>
> ***Dao*** is a way of godliness.
>
> ***Dao*** is a narrow way.
>
> ***Dao*** is a broad way.
>
> ***Dao*** is a glorious way.
>
> ***Dao*** is a suffering way.
>
> ***Dao*** is a risky way.
>
> ***Dao*** is an exacting way.
>
> ***Dao*** is an illumined way with "a lamp unto my feet/light upon my path."
>
> ***Dao*** is a sublime way.
>
> ***Dao*** is an unpredictable way.
>
> ***Dao*** is an adventurous way.
>
> ***Dao*** is a low way. But on the ***dao*** highway, the "low road" is the "high road."[102]

> *Dear friend, take my advice;*
> *it will add years to your life.*
>
> *I'm writing out clear directions to Wisdom Way,*
> *I'm drawing a map to Righteous Road.*
>
> *I don't want you ending up in blind alleys,*
> *or wasting time making wrong turns.*
>
> *Hold tight to good advice; don't relax your grip.*
> *Guard it well—your life is at stake!*
>
> *Don't take Wicked Bypass;*
> *don't so much as set foot on that road.*
>
> *Stay clear of it; give it a wide berth.*
> *Make a detour and be on your way.*
>
> PROVERBS 4:10–15 (MSG)

**Ad Astra:** God is a God of *dao* people on the move. At Beersheba God says to Jacob: "I will go down with you into Egypt, and I will also surely bring you up again."[103] Every journey, every coming and going, every mission is a discovery of some truth that you weren't previously aware of. There are many truths, but only one Truth. The Way leads to The Truth which brings The Life.

In the *dao* life, there will be "no way" situations: blocks in the way, detours on the way, disruptions to the way. When we are summoned to keep going, we will want to say, "No Way." Not "doubtful." Not "unlikely." Not "where there's a will there's a way." But NO WAY, Yahweh.

But the truth of ***dao*** is that, in the face of NO WAY situations, God will make a way.

The Story is full of teenagers facing No Ways. David, no more than fifteen years of age, is chosen to go up against the giant Goliath. No way, David, everyone said. "He's too big to hit." But Yahweh said, "David, don't listen to everyone. Trust me. He's too big to miss."

But God . . . Made a Way.

Mary, a teenager, was told by an angel that she would conceive a son who would save the world. Virgins don't get pregnant. What about my reputation? No Way can this happen, thought Mary.

But God . . . Made a Way.

Joseph, a teenager, was sold into slavery by his own brothers. Then he was betrayed by Potiphar's wife, and put into prison for life. No Way was here any way out.

But God . . . Made a Way.

Daniel, a teenager, torn from his family and kidnapped to Babylon. Daniel opened his window toward Jerusalem and displayed his faith in defiance of Nebuchadnezzar. That's what got him thrown into a lion's den. No Way could he survive this.

But God . . . Made a Way.

Gideon, the youngest of a poor family from the smallest tribe of Israel (Manasseh), is hiding out when God calls him out of hiding. No Way am I the one who want for this mission, Yahweh.

But God . . . Made a Way.

Twelve of the most famous Israelites were chosen to go

out from the wilderness of Paran and spy on the Land of Canaan. For 40 days Shammua, Shaphat, Igthur, and Geuel collected samples of the "milk and honey" flowing from this land of "milk and honey." But they also came back and said "NO WAY." These Canaanites are so big they make us look like grasshoppers.

Caleb and Joshua came back and agreed, "No Way." But they trusted God enough to say, "But God will make a way."

> *The Old Testament begins with a man walking with God and the New Testament has Christ's life here ending with a walk along the Emmaus Road.*
> ENGLISH WRITER AND CENTENARIAN RONALD BLYTHE[104]

One of the most important theologians of the fifteenth century, and the German thinker who brokered Renaissance humanism into the bloodstream of German culture, was Nicholas of Cusa (d. 1464). Cusa delivered a sermon on "The Way" that deserves the status of a classic. It is worthy of memorization:

> Paul said that we exist in God and move in him, for we are wayfarers. The wayfarer takes his name and his existence from the Way. The wayfarer who walks or moves in the infinite Way, if he is asked where he is, says, "On the Way"; if asked where he moves, replies, "In the Way"; if asked why he moves, says, "Because of the Way"; and if asked whither he goes, says, "From the Way." Accordingly,

the infinite Way is called the place of the wayfarer, and this is God. Therefore, this Way, outside of which no wayfarer is to be found, is an existence without beginning or end, and from it the wayfarer takes all that he is or has, and through it he is a wayfarer. The fact that a farer begins to be a wayfarer on the Way adds nothing to the infinite Way itself, nor does it make any change in this Way, which is eternal and immovable."[105]

If a ***dao*** human is a wayfarer, then faith needs footpaths. We may not know where we're going, but we know who we're going with.

JESUS HUMAN

## 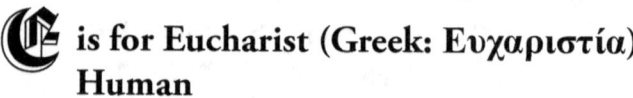 is for Eucharist (Greek: Ευχαριστία) Human

*Gratitude is the heart's memory.*
FRENCH PROVERB

Two of the most healing words any human can hear? "Thank you."

"Thank you" in Greek is "eucharistia," and Thank You is one of two sacraments (at a minimum) in the traditions of Christianity. But a "thank you" isn't truly sacramental or *eucharistic* without a story to go with it. And the story that wraps the "thank you" in Christianity is the story of Jesus' "Last Supper" with his disciples, where he said:

This is MY body,
> which is given for YOU

This cup is the new covenant in MY blood,
> which is poured out for YOU.[106]

The giving of thanksgiving is for the benefit of OTHERS ("FOR YOU"). The essence of *eucharist* is self-giving and self-sacrifice, not posturing or positioning. Yet in the story even the disciples don't get it, for immediately after the *eucharist* they engage in a contest over who's "the greatest" among them.[107]

The first thing to come between humans and God was food. The First Adam fell from his humanity from eating

# ABECEDARIUM OF A JESUS HUMAN

a proscribed meal he was forbidden to eat. The Last Adam showed us how to rise to our humanity from eating a prescribed meal we are bidden to eat. Charis (grace) inevitably leads to *eu-charistia* (thanksgiving) which gives rise the charismatic life (Spirit-gifted).[108]

The Jesus story revolves around food and tables, just as the *eucharistic* human's life will revolve around food and tables.[109] In fact, the parables of Jesus were not delivered in his preaching to the crowds but when his disciples and others were gathered over a meal. The parables are what Martin Luther called *Tischreden*, "table talk."

Whereas in Jesus' day, who is not at the table is as important in defining the table as who is there. Jesus is unique in his table manners and table hospitality. The Jesus story on earth begins in a stable table and ends in an Ascension table. In a world today that is obsessed with the "Marks of the Beast," Jesus gave us six Marks of the Feast, the marks of *eucharistic* living. These six Marks of the Feast were what got Jesus killed.

> **First**, he includes at his table society—the undesirables and the unseen, the discarded, and dislocated. Jesus stayed away from head tables and gravitated to end tables, tables on the margins with the marginalized.
>
> **Second**, he excoriates the elite for a closed table to the expendables and undesirables[110] and for only opening it to those advantageous to their standing. In doing this Jesus literally turns the tables upside

down even more than he overturned the tables in the Temple: he includes the excluded and excludes the included insiders.

**Third**, Jesus crosses boundaries by inviting to his table "sinners" and others whose presence normally contaminates the occasion. Eating with unwashed hands doesn't defile the meal. To marginalize is sin. Here is a typical Jesus guest list: "But when you give a banquet, invite the poor, the crippled, the lame, and the blind. And you will be blessed, because they cannot repay you."[111]

**Fourth**, Jesus' hospitality is indifferent to status, honor, and wealth, and he gives the best seats at his table to the feral and forgotten, to outsiders, outcast, outliers, and the out of bounds. These four table manners became the key feature of the community that would bear his name.

**Fifth**, at every table Jesus is head and host.

**Sixth**, we eat last.[112]

◇

*He who eats alone is dead.*
VARIOUSLY ATTRIBUTED TO LEONARD DA VINCI,
JEAN PAUL SARTRE, AND JEAN BAUDRILLARD

**Hospitality That Heals:** The default setting for the early church was ***eucharistic*** living, weekly thanksgivings around a

## ABECEDARIUM OF A JESUS HUMAN

common meal, usually culminating with a celebration of the Lord's Supper. ***Eucharist*** is the most intimate act Christians engage in as a community, then and now. For the first 250 years, followers of Jesus gathered in households to eat together and practice thankfulness or "***eucharist***." They came together as an "ecclesia," which meant community, not place. And since the community gathered most often at table, ecclesia meant table fellowship or ***eucharist***. When Christians gathered outside homes for worship, it was in unconsecrated, functional places where ecclesia still meant community. Only gradually did ecclesia come to mean place or building and not ***eucharistic*** community.

For the earliest Christians, there was a sacred presence and person, not a sacred place. All sacredness inhered in Jesus. The notion that certain places were "sacred" was pagan. The Temple was not "sacred," only the presence of God in the holy of holies in the temple was sacred. In pagan culture, sacred places required priestly intermediaries. The early Christians vehemently denied this. The only sacred place was the person of Jesus who invited us to be ***eucharist*** "in remembrance of me." There was no sacred ecclesia, only a sacred Christos. Divinity cannot be "housed" or "localized" in a place. Divinity can only be housed in a person for whom humans live thankfully and ***eucharistically***.

From 50–150, there is no architectural evidence of gatherings, only literary.

From 150–250, Christians needed larger and more complex places for ***eucharistic*** gatherings, so they started converting structures for assembly and worship.

JESUS HUMAN

From 250 on, Christians start building de novo and new buildings in the form of basilicas which popped up in Jerusalem, Syria, Rome, Asia Minor, and Greece. The shift from the sacralization of person to place had begun, and the table/altar became a lectern/pulpit.

At the very beginnings of Christianity, temple and table were both central. Believers met in the temple for worship, where the priests chanted psalms and sacrificed animals. But they met at home to celebrate *eucharist*, the liturgy of the table.

> Day by day, as they spent much time together in the temple, they broke bread at home and ate their food with glad and generous hearts.[113]

> The first Christians did not come together primarily to worship but to *eucharist*, to eat a sumptuous thanksgiving meal together.

> They devoted themselves to the apostles' teaching and to fellowship, to the breaking of bread and to prayer.[114]

They came together to experience the joy of *eucharist*, eating The Lord's Supper on The Lord's Day and, while eating, share in grand thanksgiving bathed in prayer. The teaching could take place before the meal, after the meal, or even sometimes during the meal. In Greek, the breaking of bread/fellowship (no "and") are simultaneous activities. So, their *eucharistic* "devotion" was to three things: fellowship around meals, prayer, and apostles' teaching. The German theologian and Near Eastern scholar Joachim Jeremias (1900–1979) argued that the core *eucharistic* concept of anamnesis ("Do this in memory of me") is given as a reminder for God more than a remembrance for us. Like the rainbow, which is a reminder not to us but to God not to flood the earth, the *eucharist* was a reminder to Jesus to return to the earth and join us at The Messianic Table.

The French Jesuit priest Henri de Lubac (1896–1991) called the *eucharist*, in a poetic phrase, a "tangible sign and deep reality." Not "deep magic" but "deep reality," ordinary reality deepened and divinely dimensioned by the extraordinary faith community gathered in the name of Jesus to give thanks for his life, death, resurrection and ascension.

> *What is given away feeds again and again,*
> *while what is kept feeds only once and leaves us hungry.*
> LEWIS HYDE, THE GIFT (1983), 65.

After the destruction of The Temple in 70 CE, the rabbis (collectively known as the "Sages of Blessed Memory") and the architects of the Mishna and the Talmud rebooted Judaism not around the Temple but around the Table. Two tables, to be exact. The Table in the public space (synagogue) at which the sacred Scriptures were read, and the table in the home where food was served to multiple generations. The word synagogue simply means "gathering together," so a synagogue was a designated public hall or outdoor gathering space.

The table is the new venue of the temple in the liturgical life of Judaism. The Temple has not ended. Jesus became embodied Torah and embedded Temple, and at Pentecost the temple burst out, centripetally, and we now become the temple.

Where priests presided at an altar, the rabbis (not a vocation found in the Hebrew Bible) presided at a table. Every synagogue must have an ark, where the Torah scrolls are kept. Every synagogue must have a table, from which the scrolls are read. Other than that, synagogues were free to take the architectural form of the communities where they're located. The original idea was for the synagogue to be the tallest building in town, but that was quickly abandoned. Jews learned to keep their heads down and not stick their architectural necks above others.

Parents presided at the table in the home where everyone studied and prayed and ate together. One of the most sacred Jewish holidays, Passover (Pesach), is not celebrated in the synagogue at all: Only around the home table presided over by the father and mother who lead the liturgy (Haggadah or "narration") recounting the story of God's liberation of Israel from slavery and God's continued presence in the lives of the people. The liturgy starts with the youngest member of the family posing four questions about the story which are answered during the extended meal.

Christians reframed and re-signed the animal sacrifices offered at the temple to be the life sacrifices offered at the synagogue and home. "Sacrifice" comes from the words "sacer" (sacred) and "facere" (make). To "sacrifice" something

# ABECEDARIUM OF A JESUS HUMAN

is to make it sacred. What Christians did was to make sacred their whole life, a *eucharistic* thanksgiving offering to God. They made everything they did, and everything they were, sacred. All of life became a holy and "living sacrifice."[115] You no longer sacrificed an animal to make your offering sacred. You made sacred your whole life, and the *eucharist* was the celebration of that sacred offering. *Eucharistic* eating is *eucharistic* living. Food is life. And life is daily gratitude for food.

We began this letter of the alphabet with a quote from Jesus: "This is my body." But since Jesus was speaking either Aramaic or most likely Hebrew, his sentence "This is my body" would have included no word the equivalent of the "is" as in "This is my body." It is linguistically impossible to say, "This IS MY BODY" in Hebrew or Aramaic.[116]

So, what would Jesus most likely have said? "This Is Me." NOT "This is my Body" but "This is Me." In other words, "This" is My Self in its Totality. "This" embraces all the activity that is taking place around the table. "This" is My Total Self in all its Corporality. You can't separate Jesus' personal, corporeal body from his corporate, communal body as expressed in table/fellowship and in Christ-body community (koinonia).

"This" in "This is Me" refers to the communal breaking of bread, not just the flesh of Jesus but the whole action of his physical presence in hosting this entire meal with his disciples. Paul's Greek word is "koinonia," and ours is "communion." "This" is the whole table time with his disciples. "This" is "koinonia," or "communion," not just the bread

## JESUS HUMAN

that he is breaking but the koinonia fellowship that breaks bread with the dead and the living.

After "This is Me," comes four animations of "This is What I'm Really Like." The four features of living **eucharistically** are:

1. Offering
2. Thanking
3. Breaking
4. Sharing

First is the freedom to offer. Second is the trusting to thank, which means prayer is a condition of continual gratitude, seeing those around you and learning to say thank you for them. Third, obedient even to breaking, a "breaking" for Jesus which will occur on the cross. Fourth, loving to share in self-giving love, and a willingness to give yourself away and sharing his resurrection life.

---

*In Love's service, only wounded soldiers can serve.
The unwounded life bears no resemblance to the Rabbi.*

BRENNAN MANNING[117]

---

1. Life Offered—your life is in your hands. You have the freedom to clench and clutch and keep it to yourself or to open your hands and freely offer it to God.
2. Life Lived Thankfully—gratitude that is a gift, not bait, is built on a life of trust and obedience.
3. Life lived Broken—woundedness makes us stronger

in the same way adding impurities to a material (e.g., aluminum) can strengthen it, stiffen it, and make it serviceable. Pure aluminum is too soft to be of any use without impurities.

4. Life totally shared—this is Love

A *eucharistic* human turns their home into a liturgical paradise of offering, thanking, breaking, and sharing. A *eucharist* human practices radical hospitality in a culture that sees Christians as fools and frauds, in much the same way as the early church faced. There are two imperatives of faith formation in a *eucharistic* human: kudos and koinonia, two Greek words meaning praise and appreciation (kudos) and connection and community (koinonia). To grow in grace and in the image of Christ, every human heart needs Kudos + Koinonia: appreciation and integration.

Meal traditions represent far more than the routine act of eating. Instead, meal practices offer means through which a society's social norms and values can be enacted and reinforced.

Jesus' "last supper" ended with a lifting up of two key elements in the Passover meal: bread and wine. And with these two elements, he introduced a whole new world with the exact same words God used to introduce the First Adam to his world: "EAT."

A Jesus human life is a life of *eucharist*. It's so important that I often sign-off my letters: "*Eucharistically* yours."

## J is for FUBAR (Pop Culture) Human

*The best proof that there's intelligent life in the universe is that it hasn't come here.*[118]

SIR ARTHUR C. CLARKE (1917-2008)

"To err is human," Alexander Pope famously said. To blame others is even more human, some wit added.

How do you say "sin" to a culture that does not know the word? Maybe you try **FUBAR**.

The only thing worse than the horror of the suffering endured by humanity is the horror of the suffering incurred by humanity. Sin is not the patrimony of humanity but the defacing of humanity, our blemish not our birthright.[119] Ignatius of Loyola, the sixteenth century Spanish priest who founded the Society of Jesuits, liked to call the devil "the enemy of human nature."[120] What is specific to human nature—as God designed it to be—is to be in relation, a relation of mutual respect and appreciation, living and working with others. This is exactly what the enemy has successfully destroyed.

We don't need the Bible to tell us that "all have sinned and fallen short of God's glory."[121] We don't need God to appear in human form to tell us that humans, left to their own devices, will mess everything up. "All we like sheep have gone astray," says the First Testament.[122] The Second Testament adds, "If we say we are without sin, the truth is not in us."¹²³ Every Third Testament is a singular witness to the truth spoken by Testaments One and Two. Every human is a **FUBAR** human.

Yours truly especially. My first driving of a car occurred at age twelve in a large, congested southern city at night while my fifteen-year-old date was sitting in the passenger seat with the convertible top down and the thirty-year-old owner of the car (who assumed because of my looks and demeanor I was licensed to drive) was busy in the back seat making out with his teenage girlfriend. What is wrong with this picture? What could go wrong? Wrong way.

To be sure, sin is not the morally trivial matter we like to make it as in "sinfully" chocolate or "Devil's Food Cake." Sin is more than human suckitude, a "toxic trait," or that Romans-7 moment which we all experience daily: "The good I want to do I don't do; the evil I don't want to do, is what I do."¹²⁴ Sin is a theological way of talking about the unavoidable human condition of falling down on life, failing each other, fouling our nests, and not fearing God. It is ironic that Augustine is not fashionable in academic circles today because of his belief that humans are born with negative predispositions, when evolutionary scientists take this for granted on a daily basis.

The Jewish and Christian understanding of sin¹²⁵ as a breaking of covenant and a violation of relationship (more than a violation of divine law) is not found anywhere else in the ancient world.¹²⁶ Sin is more than moral wrongdoing.¹²⁷ Sin is a trespass of trust, a taint of faith, which necessitates taking seriously repentance, forgiveness, and restoration.

## JESUS HUMAN

> *I come not to call the just but sinners.*
> JESUS[128]

There are always the exceptions. Just like every farmer knows that a percentage of the seed spread is bad seed, so a percentage of humanity is "born bad" with sociopathic traits and psychopathic tendencies, "bad people" one writer has called "the train drivers to Auschwitz."[129] Whether the church attracts more than its fair share of these "train drivers," or whether the church itself produces the train drivers, is another question entirely. The perversion of the best yields the worst. Or in the words of one Roman poet and philosopher, "*Tantum religio potuit suadere malorum*" or "nothing is more potent than religion to prompt people to evil acts against each other."[130]

Some days evil is so abounding it is easier to believe in the devil than believe in God. Some days it is easier to say with Charlie Brown, "Dread one day at a time" than it is to sing, "One Day at a Time, Sweet Jesus."

> *Human stupidity is a bottomless abyss,*
> *and the ocean I see from my window*
> *seems to me quite small in comparison.*
> MISATTRIBUTED TO FRENCH NOVELIST GUSTAVE FLAUBERT (D. 1880)

But Jesus doesn't say to the fallen woman "You're fallen." Jesus says, "You tripped. Let me help you up." The reason why we fall, fail, and foul is because we turn down and trip up on our humanity and go tripping after God's divinity instead: "The day that you eat of it,... you shall be as gods."[131] Instead of choosing life from the tree of life, we chose death from the tree of death: "The day that you eat of it, you shall surely die."[132] The Story of the Scriptures is one unending invitation to "Choose life."[133] God gave us life, but we must choose life. We can choose not to live life, and many people do. They stifle life. They tame life. They tranquilize life. They devilize life. They deaden life. Jesus sets us free to experience life in all its human fullness.

Sin "deforms" what is beautiful in us. And most of our de-forming is due to our attempt to form ourselves (self-forming) rather than allowing for God-forming. Sin steals life from the sinner. That is what sin is: a thief of our humanity—our talent, our time, our ties that bind us together. Our sins against God are always part of our sins against each other. Sin is literally a "crime against humanity."

*I like committing crimes.*
*God likes forgiving them.*
*Really the world is admirably arranged.*
ENGLISH POET W. H. AUDEN (D. 1973)[134]

Soldiers in the Second World War created their own name for sin in the form of the sarcastic acronym "What a SNAFU!" SNAFU was military slang for "Status Normal: All F***** Up." The Marine Corps tried to restrict the use of the "f" word, leading to the military allegation whenever the wildly popular staple "monkey butter" was in short supply:

## JESUS HUMAN

"They took away peanut butter and now the 'f' word. So you can starve to death but not tell anyone about it."

The normal situation for the human species is that we all "f*** up." Without divine help, SNAFUs will turn into train wrecks, Pandora's Boxes, Charlie Foxtrots, or what the military again snidely coined as **FUBAR**: "F***** Up Beyond All Recognition" (or alternatively BTFO as in "Blown The F*** Out"). If you can come up with a better definition of "sin" that SNAFU and **FUBAR**, the more power to you. Hamartology is snafuology.

"I'm afraid you have humans." These are the words of a cartoon, where a Saturn-like planet, wearing a head-mirror on its ring, gives a diagnosis of extinction to the planet Earth.[135] That Dantesque sentiment has echoed down the corridors of human history. The Italian Renaissance philosopher Niccolò Machiavelli wrote multiple meditations on human nature: "The Ass," "The Prince," "The Discourses on Livy." He found little to like in humanity, little worthy of redemption. British historian Thomas Babington Macaulay, after reading the Scottish philosopher James Mill's optimistic paean to humanity called *Essay on Government* (1828), shook his head in wonderment and asked the author: have you ever met a human?[136]

◇

*A human is born by falling from between the knees of its mother.*
ALWAYS BUT FALSELY ATTRIBUTED TO ROMAN POET HORACE (D. 8 BCE)

Life is not plans and maps. Life is falling. Life is freefall.

## ABECEDARIUM OF A JESUS HUMAN

All fall. All fail. But grace turns all fails and fallenness upside down, and overrides gravity with levitation and life.

Grace exerts a levitational force on everything that draws us nearer, nearer to God and drives us closer to the wounded, the broken, and the lost. As Dietrich Bonhoeffer reminded us, this is not a fallen world; it is a fallen-falling world.[137] But what we need to be reminded of is this: we serve a risen-rising Christ.

John Newton's headstone, written by himself, which can be seen today in the churchyard of Olney Church, reads:

> John Newton, once an infidel and libertine,
> a servant of slaves in Africa, was, by the rich
> mercy of our Lord and Savior Jesus Christ,
> preserved, restored, pardoned, and appointed
> to preach the faith he had long labored to
> destroy!

In his old age, when he could no longer see to read, the author of "Amazing Grace" heard someone recite this verse, "By the grace of God I am what I am" (1 Corinthians 15:10 NIV).

John Newton remained silent a short time, and then said:

> I am not what I ought to be. Ah! how imperfect and deficient.
> I am not what I might be, considering my privileges and opportunities.
> I am not what I wish to be. God, who knows my heart—knows I wish to be like Him.
> I am not what I hope to be. Before long, I

> will drop this clay tabernacle, to be like Him and see Him as He is!
>
> Yet, I am not what I once was—a child of sin, and slave of the devil!

Then Newton concluded his stream of thought:

> Though not all these—not what I ought to be, not what I might be, not what I wish or hope to be, and not what I once was—I think I can truly say with the apostle, "By the grace of God—I am what I am!"

At the age of 82, Newton acknowledged, "My memory is nearly gone. But I remember two things: that I am a great sinner—and that Christ is a great Savior!"

##  is for Guanxi (Chinese: 關西) Human

*Guanxi* is a form of socio-political Jenga, a block-puzzle game of stacking and interlocking relationships, a circuit-board of connections that are easily toppled, misperceived, misjudged. *Guanxi* is the first word learned by any person wanting to do business in China. Cracking the *Guanxi* Code is the beginning task of any person wanting to live in China. Good or bad *guanxi* shapes your destiny, and your skill at playing the *guanxi* game or handling the *guanxi* nexus determines success or failure. The Hasbro game of Jenga measures physical and spatial skills. The *Guanxi* game of Jenga measures relational and social skills.

The word literally means "connections." It's a word that underlines the importance of looking at life as a matrix of relationships. Or what the West calls "networking." The four foundational corners of business networking are trust, bonding, mutual relationship, and empathy. Nevertheless, the points of view in which these dimensions are understood and consolidated are extensively disparate in the East and the West.

The West talks of "social capital" or "relationship capital" but in China the form of wealth that can be accumulated and leveraged is "*guanxi*." The old *guanxi* was behind closed doors. The new *guanxi* is up front and above-board. Whether old or new, the *guanxi* human understands that anything in isolation dies; anything with connection thrives. The future belongs to those who have the connections.

We are already seeing the ***guanxi*** future form in the increasing popularity of group dancing, mass singing, gaming conventions, tribal gatherings, cosplay contests, communal tables, reading groups, and Pentecostal expressions of faith.[138] Human development entails both personal development and social maturation, or the build-up of social capital. You can only be whole in parts. You can't separate the parts from the whole.

There are two ways to look at the church. One way is to say we are individuals who are bound together in a faith community. A second way is to say we are a community of individuals of faith. These may sound like they are basically the same idea, but these two definitions describe very different realities.

◇

*Within that household the human spirit*
*has both roof and hearth.*

CATHOLIC WRITER HILAIRE BELLOC (D. 1953) ON WHAT IS "CHURCH"

**YOYO? (You're On Your Own?):** Which are we? Individuals bound in a community of faith, or a community of individuals bound in faith? What makes a person who they are? Not beliefs, or even behavior. But relationships. Our "worth" resides not in our principles but in our relationships, our connections, which is the essence of ***guanxi***. In fact, this notion of a person as an "individual" as we know that word "individual" today is only of modern vintage. It has only been on the scene for the past 500 years. The very word, individuum, denotes a solitary oneness enclosed

# ABECEDARIUM OF A JESUS HUMAN

upon itself. For the modern individual, any relations are secondary additions, which do not belong to his or her being. This is so not what the Bible means by "church" or "individual."

Jesus humans find their identity in community first, a community which conceives individuals and conceives Christ. But a **Guanxi** Jesus human elevates hearing to a "social sense," in the words of British neuroscientist Sophie Scott, and understands music as a ***guanxi*** glue.[139]

Whether a **Guanxi** human will use connectedness for social control or social capital remains to be seen. British musician and visual artist Brian Eno argues that "the new American approach to social control is not so much the control of what we think, but the control of what we think about." Eno says we have gone from "propaganda" to "prop-agenda."[140] Social control or social change.

JESUS HUMAN

# 𝔥 is for Hehe (Mandarin: 呵呵) Human

◇

*Whoever is near us and needing us must be our "neighbor": it does not matter whether he is related to us or not, whether he is morally worthy of our help or not. The love of Christ knows no limits. It never ends. It does not shrink from ugliness and filth.*

ST. TERESA BENEDICTA OF THE CROSS,
A.K.A. EDITH STEIN (D. 1942 AT AUSCHWITZ)[141]

The great unresolved question of the human species: how to get along with one another. We have solved other less important questions, like how to grow enough food to feed the planet.

***Hehe*** is portrayed as the essence of Chinese culture, where fifty-six different ethnic groups needed to learn to live together. They found common ground around this Confucian concept of ***Hehe***. The Chinese character for peace and harmony (hé) depicts rice stalks (right side) and a mouth (left side). The ideogram makes clear that peace cannot be separated from food security and communication. So while "he" alone just means "peace", the doubling of "*hehe*" intensifies and emphasizes that meaning in Chinese. The repetition creates a sense of profound tranquility and accord. It's used to denote relationships or situations marked by cooperative mildness, calm, and lack of friction. The traditional meaning was along the lines of "harmonious and gentle". Over time, it came to simply mean "peace" and "harmony" in Chinese culture.

In the ***Hehe*** worldview there are three key harmonious relationships: First, harmony between humans and nature. Human life is a part of nature and natural life. Second, harmony among people, where we bring together into harmony our amities and antipathies so that our communal values might cooperate and harmonize in a global village. Third, harmony within oneself, which issues first in "***junzi***," the virtuous person, a prerequisite to "***ren***," the acme of humaneness and harmony. The world-famous Chinese cuisine "Kung Pao Chicken" is an expression of ***Hehe*** . . . multiple layers of flavor like sweet, sour, salty, and spicy that combine harmoniously.

Some of the most incisive words written on the Holy Spirit come from Jonathan Edwards, who did not know the concept of ***Hehe*** but sensed its importance: "It was made especially the Holy Spirit's work to bring the world to its beauty and perfection out of chaos: for the beauty of the world is a communication of God's beauty. The Holy Spirit is the harmony and excellence and beauty of the deity. Therefore, it was his work to communicate beauty and harmony to the world, and so we read that it was He that moved upon the face of the waters."[142]

In the West, humans are encouraged to live a "balanced" life. In fact, the West has reframed Yoga away from "harmony" to "balance" as its primary metaphor. "Balance" conveys a balance beam or balancing scales where you must "even things out" or "equalize" the weight. If you are working too hard, like weights on either end of a bar bell, you must "even things out" by play or leisure. By this definition Jesus didn't live a balanced life.

I admit: I am temperamentally allergic to the word "balance" which often means get rid of the weird and wonky, the lopsided and topsy-turvy. But that's where the art is; that's where the creativity is; that's where the imagination flourishes.[143] As much as I despise the metaphor of "balance" I love the metaphor of harmony or equilibrium. Life is not a balancing act. Life is a dance floor: a dance in the park, a dance in the dark, a dance in the rain. All dances are tipsy, dizzying, askew.

In martial arts, the most dangerous moment for a participant is when that person is in a position of balance. Balance is precarious, the most likely place to get injured and the posture that leads to defeat. In the language of martial arts, the winning position is a posture of rooting and sinking into the ground.

Our music and melodies are not just how we speak to God, but how we speak to "one another." Here is St. Paul to the church at Ephesus: "Speak to ONE ANOTHER with psalms, hymns and spiritual songs. Sing and make music in your hearts to the Lord."[144] How did we miss this all these years? A Jesus human communicates to "one another" in notes and chords, vibes and melodies. What's your daily music? Classical music still has a hold, not only in the West but in the East. To hear 80+ musicians playing together in harmony at the top of their form is itself a rapture.

# ABECEDARIUM OF A JESUS HUMAN

*Christian truth is symphonic. Symphony by no means implies a sickly-sweet harmony lacking all tension. Great music is always dramatic: there is a continual process of intensification, followed by a release of tension at a higher level.*[145]

SWISS THEOLOGIAN HANS URS VON BALTHASAR (D. 1988)

The Austrian-British philosopher Ludwig Wittgenstein (d. 1951), liked to say to his students: "I'll teach you differences."[146] Traditional scholastic theology focuses on distinctions and differences. In the tradition of the Far East, or Asian-ness, it is characteristic to search for creative harmony rather than distinctions. Asian-ness asks: What truths are to be found in Hinduism, Islam, Buddhism, etc.? How we are to evaluate them, and how we are to work together?

One of the most difficult challenges in the world today is attaching an "e" to human. How can humans be more "humane." What does it mean to be a "humane" human? I discovered one person who was attaching the "e" to human in Surabaya, Indonesia.

I live in an archipelago of a little over 700 islands (that's low tide; high tide only about 172 islands) known as the San Juan Islands. Indonesia is an archipelago of 17,000 islands. It is the largest Muslim nation in the world, the fourth largest producer of coffee in the world, and the source of the most expensive coffee on the planet—the infamous Kopi Luwak coffee beans harvested by a civet cat.[147]

The largest city in Indonesia is Jakarta, where Muslim-Christian relations are at best problematic, at worst bitter and bloody. The second largest city in Indonesia is Surabaya, where Muslim-Christian relations are warm and friendly at best, aloof at worst. The difference between these two Muslim cities is one man: Alex Tanuseputra. He has spent his life giving that word human an appendix, and he has shown me what it means to be a Jesus kind of human.

Born 01 June 1941, Tan List Gwan was the second of four children. Forced to change his name to Alex Tan, after Indonesia gained its independence, his name changed a final time to Alex Tanuseputra. The child of Christian parents, Alex's rocky road to faith ended with his being a one-man-band evangelist traveling the roads of Mojokerto on a bike: he led worship, played the trumpet and the accordion, and preached. His specialty was the prison population in the city, especially the political prisoners that everyone was afraid to visit.

Alex could not escape the call to plant a church in Surabaya. So, he drove a taxi by night and preached by day. From hard work and shrewd investments, Alex moved from a bicycle as his primary means of transport to vintage cars, with which he loved to tinker and touch up.

One day, as he was repairing a buddy's car, he realized that the rest of his life he would be repairing and restoring not just the physical vehicles of his Muslim buddies, but their very souls. He could either treat them as objects or subjects, enemies or friends, problems or peers. He was struck by the thought that God wants us to prosper, but God wants us to prosper together. When he decided to treat Muslims as friends, not enemies, everything changed.

## ABECEDARIUM OF A JESUS HUMAN

He befriended the imams. When they built a mosque, his church contributed a stained-glass window depicting some Abrahamic scene. He routinely referred to God as "Allah," Arabic for "God," which got him ousted from a denomination in USAmerica and declared a heretic. He started community development projects in the poorest Muslim neighborhoods of Surabaya, and improved housing for people regardless of their religion. He even opened up a medical clinic with free dialysis for anyone, and attached to the clinic a residence inn for the family members to stay while their families were receiving treatment at the clinic.

Under the tutelage of Alex Tanuseputra in the Muslim heartland, Bethel has grown to be one of the largest Christian churches in the world. They dream of building an outdoor stadium larger than most of the football stadiums in the US. But this one man is also responsible for Christians and Muslims being able to live together in respect and harmony in the second largest city of the largest Muslim nation in the world. Surabaya is not Shangri-La for interfaith relationships. But it's a powerful step in the right direction, and a testimony to what putting an "e" at the end of that word "human" can do.

When we think of harmony or harmonious difference, it is better not to think of "multi-tasking" which is randomly juggling many things at once, and to think of "simultaneous inclusion"[148] which carefully jigsaws diverse items into a coherent place and pattern. We can do many things at once while at the same time focusing on one thing we are doing.

## JESUS HUMAN

*Jesus is the symphony, the harmony of the Father.*
CLEMENT OF ALEXANDRIA (D. 215)

What a magic moment for eight-year-old Remi, who has a muscular disorder so that one side of her face doesn't match the other side. Miranda Lambert sensed her uniqueness in an October 2019 Wichita concert, and brought her up on stage during her anthem to difference "All Kinds of Kinds." But let's be real. The truth?

People don't really like "difference." Humans like "sameness," which is the basis for all homeowners associations, condominium boards, Hollywood celebrities, zoning ordinances, franchises, and twitter. We like the "idea" of difference but we enforce conformity and sameness and uniformity with all the might at our disposal. Dominating, controlling forces seek homogeneity. But the same Spirit who calls us to the exclusivity of the Lord Jesus Christ calls us to an *unconditional love* for all peoples and the diversity of their religious experiences.

The Holy Spirit may work in a wider human register than the one we are comfortable with. It seems that for Jesus to live, work, and play successfully with others requires an intellectual commitment to a type of social order in which others are given the freedom to follow different paths and pursue contradictory ends. To be fully human, to be created in God's image, is not just TO THINK and be able to use our gray matter, but TO THINK DIFFERENTLY and to come to very different conclusions about some gray-matter things.

Human beings will learn to live together in peace and

harmony or they will burn together in hatred and war. The choice is ours: live in Harm or Harmony. When you sing in harmony with a congregation and there is such togetherness and concord that the hairs stand up on the back of your neck and your spine shivers, that's the sublimity of community.

---

*Those who love their dream of a community more than the Christian community itself become destroyers of the latter, even though their personal intention may be ever so honest and earnest and sacrificial. God hates visionary dreaming; it makes the dreamer proud and pretentious.*

THEOLOGIAN DIETRICH BONHOEFFER (D. 1945)[149]

##  is for Humanist (English) Human

One of the biggest re-framings required by our abecedary of global citizenry is the re-signing of the word "*humanist.*" Very simply, a *humanist* human is a humane human.

> *In a hidden and mysterious way [the Incarnate Logos] . . . vivifies every aspect of authentic humanism.*
> JOHN PAUL II (D. 2005)[150]

Maybe it is time to renew humanism.[151] Humanism has an august and esteemed history. There have been many different kinds of "humanism" over the years, and many "humanisms" proved more dehumanizing than humanizing. Historically, humanism could be supernaturalist or naturalist, theistic or atheistic (or agnostic). A *humanist* could be a realist or a philosophical idealist, or even a pragmatist, depending on whether one's brand was secular humanism, scientific humanism, Marxist humanism, Catholic humanism (with Aquinas their hero), literary humanism, religious humanism. There is a grand tradition in Christianity of humanism, most highly represented in the Erasmian brand of humanism.[152]

"Christian *humanists*," as they called themselves, thought that classical learning helped people to attain moral excellence. History shows how "humanism" is often where the inhumanity of humanism comes into full view, whether on the utopian or apocalyptic ends.[153] The words "Hitler" and "Nazi death camps" proved wrong this belief that highly

## ABECEDARIUM OF A JESUS HUMAN

civilized and rationalized societies would be the most moral societies. So did before them the Roman circus, Aztec sacrifices, Inquisition bonfires, and Revolutionary America slave ships.[154] There is a story of Mahatma Gandhi's visit to England in the 1930s to make the case for Indian self-rule. A reporter allegedly asked him what he thought of Western civilization. Gandhi, who had just visited the London slums, replied, "I think it would be a very good idea."[155]

At its best, humanism is partly responsible for getting books into churches and into the hands of the common people. Queen Elizabeth in 1559 issued injunctions reaffirming both her father's order of 1538 requiring the placing in all churches on "one book of the whole Bible of the largest volume in English," and her half-brother Edward VI's additional edict (The Royal Injunctions of 1547) that the *Paraphrases of the Gospels* by Erasmus were to be "sette up in some conueninet place, with in the sayed Churche . . . whereas their Parishioners maye most commodiously resorte unto the same, and reade the same."

In other words, humanism is partly responsible for churches being forced to have the cutting-edge technology of the day as part of their ministry to the community. The Bible, *The Book of Common Prayer*, Sternhold and Hopkins metrical psalter, the *Paraphrases of Erasmus*, Foxe's *Book of Martyrs*, and John Jewel's *Works* became the nucleus of book collections many often chained to reading desks or in the back of churches. These "chained books" to desks were called "Desk Libraries" and were available to the masses.

Christianity's brand of humanism is also the origin of

the concept of "human rights," which was expanded by the Reformation and the Enlightenment to include toleration, freedom, justice, and equality, although it took centuries to extend human dignity and individual rights beyond boundaries of race, gender and class.[156] The values that Western culture esteems most today are in fact derivatives of Christianity in its most **humanist** forms, no matter how hard twenty-first century culture seeks to break free from Christianity's moorings.[157]

Yet we can't give up the word "humanism" to the atheists and the secularists. "Adam" is the Hebrew word for "humanity." It is time to bring to life a new form of Christian humanism, a Jesus humanism. Call it Holy Humanism. Call it Jesus humanness. Call it Jesus humanism. Call it whatever. I prefer Jesus humanness instead of Christian humanism because Jesus heightens my humanity, not dims it. Jesus exposes the superficiality and selfishness of our humanistic definitions of being human. Jesus also checks the naive optimism of **humanist** views about human goodness, a feature which even hard-core **humanists** like Stefan Zweig (d. 1942) finally admitted was a "beautiful error."[158]

Does Jesus humanness mean faith in humanity? No.

Does Jesus humanness make the most of human life through human abilities and action alone? No.

Does Jesus enhance the beauty of the earth, the culture, each other? Yes.

Does Jesus help us see life in color, not just black and white? Yes.

# ABECEDARIUM OF A JESUS HUMAN

*Humanism is not humanism until it meets the answer to all its questions in Jesus Christ. It is only a hint of possible glory until it sees itself in Him.*
METHODIST THEOLOGIAN LYNN HAROLD HOUGH (C. 1971)[159]

We have a choice: grow toward wholeness in humanness; or dissipate the resources God has given us. Ralph Waldo Emerson went too far in the divine direction: "Every man is a divinity in disguise, a god playing the fool." James Branch Cabell went too far in the "worms with wings" direction: "Man is a parasite infesting the epidermis of a midge among the planets."

True humanism, or Jesus humanness, is realizing that the human needs the divine to be human. True humanism is the belief that Jesus was the Last Adam who came to do what the First Adam failed to do: to show us how to be fully human in life and in death, and to convince us that everything he did we could do when the divine participates in the human.[160] T. S. Eliot was right: "If you remove from the word 'human' all that the belief in the supernatural has given to man, you can view him finally as no more than an extremely clever, adaptable and mischievous little animal."[161]

The danger in any other form of humanism than Jesus humanism is some half-baked humanism, some multi-faith fusion, or the loss of faith's ritual-based particularity. There is a difference between the universality of the mystery of Christ and the universality of Christianity as a religion. Yes, there is a need for "universals" but not without the "particulars."

JESUS HUMAN

***Humanists*** tend to the "universals" and neglect the particulars. Humanism in history has been all universal. For example, David Halberstam's *The Coldest Winter* (2008) has a chilling quote from Mao Tse-Tung, the Chinese dictator who saw himself as a revolutionary ***humanist***. Halberstam says that Mao Tse-Tung, lost in the big picture and the universals, was "emotionally immune to the loss of life." In the exact words of Mao: "The death of ten or twenty million people is nothing to be afraid of."[162]

Jesus humanism teaches that human beings are precious, not expendable, that every human being is unique, created in the image of God, and that each glorious one of us has been honored with a mission and an appointment. That's Jesus humanism.

## **I** is for Ikigai (Japanese: 生きがい) Human

***Ikigai*** (pronounced in three syllables I-ki-gai) is a Japanese concept that means "a reason for being." The word "*ikigai*" is usually used to indicate the source of value in one's life or the things that make one's life worthwhile. Iki means life; gai means value and meaning.[163]

> *Christ is all that matters*
> *and he lives in all of us.*
> APOSTLE PAUL (D. 57)[164]

"Things" are part of our reason for being.[165] One of the prime languages of the divine are God-made things. God created things, and God creates with things. The Apostle Paul insisted that "things" reveals the glory of God to the point where no human is "without excuse:"

> For what can be known about God is plain to them, because God has shown it to them. For his invisible attributes, namely, his eternal power and divine nature, have been clearly perceived, ever since the creation of the world, in the things that have been made. So they are without excuse.[166]

There is light that is not "Christian" light, and people will be judged on that basis. God placed divide codes of transcendence through all creation, signifying forms of presence that testify to God's beauty, truth, and goodness.

## JESUS HUMAN

A key difference between Eastern and Western art is this one word ***ikigai***. Western sculpture revolves around the concept of the self, and the ability of a sculpture to express the voice of the artist. Eastern sculpture prizes the ability of an artist to give voice to the material and muffle the voice of the self. Artistic traditions going back to the *Sakuteiki*, an eleventh-century treatise that some say is the oldest gardening text in the world, instructed readers to "obey the request of the stone." Or as American artist Isamu Noguchi (d. 1988), son of a Japanese poet, once put it, "I tried to look into a rock and find a rock."[167]

> *The point of art is not to reproduce the visible, but to make visible.*
> PAINTER PAUL KLEE'S (D. 1940) FAMOUS APHORISM[168]

In Jesus' incarnation, God matters. And by Jesus' incarnation, God sanctifies matter and God loves mattering. God is Spirit, but Spirit matters. The heart of matter is this: there is a heart of matter. Material things convey meaning and healing.[169]

What makes humans so unique is the size of their brain, and the size of the neocortex within that brain. But an equally good case can be made for the human hand, and its distinctive features, as what makes humans human. The thumb is rotatable and long enough in proportion to the other fingers to make it an "opposable thumb" which enables precise and steady contact and fractional finger movement for the creation of hand-made items. Before there was a rule of law

# ABECEDARIUM OF A JESUS HUMAN

there was a rule of thumb, which governs by experience and practice. The hands also became an organ of communication, so that before the emergence of spoken language there was sign language. Combined with bipedality, these are arguably what made humans so different from our nearest kin in nature.

The Polish word *podziw* means wonder, respect, adoration for the Mystery of Being, and the majesty of divine and human creations. Polish-American poet Czeslaw Milosz knows the word *podziw* well as a form of love. In his unpublished diary, he wrote a self-confession as to why he writes which summarizes *podziw*: "I write because I am in love with the things of this world and I am trying to find the words which would capture be it the smallest part of its richness and immensity."[170] Milosz is not arguing for a new form of animism, where all material things have a spirit that must be respected to the point where if you kick a table, your apologize to it; or as Japanese consultant Marie Kondo would have us do, if you declutter your stuffed animal be sure to cover its eyes before you throw it into the trash.[171]

In the industrial world, the importance of personal craftsmanship was minimized. Theologian and artist Makoto Fujimura reminds us that "It may be hard to imagine, but before around 1800, almost every human product in the world was handmade. Every object was unique and wrought with time, sweat, and effort by artisans who had trained decades to master their craft."[172] To be human is to make a living, to make meaning by making—making use, making

JESUS HUMAN

up, making do, making it. The salvation story is one of remaking.

---

*Your hands are the instrument of your mind.*
MARIA MONTESSORI'S DEFENSE
OF HANDS-ON OVER HEAD-FIRST LEARNING[173]

---

For Fujimura, "making" is not some makeshift "fixing." Like kintsugi, all great art resurrects broken matter into something glorious and new. Making is creating toward the telos of healing.[174] Human "making" must echo the Creator's original "making" which was a "making" by love and vibrancy. Making is "resurrection" movement toward the new creation, or what Fujimura's theology of making calls "making-as-resurrection."

**Is the Future Handmade?** The "artmaking" process is a "handmaking" process which makes us all "makers"—we "make" by walking; we "make" by talking; we "make" by reading; we "make" by worshiping. As "makers," humans are artists whom Fujimura calls "pollinators of the good, true, and beautiful." This is profoundly symbolized in the Book of Leviticus where the bodily extremities–right thumb, right big toe, right ear lobe–are touched with oil/blood upon induction into priesthood.[175]

How do we cut through the crush of consumerist clutter? How do we keep making in a world of unmaking, and to bake into what we are making the wounds and losses of our past? To live a "making" life we need to rediscover the slow (it takes time to make something), and to celebrate the beaten and weathered and rustic and worn, a Japanese aesthetic known as *wabi-sabi*, a world-view based on three principles: "nothing lasts, nothing is finished, and nothing is perfect."[176]

*The first draft of anything is [trash].*
NOBEL LAUREATE NOVELIST ERNEST HEMINGWAY (D. 1961)[177]

For the **Ikigai** human, devotional objects, relics, and story-filled makings keep faith breathing and vital. Philosopher Jacques Derrida liked to talk about "traces" of divinity that are found in material culture. The philosophical founder of semiotics C. S. Peirce described them as "absence of presence." The divine becomes real through the five senses, including touch. Of course, humans can take a good thing too far. But we have not yet connected to all the faith resources of embodiment that are there for the taking and making.

I love to look at pictures of isolated villages with the lights on nestled in valleys and hugging the shorelines. I long to visit more remote small towns and villages around the world which have been inhabited for generations and centuries. The mystery of people living here and making a living here is . . . romance.

The Charm of Making, an incantation repeatedly uttered by both Merlin and Morgana in the 80s movie *Excalibur*, is the spell that "makes" and "conceives." The Old Gaelic dialect translates to "Serpent's breath, charm of death and life, thy omen of making." Even the serpent knows we were made to make. Conception is our vocation as humans, our calling as incarnators. When we stop making, we lose our calling and seek alternative "makings" in drugs, gambling, sex, shopping, and plastic surgery.

ABECEDARIUM OF A JESUS HUMAN

 **is for Jubilee (Hebrew: לבוי) Human**

There are over 2000 continuous camp-meetings still in existence in North America. Every summer I accept an invitation to preach at one of them, partly because I myself am a camp-meeting baby ("more souls made than saved at camp-meetings," the old saying went) and some of my most precious childhood memories come from their sawdust tabernacles, meal lines, white-hankey testimonies, and rapturous singing. But also, because I am researching and writing a camp-meeting memoir called "Beulah Land."

---

*You shall no more be termed Forsaken, and your land shall no more be termed Desolate; but you shall be called My Delight Is in Her, and your land [shall be called] Married (Beulah); for the Lord delights in you, and your land shall be married . . . And as the bridegroom rejoices over the bride, so shall your God rejoice over you.*

EIGHTH-CENTURY BCE PROPHET ISAIAH 62:4-5

---

**Beulah Land:** "Beulah" is the Hebrew word for "married," as in wedded to a state and place of earthly paradise. The people of Israel were married to Yahweh and to the land God had given them. The phrase "Beulah Land" became a sign and symbol of heaven, and the promise of *jubilee* one day. The closest to heaven on earth, for many of our nineteenth- and twentieth-century ancestors, was camp-meeting time or "*jubilee*." Even the camp-meeting choruses collectively were called "*jubilees*," and many of the songbooks proclaimed "*Jubilee!*" on their front cover.

One of the most important musical groups in USAmerican history, founded in 1871 as an acapella group from Fisk University touring the path of the underground railroad and singing spirituals and *jubilees*, named themselves the *Jubilee* Singers. "This is the year of *Jubilee*; The Lord has come to set us free." These lyrics are found in a song traced to the year 1863 when slaves in the secessionist states were freed from bondage. The word *jubilee*, found in pre-civil war black church papers and products, has a traditionally happy, hopeful connotation. Several other music groups called themselves "*Jubilee* Singers" before the turn of the century.

A favorite "*jubilee*" in camp-meeting worship was the spiritual "Dwelling in Beulah Land," which compares the delights of being married to the ecstasy of living in the kingdom of God or "*jubilee*." *Jubilee* is named after the ram's horn trumpet which announced the 50th year celebration of liberation called *Jubilee*. Seven is a number which symbolizes completeness (in fact, the Hebrew "seven" is spelled with the same consonants as the word "complete/full"). There are seven fixed sacred times known as "the appointed festivals of the Lord, which you are to proclaim as sacred assemblies."[178] Seven times seven, perfection times perfection, is the ultimate in fullness.

One of the surprising features of the Genesis creation story is the prominence of the number seven. Raised on over 700 references to the number seven in the Bible, not to mention seven deadly sins, seven virtues, and seven sacraments, it is hard to realize how unusual a number seven was in the cultures of the ancient world. Everything was ten or twelve or three.[179]

But the Hebrews elevated seven to the status of perfection and holiness and completion. First three days, "evening to morning," God creates context. Next three days, "evening to morning," God creates creatures to live in the context. But the seventh day isn't framed in "evening to morning," suggesting an endless Sabbath, which is the essence of *Jubilee*.

**The Eighth Day:** Adding a day to Sabbath symbolized a whole new beginning, which is why the cutting of the covenant took place on the eighth day of the birth of every male child (including Jesus). This is why most Christians do not keep the Sabbath, but the "Next Day" after the Sabbath, the Eighth Day, a mini-*Jubilee* that glorifies the work God completed on the Eighth Day and proclaims the new creation that flows from the resurrection life. We live, now, in that Eighth Day.

In some Reformed traditions (e.g., Lutheranism), Baptism is said to be the Eighth Day of Creation (hence 8-sided baptismal founts). God makes on this eighth day a new kind of human, recreated in water to be perfectly righteous through the imputation of grace. Hence Sabbath is regeneration of the imputed human in us. Sabbath is not the spiritual adjunct of hammocks and lawn chairs, winters nights, and summer siestas. Sabbath is resetting and restoring the original image of God in humanity.[180]

Adding one more day, an eighth day, to seven times seven or the completion of completion, symbolized not just a new beginning for creation but the beginning of a new creation, as conveyed in the ***Jubilee*** Year when all slaves were set free, all prisoners released, all debts were forgiven, all land was restored to its original owners, and all the earth was given a sabbath and allowed to lie fallow. Even loans close to the ***Jubilee*** year were adjusted accordingly.

> And you shall count seven weeks of years, seven times seven years, so that the time of the seven weeks of years shall be to you forty-nine years. Then you shall send abroad the loud trumpet on the tenth day of the seventh month; on the day of atonement, you shall send abroad the loud trumpet throughout all your land. And you shall hallow the fiftieth year, and proclaim liberty throughout the land to all its inhabitants; it shall be a ***jubilee*** for you, when each of you shall return to his property and each of you shall return to his family.[181]

**Five-Point Mission Statement:** In his inaugural sermon in his hometown of Nazareth, he was given the scroll of Isaiah from the ark and unrolled its ten feet of papyrus until he found this passage, a mash-up of Isaiah 61:1–2 and Isaiah 58:6:

> The Spirit of the Lord is on me,
> because he has anointed me

## ABECEDARIUM OF A JESUS HUMAN

to proclaim good news to the poor.
He has sent me to proclaim freedom for the prisoners
and recovery of sight for the blind,
to set the oppressed free,
to proclaim the year of the Lord's favor [a.k.a. *Jubilee*].

In this five-point mission statement, Jesus both summarized his ministry as *Jubilee* and presented himself as *Jubilee* incarnate. Jesus as *Jubilee* means:

1. good news for the poor
2. healing for the sick
3. release for prisoners[182]
4. liberty for oppressed[183]
5. *Jubilee* Sabbath

Jesus' stories don't moralize about *Jubilee*; they make *Jubilee*. Jesus' teachings don't give us metaphors about *Jubilee*; they establish *Jubilee*. They perform what they proclaim. To live the story of Jesus is to live *Jubilee*. And to live *Jubilee* is to participate in *tikkun olam*, the Jewish concept of repairing the world.

**Kingdom Dreams:** Jesus told his disciples to say when they healed the sick, "the kingdom of God has come near to you."[184] The kingdom is a presence, a resplendence, a person. Jesus didn't spend his time talking about "God is like this," but "the kingdom of heaven is like this." How to be kingdom? How to recognize kingdom? How to become kingdom? Come to Jesus and enter the kingdom of *Jubilee*.

We don't bring about God's kingdom. We don't build God's kingdom. We bring God's kingdom into people, and bring people into God's kingdom. We introduce people to the King of kings and Lord of lords, the King of God's kingdom. We help people enter the kingdom and receive the gift of kingdom. We help people become kingdom and be kingdom by becoming "witnesses" to the kingdom, "watchers" of the kingdom, and "good news" uplifts of a kingdom above brought to us below in the story of Jesus' birth, death, resurrection, and ascension.

Evolution is but one among many metaphors, and not always the best one,[185] for God's gift of agency to God's creation, especially the super-agent of creation named "human." Whether Christian, Jewish, Muslim Sikh, or Hindu, humans are *khalifah* (stewards, trustees) of the Earth. But the story of humanity has a plotline that shapes the contours and chapters of the story. And the one string that threads the whole story into one tapestry, from beginning to end, is the desire for a relationship with God and all of creation that the Bible describes as "*Jubilee*."

Pentecost is a mini-*Jubilee* of rejoicing and powering up, fifty days after Easter. The Holy Spirit is the Body-Building, Power-Lifting Spirit of Christ: "If I be lifted up . . . I will draw all people unto me."[186] If we lift Jesus up in the power of the Spirit, Jesus will take it from there. Once you see Jesus, you can't unsee Jesus.

## ABECEDARIUM OF A JESUS HUMAN

**Kingdom Is *Jubilee*:** "Kingdom" has replaced "gospel" and even "Jesus" in the lexicon of much of the church. On the one hand, "It would take a sceptic with nerves of steel to deny the centrality of the kingdom of God in the preaching of Jesus."[187] That said, there are things that we perpetuate about kingdom that argue for a more proper focus on "*Jubilee*" than "kingdom."

1. Jesus never defined the kingdom. He never gave us a clear and concise definition of what he meant by "kingdom." He did define the identity of those who entered it.

2. In the phrase "kingdom of God," not only is "kingdom" unclear, but Jesus never gave us a theology of God. Never once did he offer a definition or doctrine of God, only images of a "kind" and "merciful" and "perfect" Father that he conveyed through stories.

3. Jesus made the kingdom of God about life and healing, not politics and economics, which is what people hear when they hear "kingdom." The kingdom is about deliverance from what is preventing us from being alive. And what does it mean to be alive? It means to be a fully alive human being, and to find in every time the truth of William Wordsworth's "bliss was it in that dawn to be alive!"[188]

## JESUS HUMAN

> *For the glory of God is a living human being; and the life of the human consists in beholding God. For if the manifestation of God which is made by means of the creation, affords life to all living in the earth, much more does that revelation of the Father which comes through the Word, give life to those who see God.*
>
> "THE GLORY OF GOD IS A PERSON FULLY ALIVE."
>
> IRENAEUS (135-202)[189]

4. Jewish studies scholar Marc Zvi Brettler, an expert on metaphor and the Bible, has written a monograph proving that "God is King" is the predominant metaphor for God in the Hebrew Bible. It appears much more frequently than metaphors such as "God is love"[190] or "God is Father."[191] Jesus moved "God as Father" to the center stage and "King" dropped out.[192] Jesus consistently preached the kingdom of God, but at the heart of that kingdom was the divine Father, not the King. At the core of Jesus' preaching of the kingdom was his intimate experience of God as the loving, trustworthy "Abba" ("Father dear" or even "Daddy").[193]

5. Jesus IS the kingdom. Origen (c. 185–254) called Jesus "the kingdom in person, *auto-basileia*."[194] When a life is dedicated to the Jesus, there is the **Jubilee** of merry-making, mercy-making, peace-making, and prayer that **Jubilee** will come crashing down on every person we meet and bring them to life.

## ABECEDARIUM OF A JESUS HUMAN

Irenaeus of Lyons' pronouncement, "The glory of God is a person fully alive," is well-known. But this first half of a larger quote is a misquote, since the word "fully" was never a part of the original. Of even greater significance, the second half of that quote, the part that brings together the human and the divine, is seldom cited: "And the life of the human consists in beholding God." Some translations render it "The Glory of God is a fully living person,"[195] which is why in the Latin mass the Prayer After Communion asks for the "grace of living fully" or in another way of reference, a fully human being, a fully graced humanity, a ***Jubilee*** human.

is for Jyuuten or Juut (Japanese: ジュウテ) Human

*The battle for civilisation will pivot on the outrageously simple challenge of living a day well.*
BAPTIST BRITISH THEOLOGIAN IAN STACKHOUSE[196]

***Jyuuten*** is a Japanese word that has come to mean the rejuvenation or uplift of humanity and service of others. It has been abbreviated and appropriated as the brand name "***Juut***" by a salon spa, but that does not diminish its electrifying eloquence. Both ***Jyuuten*** and ***Juut*** derive from Juten, a Japanese word meaning priority replenishments and ritual renewals.[197] Or, as brand-meister David Wagner first put it, a "***juut***" human is a "daymaker"—someone who "makes a day" for another person by prioritizing daily rituals of doing or saying something magnanimous and kind.[198]

The first step of a ***Juut*** human is to see each other, and to value each person as the bearer of moral recognition. We look away from things we don't like to see, and hide things we don't like to come out of the shadows. Like poverty. To "see" the poor is to reclaim their humanity. The new-world community is first a community of humans, not a collective of countries or cultures or states or tribes.

There are all sorts of "divides" out there that we are good at not "seeing." These divides themselves are dividing. There are digital divides, electrical divides (2.5 billion of the world's people still don't have electricity), hunger divides, housing divides, sanitary divides, and educational divides. Some of our sacred shibboleths deepened the divides without our even thinking about it.

Take the phrase: "No Rights without Responsibilities." Would any of us want to live in a culture like that? A culture that refused to offer to its most vulnerable and weak (like the mentally ill, children, animals) citizen's rights without responsibilities? We don't help people around the world because they are Christian or might become Christian. We don't only help people who are worthy of our help. We don't help people because of who they are but because of who we are. We help people around the world because WE are Christian, because we follow Jesus.

The dignity of all human life is not self-endowed, or self-determined, or self-regulated, but bestowed by the Creator which assures the sanctity of all human life as a sacred value. A *Juut* human is not just magnanimous and kind to kin and kith, but to the full spectrum of humankind. Hitler was warm and kind to family, fans, visitors, children, and animals. But to the rest of humanity, *Juut* never kicked in. In *Mein Kampf* (1925) Adolph Hitler dismissed Jews as a "spiritual pestilence" and thus worthy of eradication. Hitler also wanted to eliminate mental illness entirely, and he found "scientific" justification for the removal from the gene pool of "*lebensunwertes Lebens*" (lives unworthy of life).

Hitler's Law for the Prevention of Offspring with Hereditary Diseases, passed in 1933, actually drew on US eugenics laws. Nazis used this eugenics platform to identify

JESUS HUMAN

people fit for sterilization or extermination: "feeble-mindedness, bipolarism, schizophrenia, epilepsy, Huntington's, heredity blindness and deafness, severe malformation, and alcoholism." The list lengthened with homosexuals, Romani people, and Jehovah's Witnesses, all of whom were swept up with the Jews to be wiped out, called the Final Solution. Even having been married to celebrated Austrian novelist Joseph Roth didn't protect Friedl Reichler, diagnosed with schizophrenia, from being gassed by the Nazis in 1940 as part of their euthanasia program. The irony of physicians sterilizing, mutilating, and murdering "useless" people after swearing an oath to "Do No Harm" went unnoticed. Hitler killed more than 75% of the schizophrenics in Germany between 1933 and 1945, even though schizophrenics almost never reproduce. Preserving our common humanity begins at the bottom not the top, with building up the common person, the common good, the commons.

In the second century, pagan philosophers were already complaining that Christians had no standards at all and would let just anyone into their group. Christianity was not about being a creedally-exclusive community keeping tight borders, patrolling for outsiders and debarring dissenters from right doctrine. It was a universal gift of a way of health and healing for all, a via universalis, open to all no matter who or what or where.

A *juut* humanity calls for the emergence of a new sense of global citizenry based on the awareness that we all share the adventure of human life; we all are blessed with the same precious gift of human existence; we all take the risk that all our hopes could be in vain; we all must learn to value more than just ourselves. Such a global citizenry might evolve from a moral matrix where our core global responsibility is the avoidance of harm, not primarily the increase of prosperity. This global moral matrix that governs rehumanized relationships is bound together by five threads:

1. moral status goes to individuals, not to clans or states of social institutions;
2. moral status goes to all individuals—regardless of class, color, sex, education, disability, religion, or national origin;
3. every human being offers moral status to every other human being
4. a dedication to the protection and preservation of the "10 Fundamental Rights" of every human being:[199]
    1) physical movement
    2) ownership of property
    3) freedom from torture
    4) fair trial
    5) non-discrimination
    6) physical security
    7) speech/association
    8) minimum education
    9) political participation
    10) subsistence
5. a Magnanimity Manifesto for a global civil religion for a "humane world." German Catholic philosopher Josef Pieper defines magnanimity as "the expansion

of the spirit toward great things: one who expects great things of himself and makes himself worthy of it is magnanimous."

> One who is magnanimous completely shuns flattery and hypocrisy, both of which are the issue of a mean heart. The magnanimous person does not complain, for his heart does not permit him to be overcome by an external evil. Magnanimity encompasses an unshakable firmness of hope, a plainly defiant certainty, and the thorough calm of a fearless heart. The magnanimous person submits himself not to the confusion of feelings or to any human being or fate—but only to God.[200]

*We need to stop boxing God into little confined, man-made spaces and then claiming that we own the land rights. God left the temple a long time ago to take up residence in a new one: one constructed from people.*

BRITISH BROADCASTER RHIDIAN BROOK[201]

A *Juut* human embodies a magnanimous spirit towards oneself, toward others of all stripes, and toward every aspect of creation. The kind of *Juut* magnanimity found in the note Woody Guthrie appended to "This Land is Your Land" in 1940:

> This song is copyright in US, under seal of copyright #154085, for 28 years, and

anybody caught singin' it without our permission will be mighty good friends of ourn, cause we don't give a dern. Publish it. Write it. Sing it. Swing to it. Yodel it. We wrote it, that's all we wanted to do.[202]

There would have been no Woodie Guthrie (Huntington's Disease) if we had exercised our ability today to genetically test and reject embryos.

JESUS HUMAN

# 𝔎 is for Komorebi (Japanese: こもれび) Human

> *Whoever dwells in the shelter of the Most High*
> *will rest in the shadow of the Almighty.*
> *I will say of the Lord, "He is my refuge and my fortress,*
> *my God, in whom I trust."*
>
> PSALM 91:1–2 NIV

**Komorebi** is an untranslatable Japanese word that refers to the sunlight that falls through the trees creating dancing shadows on the ground and in the surrounding space.

To highlight the world of shadowplay conjures up the shadow culture of Platonism, which thinks of everything worldly as a shadow of its better self. But have you ever tried to sit in the shelter of your own shadow? Every human finds life and hope only under the shadow of the Almighty, who appears nowhere but shadows everything.

This does not mean humans are spared the walk through the shadow of the valley of death.[203] Indeed, human life is a dance of the shadows. Here comes the sun. The greater the sun, the more the shadows. A faith without shadows, without the contrast of light and dark, or what artists call chiaroscuro, is an artificial, fluorescent, floodlight faith. The Son brings life, but life brings shadows. The more you move forward, the greater the shadow lengthens, a shadow which remains invisible until you stop and look back.

To attack the shadow is a life of shadow-boxing: "I do not run aimlessly," Paul asserts; "I do not box as one beating the air;" or as another translation puts it, "I am no shadow-boxer, I really fight."[204] To assimilate the shadow, as Carl Jung would put it, is to refuse to vagabond or shadow-box your way through life. A Jesus human is not a noncombatant with evil. A Jesus human probes into the shadows, faces the worst headwinds, and crosses the finish line with the promise "I have put my words in your mouth and covered you with the shadow of my hand."[205] In the midst of the worst inhumanity, buds of humanity spring forth like jonquils in the spring.

In the artistic world of Japanese gardens, there is the aesthetic standard of "miegakure." Also known as "hide and reveal" or "hidden from ordinary sight," the secret of a Japanese garden is that it is not afraid of overlapping shadow and sunlight, interlacing hiding and revealing. That is why a little Japanese garden looms so large in the imagination and intuition. **Komorebi** and **Miegakure** bring dazzling depth and breathtaking surprise to the life of humanity.

The **komorebi** human walks in the shadow of God.

##  is for Le (Mandarin: 乐) Human

Berkeley historian Michael Nylan, in his *The Chinese Pleasure Book* (2018), traces the evolution of pleasure theories in early China over the course of a millennium and a half, from the fourth century BCE to the eleventh century CE. To signify acts of pleasure-seeking, pleasure-taking, and imparting pleasure, a wide range of thinkers during that time deployed the single graph, **le**. They freely borrowed from one another, sometimes to differing ends, but often with the same goal of arriving at the most versatile model of the human condition. Undergirding their rhetoric was always the dual presumption that pleasure matters a great deal to most people, and people seek pleasure in all areas of life.

God created humans for God's pleasure. Humans exist to bring God pleasure. At the two summit moments of Jesus' life, his baptism and his transfiguration, Jesus heard from the heavens the best thing anyone can hear: "You bring me great pleasure."

It is time to take pleasure seriously. This Chinese word "*le*" many scholars translate as "joy" or "happiness" or "pleasure." But from the fourth to the eleventh centuries Chinese thinkers used the character not to indicate immediate, satisfied gratification but the engagement in, in Nylan's words, "activities that promise deeper satisfactions in return for steady, long-term commitments."[206]

# ABECEDARIUM OF A JESUS HUMAN

*If Christianity has a future as a living voice regarding what a human society, what a human culture and what a human life should be, we may be in a critical moment for trying to determine how that voice is heard and what precisely it is saying.*

ORTHODOX THEOLOGIAN DAVID BENTLEY HART[207]

*Le* can also express the joy of "inducing good men to serve in office through suitable politicking." In other words, the pleasure of "*le*" is the pleasure of table time, listening to music, participating in the arts, learning new knowledge, hanging with friends, traditioning the family story. *Le* is the pleasure that is derived from fostering health and hospitality in an erratic world of chaos and uncertainty. *Le* is the shaping of a Jubilee life in an inhumane world of bedlam and pandemonium.

Now called the "change particle," the character for "*le*" at the end of a sentence indicates that there was a completed change acted out in that statement. "I ate grits and apple butter for breakfast" means not that you eat grits and apple butter every morning, but that in that specific breakfast in question this is what you actually ate. "*Le*" symbolizes embodied and enacted change that issues in the satisfaction of completion.

In the lineage of the Chinese language, "*le*" meant more than the pleasure of a belly filled, but the pleasure of a culinary experience of food, family, friends. The pleasure of "*le*" was contrasted by classic Chinese thinkers to anxiety and worry. For us, the opposite of pleasure is pain. For Asians, the opposite of pleasure is stress, vexation, and irritation. What pleases God is not the absence of pain but trusting God with our future and the casting of our cares on God. A *le* human is one, like Peter, who makes the journey from "Master, don't you care that we perish?"[208] to "Cast all your cares upon God, for God cares for you."[209]

---

*The worst of times demand
the most dedication to pleasure.*
BONN UNIVERSITY MEDIEVALIST IRINA DUMITRESCU[210]

---

ABECEDARIUM OF A JESUS HUMAN

###  is for Logos (Greek: Λογότυπα) Human

The Greek word "*logos*" is so complex a Greek word that one scholar has compiled ten different senses of the word: computation, proportion, explanation, inward debate, narrative, utterance, voicing, subject matter, wording, and Wisdom of God.[211] David Bentley Hart, in his literal translation of the New Testament, says that "***Logos***" is untranslatable and so leaves it in Greek—unfamiliar and complex.[212]

There must be as many different definitions of ***Logos*** as there are recipes for cooking ramen. ***Logos*** is most often translated "word" or "reason" in line with Plato who contrasted *muthos*, the realm of myth suitable for poets, children, and old women (he said), with ***logos***, the realm of true rational thought and argument. The problem with all these definitions of ***logos*** is that there is a component of sound in the Greek, as in "voice" or "hearing." That's why John Calvin used the word "speech" rather than "word" in several places to translate "***logos***."

In ancient Egypt, Ra and Aton were principal names for the Creator. Several Hebrew names for God contain the sacred sound "ah." These include Jehovah, Yah, and Eloha. The word Eloha is especially interesting. In Aramaic, the language spoken by Jesus, the word for God was Alaha—a derivative of Eloha. The very same word for God exists in Arabic—"Allah." The Hawaiian or Polynesian word aloha may be related to Eloha, Alaha, and Allah. As well as 'hello'

285

and 'goodbye,' the world aloha can mean love. In Hebrew, of course, the unspoken name for God is "Yah-weh."

In Matthew 24:35's "Heaven and earth will pass away, but my words will never pass away," "words" is "logoi" which literally means something spoken. Not just something read, but spoken, and spoken means sound. Hence the significance of the English children's round (based on a German folksong) that goes:

> All things must perish from the sky.
> Music alone shall never die.

Our ancestors sang, or hummed, or whistled as they worked. Today we outsource our singing, humming, and whistling to playlists, our lips locked tight by earbuds. What do we lose when we let other people sing our songs? We lose our humanity. We lose the sound of the universal within us. We lose our voice, the voice of a matchless human, the voice of humanity that rings true. Less the music, less the love.

> *If music be the food of love, play on,*
> *Give me excess of it; that surfeiting,*
> *The appetite may sicken, and so die.*
> WILLIAM SHAKESPEARE, *TWELFTH NIGHT*, ACT 1.1

**Discover Your DNA:** The only translation that could topple the Greek original is the one proposed by Nazarene biblical scholar Troy W. Martin and mentioned earlier: Divine DNA. DNA is an abbreviation for deoxyribonucleic acid, a molecule that codes genetic information in all living organisms.

The exact structure of DNA was only discovered in 1953, after a long search for the carrier of genetic information which defines the fundamental and distinctive characteristics of someone.

Jesus is Divine DNA. "I am the Root and the Offspring of David," the angel testifies to the churches, "and the bright Morning Star."[213] The early Christian apologist and philosopher Justin Martyr (100–165), in both his First Apology and its supplement known as the Second Apology, brought the Jewish and Greek traditions together in his concept of ***Logos***, which he argued is fully expressed in the person of Jesus Christ but is evident in traces throughout other tribes and traditions and intellectual treasures.

The greatest treasure among the Hebrew people was their children. They were proof of the "seed" of their ancestors, and an assurance of their ongoing presence. At a time when the greatest curse was childlessness, and barrenness an automatic cause for divorce, the Divine DNA was injected into the human bloodstream.[214]

The biblical language of "born again" and "adopted heirs" of God support the divine DNA aspects of this word ***Logos***. For ***Logos*** making us heirs, there is Romans 8:16–17:

> The Spirit Himself bears witness with our spirit that we are children of God, and if children, then heirs—heirs of God and joint heirs with Christ, if indeed we suffer with Him, that we may also be glorified together (NKJV).

For ***Logos*** responsible for our adoption story, there is Ephesians 1:5:

> God decided in advance to adopt us into his own family by bringing us to himself through Jesus Christ. This is what he wanted to do, and it gave him great delight (NLT).

For ***Logos*** responsible for our being "born again" in the Divine DNA, there is John 3:3, 5 and 1 Peter 1:3:

> Jesus answered and said to him, "Truly, truly, I say to you, unless one is born again he cannot see the kingdom of God."

> Jesus answered, "Truly, truly, I say to you, unless one is born of water and the Spirit he cannot enter into the kingdom of God.

> Blessed be the God and Father of our Lord Jesus Christ, who according to His great mercy has caused us to be born again to a living hope through the resurrection of Jesus Christ from the dead.

For ***Logos*** responsible for our transfiguration as "new creatures in Christ," there is 2 Corinthians 5:17:

> Therefore if anyone is in Christ, he is a new creature; the old things passed away; behold, new things have come.

***Logos* or Chaos:** One of the major breakthroughs in the world of genetics is Heritable Gene Editing (HGE). These are edits to human genetics that can be passed on, by procreation, to future generations, thus entering and altering the human gene pool and changing forever the genetics of the human species. Sixty nations now outlaw it, but as of 2023 it will be legal in some countries. The domino effect will take place.

There is only one HGE that is incontestable and non-controversial: The Incarnation of **Logos**, the recombinant engineering of fallen humanity into the divine DNA.

JESUS HUMAN

##  is for Mirrorworld (Economics) Human

***There's Always MAAMMA:*** Meta/Alphabet/Amazon/Microsoft/Apple (MAAMA)

In the world of the twenty-first century, there may be no God, but there's always MAAMA. And MAAMA will not be ignored. In the S&P500, a weighted stock market index tracking performances of 500 large companies listed on exchanges in the United States, the five MAAMA stocks accounted for 21.7% of the total.[215]

John Murray Spear (d. 1887) was a New England clergy who, in 1853, thought he could bring about the Second Coming through technology. Variously called the "Mechanical Messiah," "New Motive Power," and "God Machine," he started building a steampunk machine out of magnets, zinc, copper, and a dining-room table. Spear believed his new Jesus Robot could "revolutionize the world and raise mankind to an exalted level of spiritual development."[216]

This Jesus Robot would be a metal and magnet incarnation of the divine, and be "Heaven's last, best gift to man."[217] He even designated one of his followers the "New Mary." She had gathered with him and others at High Rock Hill in Lynn, Massachusetts, to give birth to this electric Jesus. When it failed to be born after a flamboyant ritual, Spear announced his "retirement" and disappeared.

The idea that technology can save us, that humans can build a God Machine, where the deus ex machina becomes a techna ex machina or even a machina ex machina, is not new. Steve Jobs called his new invention the "Jesus Phone" before it became known as the "iPhone," because he believed it was the Second Coming of technology.[218] When the iPad was introduced, *The Wall Street Journal* quipped that the last time there was this much excitement about a tablet it had some commandments written on it. Each successive wave of digital technology has carried along with it millennial hopes and dreams.

The first great wave of digital technology? Web1.

The second great wave of digital technology? Web2 & social media.

The third great wave of digital technology that is about to hit the world like a tsunami? Web3 and ***Mirrorworld***.

***Mirrorworld*** is a digitized, melded, doppelganger world built on blockchain and subject to the power of algorithms. It is the primary focus of The Big Five, who each in their own way is creating a MAAMAverse. ***Mirrorworld***[219] is a melding of the virtual and the real, the digital lifeworld and the physical until everything will have a digital 3D twin.

Will it be humanity's greatest achievement? Or will it be but another metal messiah? Will our bodies become so augmented and cyborged that humans will no longer think or feel or act in ways that humans have conceived and conducted themselves all through history? Brad Smith, President of Microsoft in 2019, warned that face-recognition technology "means every time you walk into a store, a retailer knows when you were in there last, what good you picked out, what you purchased."[220] When MAAMA makes face-recognition universal, will MAAMA be the beckoning of a "Brave New

JESUS HUMAN

World?"²²¹ When MAAMA wires everything in your house to MAAMA (your stove, fridge, security, heating), who ultimately is in control of your house? Will MAAMA prove that people are better than pixels, or will it go the other way?

◇

*Mirroworlds immerse you without removing you from the space.*
*You are still present, but on a different plane of reality . . .*
*We can pick up a pencil and use it as a magic wand.*
*We can turn our tables into touchscreens.*

FILM DIRECTOR KEIICHI MATSUDA²²²

MAAMA's dramatic progress has some traumatic consequences to our common humanity. First, social media has fractured public opinion into tiny and isolated silos. Back in 1979, cultural historian Christopher Lasch (d. 1944) warned of an increasing "balkanization of opinion"²²³ which would unleash centrifugal forces on culture. Political scientist Francis Fukuyama pushed Lasch's critique even farther, writing that the "irresistible impulse toward the protection of ever narrower group identities" is increasingly creating fissures in society and silos of separation.²²⁴

Second, social media's forces of homogenization have led to standardized sameness, as well as damaging body images on kids and adults. The Internet may provide free access to the treasures of humanity, but only if that's the way you use it. The way it is being used now is often in more humanoid than human ways. There is now such a thing as the "Instagram face" or "glamazon face," a perfect face on a perfect body serving perfect meals and going on perfect

## ABECEDARIUM OF A JESUS HUMAN

holidays. This is a uniformity so tyrannical it may as well be a tank template with which to go through life. AI/VR technologies will replace humans with even automaton appearances, as AI programs[225] themselves become virtual human beings who will learn and evolve, get degrees and aspire to become more human as real humans become less human and dehumanize each other.

Jesus humans do not judge themselves by their instagrammability; nor do they judge themselves according to themselves, but according to the Word of God. If we judge ourselves according to ourselves, no wonder we all think we deserve a reward for doing nothing. Besides, as French Symbolist poet, novelist, and literary critic Remy de Gourmont's (d. 1915) "La Dissociation des idées" insisted: a work of art is valued and judged first of all for what makes it different, not from what makes it like that which surrounds it, and from what makes it like it is.

"I am the vine; you are the branches." Jesus didn't say "You are the branch." There are many "branches" in the vine of Christ, and each branch is different from the other even though juiced by the same source. No Jesus human is algorithmic. For example, every Jesus human has a different EQ—some go down in the valley as much or more as they go up on the mountain. Others live in the valley and look up at the mountain. A few reside on the mountain-tops.

Every Jesus human is an original work of art, not a cog in a STEM machine. STEM (Science, Technology, Engineering, Math) must gain STEAM by adding the arts to the mix. The great choral conductor Robert Shaw (d. 1999) made an offhand commencement prophecy. In pre-modern, medieval worlds, it was the church that saved the arts. He challenged the graduates to reverse roles. In the future, he prophesied, artists and the arts would be the ones to save the church.[226]

> *The creation of art is not the fulfillment of a need but the creation of a need. The world never needed Beethoven's Fifth Symphony until he created it. Now we could not live without it.*
> ESTONIAN-AMERICAN ARCHITECT LOUIS I. KAHN (D. 1974)[227]

The third threat to a common humanity is the way MAAMA monetizes engagement. How many hits determines how much money you make. As every infant knows from the get-go, the #1 driver of engagement is enragement. So, algorithms work to bring to you posts that will enrage you and then directs you to community silos of like-minded people that feed each other's rage and gets you engaged.

The fourth threat to our common humanity caused by MAAMA is the fueling of Metahumanism. Big Tech is partnering with Big Pharma for joint ventures that will make metahumanism easier go down the gullet of eugenics. It has almost become commonplace among AI pioneers that we are entering a world where humans lose their power to artificial intelligence forms. I wish I could say I invented the word "Contelligence." It's actually the result of a typing error, but apparently a certain psychologist and neuronaut named Timothy Leary[228] (d. 1996) may have already penned the word, although with a different construction and meaning:

(Consciousness + intelligence) The combination of awareness and computational power required in an Artificially Intelligent network before we could, without loss of anything essential, upload ourselves into them.²²⁹

This is the point of singularity, when the difference between born and made is obliterated.

"The Black Box" is the name given to that portion of AI that is beyond human comprehension. But what about human control? Might the Black Box be another Black Death like the one of 1348–9 that annihilated more than 40% of the European population in little more than 18 months? Might the "Black Box" be another black hole—a force so attractionally dense that nothing can resist its pull? Might the "Black Box" be a blackout for humanity?

The dangers of technology are graphically animated in the 1985 Shadow Project. Artists across the US painted "shadow remnants" on sidewalks and steps over which people would be walking. These shadows were designed to help us remember those who had been vaporized in the Hiroshima devastation. The demonic impact of technology was experienced as those obliterated were made into shadows people had to step on and across on the streets of the US.

What may be known one day as the Fourth Place, MAAMA's digitized place of the *Mirrorworld* is always on, always drawing you in, always addictive. Logos logs on this new digital continent. Jesus is Lord of the *Mirrorworld* too. And a Jesus human will be where Jesus is.

JESUS HUMAN

# M is for Mandorla (Italian) Human

*Mandorla* is the Italian word for almond, one of the most symbolically significant fruits in the Bible. Not figs. Not grapes. Not olives. Not apples. Almonds, which are generally considered nuts but are technically a drupe fruit like a peach, apricot, cherry, plum, or olive.

The almond tree is known as the "Alpha and Omega" tree: it is first to blossom, last to fruit. Almond in Hebrew means "the awakening one", because the almond tree is the first tree to awaken from the sleep of winter and blossom, testifying to the powerful impact of light and Jesus as the first fruits of a new humanity. The almond tree is also the last to reach fruition, almost seven to eight months after flowering.

What was the Tree of Life? No one knows for sure, but the semiotics of the story suggest an almond tree.

What was Aaron's rod? An almond branch with buds, blossoms, and fruit.

What was the Golden Candlestick? An Almond Tree with buds, blossoms, and fruit.

Where was Mt. Sinai, where Moses received the divine tablets? One preferred location is Jabal al-Lawz, also known as the "mountain of almonds" or "almond mountain."

What did Jeremiah see when his tongue was singed by the fires of heaven? An almond branch.

What is the symbol of Judaism? A menorah, which is an abstract image of the almond tree.

# ABECEDARIUM OF A JESUS HUMAN

What was the tree of Jesse, Jesse of Bethlehem, father of David: "And there shall come forth a rod out of the stem of Jesse, and a branch shall grow out of his roots?"[230] We know it was a fruit tree. But what kind of fruit tree? Most scholars think it was an olive tree. Equally possible is an almond tree. The Hebrew word for BRANCH is "Netzer". The boyhood home of Jesus was Nazareth, called "Net-zeret" in Hebrew. It means "The place of the BRANCH," which takes on significance in light of the fact that the Messiah was often referred to as the BRANCH.[231]

The golden lampstand within the holy place symbolizes the tree of life in the garden of Eden.[232] The floral imagery permeating through the temple also symbolized the first temple, the Garden of Eden.[233]

Overlapping circles form an almond-shape, which in the art world is referred to as *mandorla* or literally "vesica pisci" meaning "vulva fish."[234] In the historic art of Christianity, a halo over a dead person means a saint. A *mandorla* around a scene or setting means a haloing of a scene or a holy moment or holy space—like Jesus' birth, baptism, crucifixion, resurrection, or ascension. It is in the *mandorla* that Jesus is depicted, and it is in him that opposites find connection. A bow is a branch whose ends are bent together by a string, and it is the tension that makes music, as in a violin, or brings death, as in a bow and arrow. The *mandorla* is a metaphor of opposites finding connection is Jesus.

Hildegard of Bingen, who was given the rare "Doctor of the Church" title reserved for theologians who made a significant impact, did many *mandorla* paintings. Her vision

## JESUS HUMAN

of the cosmos changed to reflect the science of her age. In Scivias, her first work of visionary theology, the universe appeared as a ***mandorla***—shaped like an egg or almond. She later moved to a sphere.[235]

> *A human is the only creature to exhibit both a natural disgust for existence and an overwhelming desire to exist: He despises life and fears nothingness.*
> FRENCH POLITICAL PHILOSOPHER ALEXIS DE TOCQUEVILLE (D. 1859)[236]

The ***Mandorla*** has many things to teach us about what it means to be human. Three stick out.

**Double-Ring:** First, the ***mandorla*** is creativity's fertile crescent. Like twisting strands of DNA, opposites dance the ***mandorla*** across the landscape of faith. In the past, I've called it faith's "double ring" or "stereo vision" or "surround sound" or used the stereogram to showcase how orthodoxy is paradox. J. R. Briggs calls it "The Sacred Overlap."[237] The word for this in physics is "Superposition," a mix of both states at once, like zero and one. The Chinese word for "contradiction," *maodun*, contains both a spear and a shield. Dualities don't have to buck down into dualisms.

In a Jesus universe there are always two poles of reference, and this is what brings depth to life and what brings mystery to faith.[238] Augustine said we encounter ourselves as question. I think we encounter ourselves as paradox. Biblical contradictions can only be resolved not in principle but in practice. Biblical faith is a paradoxical world which is never resolved, only lived out. The energy of the paradox is very different from the energy of the oxymoron. The Talmud blesses the contradiction with the words that end the conflict between the House of Hillel and the House of Shammai: "*elu ve-elu divrei Elokim hayim*—both of these are the words of the living God."[239]

A key concept in patristic thought (especially among the Greek fathers or Cappadocians) is of humanity as a "meth-or'-i-os" being. The root metaphor of "*methorios*" is the common area between two entities, the part that participates in the realities on both sides. Humans are "*methorios*" by participating in the divine image or imagination of the Creator and as a creation of that Creator. Humans don't merely get to "imagine" the divine but to participate in the divine imagination. A Jesus human lives in a dynamic state of betweenness, both/and-ness, even bringing together Augustinian moral tolerance and Pelagian moral severity. The world of a Jesus human is an interregnum between an old world passing away and a new world still being born.

English poet Matthew Arnold's "Stanzas from the Grande Chartreuse" (1851) was written after he visited in 1850 the seventeenth-century monastery in Grenoble in the French Alps, famous as the headquarters of the Carthusian order of Catholic monks who introduced the world to the 130-herb green liqueur (and color) "Chartreuse." It was also most likely the first poem of his married life with Frances ("Flu") Lucy.

> Wandering between two worlds, one dead,
> The other powerless to be born,
> With nowhere yet to rest my head,
> Like these, on earth I wait forlorn.

## JESUS HUMAN

> Their faith, my tears, the world deride—
> I come to shed them at their side.[240]

Jesus' double rings reflect the double helix of the LOGOS, the divine DNA: Saint/Sinner, easy yoke/light burden, innocent dove/wise serpent, Lion/Lamb, Immanence/Transcendence, Come and Live/Come and Die, "Those who are not against us are for us"[241]/"Those who are not for us are against us,"[242] Prince of Peace/Wields Sword, God is One, God is Three.[243]

◇

*He who exalts himself will be humbled, and*
*he who humbles himself will be exalted.*
JESUS[244]

**Multi-Generational God:** Second, often overlooked in the biblical image of the ***mandorla*** is the presence of bud-blossom-fruit. Aaron's rod which became a branch has these three features. The Golden Lampstand has these three features. Why the biblical insistence on these details, even in its most sacred spaces?

God cares, not just about the fruits. God cares about the buds and blossoms too. God cares about the bud that you can see now but that you may never see come to fruition in your lifetime. God cares about the buds that have moved to blossoms, but may never come to fruition in your lifetime. Yes, by your fruits you know them, but the "them" Jesus refers to in his Sermon on the Mount is not everyone, but false and genuine prophets.[245]

## ABECEDARIUM OF A JESUS HUMAN

God knows us by our buds and blossoms, not just our fruits. Jesus' whole ministry was not about just "fruits" but about buds and blossoms. He was planting buds and blossoms that would not come to fruition in his lifetime. In fact, if your mission can be completed in your lifetime, it isn't a big enough mission. The only "by faith" the Book of Hebrews mentions about Joseph were the buds of his bones.[246] A dying Joseph trusted in God's promise of a new future enough to ask his brothers to take his bones with them on the Exodus and not leave them in Egypt.[247] "Moses took the bones of Joseph with him."[248] Joseph envisioned a future as big as God's promises, and wanted to be a part of it, even if it was only his bones that would make it there.[249]

Jesus humans start and support ministries whose benefits and blessings they will never get to see or taste its fruit. The high point of your life does not come in your lifetime.

---

*I don't know whether my God-given dreams will be fulfilled in this lifetime or whether my tears and prayers are watering them for future generations. . . . I simply do not know. But then, being all-knowing is not my job.*

AUTHOR/MENTOR DR. ALICIA BRITT CHOLE[250]

---

Tibetan Buddhism built an academy (seminary) and learning center at a place called Larung Gar, a high plateau in Tibet where Tibetan Buddhist masters gathered to teach and write about how to spread their faith across China. Soon more than a thousand Han Chinese disciples moved there to study and live and someday spread across China teaching

JESUS HUMAN

Han Buddhists how to form study groups. The Chinese government has done everything to shut them down. They sent in bulldozers to demolish homes. They barricaded roads that led to the city, preventing tourists and pilgrims from coming. They banned the publications coming out of Larung Gar which sought to fight the materialism and atheism coming out of the emerging Chinese culture.

When asked how they were handling the government's opposition and prosecution of the faithful, one Tibetan master said that the government can give it their best shot, but nothing can stop Tibetans from reaching out to Han Chinese. In a paraphrase of his words, the Chinese Communist Party has only been in existence for 100 years. The Larung Gar community is taking the long view and planting seeds of Buddhism that will come to bud, blossom, and fruition for many generations to come, over many lifetimes and centuries.[251]

Why the "God of Abraham, Isaac, and Jacob?" We are tutored to think multigenerationally, to the third generation (which was as far into the future as they could think). Long before EA (Effective Altruism) was a name much less a movement,[252] biblical metaphors taught us to form caring circles not just around locals ("short-termism") but to care about people far from us and far into the future ("long-termism"), with actions and investments that will reverberate beyond our lifetime and throughout eternity. The danger comes from separating the long-run from the short-run, and not binding them as tightly as possible.[253]

Two people who gave up trying to change anything

in their lifetimes and dedicated themselves to writing for posterity: Clement of Alexandria and Moses Maimonides. They trusted that they would be discovered by an intelligent readership in the future and that they would benefit from their insights. J. R. R. Tolkien took a different strategy. Over a 45-year period, he painted images of this tree he named "The Tree of Amalion." The Amalion tree bears on its limbs a whole garden full of buds, blossoms, and flowers, representing for Tolkien all of the stories and poems and writings he could not bring to fruition in his lifetime. A Tree of Tales—Unwritten Tales, Lost Tales, To-Be-Found Tales.

> *You do not need to complete the work, but neither are you free to desist from it.*
> RABBI TARFON (D. 130) OF THE SCHOOL OF SCHAMMAI[254]

**Triquetra:** Third, the ***Mandorla*** teaches us The Ultimate Trifecta, The Trifecta of Truth: the grafting of two opposites is carried out by a third, the trialectics of a *tertium quid*. Depth perception only comes when you look at life cross-eyed. With both eyes open to receive what's there, what's in-between will pop out if you're patient enough. That's trialectics. Three is Truth.

"I am The Way, The Truth, and The Life" is saying the same thing as "The Word, Became Flesh, and Dwelt Among Us."

## JESUS HUMAN

> The Way ("The Word is a lamp unto my feet, and light unto my path")
>
> The Truth ("Became Flesh"—Truth is a Person)
>
> The Life ("And dwelt among us")

In the overlap of opposites in the ***mandorla***, there is a third, which is the fish, the ichthus, the sweet spot of life. Call it harmonious difference, call it connected differentiation, call it "complexio oppositorum," call it the quiver of the bow . . . it is the source and font of creativity and imagination.[255]

The Rule of Three is the Rule of Life. The Rule of Three is the Rule of Creativity. All Creativity is a Three-Dog Night. Or as Sherlock Holmes would put it, that's a three-pipe problem. Abstract artist Jasper Johns once claimed that the way to make art is first to take something, then to do something to it, and finally do something else to it—a three-fold palimpsest.[256]

There is a "triunity of the universe." The mark of the Trinity is everywhere ("Vestigia Trinitatis") as the early church called it: "footprints of the Trinity."

> Time: past, present, future
>
> Space: height, width, depth
>
> Light: particle, wave, beam
>
> Matter: energy, motion, phenomenon

Word, Worship, Witness is the way of life for a human.

# ABECEDARIUM OF A JESUS HUMAN

*Upon three things the world is based: upon Torah, upon divine worship, and upon acts of benevolence.*

JEWISH HIGH PRIEST SIMON THE JUST (D. 273 BCE)
ON WORD, WORSHIP, WITNESS

## M is for Monozukuri (Japanese: ものづくり) Human

*Monozukuri* is the art, science, and craft of making things with a spirit of perfection and pride. Often mistranslated as "manufacturing," it is the quest for superior craftsmanship and the quest for excellence in anything that is made. In some ways it embodies the spirit of Japanese culture itself, whether in gardening or gourmandry.

Jesus calls us to be perfect as his Father is perfect. What an impossible dream. Yet if God's nature is love, why shouldn't we practice perfection in love?

If righteousness is found in relationships, not rules, why shouldn't we practice perfection in our relationships? Why should we want "the perfect wedding" and not "the perfect marriage?" Why should we subscribe to "Word Perfect" and not the "Perfect Word?" Why shouldn't we practice perfect love that overcomes evil with good, that prays for those who persecute us, that loves those who hate us, that forgives those who offend us, and forgives ourselves for harboring in our heart's resentment and malice toward those who scorn and detest us for our "ignorant, antiquated beliefs." "If you want peace in your heart," Ignatius of Loyola (d. 1556) instructed his followers, "You have to say, 'Please forgive me, again and again.'"[257]

#  is for Natsukashii (Japanese: 懐かしい) Human

***Natsukashii*** is a Japanese word used when something evokes a fond memory from your past. It's a word you exclaim as a smile creeps across your face. For instance, when you hear a song you loved as a teenager or when you come across an old train ticket stub in your pocket or when you want to bottle the elixir of this one rare day of total joy and keep it as a memory.

In some cultures, nostalgia is often full of sadness. But ***natsukashii*** – which derives from the verb "natsuku", which means "to keep close and become fond of"–indicates joy and gratitude for the past rather than a desire to return to it.

In Japan, ***natsukashii*** is a reminder that you are fortunate to have had the experiences you've had in life. The fact that you cannot return to those experiences makes them all the more poignant. "A positive frame put around longing is the essence of ***natsukashii***," said Christine Yano, professor of anthropology at the University of Hawaii, whose research focuses on Japanese popular culture including anime and manga. "It's part of the emotional foundation of Japan. A glass half empty is a glass that's full and beautiful. I think in Japan, nostalgia has to do with an aesthetic," she continued. "This is the aesthetic that sees beauty in imperfection, in something not being quite complete, in longing, in yearning, in evanescence, in impermanence, wistfulness, in melancholy. It is an aesthetic invested with emotion and beauty at the same time."[258]

Aesthetic concepts in the traditional Japanese arts were developed in pre-modern Japan. One of the earliest to emerge was wabi-sabi, a Japanese philosophy rooted in Buddhism that finds beauty in imperfection and impermanence; examples include deliberately misshapen bowls used in tea ceremonies and bonsai trees displayed even after they've shed their leaves. Yano suggests that Japan's approach to nostalgia is akin to wabi-sabi—but it's life, rather than objects, that's being celebrated for its imperfections.

Sumie Kawakami, a writer who teaches liberal arts at the International College of Liberal Arts (ICLA) at Japan's Yamanashi Gakuin University, echoes that sentiment. She describes **natsukashii** as a bittersweet form of reminiscing. "We miss the time—but it's better that way," she said. In today's digital age, people seem to be more obsessed than ever with nostalgia. But in Japan, paying tribute to the past goes far beyond sharing the occasional #ThrowbackThursday post on social media or binge-watching an '80s TV show reboot. On any given night of the week, Tokyo businessmen can be found blowing off steam in yokocho, traditional alleyways containing bars and restaurants. These cramped, cash-only establishments surrounded by glowing lanterns and cigarette smoke are a portal to another era, as they were originally part of black markets that cropped up in the city following World War Two. Kawakami compares the sentiment to the English phrase "the good old days". "But there may be a slight difference," she noted. "When Japanese say *'natsukashii'*, they want to confirm that togetherness, rather than simply being nostalgic to a particular event or person. [It's like] 'Yeah, we were together on this!'"

In his structuralist perception of cultures as languages, which has inspired so many semiotic studies of signs and symbols, Levi-Strauss has taught us that the liberal belief in "progress" that informs the social theories of Marxists and liberals is colonialist and valorizes Western "advancements." Different cultures will develop different accents and accelerations, which will give them different destinies. The Jesus vision of what it means to be human accommodates and encourages differences between human societies.

JESUS HUMAN

##  is for Ostranenie (Russian: Остранение) Human

***Ostranenie*** is the fundamental task of preaching making the familiar strange so that what seems obvious or evident begins to seem perplexing and puzzling.

Jesus was a master of ***ostranenie***, even of making the familiar strange twice over.

> *Clear prose indicates the absence of thought.*
> MEDIA THEORIST MARSHALL MCLUHAN (D. 1980)[259]

***Ostranenie*** is a Russian word *strannyi* which means "strange." The adjectival Russian noun for strange is "*stranno*." The philosophy of ***ostranenie*** is that the familiar must be made strange before it can be fresh again. Only strangeness has the power to tear apart the veil of familiarity. For God's mercies to be made "fresh every morning," a Jesus human must put on ***ostranenie*** glasses to shield them from the blinding light of familiarity and find beauty in things that we often overlook or disdain.

At twenty-four years of age, a literary theorist named Viktor Shklovsky wrote an article "Art as Device" in which he elevated ***ostranenie*** to a philosophy of communication and education in which "making strange" or "defamiliarization" was the key to unlocking access to all things hidden and forbidden.[260] Other cultures known for their storytelling mastered the art of ***ostranenie*** under different names. Irish storytellers called it *seanchaidhthe*, the skill of telling everything obliquely, "leaving things to the listener as their words 'dance in the space at one with the fire.'"[261]

Once accessible, Shklovsky's concept of **ostranenie** began to spread. It inspired semiotician Umberto Eco with his "A Theory of Semiotics."[262] Novelist and essayist Martin Amis is perhaps the most prominent practitioner of **ostranenie** in contemporary anglophone literature.[263] For Amis, "*ostranenie*" or what he champions as "Martianism" (anagram of Martin Amis) is but a sophisticated formulation of what has always been true: "seeing the world anew, as if it were new, is as old as writing." Emily Dickinson might have called **ostranenie** "slant interaction" after her "slant rhyme" technique.[264]

> *Automatization eats things, clothes, furniture, your wife and the fear of war.*
> RUSSIAN LITERARY THEORIST VIKTOR SHKLOVSKY (D. 1984)

Kurt Vonnegut's writings were riddled with **ostranenie** before he knew its name. In *Slaughterhouse Five* (1969), a war documentary is watched backwards. Mark Twain's prose poem "War Prayer" (1905) deployed an **ostranenie** of belligerence to decry warfare and blind patriotism.

> Lord our God, help me tear their soldiers to bloody shreds with our shells; help us to cover their smiling fields with the pale forms of their patriot dead; help us to drown the

JESUS HUMAN

> thunder of the guns with the shrieks of their wounded, writing in pain. [265]

Jonathan Swift defamiliarizes war and religion at the same time. Gulliver describes the reasons for war to the Houyhnhnms in ways that turn the sublime into the absurd:

> Difference in opinions has cost many millions of lives for instance, whether flesh be bread or bread be flesh, whether the juice of a certain berry be blood or wine.[266]

---

*Why, let me ask, should a hen lay an egg which egg can become a chicken in about three weeks and a full-grown hen in less than a twelvemonth, while a clergyman and his wife lay no eggs but give birth to a baby which will take three-and-twenty years before it can become another clergyman? Why should not chickens be born and clergymen be laid and hatched? Or why, at any rate, should not the clergyman be born full grown and in Holy Orders, not to say already beneficed? The present arrangement is not convenient, it is not cheap, it is not free from danger, it is not only not perfect but is so much the reverse that we could hardly find words to express our sense of its awkwardness if we could look upon it with new eyes, or as the cuckoo perhaps observes it.*

ENGLISH NOVELIST/SATIRIST SAMUEL BUTLER (1882)[267]

---

Defamiliarization is different from deconstruction. Askew is not always askance. Deconstruction can become dogmatic skepticism—less a "slant" than a slit and slice. Defamiliarization is a playful hopefulness; an aspiration toward sympathy and wholeness. For those for whom the

## ABECEDARIUM OF A JESUS HUMAN

Bible has become overfamiliar, overripe, or unremarkable, they don't need deconstruction but defamiliarization. They need to read the Bible strangely, and to hear the Bible differently, especially when the church has swung from cognitive estrangement from the world around it to cognitive assonance from the world around it.

English philosopher Simon Critchley argues that there is something more important in life than answers—clarity and focus are what is most needed amidst the trials and tumults of life:

> What we need are multifarious descriptions of many things, further descriptions of phenomena that change the aspect under which they are seen that light them up and let us see them anew. . . . We might feel refreshed and illuminated, even slightly transformed after a moment of clarification, but we aren't going to stop scratching that itch.[268]

In short, what is better than answers is "clarity and focus." But paradoxically that only comes from bringing in difference and disagreement—different perspectives, different angles, different cultures, different people. True clarity and focus only come from letting your eyes become unfocused and unclear. The center position is not the best vantage point for a clear view. The margins and edges and peripheries are what bring clarity and focus. Truth leans on ***ostranenie*** to keep it alive.

Jesus was a master of ***ostranenie***: "You heard it said, but I say." With this refrain of words, Jesus was ritually reframing, making the familiar strange so that the old could become new. He was not about taking things out of the picture but repositioning things in the picture. When you're reading the Bible, you can never make it out to be thicker and richer than it actually is.

Mary stood at the edge of a crowd one time and said somewhat shamefacedly that her son was "beside himself." Are we strange enough, odd enough to appear, even to our mothers, "beside ourselves?"

**Ostranenie** has the power to make you feel like you've been hatched from an egg and now look at the world with baby eyes: wonder all around; all things new.

# ABECEDARIUM OF A JESUS HUMAN

 **is for Paraklesis (Greek: Παράκλησις) Human**

*Paraklesis* is most often associated with the atonement and the sacrifice of Jesus on the cross. But it literally means to "come alongside someone," especially someone in need of help. It is that "coming alongside someone," that response to urgent supplication for assistance, that involves some sort of sacrifice—of time, endowments, energies, enduements.

"Sacrifice" is no longer a good or popular word. "Give it up for" now means to pep up and applaud, not lay it down and forfeit; not "lay down what's in your hands" but "put your hands together and clap your hands." Even our theological brooms are sweeping "sacrifice" away. Reports from the frontlines of interviewing prospective candidates for ministry on various denominational fields reveal the same findings: very few new seminary grads want to talk about the cross. As one graduate of a high-powered seminary said, "I don't like to talk about the atonement. I'm uncomfortable with cross language." It seems that the 1993 Re-Imagine Conference in Minneapolis was prophetic when its main speaker claimed, "I don't think we need a theory of atonement," and, "I don't think we need folks hanging on crosses, and blood dripping, and weird stuff." There is an old story about the banner over the entrance to a university, "We preach Christ crucified." The ivy eventually grew over the word "crucified," then Christ, then preach. Until all that was left was "WE."

Whenever I see the image of a pelican plucking her

breast, the ancient Christian symbol of lay-it-down, sacrificial love, I think of Frederick Buechner's definition of sacrifice: to make something holy by giving it up for love.[269] Is there anything good in life that does not require someone's sacrifice, sometimes (but not always) mine. Faith, marriage, family, athletics, friendships, artistry, and career success all require sacrifice at one level or another. Even sunsets require the sacrifice of some of those 10 to the 80th power of atoms contained in the universe. "The natural world is a symphony of self-sacrifice," novelist and essayist David James Duncan observes. "The sun sacrifices itself to keep this whole planet going. These little sunflowers growing in my yard here, they spend the summer collecting those solar rays and then they spend the winter feeding their faces to birds."[270]

Maybe Ralph Waldo Emerson was wrong: "The purpose of life seems to be to acquaint a man with himself."[271]

Maybe Austrian poet Rainer Maria Rilke was wrong: "The purpose of life is to be defeated by greater and greater things."

Maybe Jesus was right: "The purpose of life is to be inspired by greater and greater things." Those individuals in history who have been willing to commit acts of greatness in pursuit of "greater and greater things" did not do so without sacrifice.

The more Martin Luther King, Jr. suffered, the better it became for black Americans.

The more Aleksandyr Solzhenitsyn and other Soviet dissidents suffered, the more they won the hearts of the USAmerican people.

## ABECEDARIUM OF A JESUS HUMAN

The more Nelson Mandela suffered, the more the united future of South Africa was secured.

Russian emigre Princess Kubowsky wrote novels and memoirs under the pseudonym Croisé Jacques.[272] She told screenwriter and journalist Frederic Michael Raphael concentration camp stories, as well as stories of the two million Jews who had already been operated on, burned, shot, tortured, and buried alive before the Holocaust.[273] One of her stories concerned a Russian woman, "a writer, not Jewish, who was in one of the camps. A girl of fifteen was included in a list of those who were to die. When she began to cry, the woman said, 'Don't take it so hard. Death is not such a terrible thing. If it will help you, I will come with you.' The woman took the girl's hand and they went into the gas chamber together."[274]

One of the greatest paradoxes of life is this: joy is born of suffering, and renewal is hammered on the anvil of sacrifice.

One of my heroes is Eivind Berggrav (1884–1959), the Norwegian Lutheran bishop who resisted the Nazi occupation of Norway and refused to cooperate when he was instructed to change the liturgy to reflect the racist politics of National Socialism. At one point, the Nazis put him under house arrest, but he kept converting the guards. When threatened by his Gestapo interrogators, "We will have you shot," the bishop calmly replied, "Go ahead. Shoot me—and what will you do then?" That kind of confidence only comes from a **Paraklesis** Human.

JESUS HUMAN

# P is for Pax (Latin) Human

*We came in peace for all Mankind.*
ASTRONAUT JAMES ARMSTRONG STEPPING ON THE MOON, 20 JULY 1969

When two astronauts landed on the moon, their declared mission was not to conquer it or colonize it for one country, but to come in peace for all humanity.[275]

German philosopher and social critic Theodor Adorno (d. 1969) once traced the straight line between the slingshot and the atomic bomb. The power of force is a farce. It is time to end all the wars we are now fighting—war on terror (which started out as "Operation Iraqi Freedom"), war on drugs, war on sugar, war on crime, war on climate change, war on poverty, war on homelessness, war on heresy, war on inflation, war on fat, war on religion, war on pronouns, war on the West, war on COVID, war on war, war on meat, war on meaninglessness.

This is not to mention the hundreds of culture wars being fought at this moment, a warfare that is now as much within the church as without or between the church and the world. British cultural theorist Terry Eagleton defines "culture" as "that which you're prepared to kill or die for," and suggests that all the huffing-and-puffing, fee-fi-fo-fumming of the church against culture may have been misguided. Whether Christianity should have invested in the culture wars is another conversation, especially since Jesus can be incarnate in all cultures, the ways of the cross will always be different from the ways of the world, and only love is worth dying for. But if Christianity is "in retreat," it's a retreat that perhaps never should have started as a campaign to begin with.

*For though we walk in the flesh, we do not war according to the flesh, for the weapons of our warfare are not of the flesh, but divinely powerful for the destruction of fortresses. We are destroying speculations and every lofty thing raised up against the knowledge of God, and we are taking every thought captive to the obedience of Christ.*

APOSTLE PAUL[276]

Even the church, in the wrong hands, can turn into an instrument of war.[277] It is understandable why we turn everything into a war. We live in a world where nothing is working and everything is destroying us. My Appalachian Gramma used to comment on all the "vim and vinegar" in her grandchildren. Now there seems to be more venom than vim in everyone. What is Twitter but a blame and shame machine? We displace on others the blame for things not working, even though we know it's not working for us either. And we declare war on what is not working.

One way out of this arms race of wars is to abolish the metaphor of "war" itself. This is a metaphorized culture, which makes part of our problem a metaphor problem.[278] Why must everything be war? Not just "armed conflicts" as war, but everything that happens is or needs to be a war: computer hacking is war; "disinformation" is war. Michel

JESUS HUMAN

Foucault's contention that "the history which bears and determines us has the form of a war" suggests that even the history of ideas and arguments takes the form of a war. Maybe it's time for metaphors that encourage thoughts about peacefare, not warfare.

The two biggest problems with the "war" metaphor are, first, it requires a winner and a loser. No "war" is over until it is "won," and the enemy vanquished. All our "wars" share the same fate: because of the human condition, they are never "won." This means there is no war that will ever be over. Second, all wars are escalatory. All wars always tend toward total war and the extermination of opponents. Not just their shunning and shaming, but their annihilation.[279]

Giving up the metaphor and mindset of war may be one of the most difficult of tasks for the Jesus human. The moral theologian Richard Hays, exploring the moral vision of the New Testament, recognizes that the call to nonviolent peacemaking, while not easy, stretches people beyond what is typically considered "realistic" or "natural." He wrote: "God broke through the borders of our standard definition of what is human and gave a new formative definition in Jesus."[280] This is why it is important to have honest conversations about whether metaphors like "crusades" and "co-belligerents"[281] are helpful in promoting a just and ethical society.

# ABECEDARIUM OF A JESUS HUMAN

*The only people on earth who do not see Christ and his teachings as nonviolent are Christians."
Or did someone else say it?*

WIDELY ATTRIBUTED TO MAHATMA GANDHI[282]

We are hardwired as humans for peaceful resolution. But according to Christopher Blattman, there are five logics that can override the human and make people turn to inhuman violence.[283] This five-fold rationale for war includes:

1. "Unchecked interests"
2. "Intangible incentives" like ideals and values
3. "Uncertainty" which results in fatal miscalculations
4. "Commitment problems" or the failure to honor promises
5. "Misperception" caused when everyone talks past each other and no one listens

When ancient Christian burial grounds in Rome record in the inscriptions that someone died "in pace" or "in peace," it means they died as a member of the church, which is Christ's peace. To be a part of a Jesus community is to share Christ's peace. Every church to which Paul wrote was in the midst of a fight about something. Our churches today are no different. But we still can share the peace of Christ.

The word "martyr" originally meant "witness." The first Christian "martyr," deacon Stephen, was called a "martyr" not because of the way he died but because of the way he lived and testified to the resurrection of Jesus all the way to the end. The first apostles likewise were called "martyrs" even before they were persecuted and killed, because they spent their lives witnessing to a risen, rising, reigning, and returning Lord even when it was the most difficult thing to do. Part of peacefare is to see martyrdom as a way of living, and the martyresque life a way of overcoming evil with good.

Part of the martyresque life is refusing to separate the "in here" and the "out there." Paths to peace "in here" cannot bypass "out there," and vice versa. "In here" and "out there" cannot be separated. For example, in a Jesus Peace, inner peace and "peace on earth, good will to all" are connected in a "peace that passes all understanding." The path to peace "in here" cannot bypass peace "out there," nor can the "out there" ceasefire ignore the "in here" peace be still.

*What do I love when I love God? Do I not love Love?*
AUGUSTINE OF HIPPO[284]

In 1226, St. Francis of Assisi had a complaint about the world. The legend is he sighed, "Love is not loved."[285] The world's landscape needs lovescapes more than battlefields. Summoning all martyrs to move the world from a war zone to a place of peace where humans less "war against" than wrestle, struggle, lift up, advance, witness, exorcize, resist, refuse, defy, dissent, endure, or pray. Jesus is a fighter. Or as the Salvation Army puts it, followers of Jesus are "in the fight" for life against death. But Jesus fought with metaphors and narratives and signs and wonders that disarmed, diluted, and denatured the weapons of his day.

Warfare has created plenty of new ways to die. Peacefare creates plenty of new ways to live.

##  is for Pentimento (Italian) Human

> *It is imperative that we wear the coat God has tailored for us. It is of utmost necessity that we resound and resonate as the poem we were written to be. We are able to do this, we should do this, because this is who we really are.*
>
> APOSTLE PAUL[286]

"***Pentimento***" is from Italian (via Latin) meaning to repent. A ***pentimento*** (plural pentimenti) is an alteration in an original, prime version of a painting showing that the artist has changed his mind as to the composition during the process of painting. The word derives from the Italian *pentirsi*, meaning to repent.

The more highly skilled the artist (Rembrandt, Titian, Caravaggio), the more likely they were to compose right onto the canvas as opposed to making preliminary drawings, which means most ***pentimenti*** are found in the greatest masters of art. The more you are committed to greatness (and saintliness) in your art and life, the more you will repent.

In the world of art, ***pentimento*** is an underlying image in a painting, as an earlier painting, part of a painting, or original draft that shows through, usually when the top layer of paint has become transparent with age. In human lives, we do one thing, "gloss" over it, move on and voila! Behold! Before long, the top layer peels back and, again, we are transparent. A "***pentimento***" moment if you would.[287]

In the art world, the technique of chiaroscuro (another Italian word) brings out certain features and hides others within plain sight. Repentance is a form of chiaroscuro: not a set of flood lights that forever drive away the night, or a turning on of fluorescent lights that bathe everything in a sick-blue haze that drives away the dance of nuance and subtlety, shade, and shadow. Life is a long chiaroscuro of repentance, and the illuminations that follow from indirect lighting feature the play, the drama, the tango of light and shadow that is the constant of a life of repentance.

*God, at the end of prose, somehow be our poem.*
PRAYER OF AUSTRALIAN POET LES MURRAY (D. 2019)[288]

Dominic Johnson is an evolutionary biologist and a political scientist. He argues that the sense of justice whereby the good get what they deserve and the evil get their "just" desserts is biologically hard-wired in the human species. He is himself an atheist, and argues atheism must find ways to accommodate what he calls the "belief instinct," the sense of something "out there" to whom we owe an accountability for our actions.[289] Thirty percent of those in the US unaffiliated with any church or synagogue or mosque still believe in some judgment in some kind of hell. The religious impulse goes deep.

Everywhere you go in the church today, the #1 word that pops out is "justice." It's a word that is circulating in every corner of society as well. We owe justice here. We need to bring justice there. But when is the last time you heard about justice from a Just God? What about justice in our relationship with God?

"The fear of the Lord is the beginning of wisdom."[290] One might also argue that the fear of God is the beginning of humanity. The Hebrew word for fear (**yirah**) comes from the root (y-r-a), which ranges in meaning from the negative emotion of fear, to the positive attitude of revere and respect, to the moral response of obedience and relationship.

Regardless of which meaning, there is present in all of them an element of accountability to God's justice. The Tent of Meeting, where people gathered to praise and worship, was also the woodshed where God hauled the people to talk turkey with them. Today we would call it being "summoned to the principal's office" or in Christianese, time for a "come-to-Jesus meeting." There is a Day of Reckoning on the horizon for every human.

<u>**"I Reckon"**</u>: ***Pentimento*** humans have a penitential sense that they will stand before their Maker some day and give an account of their lives: "The end of the matter, everything having been heard: fear God and keep His commandments, for this is the whole human being."[291] Or in some of the concluding words of the Bible: "And I saw the dead, great and small, standing before the throne, and books were opened. Another book was opened, which is the book of life. The dead were judged according to what they had done as recorded in the books."[292] Jesus humans take into account that one day they must give an account. To be a Jesus human means to sign on for a lifetime of repenting, a lifetime of wanting

## ABECEDARIUM OF A JESUS HUMAN

the truth enough to regularly re-formulate beliefs, re-frame understandings, and re-sign actions.

God is a God of justice, but justice is a two-edged sword. There will be a Day of Judgment for each of us. Humans are accountable for the gifts God has entrusted to them, and for the dividends of that divine investment. Jesus taught that some will be welcomed and some dismissed.[293] Some universalists and even some justice junkies claim that even Hitler will be in heaven because he suffered from "disorders of the mind within,"[294] but the Apostle Paul insisted that we all are "without excuse."[295] The gates of hell may be locked from the inside, which makes hell something we do to ourselves. But the gates still click.

◇

*If somebody has obtained purity, everything is in submission to him, as it was to Adam, when he was in paradise before he disobeyed.*

HERMIT ABBA PAUL OF THEBES (D. 341)[296]

Repentance is often seen as a turning away from sin, and purity as being free from sin. But repentance is more than a necessary step on the path to purity. "Purity" does not simply mean moral cleanliness or righteousness or the imperfection behind what one of the three original "Pussy Riot" activists and singers, and the one who was convicted in 2012 of "religious hatred" for the Russian state, admitted when she said, "Antigovernment punks may not have much craft, but even when our music technically sucks, we still have an insane purity of impulse."[297] The basic meaning

327

of purity is "the real thing" or making the main thing the main thing, which strikes at the heart of human integrity and authenticity.

A ***Pentimento*** human is a pure human. One seldom hears that word "pure" or purity anymore, except in the oxymoron "pure evil" or in the beatitudes cliche "pure of heart."[298] But humans are enjoined in the First Testament, "A pure heart create for me, O God, put a steadfast spirit within me,"[299] and in the Second Testament, "All who have this hope in him purify themselves, just as he is pure."[300]

A ***pentimento*** human's purity is not naive innocence or virginal credulity, but a second naivete[301] that comes from maturational ripening and life-seasoning. Real purity is the cleanliness that comes after getting dirty, the authenticity that emerges after the ***pentimento*** peeling back of dirt and grime. The Greek word for "purity," *katharos*, means cleansed from impurities, stripped of messiness and confusion. Flannery O'Connor conveys this forcefully:

> The phrase *naive purity* is a contradiction in terms. I don't think that purity is mere innocence; I don't think that babies and idiots possess it. I take it to be something that comes with experience or with Grace so that it can never be naive.[302]

*Like a morning star in heaven and a palm tree in paradise, so is a pure mind and a gentle soul.*

EVAGRIUS PONTICUS (D. 399)[303]

# ABECEDARIUM OF A JESUS HUMAN

Richard Reinhold Niebhur, the son of H. Richard Niebuhr, was a theologian like his more famous father Reinhold Niebuhr (d. 1971). He lived to age 90 (d. 2017). When he retired from Harvard Divinity School in 1960, he wrote about "The problem of preaching at Eastertide:"

> It is a relatively easy thing to muse on the story of the first Easter, for it is not Easter as such that is a scandal. The difficulty arises at the juncture in which the humanity of Christ and our own humanity are equated or not equated, at the juncture in which we either we do or do not recognize ourselves in him and him in ourselves.

What is required, he argued, is the image of Christ as the one:

> in whose own humanity our own image is reflected and simultaneously freed of its distortions. Unless the gospel is uttered in such a way that it evokes in us not only a sense of our individuality but also of our humanity, there is little point in dwelling on the Christ who is for us.[304]

JESUS HUMAN

# ℙ is for Pentecostal (Greek: Πεντηκοστιανή) Human

*For what human being knows what is truly human except the human spirit that is within? So also no one comprehends what is truly God's except the Spirit of God.*

APOSTLE PAUL[305]

The Holy Spirit is software in action—Jesus software, divine software in human hardware.

If you want to see the invisible hoist a sail or throw up a flag. Suddenly the invisible becomes visible, and the wind becomes watchable. In life, you see the shape of the invisible by hoisting hypotheses and launching adventures and risking safety.

Sometimes inventions find their inventors–aspartame, ScotchGuard™, microwave. But you have to be looking. You can look for one thing and find another but only if you're still looking. The shape of the invisible is found by looking at the visible with discernment, discretion, and care. If you want to see God in your life, put some wind in your sails.

Resurrection is more than an event. It's a life, it's a life-story, it's a life-line to the eternal. Jesus' resurrection presence is the ongoing Tree of Life growing in each person and in each community. "The Lord be with you." How many times have we heard or said these words without realizing that the ultimate blessing is God's BEING WITH us, not doing something for us? Especially when we remember we have a God who says, not only "I know you by name," but "I have inscribed your name on the palm of my hand."[306]

Dom Paul Delotte is one of the three most important figures from the French Abbey of Solesmes, one of the centers of monastic life and culture, famed for its Gregorian chant. His writings are being translated into English for the first time. He makes this extraordinary statement, "We are 'the Lord'." And then he explains what he means: by "We are 'the Lord':"

> Each one of us must be a new edition of the life of the Lord, and not only in the sense that our actions must be conformed to those of the Lord himself, but in the sense that the life of our Lord must be active within us. There must come to pass in us what was in the Lord, whose whole nature was in the grip of the Word. Everything in us must be brought into unity in Our Lord Jesus Christ: for what is the living and active principle, the unique agent, that sets everything in motion and applies it to the task? It is he.[307]

We live in a world of collective PTSD.[308] Fear and isolation are exploding rates of addiction and mental illness. The Holy Spirit works amidst chaos as well as order; desperation as much as hope, fear as much as courage. In fact, the Holy Spirit preserves and protects the intellectual space for skeptical questioning and alternative viewpoints. Humans need frisson to keep alive and growing. A know-it-all posture which snuffs out doubt and disillusionment, ambiguity, and mystery smothers the Holy Spirit, a sin close to "unpardonable."

> *Even in slight things, the experience of the new is rarely without some stirring or foreboding.*
> LONGSHOREMAN/PHILOSOPHER ERIC HOFFER[309]

**<u>Stirred, and Shaken:</u>** This is the stirring function of the Holy Spirit, and the stirring-stick role of the Pentecost human. This is why when I preach ordination sermons I often give the gift of a stirring stick to the candidate for ordination. There is no healing at the Pool of Bethesda until the waters are troubled or stirred. Stirring is the key to great compost, where you combine nitrogeny "green" things and carbony "brown" things in a three-foot square minimum pile that is watery. But if you want that pile of trash, the mix of grass and vegetables and chipped branches and dog hair to come to life, you have to do one more thing. You have to stir it. You have to give it air and wind and breath. You have to turn your pile to make it compost. You have to fork it and stir it and bring the center and the edges together. The Scriptures over and over again enjoin us to "stir up your faith"[310] and "stir up your mind"[311] and "stir up love and justice"[312] as one kindles a fire to keep it going.

Easter is the story of the risen and rising Christ, and a risen and rising humanity. Resurrection is the promise that a Jesus human version of you is not only possible but rising in you right now . . . if you give the Spirit the reins in life, and let Jesus reign. Jesus rose from the dead once, but he rises in us daily and restores in us our true humanity if we keep stirring.

◇

> *Every morning, Justin Welby, Archbishop of Canterbury, an establishment man to his Winchester-and-Oxford educated fingertips, puts his breakfast aside for a moment, tilts his head skywards, opens his mouth, and speaks in a language no living human knows.*
> THE TABLET, 06 AUGUST 2022, 12.

JESUS HUMAN

##  is for Qubit (Physics/Scientese) Human

The future is one of *qubit* (quantum bit), quark (basic component of matter), and other quantum quickenings that no one fully understands what they are or what they mean. The future is already here. Chinese beggars now display QR codes.

Quantum is the smallest measurable state currently known to science. ***Qubit*** is the smallest level of quantum information and the basic unit of information in quantum computing. Innovation and imagination find their greatest hospitality in the micro part, not the macro whole; the quantum, not the gargantuan.[313]

*Great theater is rarely originated in large houses*
SINGER/SONGWRITER IAIN MACKINTOSH (D. 2006)[314]

The First Quantum Revolution brought us nuclear weapons and power, as well as laser weapons. We are now in the Second Quantum Revolution, which utilizes quantum-mechanical properties like quantum entanglement, quantum superposition, and quantum tunneling for practical applications. The Second Quantum Revolution is bringing us all sorts of new things, the most significant of which may be Quantum Computing, with building blocks not of sand, metals, and silicon, but atoms, ions, electrons, photons, and molecules. Quantum-powered AI is being spurred by DARPA (Defense Advanced Research Project Agency), which brought us the Internet. DARPA is now partnering with the private sector to create an easy way to use practical quantum supercomputers. How far and fast quantum computing will change everyday human life is up for grabs. But if "Amara's Law" is correct, we will overestimate what this technology can achieve in the short run and underestimate its revolutionary impact in the longer run.[315]

QED—or Quantum ElectroDynamics—first conceived in 1949, is the standard model of particle physics. It is a theory of the very small (the standard model) that clashes with Einstein's theory of the very large known as general relativity.

String theory bridges the gap between the very small and the very large. Vibrating strings of energy is what comprises the universe, with different modes of vibration as electron strings play a different note from a photon string or a quark string. What makes reality even more incomprehensible, string theory only works in at least an eleven-dimensional universe, not three of space and one of time.

Thus, the critique of those strung out on string theory as too impossible to be true. In 1986 Paul Ginsparg and Sheldon Galshow contended that string theory "depends for its existence upon magical coincidences, miraculous cancellations, and relations among seemingly unrelated (and possibly undiscovered) fields of mathematics," raising the question of whether "mathematics and aesthetics supplant and transcend mere experiment." In other words, scientific theory is becoming more aesthetics than trial and error.

String theory still dominates the scientific horizon, since it's the only game in town. But the critique still lurks in the background. Again, Ginsparg and Glashow: "Contemplation of superstrings may evolve into an activity as remote from conventional particle physics as particle physics is from chemistry, to be conducted at schools of divinity by future equivalents of medieval theologians."[316] Argentine poet and essayist Jorge Luis Borges (d. 1986) is famous for his insight that the greatest philosophical and scientific constructs are not the result of refined reason but masterpieces of the imagination and mindful meditation.

> *To understand the universe in a deep sense, minds count more than galaxies and planets . . . We have more to learn from the poets than from the scientists when it comes to problems of the purpose of the universe.*
> THEORETICAL PHYSICIST FREEMAN DYSON (D. 2020),
> SON OF CHURCH MUSICIAN/COMPOSER SIR GEORGE DYSON (D. 1964)[317]

We are living in a blind-faith world where no one understands how the new science works, and no one understands how the new technology works, but we use it and trust our lives to it all the time. **Quantum** mechanics is so weird and anti-intuitive that famed theoretical physicist Richard Feynman (d. 1988) once remarked, "I think I can safely say that nobody understands quantum mechanics."[318] We build airplanes all the time without fully understanding aerodynamics and without knowing exactly how they work, since computers are now programming computers to program the computers that build the plane. Humans exercise blind faith almost every hour of the day.

If "***quantum***" is one of the woolliest words in science, faith is one of the woolliest words in theology. But wooly doesn't mean weak and wimpy. Faith is fierce. To "live by faith,"[319] as the "by faith" passages of Hebrew 11 itemize, is to topple walls, part waters, quench flames, blunt swords, shut the mouths of lions, and conquer kingdoms. Humans stand on something we don't see or understand called "faith," but faith is the victory that overcomes the world. Faith can never make a comeback, because it never goes away. Faith can go awry, but not away. Everyone has faith in something (for good or ill). You can't start the day without it.

Just as nothing is stronger than faith even though we can't see it or understand it, so the invisible **quantum** world is stronger than we can imagine even though we can't see it or understand it. "We think of **quantum** systems, especially in **quantum** computing, as very fragile,' says Natalia Ares, a physicist at the University of Oxford. "That this result demonstrates that **quantum** systems can in fact be unexpectedly robust is an encouraging finding, and bodes well for potential future advances in the field."[320]

A **qubit** human understands the power of faith, even mustard-seed, **quantum** faith, to move mountains and save humanity.

---

*Christ did not say, "You shall not be perturbed, you shall not be troubled, you shall not be distressed," but he said, "You shall not be overcome."*

JULIAN OF NORWICH, *XVI REVELATIONS OF DIVINE LOVE* (1670), 68, THE EARLIEST SURVIVING ENGLISH-LANGUAGE WORK BY A WOMAN

## R is for Ressourcement (French Vatican) Human

Out of the papacy, which is the world's most ancient dynasty, and from the Vatican, which is one of the world's most successful global corporations, comes this French word "***ressourcement***" which means literally "a return to the sources" but which has come to mean revisiting the past toward the end of facing the future.

Theologian and priest David Tracy[321] (d. 2022) coined the phrase "hermeneutical retrieval" to describe when you recover a past tradition from its original sources and insights and appropriate it to your current setting. In the process of ***ressourcement*** and retrieval, the tradition is incarnated in a way that makes it ever ancient, ever new. Like the one-eye back, two-eyes forward faithful householder who brings forth the old and the new,[322] the old of a critical sense of the past must be yoked to the new of a sanctified imagination for the future.

It is not by accident that this bringing of the past and the future together called "***ressourcement***" comes out of the Roman Catholic and not Protestant traditions. Protestantism separated the living from the dead, who were no longer part of the prayer life of the living, and could not intercede in heaven for their dear ones still living.[323]

**That Was Now: This Is Then:**[324] Every epoch should carry echoes of earlier epochs and eons. But new contexts demand new language; new settings demand new speech; new worlds require new words. A church that is on the move and in mission is less focused on restoring yesterday than on restarting tomorrow. Besides, you can't restore the past. But you can restart the future by revitalizing the past. In fact, antiquity can make change and innovation easier because it lends aura and authority to what appears strange and daring. A spoonful of oldfashionedness can make the medicine of newfanglements go down.

God breathes in "Let there be" and breathes out "And there was." In the same way, human intention becomes invention because we're made in God's image. To convey this convergence of in/out, history/novelty, ancient/future, and tradition/innovation, the writer of the Hebrews uses the metaphor of a kedging anchor[325] that doesn't hold firm in the depths of the sea, but it is cast forward into the future to direct our journey, or even cast upward to the heights of the heavens where we are lifted up to the heights in the hope that has been fulfilled in Jesus.[326] On the catacomb walls you find drawings of the ship, one of the earliest metaphors for the church. You also find the pictures of the anchor, the symbol of "the faith once for all delivered to the saints" (tradition).

My favorite analogy of ***ressourcement*** is the swing and the new theory among physicists about how the swing works. Previous theories revolved around the principle of "parametric instability," which pivoted the action of swinging at the middle of the arc, and the rocking forward into a higher center of gravity. Grinnell College physicist William Case, while watching how children actually swing, has now

# JESUS HUMAN

posited a new principle called "driven harmonic oscillator" or what I call "parabolic harmonious oscillation." The key to the swing is not in the middle of the arc, but at each end of the arc, where and when the swingers do two opposite things at the same time: lean back (ancient) and throw their feet forward (future).

*Best man
in the wedding of the sailor
to the sea*

METAPHOR OF AN ANCHOR FROM SAM WILLETTS' "THE WEDDING"[327]

Confucianism is all about realizing Ren, or learning what it means to be a "true human." All four core Confucian classics[328] include the formula "Ren zhe ren ye," literally "to be ren is to be a man." This means that ren is the quality that makes a person a true person. It is for this reason that many translators choose "humanity" or "humanness" to render "ren." But understanding what is genuinely human in the Confucian theory of ren requires knowing ren's cluster of underlying metaphysical and psychological beliefs. The Four Cardinal Principles of Confucianism are:

- Ren: Benevolence, humanity, love, kindness, human-heartedness
- Yi: Righteousness, justice, morality, appropriateness
- Li: Propriety, ritual, etiquette, manners, decorum

# ABECEDARIUM OF A JESUS HUMAN

Zhi: Wisdom, knowledge, intelligence, understanding

In the same way, a ***ressourcement*** human brings together a cluster of virtues and features that enable the recovery of the past and the embrace of the future. The 6-R Taxonomy of a ***Ressourcement*** Human includes resilience, redundancy, randomization, rapture, resonance, and reason.

**Resilience:** Resilience is the adaptive ability to cope with change and bounce back from adversity in healthy and future-friendly ways.[329] "Rise Above Adversity" was the motto of Tuskegee Airmen, USAmerica's first all-black aviation unit.

For Friedrich Nietzsche, stupidity was almost the opposite of resilience. He argued that stupidity was the top danger of institutions, because they resist the adaptiveness that's necessary in order to keep them going in the face of accelerating and exponential change. A resilience human is one who is "undergoing treatment" all the time, as we undergo procedures that change us from the inside out.[330]

The history of communications is a case in point. Humans went from gesticulations to signage; then from articulated language (Homo erectus) to spoken language (Indo-European languages, 5000 BCE); then from written word (Sumer, 3500 BCE) to printed word (moveable ceramic type, Pi Sheng, 1041); then from broadcast (radio, Fessenden, 1906) to digital (telegraph, 1827; Internet, 1991). Each new communications technology replaced entirely earlier ones, but in another sense the old truism holds: there is nothing new under the sun, only new adaptations to changes brought about by deeper understandings.[331] Some things never change. What is Amazon but a department store like Macy's except an online department store?

Hence resilience needs consilience. A consilience approach believes that unrelated, independent, radically different fields of knowledge can converge to create a more comprehensive understanding of the world.[332] In a densely interconnected universe such as ours, to understand one thing, one cannot ignore anything and must try to understand everything.

When resilience and consilience come together, humans can create communities that withstand being whipsawed and whiplashed by pummeling change. Strong communities of faith cultivate education that builds tribal identity while focusing on global understanding. It fosters skills of adaptation that accompany exposure to difference. Another way of talking about this union of resilience and consilience is "antifragility" as coined by the Lebanese-American risk theorist Nassim Nicholas Taleb. The difference between resilience and antifragility, according to Taleb, is that "the resilient resists shocks and stays the same; the antifragile gets better."[333] Resilience is a punching bag. Antifragile is putty or pottery clay.

ABECEDARIUM OF A JESUS HUMAN

*Our language can be seen as an ancient city: a maze of little streets and squares. Of old and new houses and the additions from various periods; and this surrounded by a multitude of new boroughs with straight regular streets and uniform houses.*
AUSTRIAN PHILOSOPHER LUDWIG WITTGENSTEIN (D. 1951)[334]

**Redundancy:** Redundancy is the duplication of components or functions in a system to increase reliability, withstand setbacks and weather storms. Redundancy is the apex of risk management and succession readying. It is not a guarantee that bad things will never happen, but it can help to reduce the risk of unexpected disruptions. By building redundancy into life systems, like multiple skills, multiple sources of income ("side hustles"[335]), humans can be more prepared for whatever the future may hold.

The key to redundancy is the ability to think in multiples and to prize preparedness over planning. Planning is control. Preparedness is surrender, but an active not a passive one. No marshaling forces. No strategic plans that lock you in for years upon years. No nailed-down campaign tactics that cannot take into account the movements of others around you and the shifting sands of our world.

In the active surrender of redundancy, you save your life and find new life—compassion on yourself and passion for others. You find yourself preparing for the trials that beset us all, not as misery that has no meaning, or muddles that have no exit, but as mirrors for identity and as avenues for mission. In active surrender you set the future where it belongs, well in front of you. And you can see God around you right now with every step you take.

Lightning strikes, not at random but at what's most prepared and ready to receive the charge. Spirit comes upon those most ready and prepared to receive the fire. Redundancy readies us to connect, and preps us for the charge.

**Randomization:** A rut is a self-created exile from living. The key to *ressourcement* is staying out of ruts, routing and flouting the routines that grind out graves, keeping fresh and excited to receive the new. Did Jesus ever have a "to do" list, or did he live more "as he passed by?"

British novelist and Oxford professor Hermione Lee describes two kinds of reading: "Vertical" and "Horizontal."[336] Vertical reading is professional, orderly, productive and prescribed. Horizontal is private, anarchic, random, and promiscuous. For *ressourcement* to flourish, the horizontal and vertical must merge. The private and the productive become one. Another way of viewing randomization is how Søren Kierkegaard does in his book *Either/Or* (1843). Kierkegaard makes the case for crop rotation in life to curb boredom, keep the mental fields fertile and full of nutrients, and face the responsibilities of an ethical existence.[337]

Randomization is refined at some of its highest levels in the Japanese art of *zuihitsu*, a fascinating and unique genre of Japanese prose writing that combines informality, associative reasoning, intellectually spry speculations, and wide-ranging conversations hopping from subject to subject like frogs in a lily pond, the only thread holding it all together being the author's concerns and convictions.

*If habit is a second nature, it prevents us from knowing our first.*
MARCEL PROUST[338]

**Reason:** We live in a culture where thinking has become altogether marginalized in favor of feeling. A lot of our moral posturing, virtue signaling, and righteousness flagging is based on a penchant for feeling good about doing good without bothering about whether the good you are doing is actually doing any good.

"That's so emotional" now carries more weight than "That's so reasonable" or "That's so impactful." Apologetics forgets that today's faith needs to make emotional sense, not just rational sense.[339]

But when too many news flashes end in a head-shake response of "What are you thinking?" or "Did I just take a crazy pill?", the pendulum of non-thinking or group-thinking has swung too far. Especially in an era of "Artificial Intelligence," we need more human intelligence that comes from exercising our cerebral muscles like in the vigorous debates of an eighteenth-century coffee shop, or the table conversations about a Torah passage by five or six rabbis. When debate dies down or is squashed, gulags start popping up—intellectual gulags, social gulags, theological gulags.

Feelings are seldom found, or bound, in fine strands

## JESUS HUMAN

of logic. Our emotions are sentimental chains that tug on us, depending on who pulls first. No wonder the rise of "Radical Orthodoxy" and its rejection of modern modes of both rationalist faith and feeling faith in favor of more premodern, medieval-lived faith experiences which emphasize the importance of tradition, material culture, the body, and the sacraments.

Today the pillars of logic and reason are being toppled. Israeli historian Yuval Noel Harari in *Homo Deus* (2015) argues that "reason" and "liberalism" are Enlightenment fantasies or fictions ripe to be superseded by artificial intelligence. But there are certain foundations of the Enlightenment that we abandon at our peril: freedom of speech, freedom of religion, scientific inquiry, reason. We make a great mistake when we identify "secular rationality" with "reason." The "reason" of natural law may be quite different from the reason of "secular rationality." The default of reason is a rationality that transcends secular rationality.

---

> *The values of this Western civilization under the leadership of America have been destroyed. Those awesome symbolic towers that speak of liberty, human rights and humanity have been destroyed. They have gone up in smoke.*
> OSAMA BIN LADEN, OCTOBER 2001 INTERVIEW[340]

---

The Enlightenment enthroned reason as the foundational pillar and highest peak of civilization. In fact, the gift of France of the Statue of Liberty and its "lamp beside the golden door" had nothing to do with immigration but with the lamp of reason. The French gave no "freedom torch." They gave a "reason torch." Ironically, the first attempt in the history of the world to stamp out religious practice entirely was done in the name of reason during the last months of the French Revolution in 1793, when Notre Dame Cathedral was renamed the "Temple of Reason" and dedicated to memorializing the virtues of atheistic republicanism.

Reason needs the rapture and range of faith, and faith needs the rigor and refinement of reason.

---

*The first dictate of reason is ardently to love and revere the divine majesty, to whom we owe what we are and whatever happiness we can reach. Secondly, reason warns us and summons us to lead our lives as calmly and as cheerfully as we can, and to help all others in nature's fellowship to attain this good.*

THOMAS MORE, *UTOPIA* (1516), BOOK I, CHAPTER 16

---

When Jesus said he came to perfect the Law, he was not just talking about the Law of Moses but the Law of Nature as well.[341]

We are to give "reasons" for the hope set before us.

**Resonance:** In a culture with authentic aesthetics, the new metric of success is metrical: success is the resonance of an authentic voice. Those who never raise their voices can make themselves heard by the sheer resonance of their voice's authenticity.

The romance of resonance is partly in the Greek concept of syneidesis, which Augustine appropriated into Christian theology and the Protestant Reformers elevated to new heights. Syneidesis is a Greek word that means "conscience" or "consciousness" and is derived from the words syn ("with") and eidesis ("knowledge"). There is an inbuilt faculty that allows humans to pick up the difference between right and wrong. Resonance of the right brings conviction and duty; resonance of the wrong brings remorse and guilt. Syneidesis is another way of talking about the voice of the Spirit that good-vibes with truth and bad-vibes with evil, the inherent knowing that convicts us of sin and leads us to repentance. It is how we put on the mind of Christ, and knowing together we are consanguine with the consciousness or conscience of Christ.

The ultimate resonances of life occur not through the vibrations that hit the bones and skull, but through the vibrations of the heart. You can't truly succeed in life without resonance with Christ. Any "success" without Christ is more a succession of failures, disappointments, and sorrows. Our messes and misses can become God's successes and passes when we resonate with the Spirit.

**Rapture:** The ultimate rapture is not one that takes us out of this world, but one that takes us into this world for out-of-this-world experiences. In fact, recent research has revealed that the mind's function is partly to restrict what we experience in the world, otherwise to perceive the world in all its natural beauty and brilliance, would so capture and rapture us that we would be overcome and obliterated before we could reach maturity.[342]

Catholic Social Worker founder Dorothy Day (d. 1980)

defined rapture as "a burning fire of tenderness and love."[343] Both mythologist Joseph Campbell (d. 1987), whom George Lucas calls "my Yoda," and psychologist Abraham Maslow (d. 1970) talked incessantly about the hunger of this culture for "moments of rapture." Not something to believe in,[344] but the rapture of an experience of being alive like that described on the Song of Songs: "You have ravished my heart with a glance of your eyes."[345] Humans hunger for the rapture of a lifestory, especially the ravishment of a rapturous lifestory that snaps, crackles and pops.

The West's attraction to Buddhism is partly this romance of rapture without the straightjackets of beliefs or doctrines. The truth is that Buddhism is as creedal and dogmatic as anyone else. In fact, Zen demands disciplines of conformity and obedience that would bring screams from any self-respecting child of Western modernity.

Every rapture involves some rupture . . . sundering of our attachments and investments and attention.

The sixteenth-century Spanish noblewoman Teresa of Avila suffered from a self-diagnosed "embarrassment of raptures." She would float off into other realms of consciousness and faint when triggered by joy, remorse, beauty, and love. These kinds of "faintings" were not seen as weakness but as strength. In fact, in romance novels, "it is the greatest warriors and the greatest lovers who faint."[346]

JESUS HUMAN

#  is for Saga (Icelandic) Human

*The power is not in the light saber.
The power is in the story.*
THE MANDALORIAN

Every day, all of humanity is tending to some story, adding to a particular story for the good or ill of the rest of humanity. After all, we're all connected, part of the same story. And we're all super-spreaders.

*The Mandalorian* is a space-western television series, the first live-action series in the *Star Wars* franchise. It begins five years after the events of *Return of the Jedi* (1983), and revolves around the exploits of a lone bounty hunter whose mission is to protect "the Child." Whoever wields the thousand-year-old black-blade sword called the "Darksaber" has the power to rule the planet of Mandalore. But the power is not in the Darksaber, Moff Gideon explains to Mando during their duel in the finale of Season 2. "The power is in the story."

The human species is defined as homo sapiens or "wise human" because it is a story-addicted, story-addled species. The best **sagas** come from sages. And the most powerful sages are the best storytellers. Every great chef creates a menu that tells a story. Every great musician composes music that tells a story. Every great artist paints a picture that tells a story. "Our Story" is now on almost every great label.

Not just any story, but a grand, overarching **saga** or epic narrative that makes sense of life and the universe. It is time to buck the academic fashion that vulgarizes virtuoso visions: that says grand narratives have slithered to a halt; that builds on vignettes and blasts vivacious vistas as vexed or villainous; that any idea of global emancipation is dead in the water. The universe is vast and awing, past all imagining. It calls for an expansive and grand *saga* that can make sense of such a reality. You can hear this yearning from the streets themselves. Even in this nothing-is-true, everything-is-permissible culture,[347] the most trendy current response to something that once elicited a bobbing nod of "Amen to that!" or "For sure!" or "True Dat!" is now, "True Story."

We tell ourselves stories in order to live.[348]

We tell ourselves good stories in order to live well.

We tell ourselves Jesus stories in order to live Jesus.

Two of humanity's oldest pursuits are an evening activity and a morning quest. The evening activity is telling stories around the glow of a campfire. The morning quest is tracking and trailing in the savannah after the evening storytelling. The two are related in that you tell at night time what you tracked that morning after. In the morning you are a storycatcher. In the evening you are a storyteller.

⋄

*Religion sounds boring to some, contentious to others. To me it is a wonderful source of stories about what it is to be human.*
ENGLISH SCREENWRITER JIMMY MCGOVERN[349]

Moderns lost the ability to do both: track and tell. Graveyards became the place where the stories were stored.

Even indigenous peoples, who were known as the best animal-trackers and story-keepers, lost the skills of both. We are now in the midst of a massive revival of these two lost arts—storytelling and tracking. Indigenous peoples all over the world are hiring trackers to teach them tracking. The native bushmen of Botswana hired world-renowned tracker "Adrian" to teach them how to track in Africa. Many native American tribes, without any tradition of tracking, are only now hiring African trackers to teach them the ways of their ancestors. Few conferences are on more "bucket lists" than story-telling festivals. Graphicacy (digital literacy) has brought with it a revival of oracy (oral culture).

Some years ago, SpiritVenture Ministries (SVM) decided to bring these two lost arts—nature tracking and storytelling–into one African "Advance." We hired Callie Roos, a renowned tracker of the Big Five game in Africa, to show how to track wild animals on the ground at the Timbavati Game Reserve in South Africa. At the same time, I (Len) provided theological riffs on how to spot and track the Holy Spirit in the wilds of our post-modern culture. In the words of semiotics founder Charles Sanders Peirce, "we must not begin by talking pure ideas—vagabond thoughts that tramp the public highways without any human habitation—but must begin with people and their conversation." After Roos showed evidence of how animals sometimes track us when we think we are tracking them, we showed how the "Hound of Heaven" is often on our tracks, hunting and haunting us with the love of God and wooing us to Holy Life. To track the Spirit seeking us out of our hiding places to come into the light of God's presence is one of the greatest skills of contextual intelligence.³⁵⁰

The Bible story is story upon story, with one story nesting in another story like a matryoshka doll, where the meaning of a story can be found in another story. My Bible's Matthew-Revelation has 259 pages. Depending on how you define "narrative," 105–160 of those 259 pages are story.

Every word has behind it a back story, or what Virginia Woolf called a "beautiful cave" we must dig out and excavate, a cave full of "anecdote and memory." My home is not a man-cave but a story-cave. Everything in it tells a story, or is cleaned from the house as excess baggage. Humans fill their spaces, inside and out, with stories, not stuff. So, my house is stuffed with stories. One guest asked me after visiting my home, "What's the difference between this and hoarding?" I replied, "Consumers hoard stuff. Humans curate stories."

The Jesus story begins and ends in a cave story. An original Palestine manger was a stone trough, or ledge, or niche cut out of the wall of a stable low enough for animals to feed on the fodder. It became a wooden rack when St. Francis made the first creche in 1223. The tomb to which Jesus' body was taken was a stone cave, and his body put on a limestone ledge or slab. Early Christians were buried in the catacombs in little mangers dug out of walls by the fossores.

Jesus was a spelunker on a speleological mission. He came into our caves, was born and buried in our caves, in order to save us from cave-ins and free us from our caves to become human again. Jesus invited humans to come in from the cold—those who have disappeared into the cold caves of their possessions; those who have disappeared into the cold caves of their own consciousness; those who have disappeared into the cold black hole of politics; those who have disappeared into cold emotional caves of fear and shame that we use to numb our pain or evade dealing with our problems.

Jesus humans are speleologists too. Or in the words of Isaiah, which Jesus chose as his passage for his first sermon, we are here for a five-point mission:

> Preach good news to the poor,
> Bind up the brokenhearted,
> Recover sight for the blind,
> Proclaim freedom for the captives,
> Release from darkness the prisoners.[351]

If every word has behind it a back story, every story has behind it a root metaphor or etymon.[352] Get the metaphor right and everything else falls into place. Get the metaphor wrong, and everything falls apart. The quality of any outcome depends upon the carefulness with which the metaphors are selected and the story is told. The narraphoric[353] character of Scripture is what makes childhood readings of Bible tales have long tails. They take on a second-life inside our heads and hearts. Human lives are mapped by songs and stories, so we must choose our maps carefully.

This is as true for science as it is for religion. Early science, in the last half of the seventeenth century, was built on metaphors, which early scientists (the word wasn't coined until 1833) used to upend established and inherited notions about how things work. One scholar summarizes her findings

## ABECEDARIUM OF A JESUS HUMAN

with this conclusion: "Science is itself a literary trope."[354] The human imagination, fueled and fired by story and metaphor, was responsible for the development of early science. One of the best-known scientists of the twentieth century (second perhaps only to Albert Einstein), theoretical physicist Richard Feynman (d. 1988), pushed imagination as the key ingredient both in scientific advancement and in human understanding. Defining imagination as "the ability to see things in a new way, to see the connections between things that seem unrelated," he endorsed imagination as the essence of humanity. "Our imagination is stretched to the utmost, not, as in fiction, to imagine things which are not really there, but just to comprehend those things which are."[355]

Jesus, the ultimate art of the Almighty Artist, used stories, metaphors, signs, and symbols to communicate the truth about God.

Why did Jesus tell parables and use stories? Jesus answered the question himself. "For the same reason you put a lamp on a stand," he said. So why put a lamp on a stand? To make the light go further, and to see life better. What makes each of us human, a priceless treasure? We are the artwork of the divine, created to be the artist of our lives, the author of our story. What makes a Jesus human? Our invitation for Jesus to art and author our life story. We have the choice to be self-authored creatures or God-authored creations. God says to each human these words, in effect:

> You are not your own. You are not on your own. You are not alone, living in your own

> YOUniverse. You are precious in my sight. You are created in my own image, and I bought you with a price. Don't hang on to yourself and try to lift yourself up by your bootstraps. Let me hold you, hang on to you, and lift you up by my grace. Lose your life to find your life in me.

Sin is separation from the story. Salvation is reunification into the story. Christ is reunion. We never really know what sin is, or lift the live veil of evil, until Jesus gets hold of us. The gospel is not a self-help manual, but a Jesus-saves rescue mission. We can't be the humans God made us to be without help. We need God's help, and we need help from each other. The oxymoron "self-help groups" says all that needs to be said.

Salvation is God's transfiguration of us into what it is to be human and our re-creation in Christ. Sin is the writing our own story with fictions that give us immunity and amnesty and innocence from our complicity in the ways of the world that are cruel and unjust.

There are no unmixed motives. The best and the worst in us are a hair-trigger's distance. We all lie with stories to protect ourselves from rejection and conflict. A brother was seen pulling his sister's hair. Then he kicked her in the shins. When his mother pulled him to the side and rebuked him, she said "What got into you, son? And don't tell me the devil make you do it!" The little boy replied, "The devil told me to pull her hair. But I added the kick." We all have our own unique "kicks" we add to living below our best, to our story of being less than fully human.

There is nothing that a story doesn't make better—or worse. In a world where stories are being used for corporate branding, self-serving promotions, and red-herrings of disinformation, we need an education in the humanities more than ever to teach us how to recognize the bogus, noxious myths, the deceptive storytelling, and deconstruct the dominant stories.[356] We also need to learn how to do whole-story theology. When we don't know the whole story, only pieces and verses, missing the ligatures and links, we end up filling in the blanks with doctrines and dogmas. First, connect the dots of the story, not the dots of the doctrines. The best theology is derived out of, not delivered from, The Story.

The human story begins in a garden—a place of bounty, beauty and blessedness. By taking control of our own story, we quickly transitioned to a culture of boundaries, limits, lies, prohibitions, and morality. Corporate ethicist Susan Liautaud argues that ethics are not about doing the right things, but that "above all, ethics are about creating the story we want for our lives and all the lives we are privileged to touch."[357] But if ethics is not about "the right thing," it is more important than ever that it be "the right story." In the prophetic words of Fanny Crosby, "This is Our Story, This is Our Song:" the Jesus story of Goodness, Beauty, and Truth.

## JESUS HUMAN

*The ideals which have lighted my way, and time after time have given me new courage to face life cheerfully, have been Kindness, Beauty, and Truth.*

ALBERT EINSTEIN[358]

##  is for Satyagraha (Indian) Human

The word "*satyagraha*" is associated with Gandhi's defense of nonviolence. "*Satyagraha*" was one of the most important words to Martin Luther King, Jr., a word he learned thanks to E. Stanley Jones. But the power of that word for King wasn't what we have come to mean by it: "passive resistance." Rather, King was mesmerized by this word and built his ministry on this word because of what Gandhi really meant by it: "truth force" or "the force of truth."

If there is one word for the twenty-first century, it is "*satyagraha*:" the force of truth. Jesus didn't preach non-resistance to evil. He was resistant to evil and forceful in his resistance. What he did preach was forceful but nonviolent resistance to evil. In a culture that is governed by the love of force, God's dream would govern us by a very different set of relationships: the force of love and the force of truth.

Most of us will not be social revolutionaries of peace who periodize history by turning the world upside down as Gandhi, or King, or even their mentor Tolstoy. Though God knows we need a few.

But truth will once again be a force if we can voice truth while living it. Many people love to call a spade a spade, but few people like to dig holes. To speak about immorality, greed, and the cruelty of our species is one thing. And we need to be voices for the defeat of evil. But for truth to become a force, we will need to be a people

## JESUS HUMAN

who live in the same truth of which we speak. Jesus was not "meek and mild" when he turned the other cheek, or when he asked for humanity's forgiveness while he was being tortured and killed. He was living **satyagraha**, the force of truth. He would not let evil conquer him by turning him into its image. He would not return evil for evil and insult for insult. Crime writer and poet Dorothy L. Sayers captured this beautifully in one of my all-time favorite quotes:

> The people who hanged Christ never accused him of being a bore—on the contrary; they thought him too dynamic to be safe. It has been left to succeeding generations to muffle up that shattering personality and surround him with an atmosphere of tedium . . . a fitting household pet for pale curates and pious old ladies. He was tender to the unfortunate, patient with honest inquirers, humble; but he insulted clergymen . . . referred to King Herod as "that fox"; went to parties in disreputable company . . . assaulted indignant tradesmen and threw them and their belongings out of the temple. . . . Officialdom felt that the established order of things would be more secure without him. So they did away with God in the name of peace and quietness.[359]

But by forgiving and loving and suffering all the way

down, he showed the truth of God and love and forgiveness and other-centeredness is bigger than the worst that untruth has to offer.

*Bad times, hard times—this is what people keep saying; but let us live well and times shall be good. We are the times. Such as we are, such are the times.*
SAINT AUGUSTINE OF HIPPO, SERMON #30 (D. 430)[360]

What if Jesus' followers were known for being the kindest people, even in intense discussions? What if Jesus' followers were known as the people who cared more for their neighborhood block and all the people there than anyone else? What if all people of faith committed to no more protesting and being angry on TV? What if kindness is the force of truth? Maybe people would see that people of faith are not claiming to have the truth so much as the force of truth has a claim and a hold on us?

"***Satyagraha***" is as odd and random a notion as the bald, skinny, white-robed, gold-skinned Gandhi. But a true kind of human is different from the general ruck. A ***Satyagraha*** Human is an odd dream, a peculiar dream, a go-against-the-grain dream.

There is a phrase bandied about: "I'm just an ordinary mortal." There is nothing "ordinary" about a human being. A Jesus human is an ordinary mortal, but an odd mortal, a funky mortal, or in more biblical language, a "peculiar mortal."[361] Jesus characters play against type. To follow Jesus is like clicking that "I'm not a robot" box. To subscribe to a podcast or blog, you have to prove first that you're a human. No subscription goes through without first clicking the "I'm not a robot." box. If you confirm your ***Satyagraha*** humanity, you can proceed.

The beauty of the gospel *is* its ***Satyagraha*** strangeness. Perhaps we are afraid to acknowledge the surpassing strangeness of our God.

There is a lot to love about the Church of England. There is a lot to worry about the Anglican church.[362] But who can't but like the Anglican church's two kinds of parishes: ordinary (under a bishop and hierarchy) and "peculiar." Princess Diana was buried in a "peculiar" church.

God calls us to be a "peculiar" people. NOT ordinary. In the song that made Canadian Avril Lavigne famous, "Anything but Ordinary," she sings of a ***Satyagraha*** Human:

Somebody save my life

I'd rather be anything but ordinary, please.[363]

We all have favorite titles and favorite books. One of mine is titled *Rare Books and Rarer People.*[364] You know that Jesus liked anything-but-ordinary, "rarer people" because he chose odd ducks and "rare birds"[365] to be his disciples: only a few had ordinary jobs, only a few had compliant dispositions. Who did he call? Callous-handed, hot-tempered, foul-mouthed fishermen (why four of them?). Those greedy, spinster tax collectors (think personal injury attorneys). Those freaky, survivalist, anti-government, weapons-stockpiling, racist types (zealots). Illiterates, women with sullied reputations around town, and other women who didn't fit

## ABECEDARIUM OF A JESUS HUMAN

the stereotype for their gender (first female disciples). In Jerusalem it appears that Jesus let his disciples carry daggers for self-defense, daggers which were most likely with them at the Last Supper.[366] Yet disciples of Jesus are more inclined to give an arm than to be armigerous, more inclined to bare an arm than to bear arms, more embodiments of the force of love than the love of force.

Do you know what the ultimate is in cheap and ugly spirituality? . . . This will make you feel better . . . Feel-good, feel-better spirituality is *SO NOT* the odd dream of the covenant, not under the covenant with Abraham, Moses, nor under the new covenant with Jesus. The promise of the covenant is that we will be transformed into something unheard of, something so odd—a kingdom of priests; and something so new—holy humans; something so primal—pure humans, that other people will be threatened by these new kinds of humans. My friend Jim Carlson puts it like this: Where culture says, "You can become a Rock Star," the gospel says, "You can become a REAL PERSON." Again, watch any documentary on any rock star. It's hell being a rock star. Becoming a rock star is often to kiss being a real human being good-bye.

*Our concern is not how to worship in the catacombs but rather how to remain human in the skyscrapers.*
JEWISH THEOLOGIAN ABRAHAM HESCHEL (D. 1992)

In a world of heavily-rouged religions and heavily-rouged people, "real" people of rounded faith like Gandhi and King can seem mightily weird. But Jesus helps us become NOT

JESUS HUMAN

more straight-edged, strait-laced, ladder-backed and proud human beings . . . but more odd-shaped, more "rounded," more complete and whole as HUMAN BEINGS. "Rounded" human beings who are bent over to hear and heed the cries of this world. You can't hear them unless you bend down and show some humility.

Do your eyes pop out of your sockets when you see pictures of the hungry and homeless, the sick and the dying, the stunted young, and the blunted old? People are crying out for bread, for housing, for clean water, for medicine, for conversation, for love.

Can you hear the cries of the 850 million people who will go to bed hungry tonight?

Can you hear the cries of the 1 billion people today who lack access to safe drinking water?

Can you hear the cries of the 10 million children who will die this year before their 5th birthday?

A Jesus human dreams a **Satyagraha** Dream of righteousness and peace and justice FOR ALL—a dream for the downtrodden and upended, the overburdened and the underprivileged, the outsider and the infighter, the LGBTQI+ people . . . what is this starting to sound like? The Sermon on the Mount, maybe?

This is where the real danger of an "other-worldly," "this-world-is-not-my-home-I'm-only-passing-through" view of Jesus and his followers can be a real danger. In a passion to hold to the "doctrine" of a fallen humanity, needed-to-be-saved-into-heaven, moralistic faith begins to even blame those who suffer, who "have not." This is not the passion of Pentecost.

"Well, it's not their fault. They won't work."

"You know, it's their religion. They spend too much time praying or meditating or worshiping animals or something. That's why they have no food."

"This is clearly the consequence of their sin, who said they should have so much sex? Keep your pants on, and you won't get AIDS."

If people who read the Bible believe we are all "sinners," then that includes religious types, family-values champions, and those who are faithful to their spouses. When did selfishness, hard-heartedness, pride, and greed get taken off the list of sins? Jesus' beatitudes raised up the meek and lowly, offering them victory as their "least-of-these" stealth tactics flew under the radar of powers and principalities.

In fact, in the Jesus Dream there is no "other," only oneanother. The very category of "other" is a category mistake. Any naming of some as the "other," no matter how well-intentioned that calling out may be, is wrong. Any "othering" is too much "othering" going on when the very category of "other" is to give away the gospel itself. Jesus knew no other. Only "one another." There is only *allelon,* a Greek word meaning "oneanother." Over sixty times in the Scripture we are given the imperative of "oneanothering," or "love one another." One can no more separate oneself from oneanother than a wave can separate itself from the ocean.[367] To be is to love one another and to live for one another. The incarnation is the supreme sacrament of "oneanotherness," God becoming "one-of-us."

You might say, "Love your neighbor as Jesus." Or you might say, "Love your neighbor as yourself." Either way, you're saying the same thing. Your neighbor is yourself. And your neighbor is Jesus. Jewish philosopher Emmanuel Levinas (1906–1995) called this human solidarity, this oneanothering, a form of "expiation."[368] The call to be human is the expiating call of the incarnation to be flesh to our neighbor, to be blood and bone to our brothers and sisters.

In *The Brothers Karamazov* (1880), the dying boy Markel speaks of the nonexistence of "other," only *allelon*, only "oneanother:"

> "Everyone of us is responsible for everyone else in every way. And I most of all." Mother could not help smiling at that. She wept and smiled at the same time. "How are you," she said, "most of all responsible for everyone? There are murderers and robbers in the world, and what terrible sin have you committed that you should accuse yourself before everyone else?" "Mother," he said, "you must realise that everyone is really responsible for everyone and everything. I don't know how to explain it to you, but I feel it so strongly that it hurts."[369]

When we facetiously ask, "Am I my brother's keeper?" who are we imitating? Believing in the freedom of the

## ABECEDARIUM OF A JESUS HUMAN

individual, in the pragmatics of capitalism, does not mean we are not responsible for oneanother. NO human dies or lives to himself.

In spite of academe's fetishizing the category of the "other," Jesus recognized no such thing as an "other," only brothers and sisters and other body parts. Who is your flesh and blood? Jesus said that everyone is. Jesus redefined "family" to include the whole human family. Can you say to everyone, your neighbor and your nemesis, history's first love poem: "You are flesh of my flesh and bone of my bone; and I am flesh of your flesh and bone of your bone."[370] Or in Jesus' exact words, "Inasmuch as you've done it unto the least of these."[371]

"Inasmuch" extends to those who differ and disagree with us. The diversity of moral values across cultures has never been more visible: complex moral questions abound and surround us involving genital circumcision, honor killings, and abortion, with differing views on capital punishment, economics, and politics. A Jesus human refuses to treat other human beings as enemies, and refuses to be an enemy to anyone.

In a pop culture obsessed with the real historical origins of Jesus' family and other relationships, what did he say about his mother and his brothers? Did he give us a biography? Did he say they should be exalted? He said, if we have God's heart, we are there. We are just as important.

Leave it to Gandhi to take Jesus' "inasmuch" rule and make it into the #1 test of whether or not you are living God's dream:

> Whenever you are in doubt, or when the self becomes too much with you, apply the following test. Recall the face of the poorest and the weakest person whom you may have seen, and ask yourself, if the step you contemplate is going to be of any use to them . . . then you will find your doubts and your self melt away.

The ***Satyagraha*** Dream is a dream of peace, a shalom dream. But there is a new name for peace: justice. Peace is not the absence of conflict (that is death) or the absence of force. Peace is the presence of creative friction and the right kind of force: the truth force of justice and love. The love of God displayed on the cross of Christ is not a simple peace. It is truth peace. It unmasks the forces of secular power and religious control and shows them for what they are: destructive, inhumane, scared, untruths. We are not simply people of cute flowers and pleasant verses read from the Psalms. We are force-of-truth people. Justice and mercy seen in the blood and guts and overcoming love of the Son of Man. The biblical dream is full of conflict and force: turning swords into ploughs that furrow a path to the future, and turning spears into pruning hooks that provide fruit for a hungry and hurting world.[372] It's a creative dream. A dream that seems impossible. A dream that only with God is possible.

# ABECEDARIUM OF A JESUS HUMAN

*[We need a faith strong enough]*
*to hew from the mountain*
*of despair a stone of hope.*
LEN'S FAVORITE QUOTE FROM MARTIN LUTHER KING, JR.[373]

A Jesus human is not someone who becomes a spiritual person, or enters an enlightened state, or gets converted and joins the "born-again" brigade, or becomes a "better person" or a "better lover." God's dream for humanity is that Christ will so live in us, and we will so live in Christ, that we become "real people," well-rounded human beings. People who live and enjoy and taste all of life: love and sacrifice, friends and making friends out of enemies, becoming okay with how we are—because we live believing in the importance of everyone else, finding true love as we learn to give it all away. Going deep with God, by going deep with the world. And that "realness" and "roundedness" only comes when human nature is redeemed and restored by the healing power where love proceeds, truth follows, and grace abounds.

It's a **Satyagraha** Dream, being a true kind of human.

**is for Scenius (Urban) Human**

British musician and visual artist Brian Eno coined the word "*scenius*" to convey the "genius" that is embedded in scenes of people drawing on each other's talents and group intelligence rather than in genes of individual intelligence or isolated brains. If we knew the back-story of every "genius," all true "genuis" needs *scenius*.

The geography of *scenius* has several important features.

Firstly, there is mutual appreciation, which is like motivational peer pressure.

Secondly, there is a rapid exchange of tools and techniques, in which as soon as something is invented, it's widely shared among everyone within the *scenius* as everyone within the *scenius* is united by a common conversation and dream.

Thirdly, there are the network effects of success, which means whenever there is a success, it's celebrated by everyone within the *scenius*.

Fourthly, within the *scenius* there is a local tolerance for the novelties, which means that renegade, maverick, unusual, and revolutionary ideas are protected from tampering by a buffer zone. **Scenius**, in other words, is a flourishing space for nonconformity.

Thomas Aquinas loved to quote Aristotle, who said, "We should love both kinds of people: those whose opinions we follow, and those whose opinions we reject. For both study to find the truth and, in this way, both give us assistance."[374]

ABECEDARIUM OF A JESUS HUMAN

#  is for Sentipensante (Spanish: Sentimientos) Human

The dream of a true kind of human is a ***Sentipensate*** Dream.

***Sentipensante*** is a Spanish word meaning "feeling-thinking." It was invented by fishermen off the Columbian coast, who fused two Spanish words in an attempt to describe the secret of their success in fishing. It was introduced to the Latin American world by Uruguayan author Eduardo Galeano, who heard it used by these fishermen and then referenced it to define language that speaks the truth.[375] The word is becoming popular, and may become as popular in the next twenty years as the Nguni languages word "Ubuntu" became in the past two decades.

In a "Devi" Yoga studio in Arizona, an instructor (Geoffrey Taylor) is the originator of his own system of Vinyasa style Yoga called "***Sentipensante***" or thinking and feeling. He is leading the way for developing Yoga in Latin America and a senior teacher at studios around the globe. He is a researcher, writer, scholar, lecturer, and master-level trainer in the world of Yoga.

As early as 2006, educational consultant and professor Laura Rendón spoke at the Association of American Colleges and Universities (AAC&U) with the title of her talk, "The Pedagogy of ***Sentipensante***: Recasting Institutional Core Agreements." Rendon challenged educators to revamp their institutional belief systems in order to move beyond the monoculturalism that pervades universities with "Western structures of knowledge." Mental knowing is not the only type of intelligence—we must promote all forms of knowledge, including emotional knowledge, musical knowledge, and especially the "deep wisdom" that comes with multifaceted learning. Inspired by the writings of Eduardo Galeano, Rendon refers to a new global pedagogy as "***sentipensante***," or "sensing/thinking": a "multi-human" approach that "unites what I call the poetry of teaching and learning with the rationality of teaching and learning."[376]

The key to a **Sentipensante** Dream is it brings together two opposites that have complicated, uncomfortable, intimate relationships: feeling and thinking, heart and head, right-brain and left-brain. For example, my Ph.D. course of study was a rigorous training in discarding subjectivity, banishing any writing with feeling, and decrying emotionalism. Toward this end I developed in my studies a sceptic's tool-kit full of well-sharpened instruments of objective dissection and doubt without so much as a pound of subjectivity or a pinhead of faith. I was trained as a professional historian: good professional historians keep imagination at bay, metaphors buried, and autobiography behind locked doors.

*As he thinks in his heart, so is he.*
PROVERBS 23:7 NKJV[377]

God's Dream for a true kind of human brings together and binds together the head and the heart. In a **Sentipensante** human, note which comes first: feeling comes before thinking, which then filters the feeling. In fact, one could make the case that to think clearly, you need to get your heart pumping. That's why to learn something "by heart" is to take it to heart, which means it becomes part of your entire body. "By heart" learning is not just to memorize something, but to so integrate it into your *sentipensante* that it becomes second nature.

Here is the best thing Henri Nouwen has written, and that's saying a lot since he's written so many great things:

> The great challenge is living your wounds through, instead of thinking them through. It is better to cry than to worry, better to feel your wounds deeply than to understand them, better to let them into your silence than to talk about them.
>
> The choice you face constantly is whether you are taking your wounds to your head or to your heart. In your head you can analyze them. . . . But no final healing is likely to come from that source. You need to let your wounds go down into your heart. Then you can live through them and discover that they will not destroy you. Your heart is greater than your wounds.[378]

But a **Sentipensate** Dream means more than just the solution to a Big Head is a Big Heart. A **Sentipensate** Dream is by definition a double dream, a dream that brings together opposites not to achieve some kind of synthesis, or

## JESUS HUMAN

to maintain some dialectic, but to live the luminous and harmonious mystery of the paradox. In fact, some scholars argue that there is one feature of human cognition that separates us from the rest of creation: the human ability to hold in our heads multiple orders of intentionality and conceptuality.[379]

Here's a blazing example. Many of us grew up with a parent who had this favorite saying: "Every saint has a past; every sinner a future."

Can you hear it?

Biblical truth has poles, opposite poles that make each other necessary, opposed extremes that need each other and form a mutually sustaining relationship. Christianity is a very complicated religion, dynamic not dynastic, because of this holding together two opposites at the same time. The word Islam means "submit." The word Israel means "struggle."

Islam is derived from the root term selama, "to surrender to or obey" God. This is why Islam is a religion of law.

Judaism is based on the Hebrew word for "struggle," especially a struggle with God. This is what Judaism is—a religion of protest and questioning.

Christianity is based on the word for "little Christ," the root of which is followership, friendship, and participation. This is why Christianity is an anti-religion[380] religion of relationship. And deep relationship has an entrance requirement: a submission of oneself to another. To host the risen and rising Christ inserts into the relationship "Perfect Submission, Perfect Delight" ("Blessed Assurance").

Call this dynamic struggle the paradoxy of orthodoxy. To

## ABECEDARIUM OF A JESUS HUMAN

think the unthinkable . . . is itself a paradox; to dream the undreamable . . . is itself a paradox.

Dietrich Bonhoeffer liked to talk about "The Beyond." But it was always "The Beyond . . . In our Midst." The Beyond, The Kingdom among us, is here now. Orthodoxy says Jesus is fully human and Jesus is fully divine. That is a logical contradiction, and by definition a logical contradiction is a falsehood. What's the truth? Jesus is fully human, or Jesus is fully divine. Which is it? "Yes: Yes I believe, help thou my unbelief."

Orthodoxy says God is One and God is Three: what's the truth?

"Yes I believe, help thou my unbelief."

Orthodoxy says God is transcendent–the God beyond— and that God is immanent–the God within: what's the truth?

"Yes I believe, help thou my unbelief."

The despairing cry of "My God, my God, why have you forsaken me?" which Jesus sang from the cross (the beginning of Psalm 22) ends with the triumphant cry of "It is finished" (the ending of Psalm 22).[381]

In non-theological terms, Christians must learn to live stereoscopically, with bi-focal vision: to hold two opposite things together, not blending them or conflating them or reconciling them, but bringing them together until they symphonize at a higher level. Like those magic 3-D pictures called stereograms, where computer-generated dots and patterns that appear flat suddenly pop out, and turn into something three-dimensional when you bring two poles together and they breed in your mind to bring you to a higher dimension.

Or to a grueling headache—seeing those dimensions for the first time can be painful!

This is Truth with a capital "T:" what appear to be opposites are really lesser truths that explode in capital "T" truth when they are brought together, like a battery explodes with energy and power once its positive and negative poles are connected. The problem with one pole of truth is that it's a profound half-truth; and no matter how profound, to every half-truth there's another half.

In theological terms, this **Sentipensate** dream of a new kind of human is cruciform living: when we bring together The Word, the vertical, with the flesh, the horizontal; when the vertical energies of the universal are connected to the horizontal energies of the particular. Live without verticality, and you live a subhuman life. Live without horizontality and you live a nonhuman life. A true kind of human bears the beams of love for God, and love for neighbor. The way to the universal is always through the particular. In the words of Swiss Catholic physician and theologian Adrienne von Speyr: "Love for one fellow human being always includes love for OTHER human beings and, in the last analysis, love for ALL human beings."[382]

A true kind of human *double dreams* man-on-the-moon dreams and man-in-the-gutter dreams; a double-dare dream with one foot in the garden of Eden, and the other foot in the grave. A double dream is a dream for the poor, *and* a dream for the rich.

# ABECEDARIUM OF A JESUS HUMAN

*Serve the poor, and the rich will come.*
WHAT GOD TOLD PASTOR JOHN KING,
RIVERSIDE COMMUNITY CHURCH,
AT THE FOUNDING OF DREAM CENTER, PEORIA, ILLINOIS

The poet John Donne must have known a lot of pointy-headed people because he observed how that the head points upward, while the heart points downward.[383] A true kind of human dreams of a ***sentipensante*** faith that brings together heart and head, the up and the down, the inwardly mobile and the outwardly mobile.

A ***Sentipensante*** Dream brings together this world as a place of oppression, injustice, disease, greed, and despair, and connects it with this world as a place of beauty, art, altruism, and joy.

A ***Sentipensante*** Dream thinks big—our world is part of 140 billion galaxies[384]—and a double dream thinks small—each cell in your body has as many working parts as a Boeing 777, and you have ten thousand trillion cells in your body, each one of which contains six feet of DNA.

Call it double exposure; call it counterpoint; call it paradox; call it double-ring—a Jesus human always rings twice. Call it the Jesus flip; call it whatever: a ***Sentipensante*** human faces the miracle of a new day with two opposing dreams: Memento Mori—live as if this could be the last day of your life; but simultaneously with the dream of *Memento Mori & Carpe Manana*—live and dream as if this could be the first day of the rest of your life.

## JESUS HUMAN

A Jesus human by nature has a paradoxical mind-set. Our normal state of existence as humans is paradox and contradiction. For Gregory of Nyssa (d. 394), to be human is to be grounded in paradox. To be human is to be finite and at the same time to participate in the transcendent. This makes every human being a paradox by default, a "soaring stasis" as he put it, as "the more the soul participates in God the more she recognizes that God transcends her as much as before."[385]

In every human there are always two points of reference, not oppositional opposites but true polar opposites which mean they need each other for the planet to spin. Paradox is not oxymoronic but magnetic. A magnetic field of attraction is created by paradox, by polar opposites; antipathy and aversion are created by oxymorons.

The unified human life is a dynamic equilibrium of two sides which form a single, living reality: light and dark; waters above and waters below; earth and sea; conservation and innovation; reverence and rebellion. A faith that has "dynamic equilibrium" makes connections, leverages interdependencies, and platforms synergies. But a faith with "dynamic equilibrium" only works if there is an overarching higher mission, a meta-narrative that can embrace and embed both opposites. Orthodoxy is paradoxy.[386]

As a **Sentipensante** human, my faith is getting more simple, more childlike, and "second naivete" while my theology is getting more complex, more adult, and mature. In English we might call it "simplexity," but in Japanese the word "Shibusa" conveys the harmony of simplicity and complexity that come from the plain, subtle, nuanced, unobtrusive beauty of "Shibui."

An adult theology is one that can "rightly divide the word of truth" and see the subtle nuances and switchback complexities of the doctrinal scaffolding of faith. A simple faith is one that "becomes" (as Jesus put it) that "child" that desires only to be in the presence of the Father . . . whether working in the garage, shooting hoops, or simply "being" in a parent's presence whether "doing" anything or not. This is the desired kindling that allows that fire within to blaze anew to witness to Emmanuel, God WITH Us.

JESUS HUMAN

 is for Shalom (Hebrew: שולם) Human

> *Humanity is being taken to the point where it will have to choose between suicide and adoration.*
> TEILHARD DE CHARDIN[387]

When mind, body, and spirit are harmonized, each to the other, all with God, you enter a state of what some call health and wholeness, others call holiness, still others call ***shalom***, or what we call most fully human. A better translation of "All things work together for good" might be "God synergizes life into the harmony of ***Shalom*** for those who love."[388]

***Shalom*** is one of those almost untranslatable Hebrew words that have a cluster of meanings that pertain both to the "in here" and the "out there." In this one word, all dualities are brought together and categories like sacred and secular, clean and profane collapse. The ***Shalom*** WordCloud features concepts like completeness, wholeness, serenity, security, harmony, presence of reconciliation, and restoration. The Psalmist directs us: *bakesh **shalom**—*seek peace.[389] ***Shalom*** is not some static place of peace and quiet. ***Shalom*** is dynamic, pursuing, and seeking. There are infinite amounts of fibers and scraps of fabric that make up a community. What ***shalom*** does is weave it all together into a glorious tapestry of beauty. Every human is living art. ***Shalom***, God's peace, makes it into an exquisite piece of fine art.

The explosion scholarship of the past fifty years exploring

various aspects of "spiritual formation" is in equal measure fascinating and difficult. Difficult because humans are complex systems made up of more than spiritual components. The word "spiritual" is served up fast and unfussily. But humans are more than "spiritual beings." Humans also have physical, emotional, intellectual, and social requirements to be healthy and whole. British poet Geoffrey Hill (d. 2016), when questioned about the much-discussed difficulty of his own poetry, responded, "human beings are difficult" and that "poetry should reflect the difficulty of human beings."[390] To become fully human is to develop a holistic human formation, not just spiritual formation, that engages the totality of human difficulty, the entirety of complex systems in God's design to become the best humans we can be.

All four gospels record Jesus being "moved with compassion."[391] That word "moved" is both an emotion and a motion word. Compassion is at the heart of the God. God's first self-description beyond lordship is "compassionate" as in "the compassionate and gracious God."[392] The word compassion comes from the Greek "pasch" meaning "experience" or "suffer with." There is no true compassion without the willingness to experience someone on their terms and suffer with them. Compassion is a generosity that springs from human nature at its best while on the road of life.

Augustine had a marvelous phrase, "the whole Christ," head and members. Jesus' home town of Nazareth is derived from the Hebrew ne·tser, meaning "branch." Jesus of Nazareth did not see himself separate from his disciples: "I am the vine, you are the branches." What is more, "my Father is the vinegrower." The Incarnation goes all the way down and into the farthest branches. Branches are pruned to bear greater fruit, but only those branches surging with sap will come to fruition. If there is no sap flowing, the branches aren't pruned but plucked and burnt. There is but one fruit—the fruit of love.

When Jews say "Shabbat *shalom*–Sabbath peace" to family and friends after an exhausting week, it means far more than "have a peaceful and restful tomorrow." What is really being said is: May you be restored to wholeness on the blessed Sabbath. After a bruising and battering week, may Sabbath heal and restore your **shalom**. A **Shalom** human does not banish blemishes and bruises and brokenness, but comes clean with their neediness and helplessness and trusts God to bless others and be blessed through the cracks.

Brokers of brokenness abound. Brokers of healing are hard to find, except among the broken themselves. The story of the ten lepers is testimony to the neediness of each human in our common humanity.[393] As lepers, the ten lepers were all together. Once they were healed, they became separate as Samaritan or Jew. The Samaritan could not enter the temple with the Jew. The bonds of our brokenness make us more welcoming and human.

The day before his execution, Bonhoeffer was asked by his fellow prisoners to preach the homily for the service they patched together. Liturgically it was Low Sunday (the Sunday after Easter), but Bonhoeffer chose to preach from this text: "By his wounds we are healed."[394] At the break of dawn on 09 April 1945, he was hanged. Some of his last words were

## ABECEDARIUM OF A JESUS HUMAN

later retold by a captured RAF pilot: "This is for me the end, the beginning of life."

A ***Shalom*** human is more than the sum of their wounds. But there is truth wound around our wounds. When you graft something together, you graft wound-to-wound.[395] The story of God's love affair with humanity does not only include the "best and the brightest," with the most well-toned bodies, well-turned minds, and well-tuned temperaments. It also includes the disabled, the deformed, the weak, the wounded.

---

*The wound is the place where the Light enters you.*
ATTRIBUTED TO THIRTEENTH-CENTURY PERSIAN POET RUMI

---

We have been slow to understand this. Not until 1983 was disability removed as grounds for refusal for consideration for the priesthood in the Roman Catholic church. At least fifteen percent of the world's population lives with a disability. What a treasure trove of assets. Too often the church views these brothers/sisters as "impaired" subjects, or objects of our compassion. The world is often better at inclusion than the church, which must come to see people with disabilities not as awkward problems for ministry, but as equal partners in ministry.

There is no shortage of vocations, and God has not ceased calling. Whether we are listening is another matter. Five times Moses flashes his "That's not my gift," Get-Out-Of-Jail-Free card when God calls him out.

## JESUS HUMAN

Five Reasons Moses gives for saying No-Way to Yah-weh:
1. I'm a nobody.
2. Under whose authority do I do this?
3. I have a speech defect.
4. What if they laugh at me or don't believe me?
5. Send someone else.

The boundaries of our service are not set by our gifts or strengths. God works through rather than around human weakness. We bless others naturally with our gifts. We bless others supra-naturally with our weaknesses. God's strength is made perfect not in our vivacity but in our vulnerability. A **Shalom** human's greatest blessings in life will come not through strengths but through wounds and weaknesses.

The person in my life who has taught me more about what it means to be human than any other person on planet Earth is a person who is defined as "special needs" and seen as deficient in much of what supposedly makes us human.[396] When we remove this reflecting pool of humanity from our midst, whether through abortion or genetic manipulation, we are making the planet less human and dehumanizing ourselves. Woundedness makes us stronger in the same way adding impurities to a material (e.g., aluminum) can strengthen it, stiffen it, and make it serviceable. Pure aluminum is too soft to be of any use without impurities.

We are also throwing our "perfectness" in the face of a disabled Savior who sits at the right hand of the Father, interceding on our behalf, for a wounded world and a world-worn humanity, with wounded hands and feet. Jesus took the wounds with him into eternity. A **Shalom** human is not a perfect human but a total human.

---

> *A congregation without disabled people accepted into the life of the church is a disabled church.*
> SYSTEMATIC THEOLOGIAN JURGEN MOLTMANN[397]

---

The divine became human so that the human could participate in the divine. When Jesus ascended, he did not leave his humanity behind. He took his humanity with him into the triune relationship. Through Jesus, humans have entered the divine life. In the words of Pope Francis: "The Ascension of Jesus into heaven acquaints us with this deeply consoling reality on our journey: in Christ, true God and true man, our humanity was taken to God. Christ opened the path to us."[398]

The Apostles Creed tells us that until Judgment Day, Jesus "is seated at the right hand of God the Father Almighty." But when Stephen is stoned, Jesus stands to stand with him in his pain, suffering, and death. In your pain and suffering, Jesus stands with you, and stands to greet you when you enter God's presence. The open wounds become closed scars upon the Revelation 10:6 angelic announcement, "Time is no more." At the end of Revelation, THE LAMB WINS. The story ends with a meal: the marriage supper of the Lamb.

An old legend tells about the devil appearing to St. Martin of Tours (316–397) in the form of Christ. Martin looked him over carefully, and then asked him testily: Where are your wounds?

A Christ without wounds, or a church without wounds, or a faith without wounds, is a liar and a deceiver. We are called, like "Twin" Thomas, to touch the wounds of our world and in that touching find "My Lord and my God!"

---

*Crown him the Lord of love;*
*behold his hands and side,*
*rich wounds, yet visible above,*
*in beauty glorified;*
"CROWN HIM WITH MANY CROWNS" (1851), VERSE 3

---

Shamayim is the Hebrew word for "heaven" and denotes a component of the cosmos, the other elements being the earth (erets) and the underworld (sheol). **Shalom** Shamayim is an encounter of the Spirit that leaves you alive and aglow with life. **Shalom** Shamayim comes to humans who touch the wounds of humanity, the wounds of the poor, disabled, addicted. **Shalom** Shamayim comes to humans who hear the cries of the wounded, the cries of the poor. **Shalom** Shamayim is experienced when humans hear the cries of the earth itself, the wounds of our world. **Shalom** Shamayim comes to those who go around wading, trekking the deep for the wounds of this world and lifting them to the Wounded One. Or perhaps pulling them out towards the Wounded One?

There are two more features of the **Shalom** human that need highlighting: creation itself, and the death that each of us owes to life. Both of these are often omitted when talking about **Shalom**.

First, the nature, creational component to **Shalom**. Poet/farmer Wendell Berry insists it is a mistake to assume that there is a "divisibility between nature and humanity" while at the same time he admits it is wrong to claim that there is no difference between the two. "Our problem, exactly, is that the human and the natural are indivisible, and yet are different."[399] Inuit culture talks about the feeling of "*lilira*" when in the presence of nature: "an awed, respectful and slightly nervous feeling" toward all of creation that governs how one daily lives.

It was that "lilira" that was missing in how Europeans treated the outdoors. Artist/ornithologist John James Audubon (d. 1851) complained about the number of crows farmers killed each year, encouraging agrarians to be "less presumptuous in their stance before nature." If humans are fed from the earth, it is best not to foul the nest that feeds you. Native Americans cut down trees just like the Europeans did. Except the American Indians spared the biggest trees from cutting, honored the "monarchs of the forest" with reverence, and cut everything else. On the other hand, the Europeans cut the biggest trees first, and didn't waste time on the skinny, little trees. From a **Shalom** perspective, both were wrong. Both treated the natural world as a commodity to be exploited and used, NOT as an ecosystem and habitat of biodiversity where everything exists in relationship to everything else which must be respected accordingly.[400]

The second avenue where **Shalom** needs to proceed is in

death itself. William Gilbert (d. 1824) was an eccentric and esoteric Romantic poet. Coleridge called him a "man of fine genius" who had "unfortunately . . . received a few rays of supernatural Light thro' a crack in his upper story."[401] There is a crack in every story. And the biggest crack is death. Every crack crashes. Death is the crushing part of every human life story.

To be human is to confront death. A **Shalom** human faces up to death as well as life. Every story must have a beginning, a middle, and an end. Death is the end of one part of the human story, and the beginning of another part of the story if the human is to truly live. But no one wants a good story to end.

Death is the biggest limitation of life. Each one of us will take up residence in Terminal Café. There will be a last dance, a last supper, a last orgasm, a last football game. The bracket will close on everything. Do we want to know when the brackets close?

Death is conceived and contained in our body from the moment we were born. In his last months of struggle with esophageal cancer, which took him at age 62, interviewers would ask the brilliant polemicist Christopher Hitchens how he was. "Well, I'm dying," the great writer and critic would say. And then, after a delicious pause, "but so are you."

Is the purpose of life death? Or is the purpose of life life? Jacques Derrida introduces the term "Life Death" to critique the dichotomy between the two, life and death, and to honor the paradox that the price of life is death.[402] Some ancient stories did not end with "they lived happily ever after," but with this line: "Until there came to them that from which there is no fleeing, and praise to God, Lord of all being." A Jesus human wants their life to end in a yell, and yelp of YES! A tribute to the **Shalom** "peace that passes all understanding."[403]

*Dying is easy, parking is hard.*
HUMORIST ART BUCHWALD (D. 2007), MOCKING DEATH UNTIL THE VERY END

The last sermon preached by Bishop John ("Honest to God") Robinson (d. 1983) was preached at Trinity College Chapel, Cambridge, on 23 October 1983. The bishop was reflecting on the text from Philippians "For me to live is Christ, and death gain" (1:21). He ended his final sermon with words that proved to be his final ones:

> According to my chronology [Paul] lived nearly ten years after writing those words: others would say it was shorter. But how little does it matter. He had passed beyond time and its calculations. He had risen with Christ.[404]

The process of being a Jesus human is learning to rise with Christ and pass beyond time.

Pergamon is famous for being one of the seven churches of Asia cited in the Book of Revelation. Designated in 2014 as a World Heritage Site by UNESCO, among the ruins of Pergamon is the temple of Asclepius. Asclepius was the god of medicine in ancient Greek religion and mythology. There were many temples of Asclepius ("hospital" is a corruption of "Asclepius"). In one of them Hippocrates, the founder of medicine, taught. Over the doorway of the Asclepius temple at Pergamon were these words: "Death cannot enter here."

In the Book of Revelation there is mentioned another city, a heavenly city, a city yet to come. Over that entire city one may write "Death cannot enter here." It is more than a hope. It is more than a promise. It is more than a temple. It is truth. For Revelation 21:4 says, "Death shall be no more."[405]

Or as Paul put it, "For to me life is Christ, and death gain."[406]

ABECEDARIUM OF A JESUS HUMAN

 **is for Sobremesa/Sobramesa (Spanish) Human**

*"What is the use of a book," thought Alice before she goes down the rabbit hole, "without pictures or conversations?"*
OPENING LINES OF LEWIS CARROLL'S *ALICE IN WONDERLAND* (1865)

Alice might have asked the same question about life as she asked about a book. "What is the use of a life, without people or conversations?"

That's where ***sobremesa***, and ***sobramesa***, come in. The conversation of humanity may be part of the conversion of humanity. Food is the first thing that came between humans and God. So, it is important we get this right, especially in a world where dinnertime is almost gone. In the 60s, dinner was 45 minutes long; by 90s, it had shrunk to 15 minutes; now it's down to five minutes, without any sitting down as we eat standing up around the kitchen counter, or kids get "latchkey dinners."

Mesa means table. Sobre mesa means over, on, or across the table.

Sobra mesa means after or extra the table, or the leftovers, the surplus, the excess food. In the words of Pentecostal theologian Wolfgang Vondey, "With Jesus it is always an extravaganza. The outpouring of God's Spirit manifests an uncontainable surprise: an overflow, an excess, and a gift."[407]

*And my cup overflows.*
PSALM 23:5

For a ***sobremesa*** in Scripture, Paul has a midnight meal (*klasas ton arton kai geusamenos*) with the leaders of the church in Troas.[408] He conducts his table-talk with them until dawn, when the church leaders emerge greatly charged and comforted (pareklethesan ou metrios).[409] And no doubt exhausted. If you have never slept off several rounds of theological ***sobremesa***, you haven't lived. The "Lord's Supper" itself was a Passover meal followed by a ***sobremesa***: "when the supper was over."[410]

You can nudge people without food. But you can't nudge them far. What makes the table culture of ***sobremesa*** so difficult today is that we live in the fast lane, eating fast foods, and seeking fast bucks. Fast and furious living is causing falling levels of trust in everyone and fake everything. Like slow food and a slow kiss, slow thinking, slow reflection, and slow conversation heavy with theological sauces tastes better and are ultimately more satisfying.

One of the reasons why ***sobremesa*** may be so difficult for us is because we fail to see holiness in everyday life, the "mundane, everyday practice, as opposed to exceptional worship," in the words of historian and food expert Roger Horowitz.[411] We have come to think of the sacred and holy as belonging to worship and not to the workaday.

# ABECEDARIUM OF A JESUS HUMAN

*The whole of life is like an after-dinner hour with a cigar; easy, pleasant, empty, perhaps enlivened by some fable of strife.*
JOSEPH CONRAD IN *LORD JIM* (1900)

Duke theologian Luke Bretherton argues for a "mundane holiness" where the drudgery and trivialities become divine and true. He condemns divorcing spirituality from theology, and berates those who offer "Christian spirituality" as a consumer option or technique to be learned so one can transcend everyday life. In Christianity, "spirituality is true materiality," he contends.

Paul's advocacy of the spiritual life points to neither an ethereal, otherworldly life nor an interior realm of consciousness, but to a whole pattern of life which is truly material, truly itself, a human life as part of creation healed and fulfilled.

Bretherton points to the church year and says there are times of fasting and lament, as well as times of feasting and joy. But the clearest indicator of "mundane holiness" is the existence of ordinary time:

> It is ordinary time that is the focus of a mundane holiness and it is ordinary time that is, perhaps, the major key or predominant mode of the Christian life. . . . To refuse to live faithfully in ordinary time and constantly seek times of ecstasy or insist that all

life is a fast is to refuse . . . a definitive part of Christian discipleship.

Bretherton, a sticky-bun of a theologian, suggests five marks that should be present in all Christian spirituality:

1. It should be about relationship with the Father, through Christ, in the Spirit and not about focusing on exercises, experiences or techniques;
2. It should have a community dimension and focus, not merely individualistic or therapeutic;
3. It should not see time and place as enemies to be overcome;
4. It must show concern for ecological, political, economic, and social justice;
5. It should be eschatological, that has a right understanding of the "now and not yet."[412]

The life of faith is best found and expressed, not in trekking off to camp-meetings or their modern-day equivalents like Catalyst, Soul Survivor, or "Burning Man," but in the infinite preciousness of everyday life. In his book on the quest for a moral life, public intellectual David Brooks names the magic of table mundaneness "the technology of the table."

> After the meal we head over to the piano, and somebody will play an Adele song and people will sing. But the dinner table is the key technology of social intimacy here. It is the tool we use to bond, connect, and commit to one

another. I've learned to never underestimate the power of a dinner table. It's the stage on which we turn toward one another for love like flowers seeking the sun.[413]

A lot of scholarly energy has been given to why the French have less heart disease than most nations, especially with all those rich sauces and gravies.[414] Most have focused on restrained wine consumption. Maybe the answer lies in the whole dining experience itself, which is relaxed, slow-paced, multi-coursed, and conversation-based which is more sharing than airing. There is a world of difference between airing and sharing. Airing is a preemptive strike. Sharing is a prevenient embrace and precious grace.

Jesus lived a life like ours. Jesus mulled over the mundane until it mirrored the epic, magic, and sublime. A Jesus human mulls the mundane until it shimmers with the divine. Every table bakes a souffle, but a souffle takes lots of time and massive infusions of hot air. When we sit at the table of the eucharist, and eat some common bread and no-label wine, we are eating of the Tree of Life.

It is encouraging to our common humanity to see how the table is being rediscovered around the world. For example, the Japanese are adopting and adapting to their culture the dinner-party, the *hoomu paatei* or "home party." The Japanese Home Party Association even offers certificates to those who take its courses. The biggest problem the Japanese have had in bringing people to the table is discovering that it is not about serving but conversation.

## JESUS HUMAN

It is not about showcasing the Japanese art of ikebana, or variety of floral arrangements, but the variety of humans present unfolding and unfurling in each other's regard. The host is not supposed to stand and serve the guests, but sit down and join in the conversation.

Maybe we need to consider not just saying grace before meals, but offering grace after meals, after the ***sobremesa*** and before the ***sobramesa***. Before the meal, thanksgiving for the food prepared and about to be received. After the meal and before leaving the table, thanksgiving for the conversation and conviviality and companionship (com=with; panion from panera=bread). Especially when there is intellectual stretch and theological reach in these commonplace ***sobremesas***; especially when the tablemates have danced on the hot tin roof of controversial subjects without leaving burn marks on each other.

*The art of cookery made the brute human.*
*Civilization grew, step by step, in the kitchen.*
ELIZABETH ROBINS PENNELL (1896)[415]

##  is for Sozo (Greek: σόζο) Human

> *"I will restore you to health and heal your wounds," declares the Lord.*
> JEREMIAH 30:17 NIV

The only "art" the Sweet family hung on its walls was verses from the Bible. Some were framed in print; others were carved in wood or cast in porcelain, plaster of Paris, or ceramic. My favorite of all the "artwork" adorning our Bloomingdale Avenue house was a cheap plaster of Paris scroll of Proverbs 3:5–8:

> Trust in the LORD with all thine heart; And lean not unto thine own understanding. In all thy ways acknowledge him, and he shall direct thy paths (KJV).

The problem is that there is more to this passage than what was plastered. The verses actually end with the words:

> Then you will have healing for your body and strength for your bones (NLT).

A global humanity will rediscover and recover God's self-description: "I am the God that heals you."[416] The Hebrew term for "chosen people" (English) or "the elected people" (*peuple elu* in French) is the Hebrew phrase "*Am Segulah*," which most often translates as "treasure people" but equally can be rendered "medicine people" or "people capable of making distinctions." The Great Physician chooses to share divine life with *Am Segulah*, the "healing people," whom God treasures.

Yeshua HaMashiach (Jesus Messiah) is how first-century disciples would have called Jesus. Yeshua is the Hebrew pronunciation of Jesus. Mashiach is the Hebrew pronunciation of "messiah," which means the Anointed One. In short, Jesus Christ is Yeshua HaMashiach or Anointed Salvation. The Anointed One is our Anointed Saviour and our Anointed Healer. It was said of the Messiah that he would do certain healing functions as signs of the kingdom breaking in: sight to the blind, cleansing of the lepers, etc.

---

*Christ is the form of all virtues, the medicine of all infirmities, the example of all good works, the remedy of all evils.*
"THE SECOND AUGUSTINE" HUGH OF ST. VICTOR (D. 1141)[417]

When William Tyndale published the first English translation of the New Testament translated directly from Greek texts in 1526, he used the word "health" where we use "salvation" to translate the Greek word "***Sozo***."[418] The English word "salvation" is itself derived from the medicinal word "salve," which means to heal or make whole. To be "saved" is to be made whole, to live in health and holiness. Jesus Saves!

The connection of healing and salvation and learning was an ancient one. Engraved over the door of the thirteenth century BCE library of Rameses the Great in Thebes, a door carved with images of healing and learning and wisdom, were these words: "the house of healing for the soul." This motto

# ABECEDARIUM OF A JESUS HUMAN

for the world's oldest known library would make a great motto for every house of worship.

The words for health, healing, wholeness, and holiness are basically the same. Savior is a healing word. Holiness is a "final integration" of mind, body, and spirit and the opening of connections between the human and divine. Sanctification is a lifetime metabolizing of God's grace, not guilt or grief or despair. That is **Sozo** Jesus.

One **Sozo** Jesus story will suffice. The story of the hemorrhaging woman is the pharisaic idea of a walking nightmare.

As an unaccompanied woman, she has no business traipsing about behind Jesus and his disciples.

As a woman with "an issue of blood," she is ritually unclean. Touching her or touching anything she has touched would bring her impurity upon the toucher.

As a woman who has suffered from this malady for twelve years, she would have been religiously and socially outcast from friends and family, from her own community, and from religious life, for that entire time.

Her faith in Jesus' healing abilities mirrors that of the distraught father Jesus is following. In fact, her faith is so great that she believes just touching the fringes ("*tzitzit*") of his garment will bring about her healing. Matthew's text uses the Greek term "*sozo*,"[419] which may be rendered either as "healed" or "saved"—denoting a physical, mental, and spiritual deliverance. The woman's surreptitious touch brings her the "healing," the "salvation," the health and wholeness she longs for. It also brings her to Jesus' attention. Although technically her touch would have brought impurity to Jesus,

## JESUS HUMAN

he answers her that her faith has "made her well." Just as the abandoned paralytic is the only person Jesus looked at and called "Son," this ostracized woman is the only person Jesus looked at and called "Daughter:" "Daughter your faith has made you well. Go in peace."[420] Health and Peace, **Sozo** and Shalom, go together.

There is a difference between "heal" and "cure." Jesus didn't cure everyone who asked or needed it. Cure is to fix a physical disease or ailment. But he did heal everyone, which means to bring a state of wellness and wholeness even in the midst of sickness. And Jesus always heals, since one day we will be "healed" of all the problems of this world. The beauty of this healing is never in the death, but only in the healing that death brings.

The Latin root of word "whole" is *totius*, which means both "to cure" and "to measure." For every living thing to be "well," there has a right "inward measure" which integrates the various parts into a functioning whole. When everything is in harmony, there is wellness and wholeness. The word "integrity" comes from the "integration" of all parts of one's being into a wholeness. Thomas Merton followed William Blake in seeing wholeness and holiness as a "final integration." In the Jewish tradition there is the person known as the tzadik, the righteous person, which Rabbi Nachman of Breslov (d. 1810) defined as the fully-realized human being. We each have an Inner metric of "wholeness" and "fitness," or what science fiction legend Arthur C. Clarke called a "highly developed sense of the fitness of things."[421] When "fitness" is actualized in a person, they become a Shalom human.

Shalom embraces body, spirit, and mind. Those most ill among us may not have any physical problems. You can be physically fit and inwardly sick. The health of the spirit matters as much as the health of the body. Jesus died on the cross for our "salvation," to bring us into a "saving" state of health, holism, and holiness where our minds, bodies, and spirits are being wholly orchestrated by the Spirit.

Medical healing is the knowledge of God manifested through science. Spiritual healing is the knowledge of God manifested through faith. It is the same knowledge. It is the same God.

Trust and faith activate healing. Before penicillin, physicians were little more than faith healers. People were healed because they trusted the doctor to make them well, not because of anything the doctor did (which often made them worse). It's the same today. A lot of the healing that takes place is not because of the medicine but because people have faith and trust in their healers. If you are a person of faith who inspires trust, you can be an agent of healing for others. In 1136 Hugo St. Victor finished writing for a young student at his Abbey named Andrew *The Didascalicon* ("On Instruction"), a seven-book treatise on education that is celebrated by historians as one of the most important works of medieval educational theory which and one of the most influential treatises that shaped the development of medieval universities. Hugo instructed his seminary students that they were to see themselves as healers, and Jesus as "The Medicine:" "He is your remedy." The stories, songs, metaphors, and words of the Bible is their pharmacy of prescriptions for whatever ails the soul.[422]

One of the most beloved and buzzy words of our time is "spiritual." People claim to be "spiritual but not religious." But gnostic dangers lurk in that word "spiritual," since Jesus did not die on the cross to save our "souls" or make us "more spiritual," but to heal and save all of us—mind, body, and spirit. **Sozo** Jesus is the Mediator of Ultimate Human Well-being. "We have heard the joyful sound, Jesus saves, Jesus saves"[423] is how each radio broadcast began of Charles E. Fuller's "Old Fashioned Revival Hour" that ran from 1937 to 1968. But the rousing chorus of that children's hymn that ends "This our song of Jubilee" is even better translated, "Jesus heals, Jesus heals."

> *I have a bit of a quarrel with the word 'spirituality.' I occasionally use it as an abstract noun, spirituality being a human being's capacity for life in the spirit. But I find the word spirituality with an adjective attached to it just nauseous. If someone asks me to give a talk about 'Cistercian spirituality,' I say I don't know what that is.*
> NORWEGIAN TRAPPIST MONK AND BISHOP DOM ERIK VARDEN[424]

"No man is an island," not even in our illness and healing. Just as sickness is never a solo condition, and all illness involves more than one person, so healing is always a relational and communal journey home to health. You can't be healed in slices.

Houses of worship are most seen as preaching and teaching places, but must become as it was in the beginning and forever must be: a healing place. A place of healing, health, holiness, and wellness where broken relationships with individuals and communities and cities are healed; a place where mental, physical, and emotional health is restored. We have become better at dealing than healing, dealing with issues rather than "healing" of diseases or hearing each other out ("I don't have to listen to you;" "I don't have time to listen to you").

Jesus' mission begins, not with him preaching, or teaching, but healing. His first sermon makes this clear in his five-point mission:

> The scroll of the prophet Isaiah was handed to Him. Unrolling it, He found the place where it was written: "The Spirit of the Lord is on Me, because He has anointed Me to *[1] preach good news to the poor.* He has sent Me to *[2] proclaim deliverance to the captives* and *[3] recovery of sight to the blind*, to *[4] release the oppressed*, to *[5] proclaim the year of the Lord's favor.*"[425]

"To announce the word of the Lord's favor" is shorthand for Jubilee, the 50th year when the ram's horn is blown, everyone goes home and is restored to their rightful place, all debts are forgiven (no more foreclosure), all prisoners released, and the land goes fallow. All of creation is part of ***Sozo***. Not one iota of the universe is outside God's healing power. Every inch of the universe is touched by the healing

## JESUS HUMAN

grace of God and is restored, renewed, no longer broken, no longer shattered.

Jesus' healing is often prefaced by the question, "What can I do for you?"[426] Jesus does not use his twenty-six recorded healings to lift up his messiahship,[427] or to recruit disciples, but to simply help people and honor faith. Jesus begins his ministry where people are: in the middle of aches, ailments, and anxieties. Jesus begins his ministry showing a God who cares about you and whatever you care about and stroking your diseased body with his life-giving hands. It was a revolutionary new revelation of "power."[428]

Jesus even heals the damage done by his own followers, as revealed in the story of Malchus's ear.[429] Malchus, which means "king," was the servant of the high priest Caiaphas who advised the Jews that it would be expedient that one man should die for the people.[430] It is likely that the high priest sent him, along with soldiers and Judas Iscariot, to capture Jesus.[431] Jesus' chief apostle Peter, who had promised Jesus earlier that he was willing to die for his Lord, drew his sword and most likely went for Malchus' head but missed and cut off his ear. Jesus heals the wounds caused by the head of his church, and his church itself.

*Jesus! the name that charms our fears,*
*that bids our sorrows cease,*
*'tis music in the sinner's ears,*
*'tis life and health and peace.*
CHARLES WESLEY, "O FOR A THOUSAND TONGUES"[432]

## ABECEDARIUM OF A JESUS HUMAN

Protestant Reformer Martin Luther was haunted by the Great Judgment scene,[433] where he envisioned God saying to some at the bar of justice: "I was sick, and you did NOT visit me? Go to hell." Pastors are not employees. Pastors are healers just like physicians are healers. The medical staff taking care of the health of bodies don't practice "social distancing;" nor should people taking care of the health of the mind and spirit and body. ***Sozo*** humans are First Responders of the First Order on the world's Front Lines and Fault Lines.

The definition of a "first responder" is someone who runs towards what everyone else is running away from. Fires, explosions, earthquakes, collapsed buildings, rising waters. For most of us, the overwhelming instinct is to get as far away as possible as quickly as possible. But for the men and women who were born and bred to respond first in the event of an emergency, their imperative is to head in, not head out. Their instinct is to put hands out, not hands off.[434]

Caregiving is fundamental to human life. It can be considered a species-specific characteristic. Anthropologist Margaret Mead was once asked what she considered the earliest evidence of civilization. She answered that it was a human thigh bone with a healed fracture that had been excavated from a fifteen-thousand-year-old site. For an early human being to have survived a broken femur, living through the months that were required for the bone to heal, the person had to have been cared for—sheltered, protected, brought food and drink. While other animals care for their young and injured, no other species is able to devote as much time and energy to caring for the most frail, ill, and dying of its

## JESUS HUMAN

members.[435] Stanford Professor Robert Pogue Harrison, who has been called the "single most significant writer in the humanities today," puts it simply: "To be human means, above all, to bury."[436] Some of the holiest words ever spoken were uttered by the Belgian Catholic missionary to the lepers of the Hawaiian islands, Father Damien, also known as Saint Damien of Molokai. After many years of **Sozo** caring in his leprosarium, one week he began his weekly sermon with these two holiest of holy words: "We lepers."[437]

---

*The worst sin towards our fellow creatures is not to hate them, but to be indifferent to them: that's the essence of inhumanity.*
GEORGE BERNARD SHAW'S 1897 PLAY "THE DEVIL'S DISCIPLE"[438]

---

All of us personally know some "first responders," even if you've never met a firefighter, an EMT, or a police officer. The first "first responders" each of us meets up with and gets to know are called "Dad" and "Mom." Jesus, the expression and embodiment of God's love for all creation, was our selfless "First Responder." Jesus strode purposefully towards the sinfulness of our lives, the struggling, damaged lives of all children, even children of God, and offered himself as their means of rescue and redemption.

We are baptized into love, and what it means to be a Jesus human is to be what we are—living the love that first loved us.

People love dogs because they cannot help but show their joy with their tails. I wonder what a world would be like where human beings were free to show that too. But we tend to wait on others to do it first. What if we as Jesus followers become the first responders of joy? What if we are the bold ones who take chances with our hearts to heal the hearts of others? The Jesus Human isn't prey to others first. The Jesus Human wears her heart on her sleeve, because it is rooted and sheltered in God.

> *Reckless courage is what a person needs to be able to endure a limitless experience, one that is exposed to all kinds of risk.*
> MEXICAN NOVELIST CARLOS FUENTES (D. 2012)[439]

Holiness is not self-protection or self-preservation. Holiness is losing ourselves for God's sake and daredreaming a new world.

There are many horrors in life. And this culture is addicted to scares and scandals: just check the "New" on Netflix and decide for yourself whether or not we are now in Hannibal Lecter land. But the horror of horrors, the Horror of it all, the ultimate horror of existence, is the horror of apathy. Elie Wiesel was not the first who said, the opposite of love is not hate, but apathy:

> The opposite of love is not hate,
>   it's indifference.
> The opposite of art is not ugliness,
>   it's indifference.
> The opposite of faith is not heresy,
>   it's indifference.
> And the opposite of life is not death,
>   it's indifference.
>       ~Elie Wiesel (1986)[440]

There are so many things about John the Baptist that we don't have right. Our image of him is a wild man in the desert with a hermit's beard and a hair shirt who was almost anorexic from eating locust and wild honey. Actually, locust was a protein delicacy in the first century, almost like our prime rib today. And honey was the first century version of chocolates. So here is John the Baptist announcing "the Kingdom of Heaven is at Hand" by eating a feast fit for the Kingdom: Godiva Chocolates and Morton's Steak.[441]

---

*The locusts devour the Bedouin and the Bedouin devours the locusts.*
POPULAR PERSIAN SAYING[442]

---

But there's another thing about John the Baptist, this dividing line between the old and new covenant. You had to go out to see him. He didn't come to town to preach in the streets and courtyards. John the Baptist didn't come to you. You had to dare to go beyond the familiar, the comfortable, where the wild beasts roamed and the wilderness reigned, to see and hear him.

Jesus does not want his disciples to hunker down and keep their heads low. Disciples are not called to avoid risk, high stakes, and genuine challenges. A disciple of Jesus operates within the world of high risk. Jesus placed himself in the firing line of history. Sometimes he calls us to place ourselves in the firing line of history as well. And sometimes that gets us shot.

# ABECEDARIUM OF A JESUS HUMAN

*Orville Wright Did Not Have a Pilot's License.*
OLD SAYING[443]

I am so tired of hearing "We must not claim too much." What if we started hearing another warning: "You must not claim too little." A dare dream is a big dream, an extreme dream. Jesus taught that reality can be the daughter of dreams: Strive to Be What You Are Not, and You'll Become the Human God Wants You to Be.

St. Thomas Aquinas pulls off a stunning reversal in his *Summa*. He is talking about the problem of drunkenness, and how the church ought to reach out to people to pour their soul down the drain one drink or pill at a time. But then he suddenly draws attention to a vice that he says is even bigger than drunken excess. The problem is that of the opposite of drunken excess: "the vice of being too sober." We have become too safe, too sensible, too unenthusiastic, too placid.[444] We need a divine intoxication.

> *Men [and women] will not live without vision; that we do well to carry away with us from contemplating, in so many strange forms, the record of visionaries. If we are content with the humdrum, the second-best, the hand-over-hand, it will not be forgiven us.*
> ENGLISH THEOLOGIAN RONALD KNOX (D. 1957), *ENTHUSIASM* (1950)[445]

Few parables are more misinterpreted in the Bible than the parable of the talents. This parable is less about "using your talents wisely" than it is about risking all for the master. The hundredfold increase of "talents" for those servants who risked everything isn't a lesson in wise money management. No wise investor places his 401k on the craps table. Instead, it is a call to step out beyond the safe avenues, the accepted lifestyles, with the trust that putting everything in the hands of God is the best investment we can make. We aren't promised monetary or even tangible gain. It's not an old-earth kind of investment, because we aren't called to be old-earth kind of people. Only by giving everything over, only by putting ultimate control beyond our short reach do we find the "joy" that Jesus' parable promises a new kind of human.

Where did we get this notion of the church as a "safe haven," a "sanctuary" away from the dangers and risks of the world? The church is the place where disciples receive the "talents," the gifts of faith and forgiveness, grace and love, which enables them to become God-fearing, sea-faring risk-takers and dare-dreamers in the eyes of the rest of the world. The church is a launch pad into faith-based chaos.

The true definition of a "sanctuary" is not a safe place from risks. A true definition of a "sanctuary" is a safe place to take risks. When was is it that the church became such a "risk-free-at-any-cost" zone? Where is it that Jesus calls his disciples to follow him and he will lead us into safe moorings? How did our churches become so safe, so clean, so medically sterile? Jesus appealed to something deeply romantic in all of us by calling us to the risk-full-at-all-costs life.

Jesus does not help us transcend the human to achieve some other realm of existence beyond flesh and morality, which is essentially a betrayal of our humanity. The gospel is less a transcendence of the human than a realization of the human. Jesus calls us to live our humanity with no limits but with singular limitations. What one human being can offer another human being is almost as beautiful as what one human being can do to another human being is ugly. In fact, what studies have shown that what draws kids into terrorism isn't so much "Islamic faith" as it is what makes us human, human behavior: social networks, moments of pleasure, pressure to stretch beyond ourselves.

JESUS HUMAN

##  is for Terroir (French) Human

*Most people can name the great leaders and major battles in the past, but few can name the biggest storms, the most significant floods, the worst winters, the most severe droughts, or the ways that these influenced harvest failures, provoked political pressures or were catalysts in the spread of disease.*
PETER FRANKOPAN, OXFORD PROFESSOR OF GLOBAL HISTORY[446]

**Terroir** refers to the complete natural environment in which the grapes for wine are grown, and in which the wines themselves are produced and aged. It includes factors such as the soil, topography, and climate. It has become shorthand for talking about a "sense of place" in a world of nowhereness and placelessness.

Long established among European winegrowers, the concept of ***terroir*** is becoming more important in the U.S. and other nations, and is being used far beyond its original vinery context. Interestingly, there is no exact translation of ***terroir*** from its French language origins. It can refer to a terrain as broad as an entire region or as narrow as a few rows in a specific vineyard.

Genealogy is big business (ancestry.com; 23andme.com), because issues of identity are front and center in a culture adept at the vaporizing of identity. We hear it said, over and over again, "Be You!" But "Be You" presupposes we know who "you" is. Do we know who "you" is, and how do we know who "you" is? Then, do you know how to be you?

*Jesus may live in your heart,*
*but Grandpa lives in your bones.*[447]

One of the hardest learnings in life? Learning to be who you are; living and learning your ***terroir***. The premodern self (if there really was one) emerged out of the "commons" of family, tribe and guild, from the outside in. The modern western self was self-constructed from individual interiors outwards. The current reigning self is the internalization of the collective, the self borged and branded from consumer-celebrity culture.

The Greek word for "disciples" is *mathetes*, which also translates as "learners" or "students." One of the "learnings" from the One who said "Learn from me"[448] is to learn from Jesus your unique ***terroir***—to be who you are. John Updike liked to say that "American is a vast conspiracy to make you happy." The gospels are a "divine conspiracy"[449] to set us free to be who we are—an original creation of art. A human being is not a human "resource" but a human gemstone, a human ***terroir***, an original masterpiece of divine artistry. Incarnate faith takes the form of the faces and features, the music and meals of the cultural context in which God has placed you. But there is no originality without repetition and recurrence, and that repetition and recurrence is rooted in Jesus.

## JESUS HUMAN

> *Jesus is "the art of the almighty Artist."*
> CELTIC PHILOSOPHER JOHN SCOTUS ERIUGENA (D. 877),
> THE GREATEST METAPHYSICIAN WHO EVER LIVED[450]

The One who made us who we are is the best one to show us who we are and what we can become. "Who told YOU that you were naked?"[451] Who gets to define us? Who gets to establish our identity? "Who told YOU who you are?" The Creator told us who humans truly are. And The Creator is the only one to whom humans should listen. God puts us in our "place," and places us in a one-of-a-kind constellation of genes, cultural contexts, landscapes, streetscapes, townscapes, soundscapes, inscapes, and influences.

The more humans find their identity in Christ, the more uniquely placed a human becomes and the greater the ***terroir***. If you've met one Jesus human, you've only met one human. That's all. The paradox is that in finding one's identity in Christ, and incarnating that identity in your context, you become more yourself as you become more a "little-Christ" (Christ-ian).[452]

There is a distinctive human sense of ourselves as beings who are not yet what we might be. The #1 resolution on New Year's is the same for as long as they have been tracking "resolutions." It is not to lose weight, or to make more money. It is to "be a better person." Jesus is our best person, our best shot at being the "human" God made us to be. In running "the race set before you,"[453] not the race set before someone else or some cultural race, you thereby, with the Psalmist, "set

God before my face."⁴⁵⁴ And we "press on to toward the goal for the prize of the upward call of God in Christ Jesus."⁴⁵⁵

---

*Everyone fails at being who they're supposed to be. The great thing is to succeed at being who you are.*
FREYA'S WORD TO THOR, "ENDGAME" (2019)

*Do you know who you are—who you truly are?*
FINAL QUESTION IN "MOANA" (2016)⁴⁵⁶

---

Human identity requires being vintaged . . . and vintaged means the ***terroir*** of time and the smellscapes of the past. History is not the same as heritage: heritage is history shaped to present. To be vintaged is confront history honestly, not to denigrate our ancestors and castigate them for their mistakes and misdeeds, or to burn effigies of our predecessors who vanish behind various constructs, categories, and theories, but to cultivate a mature understanding of the past in the hope that its waywardness will not be repeated or celebrated. History-writing is an identity-forming activity.

For a Jesus human who follows the manger gift, no matter how floral, fruity, minty, nutty, pungent, sweet, or woody the smell, they all have a base of the barnyard in them.

---

*"We are the aroma of Christ TO GOD" . . . When God smells what we are doing, can he smell what his Son went through in his life through us?*
DR. JAMIE MCCALLUM⁴⁵⁷

---

JESUS HUMAN

 is for Tong (Korean: 통) Human

―――――――◇―――――――

*So many of our dreams at first seem impossible, then they seem improbable, and then, when we summon the will, they soon become inevitable.*

REAL-LIFE "SUPERMAN" CHRISTOPHER REEVE (2004)[458]

***Tong: The Impossible Dream:*** Many Korean Christians like to start the day praying together. They come to church at 5 or 6 a.m. in the dark, sing hymns as the lights gradually come on inside the church and outside, and then pray. They pray individually, communally. Each person prays their own prayer. At the same time. Out loud. They don't pray a common prayer together. They pray in common together. It's called "*Tong.*"

***Tong*** is a Korean word for sacred reading that is a form of prayer and meditation, a holistic method of praying through the Bible where intuition meets intention, where East meets West, where orality meets graphicacy, where sound meets story. Most fully developed theologically by Seoul pastor and biblical scholar Dr. Byoungho Zoh, a ***Tong*** reading of the Bible is both a rational and imaginative contemplation of the Scriptures that ushers in a Jesus-human lifestyle of holiness, justice, and peace. Zoh's many books, retreats, apps, and university are revolutionizing how people hear (not just read) The Story into a storybook life of ***Tongdok*** faith

English novelist Rudyard Kipling (d. 1936) wrote

## ABECEDARIUM OF A JESUS HUMAN

a famous poem "The Ballad of East and West" (1889). Everyone knows the refrain, which lays out the impossibility of bringing into relationship Western society, which amounts to one-sixth of the human race, with the rest of the world: "East is East, West is West, and never the twain shall meet."

Jean Paul Sartre refused the Nobel Prize in 1964 because the Nobel Prize Committee refused to *Tong*. Sartre gave two reasons for his refusal to accept the world's greatest honor. We are familiar with his first reason: a writer has a duty not to allow himself or herself to be transformed into an institution or a celebrity. But his second reason for refusing the Nobel Prize was as important to him as the first, but seldom cited: the Prize belonged to the culture of the West, and shut out the Eastern bloc. Sartre did not want to endorse such a Westoxicated snub and division.

A Jesus human looks to the East: In the East, the God-realized person is an awakened, enlightened person.

A Jesus human looks to the West: In the West, the God-realized person is a saved, healed, liberated person.

To *Tong* is to look out of both Jesus eyes. Bifocal vision will give depth to life by grafting East and West, decentering the western world and foregrounding eastern regions. Bifocal vision will bring together what is, with what might be. Carl Jung makes as a characteristic feature of intuitive people this openness to possibilities of what might be rather than what is. "Intuitives concern themselves neither with ideas nor with feeling reactions, nor yet with the reality of things, but surrender themselves wholly to the lure of possibilities."[459]

Most scientists now agree that humans have more than

five senses—some say seven, some say nine, some say as many as fifty-three senses.[460] But all say that what has been known as the "sixth sense" of intuition, the "surrender to the lure of possibilities," is available to everyone.

Intuition is a form of cosmic intelligence that the modern world dismissed as "women's intuition." The very fact that Estee Lauder now has a Men's Fragrance called "Intuition" signifies the sea change. The divorce of rational knowledge and intuitive knowledge, Reason and Intuition, must end.[461] The knowing that takes place under the radar of reason, which I like to call "cosmic intelligence," is what enables us to navigate the radioactive opportunities and obstacles of life.

***What Time Is It?*** That "never-the-twain-shall-meet" refrain is challenged by the gospel, where an Asian theologian named Jesus of Nazareth dreamed of a world where "people will come from east and west, and from north and south, and recline at table in the kingdom of God."[462] In a world where East and West are at each other's throats, God's Dream for a true kind of human is an EastWest dream. Both Jesus in particular and Christianity in general needs liberating from Western captivity and Eastern disregard.

*The only hope for the West won't come from the West.*
NEW ZEALAND CHURCH PLANTER MARK PIERSON[463]

The key to a more Eastern, ***Tong*** reading of The Story is seeing the human body as a vibroscape that needs the "sounding out" of words if the heart of God is to lodge in and beat as one within the human heart. In other words, ***Tong***

## ABECEDARIUM OF A JESUS HUMAN

is the musical modulation of the Scriptures from spirit to flesh, from vibrational being to physical being. ***Tong*** is like a song: it gets you in your "insidest inside" (in composer Edgar Elgar's phrase). ***Tong*** moves us from the tyranny of flat, artificial clocklike chronos time to our birthright of kairos time, a ticking and tocking which opens the door to curvaceous epiphanies and winding advents.[464]

> Now or Never is Chronos Time
>
> Now and Then is Chronos Time
>
> Now and Again is Chronos Time
>
> Now and Forever is Kairos Time
>
> Now and Not Yet is Kairos Time

***Tong*** moves us from imitating Jesus, to imparting Jesus, from presenting Jesus to presencing Jesus, from mimicking Jesus to manifesting Jesus as story and song. ***Tong*** teaches us that the stories about Jesus healing, or the Jesus stories about healing, are themselves healing remedies. Then and now people were changed and healed by them. The stories do what they describe.

How symbolic that one of earliest fragments of Scripture should be a song: "Sing to the Lord for he has triumphed gloriously."[465] Besides the hymnbook pivoting the Scriptures called "Psalms," there are song fragments throughout the *Torah*, in the prophets, the gospels, and the epistles. Basil of Caesarea (d. 379) wrote that the Holy Spirit "blended the delights of melody with doctrines in order that through the softness of the sound we might unawares receive what is useful in the word."[466] For John Calvin, psalm-singing was speaking to God using God's own words. The Puritans often called worship "singing psalms" . . . not one word but two.

Hence the out-loud reading of the Bible. Hence *Tong*.

**Dream Out Loud:** In the preface to *The Book of Common Prayer* (1549), which some have called "the second greatest religious book in the English language" (the Bible being the first, of course), there is this mandate for the out-loud reading of The Story in divine service:

> "All the whole Bible (or the greatest part thereof) should be read over once in the year."

In the second edition of *The Book of Common Prayer* (1552), these are the instructions for the public reading of Scripture:

> "Then shall be read two Lessons, distinctly with a loud voice, that the people may hear."

The Bible is composed for oral hearing, not silent reading. The Bible is meant to be given a "close hearing" even more than a "close reading." The Bible is meant to be heard and sounded forth, the vibrations forming a "new creature" in Christ. We forget that only in the 1940s did humankind pass a literacy rate of 50%.[467] For most of human history, we communicated orally and pictorially, not textually.

Monks aimed to so sing the Psalms that their lives became a living Psalms. The Scriptures are the soundtrack of life. In a culture where we are losing the ability to "say" much less "sing" the Scriptures, ***Tong*** is revolutionary in its power to help us come alive to The Living Story.

Certain parts of Jesus' teaching were so sacred that they were never written down, only committed to oral telling and passing on. As in the case with Samuel, Timothy knew the scriptures at a young age. St Paul marveled about Timothy "how from infancy [he had] known the holy scriptures."[468] Timothy "heard" rather than "read" the holy scriptures from his grandmother Lois and his mother Eunice, who sounded out the words to him as an infant. How important it is today to "tell" God's story to our children so that these scriptures become the soundtrack for their daily living. There is a mysterious power to hearing the Scriptures. Their very sounding is a resounding in the soul, a voice recognition of the divine.

The private, solo, silent reading of the Scripture is a recent development in the history of Christianity. St. Augustine was startled in 380 to hear Bishop Ambrose read the Bible silently. It was the first time he had ever heard it read that way. To be sure, St. Ambrose was not the first silent reader. One historian argues that "Alexander the Great, not Julius Caesar, is the first silent reader to be unambiguously recorded in Greek history."[469]

Pulitzer Prize-winning poet Robert Frost (1874–1963) was beloved to the point of being selected as Poet Laureate of the United States because he privileged sound and the speaking voice in his poetry. He called it the doctrine of "sentence sounds" and "the sound of sense." Frost argued that "pure sound" trumps subject and object, and he was especially sensitive to the "oversound" of speech that revealed itself in his mastery of the colloquial patterns of the vast soundscapes of USAmerican speech.

It is not a matter of hearing vs. seeing. It is a matter of hearing into sight. The Bible privileges hearing over seeing, but it also brings the two together. Augustine called letters "signs of sounds" and the sounds were "signs of things we think."[470] Sound becomes sight; vibration becomes vision.[471] That's what metaphors do: they bring the oral and the aural together. That is also why metaphors do more than inform our spirituality; they form our spirituality. So choose your metaphors carefully. **Tong** teaches us to trust the sensory and musical metaphors of the Bible, not just the words of the Bible.

"Meditation" is a popular concept both in the East and West. We hear from a variety of sources that it is important to "pray and meditate." However, meditation is a lot more difficult than we think it is, because our concentration breaks so easily. A prime reason why our concentration breaks is because we don't know The Story. We only know fractals and fragments. So how can we meditate properly?

**Sonant, Not Surd:** The key is 'sound' and 'ear'—reading The Bible out loud and using our ears to listen to The Bible. That's **Tong**. The human ear is a marvelous and most effective tool. When we read out loud, concentration levels go up, making it only natural that we learn and recollect The Story. We need to first read out loud in order to capture the whole story. Meditation requires a prior processing, a knowing and an understanding of The Story. The Story truly requires a slow, "read-out-loud" and "listen" receptivity. A slow, out-loud reading the Bible changes your soul in the same way exercise changes your body. We now know what David the psalmist knew first: the healing powers of sound. We now know what David didn't know: that soundscapes can change the cellular environment of a body.

Our world is de-forming and loves demoting. A storm of deconstruction has bred a cultural climate of destroying and destorying. Eroding social capital, expanding social media, declining civility, rising inequality, declining social mobility, falling educational standards and failing educational systems—all of these have at their root of malfunction an absence of **Tong**. The world cannot function properly without **Tong**.

In the tenth century a group of Arab thinkers coalesced in energy and creativity. They were based in Basra, and their theology revolved around Shia Islam. They produced a remarkable work called "Epistles of the Brethren of Purity." The twenty-second epistle is the story of the complaints by the animals against humanity. The animals bring a series of indictments against humans. All the animals are allowed to speak.

The insects are led by the King Bee (it was assumed, with Aristotle, that the head of a bee colony could only be male); the cricket, too, is heard. Aquatic species are represented by the sea serpent, dolphin, whale, turtle, crab, crocodile and frog; reptiles by dragon and viper.[472]

In the "Epistles of the Brethren of Purity," humanity

## JESUS HUMAN

gets a drubbing. Through satire, sarcasm, sermonic admonitions, and humor, humans get raked over the coals for our wastefulness, pride, cruelty, selfishness, frivolity, squabbling, oppression, violence, etc.—in short, for our inhumanity. The "Epistles" rip the veil of vanity from our hubris, and opens our eyes to see our pathological bent to put the self at the center of everything and think of ourselves better than we ought to think.

In the tradition of Christianity, Jesus reconstitutes our humanity, which has been damaged by the fall. God has a middle name—Emmanuel means God WITH Us.[473] If Jesus is God's middle name, so Jesus has a middle name: Jesus All-Things-Are-Possible Christ. Mary's words of wonderment are a prophesy of Jesus' middle name: "How can this be?"[474] If you aren't hearing or saying these words—"How can these things be?"—it's not God. Impossible is nothing if you're a Jesus human.

◇

*Ponder anew*
*All the Almighty can do . . .*
JOACHIM NEANDER (1680)[475]

**is for Ubuntu (Nguni—the name for closely related Bantu languages including Xhosa, Zulu, Ndebele, and Swazi) Human**

U-boon'-tu (as ***Ubuntu*** is pronounced) is a quality a person possesses that is based on relationships with other people. It is built on the African philosophy that the self is found in selflessness, that acting in ways that benefit others is the path to beauty, truth, and goodness. There are words that express this philosophy in sub-Saharan African cultures and languages. But ***Ubuntu*** is the most familiar.

***Ubuntu*** means, "I am because We are." We become "persons" through other people. The quest to "Be Yourself" is inseparable from the quest to "Be Ourselves." Or in a more epigrammatic way: It takes a WE to make a ME. I can't be Me without We.[476] You can't have selfies without ussies.

The Lakotas have a beautiful phrase, "*Mitákuye Oyás'i?*" which means, "all my relations," or, "we are all related." For them, it is as common of a phrase as "hello." It is deeply embedded into the culture. It is time to embrace the depth and reality of our connectedness and interdependence. To be truly human is to be a member of a community, a participatory, not predatory, part of a community.

"He's only harming himself" is impossible. When you harm yourself, you harm everybody. In ***Ubuntu*** spirituality, there is a great sense of the "great cloud of witnesses"[477] whereby ancestors are part of the family, in some places even to the point of ancestor worship.

Everyone has a DMN (Default Mode Network), which some neuroscientists call "The Me Network." Followers of Jesus have a DMN that is less a Me Network than a ME/WE Network.

There is no "other." Only "oneanother," a word which exists in Greek as "*allelon*" (oneanother). The problems of the world require a new kind of human, not one that goes around "othering," pointing out the "others," and scolding others for not embracing "othering," but goes around "oneanothering." In the words of Oliver Clement: "Genuine Christian life is an imitation of the Trinity. Just as there is one God in three Persons, so, in Christ, we are all 'members one of another'; there is, and we are called to become, *a single Man in a multitude of persons.*"[478]

The battle of the universe is between **Ubuntu** vs. Ungratefulness. Dostoevsky defined a human as "the ungrateful biped."

**Ubuntu** humans are the most ignorant persons you will ever meet in one subject. They are totally unschooled in the ways and means of egotism and hubris. All ego journeys are a trip to nowhere. Ungratefulness and Egoism are kindred spirits: I am because I am—I am self-made, I am independent, I am not beholden to anyone. In Egoism, we become "persons" by being independent of other persons. Ungratefulness has brought us to the edge of civilizational and ecological collapse. "WE" must be more than an aggregation of "I's." For a WE not to be just a mass or mob, it must be more than an amplified amalgamation of "ME's" but a transmutation of ME into something greater than the sum of its parts.

# ABECEDARIUM OF A JESUS HUMAN

All for One and One for All.

All in the One and One in the All.

Our shared humanity makes demands on each one of us, or what used to be called in evangelical circles a "burden." ***Ubuntu*** makes us feel "burdened" for humanity. These "burdens" for others are not burdensome but blessings. In "carrying each other's burdens," our own burdens become lighter, as they are lifted up by others. We're all entitled to our own opinions, but not entitled to our own facts and the burdens which come from them:

The burden of content;
> the burden of compassion;
> the burden of listening;
> the burden of love;
> the burden of touch.

You can only unite a community around love of someone or a burden for something bigger than themselves. A community united around a common love of each other is a clan. Community is not an end in itself. If it were a KKK celebration of its 100th lynching, or a Nazi dinner celebrating it's 1 millionth gassing, would qualify. A community of Jesus humans is a weird community because it's more than a social club; it exists for the people who aren't there. Togetherness is not the telos of the church. It has a mission that is outside itself, an earnest of an eternal kingdom. It is Christ become flesh, the Christbody community, Corporal Christ. The church is Jesus in his corporal form. But Paul doesn't see the church as a corporate entity for Christ to act in the world. For Paul, the church less provides Jesus with a physical agency for acting than an expression of the organic nature of community as the body of Christ where the focus is on its corporal nature more than on its ability to act on behalf of Jesus.

Two words create the most beautiful crystals in existence: "Love and Gratitude."[479] They need to be put together to produce the beauty of a common humanity. We are 70% water; the planet is 70% water. The metaphors and words we use shape the crystals of water. Words like beauty, truth, goodness, harmony, and resonance produce elegant crystals while words like hate, despair, depression, and dislike produce deformed and malformed crystals. "As you think in your heart," Jesus said, "so you are." We create the world we live in by the words we use, the stories we live by, and the metaphors we take to heart. It doesn't matter what language these words are spoken in, so it has nothing to do with vibrations. It's the meaning behind the words that produce well-formed and attractive crystals[480]

When you undergo that shift in consciousness that sees the world through the eyes of Christ, you begin to see how all things are connected. That to take care of the least and the last is to heal the whole, not just the part. God gives each of us a different mission because all our missions are one mission. All roots can be traced to the same bed, and to heal and revive one root system is to heal and revive them all.

"He's only harming himself" is impossible and should never be said. When you think you're only harming yourself with your behavior and beliefs, you're harming everyone who

## ABECEDARIUM OF A JESUS HUMAN

loves you, everyone around you. We're all connected in ways beyond measure or imagining.

Community cannot subsume the person, but the person cannot suborn the community. The human is the opposite of the hive. True community is the opposite of the collective and its wolf-pack dynamics. When everyone around you is thinking the same, sounding the same, mouthing the same pet phrases and brandishing the same cliches, the hive has arrived.

> I pray that they will all be one, just as you and I are one—as you are in me, Father, and I am in you. And may they be in us so that the world will believe you sent me.[481]

Jesus is not calling for church union here, or even praying for harmony among his disciples. Jesus is portraying the ideal relation between humanity and God as the same as between Him and his Father . . . that union of the divine and the human is possible, even though the divine is a separate category from the human.

"Let him alone." Some of the harshest words ever spoken in the Bible: "Let him alone." If you want to be alone, you can be alone. God will let you alone. But alone is not human unless it's in solitude, and even in solitude you take the community with you. And God will not let you alone, or let you be alone, for long. God seeks us in our hiding places and calls us out.

##  is for Verboten (German) Human

What you say "no" to in the future may define your humanity even more than what you say "yes" to.

It hurts to say this, because too mu+ch of too many religions have been based on more "Don'ts" than "Do's." Some Buddhist monks in Thailand who are part of the Theravadin tradition itemize 218 prohibitions they must live by. Some monks add to the list to prove their superior piety. When a religion forces you to define your life in terms of things you don't do rather than do, it is the devil on stilts. For much of my early life in the holiness tradition, my feet never touched the ground.[482]

Yet, God's first word to humans was not "No" but "Yes." "Eat Freely" God told Adam and Eve. But of all the trees one was free to eat, there was one, The Tree of the Knowledge of Good and Evil, that was **verboten**: "Don't go there." God's original blessing to humans was a "yes," not a "no."

Maybe we know that from the deepest levels of our being because one of the fastest ways to a best-seller is to name your book "the power of" and then fill in the blank. The power of positivity, the power of good, the power of belief, the power of one, the power of love, the power of myth, the power of now, the power of relationships, the power of us, the power of prayer. Seldom do you find a book on the power of evil, or as John Tierney and Roy F. Bautheister put it, *The Power of Bad* (2019). The best you can get is *The Power of a Positive No: How To Say No And Still Get to Yes* (2007).

**Burning Tongues:** Our tongues were meant to flame fires of love and hope, not fires of criticism and complaint, hate and negate. A series of shibboleths I give my graduate students is Celebrate, then Cerebrate; Praise, then Appraise; Commend, then Critique; Yes, then No.

Nevertheless, intrinsic to the human species is a preferential option for the negative, an eagerness to denigrate more than celebrate. Even in Pilate's comment "I find no fault with this man" his default mode was one of critique, always looking for the fault, eager to "size up" each other at first impression. Many Christians read their Bible "In the beginning was the Word, and the word was 'NO.'" The "do's" and "don'ts" of the Christian life have majored in the "don'ts" and minored in the "do's." How many of us grew up with the mantra "Don't drink, don't smoke, don't dance, don't chew, and don't go with girls who do?" This "don't" over "do" focus has created a flip-flop faith within a culture of the negative.

To be sure, some of the "don'ts" are valiant attempts at negative identity formation, showing us how to be "in" the world but not "of" the world by showing us what the opposite looks like. I once heard a sermon on "A Church with Piles" where the preacher taught the congregation what it meant to be a Christian: Christians don't "pile on" the sick and wounded, don't kick when a person is down; Christian's don't "pile up" treasures on earth; Christians don't "pile in" the bandwagon and follow the fads of fashion.

Even if you were spared a childhood of "don'ts," you went to school where if a teacher asked "What do you think?" you were being asked to be a critic, to be a voice of "against." To be critical about critical thinking, to be against against, is itself to be "critical." But we are instructed to study to "show ourselves approved," and that divine approval does not come from "quarreling about words," which "only ruins those who listen," but from "rightly dividing the word of truth," which has a positive not negative impact on people.[483]

But sometimes we have to give the devil his due, but no need for a bonus.[484] One of the least devil-may-care languages is German. The German language has three words for "no:" nicht, nein, and kein. But they all pale in comparison to the power of that one word "***Verboten***" which means "Forbidden." The birth story of humanity has a big "***Verboten***" in the midst of it: "Forbidden Fruit."

But sometimes "no" means no. A hard no. No yes. Just no. Sometimes there needs to be a "Wrong Way" sign posted at forks in the road. Some paths are "Not Permitted." Some boundaries are not to be crossed. Boundaries are less barriers than buzz alarms of warning, caution, and attentiveness.

The more GRAINy the future becomes (GRAIN is my acronym for Genetic Engineering, Robotics, AI, Infotech, and Nanotechnology), the more we will need to be able to say "***Vereboten***" to unbounded possibles and interminable potentials. Regress can mask itself as progress. Especially when it comes to an Artificial General Intelligence or Heritable Gene Editing gone drunk on power and a posthuman future.

We need to know our birth story, our originary genesis story better than ever if we are to read insightfully the inflections and directions we ought to go. Every grand saga is made up of small narratives . . . from soap box stories to soap opera stories to grand opera stories to genesis stories. Every human has a birth story, and deserves to be told their birth story. How well do we know the details of our birth story? How well do we know the details of the Jesus birth story? How well do we know the birth story of the universe and humanity's place in it? The biblical creation story is not the first one on the historical scene. In some ways, however, the genesis story is a corrective to the other ones, and a revolutionary one that altered the course of world history and continues to change the world through its power of re-genesis. The story of humanity is safe if it stays within the parameters of its birth story.

It will not suffice to step forward into this GRAINy future with the attitude of "Let's hope AI won't mean thought control and censorship!" or "Let's hope Quantum Computing is friendly!" Whether these tools are friendly or not, democratic or totalitarian, depends on human ability to say "**Verboten**." The first rule of health and medicine is "Do No Harm." Any technological move must be governed by human "Do-No-Harm" protocols. With all the misdirections and indiscretions of our technocratic, scientistic worldviews, it will not be easy.

Scientific and technological progress is not the same as human progress. Soren Kierkegaard observed long ago in his case for anxiety as the original sin: "Anxiety is a sympathetic antipathy and an antipathetic sympathy. . . . Human desire [is] ambivalent, torn in two directions: we are attracted to what we know is bad for us, but resist what we know to be good for us."[485] There is an old saying that humans will always do whatever is possible for them to do, but they might only do it once. The future of planet Earth depends on our ability to prove that maxim wrong. And to hear "***verboten***," not as a swan song, or a snail's pace, but as a rallying cry.

The snail is the symbol of the Slow Food movement. Every snail must labor to build its own shell. Its body boasts an organ called a mantle which secretes layers of calcium carbonate that crystallize and harden. Starting upward, it constructs a beautiful spiral shell but quickly realizes that the structure is becoming too delicate and fragile. So the snail reverses direction and adds strength and stability to its home. Every human, and every home, needs resilience, and resilience only comes from a rhythm of "Yes—Innovate," "Maybe–Consolidate," and "No–Negate/Block."

##  is for Wateca (Lakota) Human

*Wateca* was a Lakota concept that each person carried with them their own eating utensil, whether they were going on trips, visiting relatives, or attending gatherings. "Bring your *Wateca* dishes." The host is responsible for the food, not the means by which you eat the food.

Back in 2012, Carla Rae Marshall, a longtime resident of the Black Hills and citizen of the Cheyenne River Sioux Tribe, started posting #WatecaChallenge to social media to remind people to take their own dishes if they were going to cultural and family gatherings or spiritual ceremonies. This is a way to honor traditional cultural practices, as well as to reduce humanity's carbon footprint. In Lakota, ***wateca*** means to take feast food home.

Pre-colonization Lakota people received their dishes at a young age and were responsible for them for a lifetime. Their wooden bowl, buffalo horn spoon, and water bladder bag were extremely personal and were seen to have spirit that blessed the food that it held. These items took care of that person's physical well-being just like their Cannunpa, or sacred pipe, took care of their spiritual well-being.

Unfortunately, people now depend heavily on Styrofoam plates, bowls, cups, and plasticware to be provided at gatherings, meetings and spiritual ceremonies. Even more, humans now use these disposable items regularly at home.

Our dependency on single use plastic, introduced only fifty years ago, has now become a global pollution crisis with major health and social justice issues attached. Plastic is everywhere—plastic shopping bags, bottles, jugs, cups, bowls, straws, and flatware—and contribute a large portion of waste contaminating our waterways, aquatics, and ecosystems. Plastic may have made things more convenient for people, but only at great cost to our health and environment.

And at great cost to the 8.7 million living creatures on this planet. We are facing an Insect Apocalypse. Two percentages tell the story: 41% of insect species are threatened with extinction and 75% of crops require pollination by insects. No apples, tomatoes, strawberries, pumpkins, or coffee without pollination.[486]

There are 100,000 species of wasps on this planet. Only 22,000 species of bees, which suggests that wasps were the ancestors of bees and ants. Wasps that forgot how to hunt and became vegetarians are called bees. Wasps that forgot how to fly and got grounded are called ants.[487] As much as I wish Noah had seized the moment and taken care of these annoying creatures before they entered the ark, there are no "useless" creatures.

To save the planet and preserve nature's ecosystem, we have had to learn the hard way to respect and protect species we find unappealing, even species we cannot stand, have no use to us, and that may even harm us—wasps, anyone? Why can't we learn to do the same with humans, and practice unbiased appreciation beyond the metrics of our own mindsets and political persuasions?

## ABECEDARIUM OF A JESUS HUMAN

*The first man Adam became a living being: the Last Adam became a life-giving spirit. The first man was from the earth; a man of dust; the second man is from heaven. Like the man of dust, so are those who are of the dust; like the man of heaven, so are those who are of heaven. And just as we have borne the image of the man of dust, we will also bear the image of the man of heaven.*

APOSTLE PAUL[488]

By the way, archaeological discoveries at Gobekli Tepe in Turkey have demonstrated that the historical assumption that farming or husbandry came before organized religion were wrong. Traces of religion precede discovery of farming. In other words, the first evidence of humans being human is their experiences and expressions of worship. Worship and ***wateca*** need always need to be kept together.

For a deeper discussion of a ***wateca***-human, see the theology of leftovers in sobramesa.

## JESUS HUMAN

 **is for Xenophiliac (Greek: Ξενοφιλικός) Human**

A ***xenophile*** is someone who is drawn to strangers and the strange. A xenoglossophile is someone who is attracted to foreign languages and cultures. A ***xenophiliac*** human is someone who is not only NOT afraid of the unfamiliar and unknown, but is strangely warmed and attracted by them.

In a fitting symbol for the "Christian" as a ***xenophiliac***, "X" comes from the Greek letter Chi, the first letter of the Greek word *Christos* (Greek: Χριστός), which becomes Christ in English. A love for the unknown and the unfamiliar, for variety and diversity, is at the heart of who God is and who God made us to be.

The letter "X" is also the symbol for the unknown, stemming from an Arabic word for "thing" used in algebra equations, which was translated into Old Spanish as "xei" and abbreviated as "x." Any way you look at it, X, Christ, and unknown go together.

How we became a Jesus man, or Jesus woman, differs for every one of us. Jesus takes hold of each one of us in a dissimilar way, but it is the same Jesus leading us in the same direction. Jesus comes down and takes each one of us differently.

Mosses that grow profusely in the forests of the Pacific Northwest are like coral reefs in the oceans. The biodiversity of both is colossal: over 2,000 species of coral reefs, over 12,000 species of moss, dozens of which I see and touch every time I walk out my front door.

## ABECEDARIUM OF A JESUS HUMAN

Part of our dehumanization, for instance, is the loss of diverseness in the foods we eat. The stomach of a preserved 25,000-year-old human body, dug out of a Danish peat bog, revealed the contents of the last meal: "a porridge made with barley, flax, and the seeds of 40 different plants." In east Africa, the Hadza, one of the last remaining hunter-gatherer tribes, "eat from a potential wild-menu that consists of more than 800 plant and animal species."[489] Twenty-first-century humans get 75 percent of their calorie intake from just eight foods: rice, wheat, corn, potatoes, barley, palm oil, soya, and sugar.[490] Boring is the sure-fire sign of the pseudo, and a boring diet is not human but anti-human. Boring is decreation, and decreation is dangerous. "Bored to death" is more than a metaphor, especially when a Jesus human is born to life.

A Jesus human is able to embrace things that would never push their "like" button. Just because something is too difficult for me (e.g., Joyce's *Ulysses*), or not to my liking (Sondheim musicals), or beyond my endurance level (David Keenan's 808-page *Monument Maker*) or above my pay grade (*String Theory and M-Theory* by Michio Kaku) does not make them less true or wonderful.

The Latin motto of the European Union (EU) is "*in varietate concordia*." Translated into English the phrase is not rendered, as it first appears, "concord in variety" but "united in diversity." Diversity is not an end in itself, but a means to a larger end of wholeness, harmony, and peace. Marginality or difference in and of itself are celebrated as if transgressive itself is to be celebrated because it's on the margins and different (serial killers, anyone?). We love the rainbow, which is nothing but the light refracted into seven colors, all of which together make the One Light.

We need both the solitary colors of the rainbow and the solidarity of the light. This is a culture that makes orthodoxies poisonous and heterodoxies cleansing without realizing that some of the most toxic ideas in history are heterodoxies like Nazism. We celebrate diversity and difference but should never forget that it has been diversity and difference in the service of solidarity and unity that has made the biggest difference in the world.

##  is for Yada (Hebrew: עָדִי) Human

Pythagoreans liked to use the letter "Y" and its diverging branches as a prop to illustrate the choice between a life of leisure and a life of learning and struggle.

"Knowledge puffs up," Paul wrote, "but love builds up."[491] With all our education are we huffing and puffing, or are we body-building and love-lifting? The choice is between life or death. When you are out of love, you are out of life. When you are out of love, you are dead to humanity.

---

*They pretended to know it all, but were illiterate regarding life. They traded the glory of God who holds the whole world in his hands for cheap figurines you can buy at any roadside stand.*

ROMANS 1:23 (MSG)

---

One fruit of the spirit is knowledge. But "knowledge" in the biblical sense is not info or data, iotas or facts, or anything you find on the TV game show *Jeopardy*. Biblical knowledge is a "knowing" that comes from up-close-and-personal relationships with someone or something. The way to know more about anything is to deepen your experience of it, not to detach yourself from it. In fact, the "fall" of the first humans was the choice of knowledge over knowing, cognition over relationship.

*Yada* is Hebrew for "knowledge" but is better translated "knowing." *Yada* is used 950 times in the Hebrew Scriptures. *Yada* is a relationship word that means "knowing" from the inside out. Like Jesus knows us from the inside out. "He knew all people and needed no one to testify about anyone; for he himself knew what was in everyone."[492] Nathaniel asked Jesus: "Where did you get to know me?"[493] The many-times manhandled Samaritan woman, who encountered Jesus at Jacob's well, could not help but tell everyone about the first male in her life who knew her beauty from the inside out. Or in the exact words of Scripture, "Come and see a man who told me all that I ever did."[494]

---

*The way to begin healing the wounds of the world is to treasure the Infant Christ in us; to be not the castle, but the cradle of Christ; and in rocking that cradle to the rhythm of love, to swing the whole world back into the beat of the Music of Eternal Life.*

BRITISH ARTIST AND POET CARRYL HOUSELANDER (D. 1954)[495]

---

Knowledge is to write about grace. Knowing is to write grace. Knowledge is to write about beauty. Knowing is to write beauteously. The difference between "**yada**" as knowledge (as we know it) and knowing is symbolized in the two highlighted trees in our birth and downfall story: the Three of Life and the Tree of Knowledge of Good and Evil. The Tree of Life represented knowing God and breathing his daily presence. The Tree of Knowledge of Good and Evil represented our attainment of divine knowledge that could rationalize the presence of evil in a good world. Our choice to pursue knowledge over knowing led to our broken relationship with God, ourselves, each other, and creation. It also led to our universal failure in every time and place to understand the meaning of evil and suffering, and to make theodicy the most intractable of all philosophical dilemmas. We still choose the knowledge over the knowing partly because knowledge is control and knowing involves being known, which is the essence of vulnerability itself.

True knowledge requires humility: "Take my yoke upon you and learn from me, for I am gentle and humble in heart."[496] The ultimate in **yada** is nada . . . nada is Spanish for "nothing." A Jesus human always wants to know more, even though they know the impossibility of ever really knowing anything. The ultimate in "knowledge" is to acknowledge our total dependence on God. True **yada** is the awareness that apart from God, we are "nada." Apart from God, we **yada** nada. The illusion of omniscience is when you don't know what you don't know.

But there is also the knowing of not knowing what you already know. We all know more than we know. The most important thing we know that we don't know we know until someone tells us we know is this: Jesus is Lord.

In trinitarian terms: God the Creator is the song that sings itself: "All nature sings, and round me rings, the music of the spheres."[497]

Christ the Redeemer is the song that does not sing itself: "Tell Me the Stories of Jesus." You have to sing it, or it goes unsung. The Holy Spirit intervenes to draw forth and sing The Song that is humming and strumming within us in any way the Spirit sees fit.

JESUS HUMAN

*Most good painters don't know what they think until they paint it.*
ABSTRACT EXPRESSIONIST ROBERT MOTHERWELL (D. 1991)[498]

One of the most classic lines in the history of television is from Sgt. Schultz on the CBS sitcom *Hogan's Heroes* (1965–1971): "I Know Nothing!" Sgt. Schultz's signature snort "I know nothing" is a shorthand version of the Socratic paradox, which highlights one of the most insightful principles in the history of philosophy: "The only true wisdom consists of knowing that you know nothing." In other words, the more you know, the more you know you don't know.

We live in a world of folly where know-it-all boffins and buffoons pontificate on everything. Everyone is an expert. Everyone knows everything. Everyone thinks they must have an opinion on anything. Just ask them. When is the last time you heard someone confess, "I don't have a good opinion on that," or "I haven't given that much thought," or admit they have no idea what is really going on and likely to happen? Sometimes the biggest human advantage is the advantage of ignorance, which empowers us with the daring of trying something new.

I started down this line of thought because a lifelong Methodist, and dysfunctional Defense Secretary, Donald Rumsfeld (d. 2021), was mocked for saying, "I don't know." But like Sgt. Schultz and Socrates, there is wisdom here:

> As we know, there are known knowns;
> > there are things we know we know.

# ABECEDARIUM OF A JESUS HUMAN

> We also know there are known unknowns;
> that is to say we know there are some
> things we do not know.[499]

A posture of humbleness in knowing does not gift anyone with a get-out-of-jail-free card. In 1976 Charles Jewell was convicted by a San Diego court for trafficking 50 kilograms of marijuana hidden in a car he drove across the Mexico US border. He based his defense on not knowing about the stash. The court established a legal rule known as the Ostrich Instruction, which "informs the jury that actual knowledge and deliberate avoidance of knowledge are the same thing."[500] Deliberate ignorance is in some ways the worst kind of ignorance.

---

*Then the Lord answered Job out of the whirlwind and said:*
*"Who is this who obscures My counsel by words without knowledge?"*
JOB 38:1-2

---

One of the strangest political parties in US history was the "Know Nothing Party" of the 1850s. They were a strange mixture of progressivism and populism: they opposed slavery, promoted women's rights, supported workers' rights and labor unions, and government regulation of key industries. At the same time, they were anti-immigration, anti-Catholic, anti-Masonic, and anti-alcohol (a forerunner of the temperance movement). The "Know Nothing Party" got its name from the standard response of members when asked what the party stood for: "I know nothing."

But there are degrees of knowing nothing. You can still

## JESUS HUMAN

know something and basically "know nothing." And for a Jesus human knowing that "something" is a BIG THING: But this ONE THING I know . . . Jesus Christ. Knowing ONE THING was a constant refrain from the mouth of the greatest theologian in the history of Christianity:

> "For I resolved to know nothing while I was with you except Jesus Christ and him crucified."[501]

> "I count not myself to know nothing: but this one thing I do, . . . I press toward the mark for the prize of the high calling of God in Christ Jesus."[502]

---

*It is one of the triumphs of the human that he can know a thing and still not believe it.*
NOBEL LAUREATE JOHN STEINBECK (D. 1968)[503]

---

In my life story of "knowing," first I knew it all. Knowledge was the be-all and end-all. Then I knew nothing. The more I knew, the more I knew I didn't know. Now I know little about lots, because my mind sets on the one thing that opens the door to all things—Jesus. When we put on the mind of Christ, and open ourselves to the circuitry of the Spirit, our minds and spirits are constantly renewed by the One who knows everything. The Spirit can dispense knowledge and wisdom at will and to whomever. Intellectual ability is just one good among many.

> "The secret things belong to the Lord our God, but the things revealed belong to us

and to our sons forever, that we may observe all the words of this law."[504]

"Call to Me and I will answer you, and I will tell you great and mighty things, which you do not know."[505]

"For nothing is secret that will not be revealed, nor anything hidden that will not be known and come to light."[506]

"No longer do I call you servants, for the servant does not know what his master is doing; but I have called you friends, for all things that I have heard from My Father I have made known to you."[507]

Especially when visiting people who are sick and dying or in trouble, **Yada** Nada is the best posture. Instead of saying all the things people say to have something to say, the fallback bromides, the catch-all cliches that are trotted out when you don't know what else to say, maybe the best is simply, "I don't know what to say." Jesus himself instructed us, "Do not be anxious beforehand what you are to say, but say what is given to you in that hour, for it is not you who speak, but the Holy Spirit."[508] If nothing is given, say nothing. Presence is the true vernacular of healing.

Sometimes and in some people, presence can be conveyed in ways beyond the physical. After the 32nd US President Franklin Delano Roosevelt died in 1945, people stood deep and wide to watch the funeral train go by. It was a thousand-mile journey across seven states, from Warm Springs, Georgia, to Hyde Park, New York. Many people wept openly. One crying mourner was asked, "Did you know the president?" The response? "No, but he knew me." In a social media world, not everyone can know us in person. But we can know every person personally.

Biblical knowing (*yada*) is not abstract or distancing, but embracing and embodying. When you truly "know" God, you conceive Christ for the world.

*Jesus knows me,*
*This I love.*
CHURCH SIGN RE-SIGNING "JESUS LOVES ME THIS I KNOW"[509]

##  is for Zeitgeist (German) Human

In the visions of the Desert Fathers, demons often appeared to them without knees. Demons don't bend the knee. Unlike demons, we sons of Adam/daughters of Eve were created with knees to bend, but we don't like to bend them before God. We humans drop down and bow before every fad, fashion, and fame—the ***Zeitgeist*** or spirit of the age—but dislike bending at the knees for the divine—the Heilige Geist, the Holy Spirit or spirit of God. If we get it right, the relationship of culture and faith, politics and religion, Zeit and Heilige, will never be a straightforward or comfortable one.

Every lived story takes place within a particular culture where all human life is there. To be a Jesus human is live out the Jesus story in one's own context as a resident not a visitant, whether it be a high or low context culture. It is only in context that a life can be lived, or a story told.

For example, paintings of the Virgin Mary after 1100 often show her in blue robes and red shoes. Why? Blue, of course, is the color of heaven. But why the red shoes? Red seems more fit for the brothel or dance floor. But in the Middle Ages, red was the most expensive and coveted color for shoes and hence fit for the Queen of Heaven. Context is not everything, but close.

Most of Jesus' teaching was highly contextual, using parables in which people could better understand the truths of God. As theologian Stephen B. Bevans states in his classic study of contextuality, "there is no such thing as 'theology'; there is only contextual theology."[510]

The Apostle Paul understood the importance of context and *Zeitgeist*: "There are doubtless many different languages in the world, and none is without meaning, but if I do not know the meaning of the language, I shall be a foreigner to the speaker and the speaker a foreigner to me."[511]

A Jesus human lives out obedience to the Heilige Geist within a *Zeitgeist* of cultures and circumstances. We are all called to be fully here, and fully somewhere else: "in" but not "of" a culture, as Jesus put it; to participate in the particular and the universal at the same time.

* In touch with the geists of the zeit but in tune with the Heilige Geist
* Compatible with culture but not compliant or congruent with it
* Respecting a culture and its people, but not resonant with it
* In deference but in defiance at the same time
* Aspirational for many of a culture's hopes and dreams and antagonistic to its idols
* Convincing to a culture but also convicting to that culture

A *Zeitgeist* human contextualizes The Story in whatever "state"[512] they are in without condescension or disdain. The ancient Greeks looked down on anyone who didn't speak Greek. The Greek word "barbarian" didn't have anything to do with savagery or brutality. It had to do with the "baa-baa-baa" sheepishness of anyone who couldn't step up to speak the presumed greatest language in the world: Greek. Everything else but Greek was but baa-baa-baa. There are too many barbarian Christians.

In C. S. Lewis' classic satire of how a successful devil operates,[513] some of the prime seductions for humans are contemporary fads and fashions. Trends disregard ancient sources of wisdom and truth in pursuit of being "relevant" and "seen" by others, forgetting that fads fade and become the follies of tomorrow. Screwtape also lures Christians towards hell by encouraging them to see their faith not as a relationship with a Person but as a Principle to banner and badge, or a Possession to barter for blessings and favors, or even a Prop wielded as a weapon to control and conquer. What the devil fears most is for humans to develop a relationship with God and our neighbor that is humble, joyful, and self-transcending, and where all human interaction is holy, in some form or fashion.

Hell for Lewis is a hellish state of mind "where everyone is perpetually concerned about his own dignity and advancement, where everyone has a grievance, and where everyone lives the deadly serious passions of envy, self-importance, and resentment . . . something like the bureaucracy of a police state or the offices of a thoroughly nasty business concern."[514] Does this ring any bells?

Every *Zeitgeist* needs the Heilige Geist.

## CONCLUSION:
# HUMANLY POSSIBLE

*Humans have been made more sacred than any superman or supermonkey. . . . our very limitations have already become holy and like a home, because of that sunken chamber in the rocks, where God became very small.*

G. K. CHESTERTON[1]

In February of 2016, I had the privilege of being the speaker at the Maramon Convention in Kerala, India. This is the largest gathering of Asian Christians in the East. The first day I was there, they asked me to be part of a taped interview with the Emeritus Metropolitan Mar Chrysostom to be given as a gift to the Mar Thoma Syrian church in celebration of his 100th birthday.

As I was ushered upstairs into his retirement residence overlooking the luscious Pampa River, I had no idea what to expect. I waited nervously in the room off the balcony where my audience with the Metropolitan was to take place. I ransacked my brain for the kinds of questions I might ask this great leader of the Eastern church, known for his humor

## JESUS HUMAN

and love for people. Indeed, he is often called "The People's Bishop." I had started working on a book called "A Jesus Kind of Human," or as I affectionately called it to people who asked what books I was working on, "Will There Be Any Christians in Heaven?" The passage that prompted the idea for the book—Jesus' promise in John 4:12 that "whoever believes in me will do the works I have been doing, and they will do even greater things than these, because I am going to the Father"—was foremost in my mind. By "everything I do you can do" does it really mean "everything?" Did "greater things" really mean "greater things?"

I could not stop coming to terms with the fact that theosis is our humanation, not our divination. How much of Jesus' life showed us how to be the original human God made us to be? Was it everything up until the miracles, which were to give us signs of his status as the Son of God? Or were his miracles also signs of what is possible for those living out of their full humanity?

How could I ask him such a complex theological question in a simple way? I finally settled on a way of getting to the issue as quickly as I could. I would ask him: "Your holiness, Jesus weeping at the tomb shows his humanity. Did Jesus speaking 'Lazarus, Come Forth!' show his humanity too?"

Suddenly I stood up as a very frail gentlemen was ushered into the room and placed in his chair. He was assisted by two aides who stabilized his every move. As he was fussed over by the camera crew and by all sorts of adoring students, I noticed that there was a trembling of his body that created a kind of tremor in the room, almost the holy hum of a faith lived a capriccio, with light rhythmic spirit, that gladdened everyone around him without ever saying a word.

I had been briefed that the Metropolitan took the name Mar Chrysostom when he became a bishop of the Mar Thoma Church in 1953. Ordained as a priest in 1944 and a bishop of the Mar Thoma Church on 23 May 1953, Thirumeni continued his priestly ministry actively in his 99th year. But I had no idea what to talk to him about, or how to honor his seventy plus years in ministry. I had no idea whether he could even hear me, much less talk since his lower lip was trembling so much.

When they turned on the camera and nodded for me to start, I gave an official greeting on behalf of world Methodism in general, and my tribe in particular. Then I blurted out that I had been absolutely obsessed of late as to Jesus as the Last Adam and his mission to bring us back into a garden relationship with God.

Before I could ask him my carefully formulated question, the Metropolitan spoke. The first words out of the Metropolitan's mouth may be the last words I will ever hear. He said, "Everything Jesus did he did as a human. Everything." When he uttered these words, it was as if my mouth had been touched from the fires from on high. It was as if God had directly spoken to me to keep on the direction my mind was going. Jesus, the true, pure human, came to show us not what was divinely possible, but what was humanly possible.

## JESUS HUMAN

*In the immense cathedral which is the universe of God,
each man, whether scholar or manual laborer, is called to act
as the priest of his whole life—to take all that is human,
and to turn it into an offering and a hymn of glory.*
ORTHODOX FRENCH THEOLOGIAN PAUL EVDOKIMOV (D. 1970)[2]

Of course, the original design of human required the divine. You can't be human without God. That's what the Tree of Life meant in the Garden—God's ongoing gift of participation in the divine life as the essence of what it means to be human. When we tried to go it alone, without the presence of the divine in the human, we "fell" from our lofty place as the capstone of creation. Humans aren't special because of their rule or reign over creation. Humans are special because of their responsibility to care for, cultivate, and complete creation.

*Man stole the fruit, but I must climb the tree;
The tree of life to all, but only me.*
JESUS' WORDS
IN GEORGE HERBERT POEM "THE SACRIFICE" (1633)

In the Christian revolution and the Jesus story, the very notion of what it meant to be human toggled back and forth and changed forever. The gospel story is not imitatio Christi, but *in persona Christi* where "persona" is not impersonate but personate. Women and men are called to bring Christ into the world at our baptism, and become a Jesus human in whom the risen and rising Christ can live his resurrection life in the mission of a nobler humanity. As the old hymn written in 1933 by Presbyterian Alfred Henry Ackley, pianist and private secretary to Billy Sunday and publishing partner to Sunday's music director Homer Rodeheaver says:

> I serve a risen Saviour, He's in the world today
>
> I know that He is living, whatever men may say . . .
>
> You ask me how I know He lives?
>
> He lives within my heart.

**Come On, Ring Those Bells:** Sewanee Hunt is a professor at Harvard's Kennedy School of Government and former U.S. ambassador to Austria (1993–97). She tells the story of a woman named Sophia. "She lived in a little town in Croatia. She was an old woman. Every day she had one job, to go at noon to the church, to take the ropes that were tied up on the wall, untie them, pull on the ropes, and ring the bells in the tower. During the war, in village after village, when the Serb forces came in tanks, they would shoot up all the houses of the Catholics, the Croats, and then they would end up at the church. They would go to the church and shoot up the church. At the very end they would shoot the tower. Then they would roll out, and it would now be a Serb town. This old woman whose church had been shot up, every day you would find her in the churchyard at noon. There was wood splintered everywhere, but in the middle of the debris, the big bell that had been in the bell tower was lying on its side on the ground. Sophia, this eighty-year-old woman, was bent over with her old gnarled hands grasping the clapper and swinging her arms, ringing the bell. . . . No matter what the circumstances in which you are working, your job is to keep your hands on that clapper, ringing the bell."[3]

Some husband or wife is ringing a bell this morning, staying faithful to a spouse lost in depression and unhelpful pills.

Some pastor is ringing a bell this morning, trying to listen and understand the stories of people for whom seminary did not prepare him.

Some working single mother is ringing a bell this morning, working two jobs to sustain a different dream for her children.

Some senior citizen is ringing a bell this morning, refusing to grow bitter in a changing world, and praying for a better future for her grandchildren.

Some patient in a hospital is ringing a bell this morning, believing this life has meaning for them, even though they now realize they will never have a family.

Some social worker is ringing a bell this morning, trying again to bring reconciliation to neighborhoods that seem trapped in hopelessness.

Some executive is ringing a bell this morning, looking for ways to build a profitable company to employ thousands, while also benefitting the local community.

My hands were clasping that clapper while writing this book, ringing the bell, the bell of Jubilee, God's dream for this world.

# INTERACTIVES

1. Try saying these three words. Repeat these words after me: "I am holy." Say them out loud: "I am holy." Now say with conviction: "Human is holy." How did you feel saying these phrases? Talk to each other about this.

2. How can Christ live in me, and yet sometimes I feel so alone?

3. "For the past eighty years [wrote the cellist Pablo Casals at the age of ninety-three] I have started each day in the same manner . . . I go to the piano, and I play two preludes and fugues of Bach . . . It is a sort of benediction on the house. But that is not its only meaning . . . It is a rediscovery of the world in which I have the joy of being a part. It fills me with awareness of the wonder of life, with a feeling of the incredible marvel of being human."[1]

    What exercises and routines do you keep that give you a sense of "the incredible marvel of being human?"

4. Liberalism's favorite conservative is David Brooks. David Brooks' *The Road in Character* (2016) makes the case that "they had to go down to come up." Brooks portrays human nature in terms of two competing drives:

Adam I and Adam II. Adam I is ambitious, achievement-oriented, and sees life in monetary terms. Adam II is morally concerned "to love intimately, to sacrifice self in the service of others, to live in obedience to some transcendent truth, to have a cohesive inner soul that honors creation and one's own possibilities" (p. 13–22). Adam I is shrewd, competitive, productive, and "externally oriented;" but without some emphasis on the "internally oriented" Adam II, "it is easy to slip into a self-satisfied moral mediocrity." Brooks argues that "The ideal is to find a way to live a life that is both successful and meaningful, a life that is both Adam I and Adam II" (p. 22). What do you think of this typology using Adam I and Adam II as ideal types?

5. Who is on your Mt. Rushmore of humans?

6. To navigate the various weathers, windings, and waylays of life, you need a compass constant. Do you think a person can be their own North Star, or Southern Cross? Discuss the bravery and sure-footedness it takes to be one's own compass constant.

7. One of the words that didn't make the alphabet cut is F = Fika Human (Swedish). Swedish fika, pronounced fee-ka (and the Danish word hygge pronounced hoo-gah), convey the coziness and contentment and recuperation that comes from taking small breaks for coffee, pastry, and conversation during the time. "Do you want to have fika?" is a recurrent Swedish phrase, as is the declaration, "It's fika time." It's in "fika time"

where relationships are formed and deals are struck in an informal way before the formal proceedings.

The Finnish version of fika is sisu.2 Sisu is a Finnish concept described as stoic determination, tenacity of purpose, grit, bravery, resilience, and hardiness and is held by Finns themselves to express their national character. It is said to be a grim, gritty, white-knuckle form of courage that is presented typically in situations where success is against the odds. It expresses itself in taking action against the odds and displaying courage and resoluteness in the face of adversity. In other words, deciding on a course of action and then sticking to that decision, even despite repeated failures. It is in some ways similar to equanimity, with the addition of a grim kind of stress management. "Gutsy" is a fairly close translation.

Do you think either "fika" or "sisu" should have been included in the abecedary of Jesus-human qualities?

8. Discuss this one line from the 1869 hymn "Loved with Everlasting Love" by George Wade Robinson:

> Heaven above is softer blue,
> Earth beneath is brighter green;
> something lives in every hue
> Christless eyes have never seen.

Give some examples of the "something" that "Christless eyes have never seen."

9. Storytelling to a digital mindset requires an octagonal matrix of coordinates. An octagon is a sacred space, because it brings together the circle and the square, the

circle of heaven and the square of earth. Here is the octagonal matrix of the mission field today. Discuss each one and what it might mean for you and your church.

1) From Gutenberg to Zuckerberg
2) Storify, not Versify.
3) Metaphor to Metanoia to Metamorphosis
4) Make the Story a Movie in Your Mind
5) Trust the Story
6) Receive the Story First, Theologize Last.
7) Every Story Contains the Whole Story.
8) Live the Story, Sing the Story
9) Discuss this reframing of the "coming" of Christ:

> Our task is to seek and find Christ in our world as it is, and not as it might be. The fact that the world is other than it might be does not alter the truth that Christ is present in it and that his plan has been neither frustrated nor changed. . . . What is uncertain is not the 'coming' of Christ but our own reception of him, our own response to him, our readiness and capacity to 'go forth to meet him.' We must be willing to see him and acclaim him, even at the very moment when our whole life's work and all its meaning seem to collapse.
> ~Thomas Merton, *Seasons of Celebration* (1965)

10. What could go wrong? In 2018, we entered a new world. For the first time, humans didn't make machines. Machines started making humans, in this

case a gene-editing machine called CRISPR-Cas9, which He Jiankui, a Chinese biologist, built to recreate mutations in babies that confer resistance to HIV.

A small step for humanity? What could go wrong?

The gene-editing introduced new, not-intended mutations in the babies. Furthermore, these never-seen-before botched genes instead of the good ones will be passed on to the babies' offspring.

What are your hopes and fears for this new world we are entering?

11. Karen Kilby, professor of Catholic theology at one of the top-ranked universities in the UK, Durham University, writes in God, Evil and the Limits of Theology (2021): "Christian theology ought to acknowledge itself to be faced with questions it cannot answer."

    Do you agree? If so, what might some of those questions be?

12. Listen to Stephanie Gretzinger's eucharistic song, "Remember." Have you ever heard of a two table-grace tradition, a two-grace tradition at the table?

13. Who among us has not read a book where the author confidently and excitedly asserts that Marxist theory, or Darwinian evolution, or Freudian self-actualization, or any number of other worldviews is "the best" and only way to understand the world in which we live? Why are followers of Jesus not as confident and excited about looking at the world through Jesus' eyes and the Jesus lens?

14. Historian Ian Kershaw, the world's leading expert on Hitler and Nazi Germany, argues in his new book Personality and Power: Builders and Destroyers of Modern Europe (2022) that the outcome of global crises depends largely on the personal character of the humans who are in positions of responsibility and power for handling them. Does this make you worry less, or worry worse?

15. Every human soul is different. What is your soul like?

    A library?
       A catwalk?
          A mirror?
             A matryoshka doll?

16. Electroencephalogram (EEG) tests which measure electrical activity in the brain are getting more and more sophisticated. Recently, EEG research, especially the work of Dr. Dario Nardi, has revealed the existence of a "Christmas Tree brain" ("trans-contextual thinking") described this way:

    > Regardless of what stimulus enters—sight, sound, smell, etc.—the brain responds by rapidly processing that stimulus in multiple regions—including regions not seemingly applicable to that stimulus.[3]

17. This is a highly creative "asynchronous macro-state characterized by various regions of the brain firing at different amplitude and frequencies." Might this form of

# INTERACTIVES

whole-brained creativity have been the brain the original humans received from God?

18. This was written over a half century ago. How much does this still track with today?

> The modern world, which denies personal guilt and admits only social crimes, which has no place for personal repentance but only public reforms, has divorced Christ from His Cross, the Bridegroom and Bride have been pulled apart. What God hath joined together, men have torn asunder.
> ~Archbishop Fulton J. Sheen, *Life of Christ* (1958), xxiv–xxv.

19. It is stories that give us a human shape. What is one story that has shaped you as a human?

20. Where do you find the human spirit most truly alive and itself?

21. Why is the place for animals called "The Humane Society" and not "Animal Kingdom?" Shouldn't the church be more "The Humane Society" than, as it sometimes is, the "Animal House" or "Animal Farm?"

22. Discuss the importance of this tweet by Dr. Mark Chironna: "Apart from Christ we can know neither what it means for God to be God nor what is means for humans to be human."[4]

23. The founder of Focolare Movement Chiara Lubich (d. 2008) said this: "As one sacred host, from among the millions of hosts on the Earth, is enough to nourish us

with God, so one brother or sister, the one whom God's will puts next to us, is enough to give us communion with humanity, which is the mystical Jesus. My God, let me be in this world the tangible sacrament of your Love, of your being Love; let me be your arms that press to themselves then consume in love all the loneliness of the world."[5]

What does it mean to be a "tangible sacrament" of God's love? Do you have any stories of "hosts" in your life who brought out your humanity and brought you close to God?

24. "You were within me, Lord, but I was outside myself."[6] Does St. Augustine speaks for all of us in his confession that even when we are "outside" ourselves, Jesus is still within calling us home? How do you bring the "outside" and the "inside" together?

25. How does this metaphor of Jesus as a "divine fishing rod" play in your mind and spirit? What are its positives and negatives? Would you use it?

> The human beingness of Jesus Christ was, as it were, the divine fishing rod that caught the human beingness of all men and was now pulling it in, so that all the human beingness of all men would be brought into the unity of the body of Christ.
> ~Pope Emeritus Benedict XVI from *The Unity of the Nations: A Vision of the Church Fathers*, trans. Bonaface Ramsey (2015).

INTERACTIVES

26. We used to talk about "saving the lost." Is it the same thing but in a fresh way to say it this way: The mission of every Christian is to illuminate, activate, and animate Christ in everyone you meet? How much more understandable to this culture is the latter? Or do you still think the former way of talking about salvation works?

27. Theologian Cherith Fee Nordling tells of how "I wake up differently now and say, 'Jesus, what would you invite me into today that isn't what I would do by myself?'" What difference would that prayer make in your life and in the life of your church and family?

28. Elon Musk and thousands of others working in the field of AI signed on in late March 2023 to a "Pause Giant AI Experiments: An Open Letter." Here is the link to the letter issued by the Future of Life Institute: https://futureoflife.org/open-leter/pause-giant-ai-experiments/

    Read the letter and discuss whether or not you would or will sign it. Will a pause be enough? Does a pause cut it? Or do we need to cut more deeply?

29. The section on "Ressourcement" highlights the concept of resilience. Have you heard of resilience hubs that are designated buildings that provide air-conditioned places of refuge (food, water, Internet, charging stations) when heatwaves either threaten people at high risk (old, infirm) or when blackouts make it difficult. Could your church become a resilience hub?

30. Luke Bell OSB is a monk of Quarr Abbey on the Isle of

Wight in the U.K. In his book The Mystery of Identity (2022), monk of Quarr Abbey on the Isle of Wight in the U.K. writes:

> Each personal identity is a spoke in a bicycle wheel, fastened to the still, turning center who is God among us and stretching out to the rim whose extension is the space and time coordinates of individual lives. Identity in the sense of uniqueness is on the circumference where one position is not another; identity in the sense of sameness is in the center where all are one in Christ (p. 31).

How does this metaphor of the spoke of a wheel speak to you about your own identity?

31. Former British Army officer Rory Stewart was a member of Parliament from 2010 to 2019. He resigned from the government in July 2019, after voting against the government's Brexit deal. Now a Senior Fellow at Yale University, he reflects on his decade in politics using the terms we have used in this book on the need for humility and confidence:

> My central experience as a working politician was one of mental and moral corrosion . . . Sometimes it felt as if the job were reshaping the very neural pathways of my brain, enervating the qualities I required to act responsibly in the Cabinet Room. Governing was about critical thinking; politics was not.

> While critical thinking required humility, British politics demanded absolute confidence: in place of reality, it offered untethered hope; instead of accuracy, vagueness. While critical thinking required skepticism, open-mindedness and an instinct for complexity, politics demanded loyalty, partisanship and slogans: not truth and reason but power and persuasion."[7]

32. How important is it for humans to keep dancing these two opposite forces of humility and confidence?

33. We are living in a world of proliferating deepfakes. What would it mean for humans to aspire to be deepreals? How would a deepreal life change how you live your life?

34. Discuss Cambridge University scholar Rupert Shortt's contention that it may be even harder to be an atheist than a theist. In a nutshell, "justifying the belief that we are made in the image of God is challenging . . . but the alternative—that we are no more than chemical scum hurtling through the void on a piece of rock, to reference Stephen Hawking—may be just as contentious a proposition."[8]

35. To what extent does social media steal the innocence and privacy of children? How might this affect their (and our) humanity?

36. Anyone ever nod off while you're driving? Even if just for a second? You wake up, roll down the window or turn up

the radio, sometimes even slap your face. These are called "microsleeps." And the average microsleep is five seconds. At 60 mph, that's the length of a football field. In other words, you've just slept through 100 yards of driving.

That's an example of "ostranenie." Can you come up with other examples of defamiliarization that wakes us up to something old that needs to become new and fresh?

37. AI potential is promising "wingbots," "copilots," and "personal agents." Can you see how AI can become an integral and integrated part of your organic life, not just your electronic life? Or is it a dystopian danger that will make obsolete organic hardware and software?

38. Charles Haddon Spurgeon warned against the sin of what he called "ministerialism"—the tendency of ministers to lose their humanity in ministry and become ministers first and disciples of Jesus second. Here is his prayer:

> Lord, keep me from ministerialism. Keep me from reading my Bible as a minister, and from praying as a minister, and from doing the whole of my religion as if I were not myself personally, but only relatively concerned in it. Keep me from thinking that I am better than other men, or that I have any special holiness because I am called to the ministry. Keep me humble, and let me always remember that I am only a sinner saved by grace. Keep me from being proud,

and let me always remember that my primary calling is to be a Christian, not a minister.⁹

39. Are we approaching life more as a "minister" than as a "human?"

40. How important is humor to humanity? Have you ever celebrated Holy Humor Sunday, the Sunday after Easter? It is also known as "Bright Sunday." If so, how have you recognized the "days of joy and laughter" God has given us?

41. What do you think should be the relationship between faith and politics? For example, Anthony Harvey's By What Authority? The Churches and Social Concern (2001) does not argue that faith traditions and local churches should leave public policy alone. Rather, they should cease to base their political, social or economic pronouncements on theology, that is, on an attempted reading of the mind of God. Instead, they should articulate a "latent moral consensus" relying on the concern for justice that is canonic in Judaism, Christianity and Islam, and is widely shared beyond. To do this is to follow the technique Jesus used in the telling of the Good Samaritan story: this is the kind of conduct we know you already admire, and we offer it for your participation. Discuss Harvey's position and how might such a posture change the political commons?

42. The French Jesuit priest Henri de Lubac (d. 1991) reflected on the incarnation in this way: "If you do not

live, think and suffer with the people of your time, as one of them, in vain will you pretend, when the moment comes to speak to them, to adapt your language to their ear. 'Know the moderns in order to answer their difficulties and their expectations.' A touching intention. But this way of projecting the 'moderns' into an objective concept, of separating oneself from them to consider them from the outside, makes this goodwill useless."

Lubac goes on: "We must have shared their anguish, their hopes, and their defeats if we are to be able to speak to them with authority. We must have lived their life, if we are to be able to show them the way to life."[10]

Can Jesus humans do ministry and mission without skin in the game?[11] If not, how much skin?

43. Discuss the irony of how, in this "anything-goes," "everything's-relative" age, there are more heresy hunters with purity tests (of the left and right) than perhaps any time since the Inquisition? How can humans strive for harmonious difference? Does ethicist Richard Mouw's concept of "convicted civility" cut a path forward, which the President Emeritus of Fuller Seminary explains as follows: "Convicted civility does not mean that we have to water down our convictions. It simply means that we are willing to engage in respectful dialogue with those who disagree with us, even when we are convinced that they are wrong."[12]

44. If Jesus' incarnational mode requires us to be "in" this AI world but not "of" it, how do we summon the contrarian

## INTERACTIVES

courage to use this technology but not let it use us? Here are two suggestions. First, never allow AI to take human form when it is roboticized? Second, never refer to AI in personalized or human pronouns. Do you agree? What would you add?

45. How do Jesus humans deal with failure? How do you handle failure? As I finish this book, I feel deeply my own utter failure in communicating the heights and depths of what it means to be a "Jesus human." Here is Dorothy Day at age seventy-nine, forty-five years after the day she walked into New York's Union Square and began selling copies of Catholic Worker for a penny a copy. "I feel like an utter failure," she wrote. "The older I get the more I feel that faithfulness and perseverance are the greatest virtues—accepting the sense of failure, we all must have in our work, in the work of others around us, since Christ was the world's greatest failure."[13] Discuss the paradox of Jesus being "the world's greatest failure" at the very moment on the cross he is most victorious and heaven's greatest success. How comforting is it to know, as Dorothy Day liked to say, "Christ understands us when we fail"?

46. British Baptist theologian Ruth Moriarty invokes the need for a deeper wisdom, a "slow wisdom" in our fast-paced, ever-changing world.[14] She suggests some practical exercises to develop "slow wisdom:" 1) Pay attention to our bodies and emotions; 2) Listen to the stories of others; 3) Practice mindfulness in

JESUS HUMAN

which you are present to the moment without judgment or preconditions; 4) Create space for silence.

How important do you think is "slow wisdom" for our discernment today? Of these four exercises, which one(s) are you good at and who ones do you have the most problem with?

47. ***Jesus Human*** has argued that Jesus was the most fully-loaded human, the most morally load-bearing human who ever lived. But that "load" became "easy," and that "burden" became "light," because of his participation in the life of the divine and his passing on to us by his resurrection that divine participation. Discuss the ways in which Jesus lives his resurrected life in us and among us, so that we become Jesus humans.

48. What is a Jesus human? A Jesus kind of human is someone whose desires of the heart are to be:

hospitable to hope,
    constant in faith,
        extravagant in love.

49. How do the desires of your heart, and the desires of your church, match up against these faith-hope-love standards?

50. The prime minister of England, Rishi Sunak, took his 2022 Commons oath on the *Bhagavad Gita*, the Sanskrit text sacred to the Hindu faith.[15] At the 2023 coronation of King Charles III, he stands alongside a Hindu prime minister and a Muslim mayor of London

and presents himself as a defender of all faiths.[16]

Christianity is already a minority religion in England and Wales. Christianity is soon to be a minority religion in USAmerica.[17] The fact that there are now more "nones" and "dones" than "somes" and "comes" requires a whole new missional set of 'tudes, tunes, and talk. In more ways than we know, the twenty-first century is more like the first century than the twentieth. Then is now. We are them.

51. Humans are designed for the divine, and seek in vain elsewhere for fulfilling storylines and soundtracks. This human-needs-divine-to-be-human thread draws tight the biblical tapestry. It is often hidden in back-stories, missed themes, and mistranslations. Let's do a Bible study by looking at Daniel 10:19 as a case in point:

> And he said, "You must not fear, *O* beloved man. *Peace be to you*; be strong and be **courage**ous!" And *when he spoke* with me, I was strengthened and I said, "Let my lord speak, for you have strengthened me.[18]

The problem is that the word courage is not in the original. It has to be deduced from and nuanced against "strong" to be included. However, this changes the meaning of the passage. The NIV has it right:

> "Do not be afraid, you who are highly esteemed," he said. "Peace! Be strong now; be strong." When he spoke to me, I was

strengthened and said, "Speak, my lord, since you have given me strength."

52. When the red-herring of "courage" is removed and replaced by the original translation, a double strengthening suddenly appears. First, there is a divine strengthening of the human. Second, the human embracing of that divine strengthening leads to a double empowerment whereby the human can be all it was made to be through divine fortification.[19]

    How might this double-empowerment change your life?

53. Some of the most intelligent people in history, starting with Aristotle and Socrates, insisted that human wisdom was paradoxical and consisted in knowing that one knows nothing. The Roman poet Lucretius wrote in the first century BC: "As I grow older, I learn more and more how much I do not know." Give some examples of people you know who are wise and humble at the same time.

54. What are the implications of living in a world where every time you leave your house you are giving total rights and consent to anyone, anywhere, at any moment, for any reason, to photograph or film you? Can you think of other examples of how wired goes haywire?

55. Why did the angel Lucifer rebel against God? In Isaiah, Lucifer is described as being "cast down from heaven" and "brought low" (Isaiah 14:12–15; see also Ezekiel 28:11–19). Lucifer was originally called "Helel ben Shahar,"

which means "morning star, son of the dawn."

The answer to the question depends on whether you think Lucifer's rebellion took place before God created humans, or after. Most scholars say before. But some scholars argue that the heavenly rebellion was motivated by angelic jealousy of humans. Lucifer is often depicted as being the most beautiful of the angels, which may have led him to think he should have been given a higher position than humans.

What do you think?

56. *Jesus Human* has argued that Jesus is The Divine DNA. The umbilical cord that connects us to the DNA of the divine is triple-braided: Jesus, Scripture, Spirit—The Holy Braid. Once you separate one cord from the strand, the umbilical cord is cut and collapses. But if you keep the three tightly woven, the Spirit brings Jesus of the Scriptures alive to live his resurrection life in and among us. "A cord of three strands is not easily broken" (Ecclesiastes 4:12). What are steps you can take to keep that braid unbroken?

57. Are we at a time in history when it is less important to win arguments and declare victory than to build bridges of understanding and concede "Is this what you're saying? Can you hear what I'm saying?" What are you and your church doing to be bridge-builders?

58. Influencers have replaced role models. Role models were known for character and integrity. Influencers are known for clout and clicks. Is this progress?

59. Dr. Zoh's concept of "Tong" is a holistic method of praying through the Bible. How might this Eastern approach to engaging with scripture differ from traditional Western methods, and what potential benefits could it offer to people's spiritual practices?

60. If "The Bible is composed for oral hearing, not silent reading," how might reading the Bible aloud and emphasizing its auditory aspects change one's understanding and experience of the text? Do you agree with this perspective?

61. The Tong chapter discusses the integration of Eastern and Western spiritual concepts, symbolized by the idea of "bifocal vision." In what ways could this integration of different cultural and spiritual perspectives enhance or challenge one's understanding of faith and spirituality in today's globalized world?

# CONNECT WITH LEONARD

For more from Leonard Sweet:

Websites:
   www.leonardsweet.com
   www.preachthestory.com
   www.sanctuaryseaside.com

Instagram: @leonard.sweet

Facebook:
   facebook.com/lensweet
   facebook.com/preachthestory
   facebook.com/sanctuaryseaside

Twitter: @lensweet

YouTube: www.youtube.com/@leonardsweet1

Podcast: www.leonardsweet.com/podcasts

Napkin Scribbles Podcast:

   Spotify:
   https://open.spotify.com/show/2vt6wEi70dQEpW37CypfvY

   iTunes:
   https://podcasts.apple.com/gb/podcast/napkin-scribbles-a-podcast-by-leonard-sweet/id1436743015

# SCRIPTURE VERSIONS

Scripture quotations marked CEB are from the Common English Bible, copyright © 2012 by Common English Bible.

Scripture quotations marked NIV are taken from the Holy Bible, New International Version®, NIV®. Copyright © 1973, 1978, 1984, 2011 by Biblica, Inc.™ Used by permission of Zondervan. All rights reserved worldwide. www.zondervan.com. The "NIV" and "New International Version" are trademarks registered in the United States Patent and Trademark Office by Biblica, Inc.™

Scripture quotations marked TNIV are taken from the HOLY BIBLE, TODAY'S NEW INTERNATIONAL VERSION®. TNIV®. Copyright © 2001, 2005 by International Bible Society. Used by permission of Zondervan. All rights reserved worldwide.

Scripture quotations marked KJV are taken from the Holy Bible, King James Version.

Scripture quotations marked NASB are taken from the (NASB®) New American Standard Bible®, Copyright © 1960, 1971, 1977, 1995, 2020 by The Lockman Foundation. Used by permission. All rights reserved. lockman.org

Scripture quotations marked NKJV are from the New King James Version.® Copyright © 1982 by Thomas Nelson, Inc. Used by permission. All rights reserved.

Scripture quotations marked NRSV are from the New Revised Standard Version Bible, copyright © 1989, Division of Christian Education of the National Council of the Churches of Christ in the United States of America. Used by permission. All rights reserved.

Scripture quotations marked ESV are from The Holy Bible, English Standard Version® (ESV®), copyright © 2001 by Crossway, a publishing ministry of Good News Publishers. Used by permission. All rights reserved.

Scripture quotations marked NLT are taken from the Holy Bible, New Living Translation, copyright ©1996, 2004, 2015 by Tyndale House Foundation.

JESUS HUMAN

Used by permission of Tyndale House Publishers, Carol Stream, Illinois 60188. All rights reserved.

Scripture quotations marked MNT are from Moffatt, New Translation, copyright © 1922 by James Moffatt.

Scripture quotations marked JET are from the Joint English Translation, copyright © 2020.

Scripture quotations marked AMP are taken from the Amplified Bible, Copyright © 2015 by The Lockman Foundation. Used by permission.

Scripture quotations marked CSB have been taken from the Christian Standard Bible®, Copyright © 2017 by Holman Bible Publishers. Used by permission. Christian Standard Bible® and CSB® are federally registered trademarks of Holman Bible Publishers.

Scripture quotations marked MSG are taken from The Message, copyright © 1993, 2002, 2018 by Eugene H. Peterson. Used by permission of NavPress. All rights reserved. Represented by Tyndale House Publishers.

Scripture quotations marked (Dar) are taken from the DARBY BIBLE, published in 1867, 1872, 1884, 1890; public domain

# NOTES

**PREFACE**

1. This is a paraphrase of a line from Buber's 1929 collection of essays entitled *Between Man and Man* (1929 German; 1947 English; 1970 edition), 112. The literal translation is: "In every meeting between man and man the human race is set on the move."

2. Here are some of the writings of Maximus the Confessor where he talks about the new way of human life that Christianity offers:

   "The Lord has come to teach us a new way of life, a way of love, humility, and service." (*Ambigua* 41.17)

   "The Christian life is not about following a set of rules or regulations; it is about following Jesus Christ and living in the way that he taught us." (*Capita de caritate* 2.10)

   "The kingdom of God is not a place, but a way of life. It is a way of life that is characterized by love, peace, and justice." (*Homiliae in Ps.* 67.1)

3. See George Weigel, "The Catholic Crisis Over 'Us,'" *First Things*, 26 April 2023.

4. Richard Rex, "A Church in Doubt," *First Things* (April 2018), 22–23. https://www.firstthings.com/article/2018/04/a-church-in-doubt. Accessed 17 August 2023.

5. The larger quote found on page 125 is this: "We have made a wilderness of what was once a garden. We have poisoned the air and water, and we have filled the land with waste. We have destroyed the habitats of countless species, and we have driven many to extinction. We have done this in the name of progress, but what we have created is a wasteland. We are bewildered at the wilderness we have made of what is human and humane."

6. *The Trends Journal*, 21 March 2023.

7. See my *From Tablet to Table: Where Community Is Found and Identity Is*

## JESUS HUMAN

*Formed* (2019), where I contend that identity requires narrative form, or James Bryan Smith's, *The Magnificent Story: Uncovering a Gospel of Beauty, Goodness, Truth* (2017), where he says the same thing but in different words: "the stories you are living by are running your life. You are living at their mercy," adding, "the most important thing we can do is to start living into the right story" (p. 5).

8   Acts 3:15

9   https://www.youtube.com/watch?v=18ZFPqnlMaQ&t=3s. Accessed 17 August 2023.

10  Acts 3:21, CEB

11  Final stanza in the 35 stanza "The Wreck of the Deutschland," written in 1875–76, but not published until 1918.

12  Romans 6:4

13  I owe this reframing of eternal life to Alexander Schmemann, *The Journals of Father Alexander Schmemann, 1973–1983*, trans. Juliana Schmemann (2000), 78.

14  The will to kill is perpetually at odds with the will to fill. Genesis 1:28 commands, "Fill the Earth."

15  The full quote from Mark Twain is as follows: "I have not read Nietzsche or Ibsen, nor any other philosopher, and have not needed to do it, and have not desired to do it; I have gone to the fountainhead for information—that is to say, to the human race. Every man is in his own person the whole human race, with not a detail lacking; I have studied the human race with diligence and strong interest all these years in my own person; in myself I find in big or little proportion every quality and every defect that is findable in the mass of the race.... What a coward every man is! And how surely he will find it out if he will just let other people alone and sit down and examine himself. The human race is a race of cowards; and I am not only marching in the procession but carrying a banner." Harriet E. Smith, et al., eds., *Autobiography of Mark Twain, Volume 3: The Complete and Authoritative Edition* (Volume 12, Mark Twain Papers) (2015), 130. Source: https://quotepark.com/quotes/1034027-mark-twain-the-human-race-is-a-race-of-cowards-and-i-am-not/. Accessed 17 August 2023.

16  Romans 1:26, NLT. With thanks to colleague Archie Callahan for reminding me of this passage.

17  At the same time, in the words of the Nicene Creed (325), "We believe in one Lord, Jesus Christ, the only Son of God, eternally begotten of

# NOTES

the Father, God from God, Light from Light, true God from true God, begotten not made, one in being with the Father." Fully human and fully divine, Jesus' two natures are totally distinct, but wholly united in one person.

18  Some estimates go as high as 231 million killed in the wars of the twentieth century. The two world wars alone accounted for over 100 million deaths. Civilian casualties were as high as 50 percent of these deaths.

19  Troy W. Martin, "The DNA of Logos in First Peter 2:23–24," in Richard P. Thompson, ed., *Listening Again to the Text: New Testament Studies in Honor of George Lyons* (2020), 133–150. For my use of the DNA metaphor to describe Logos, see *So Beautiful: Divine Design for Life and the Church* (2009) with the double helix as an ichthus on the cover. See the trailer for the book feature the DNA symbol, https://www.youtube.com/watch?v=fXgW1SfsAkw. Accessed 17 August 2023.

20  Homo sapiens stand on top of the nature chain in terms of the ratio of brain volume to body size. Dolphins are a close second, though, beating not only the great apes but also our early hominid ancestor. An animal is considered highly intelligent if it can do 6 things: 1) remember; 2) imitate; 3) use tools; 4) understand language; 5) be self-aware; 6) be behaviorally flexible. Each one of these was once considered the unique preserve of the "human" until the gap has almost closed.

**INTRODUCTION**

1  Leopold von Ranke, *Weltgeschichte*, III, I, 160ff.

2  W. H. Auden, "For the Time Being: A Christmas Oratorio," in his *Collected Longer Poems* (1969), 156–57. For the musical setting composed by Marvin David Levy, see *For the Time Being: Christmas Oratorio for Soloists, Narrator, Mixed Chorus and Orchestra*, from the poem by W. H. Auden (1959), 81–93.

3  Walter Wink, *The Powers That Be: Theology for a New Millennium* (1999), 11.

4  From his study of the Hebrew Bible and the Dead Sea Scrolls, Geza Vermes argues that "Son of Man" is not a title but means "Human Being" in his book *Jesus the Jew: A Historian's Reading of the Gospels* (1981). Vermes argues that the phrase was used in both of these sources to refer to a human being, not to a divine being.

5  Acts 17:28, KJV

6    In the second cantata of his "Christmas Oratorio," Bach has the chorus sing: "Resound, you songs, ring out, you strings!/Shout for joy, you hearts, with delight!/The Lord is with us, the Savior is here!/He is the most beautiful of all human beings,/He is the King of Kings,/He is the Lord of Lords."

7    In one year (2020–2021), the number of Belgians applying for debaptism went from 1260 to 5237. See "News Briefing: The Church in the World," *The Tablet*, 10 December 2022, 24.

8    Matthew 25:40

9    Romans 15;3, Psalm 69:9

10    Jesus's followers "do not commit adultery: . . . they do not bear false witness: they do not . . . covet what is not theirs: they honor father and mother: they do good to those who are their neighbors: and when they are judges they judge uprightly: . . . and whatever they do not wish others should do them, they do not practice towards any one: . . . and those who grieve them they comfort, and make them their friends: and they do good to their enemies: . . . they walk in all humility and kindness, and falsehood is not found among them, and they love one another: and from the widows they do not turn away their countenances: and they rescue the orphan from him who does him violence: and he who has gives to him who has not, without grudging." *The Apology of Aristides on Behalf of the Christians: From a Syriac Ms. Preserved on Mount Sinai*, ed. J. Rendel Harris (1891), 48–49.

11    Timothy Radcliffe, *Why Go to Church? The Drama of the Eucharist* (2009), 27.

12    D. T. Niles, *In the Beginning* (1958), 38.

13    As quoted by Quincy Jones in "Jon Batiste," *Time Magazine*, 06 June/13 2022, 102.

14    John 20:22, NIV. See also Andy Johnson, "Gospel Themes as 'Glue' for Pauline Ecclesiological Images," p. 85 in Richard P. Thompson, ed., *Listening Again to the Text: New Testament Studies in Honor of George Lyons* (2020), 73–93. Professor Johnson puts it like this: "The portrayals of Jesus in the Gospels of Mark and John as the eschatological temple of God, the locale or microcosm of the new creation, and the new/true human being bear an analogy to the primary images Paul uses to depict the church and suggest a particular relationship between those images" (86).

15    John 20:21, NIV

16    Galatians 2:20

# NOTES

17 German theologian, philosopher and bishop Klaus Hemmerle (d. 1994), *Wegmarken der Einheit* (1995), as cited by Thomas Norris, *The Trinity: Life of God, Hope for Humanity* (2009), 131.

18 Jeremiah 1:5, NIV

19 Terry Eagleton is a British public intellectual but respected for his academic work on literary theory (he has written the standard text on the subject). In his book *Reason, Faith and Revolution: Reflections on the God Debate* (2009), this non-Christian Marxist combats atheists (Dawkins+Hitchens=Ditchkins) and argues for the value of faith. He calls himself a "tragic humanist" with a vision of our species as (in Swift's phrase) a "race of odious vermin" which can become human "only by a process of self dispossession and radical remaking." There is no cheery secular rationalism here, and he only sees Jesus as a political revolutionary. But Eagleton is convinced that "human" is something we become only by a "radical remaking" of ourselves, which we believe, of course, we cannot do by ourselves but only through the grace of Christ.

20 Gregory Nazianzen said this in his Oration XXXIX, which is a sermon on the baptism of Christ. The quote is from the following passage: "For it was fitting that he should be baptized, that he might plunge the old Adam entirely in the water, and might raise up the new man, as from the dead, by the resurrection that followed."

21 With thanks to Paul L. Escamilla, *Longing for Enough In a Culture of More* (2007), 3.

22 "What is good? . . . The considered life—free, creative, informed and chosen, a life of achievement and fulfilment, of pleasure and understanding, of love and friendship; in short, the best human life in a human world, humanly lived." The concluding worlds of A. C. Grayling in *What is Good? The Search for the Best Way to Live* (2003), 219.

23 GRAIN: Genetic engineering, Robotics, Artificial Intelligence, Information technology, Nanotechnology. For more on this see Leonard Sweet, ed., *The Church of the Perfect Storm* (2008) and Leonard Sweet with Mark Chironna, *Rings of Fire: Walking in Faith Through A Volcanic Culture* (2019), chapter 15, 139–62.

24 See Clare Chambers, *Intact: A Defence of the Unmodified Body* (2022), a barn-stormer of a book, "The average life expectancy of a Mr. America who won since the onset of the steroid era is 53."

25 This quote is widely attributed to Augustine's writings, but I have not been able to find it.

## JESUS HUMAN

26  Albert Camus, *The Myth of Sisyphus* (1942), 17.

27  Simone Weil, *Waiting for God*, trans. Emma Craufurd (New York: HarperCollins, 2001), 90.

28  Gerald O'Collins, *Jesus: A Portrait* (2008), 39.

29  Terry Eagleton, in his masterful *The Meaning of Life* (New York: Oxford University Press, 2007), 164–68, argues that it is one thing to have beliefs; it is another thing to have faith. What makes humans unique? The search for meaning in life, which is not a solution to a problem, but an ethical journey in agape.

30  See Keith Ward, "Contemporary Spirituality and Christian Doctrine," in *Public Life and the Place of the Church: Reflections to Honor the Bishop of Oxford*, ed. Michael Brierley (2006), 65–70.

31  Barbara Brown Taylor, *Leaving Church: A Memoir of Faith* (2006), 120.

32  John 19:5, NRSV. The original Greek is "ἰδοὺ ὁ ἄνθρωπος."

33  Of course, Jesus does both. See Carlos Fuentes, *This I Believe: An A to Z of a Life* (2005) where "C" is for Christ.

34  Anyone who has grown up in the holiness tradition knows what H. G. Wells meant when he called morality "jealousy with a halo." G. B. Shaw called moralism "one person's way of disrupting someone else's innocent enjoyment." Today's world of one "moral panic" after another was standard fare in holiness churches and households. For my re-signing of holiness, see *The Well-Played Life* (2014; revised edition 2021), 150ff; *Postmodern Pilgrims* (1999), 123–124; *The Jesus Prescription for a Healthy Life* (1996), 14–15; *The Greatest Story Never Told: Revive Us Again* (2012), 107–112.

35  The common good and the striving for excellence in life and thought and behavior are not mutually exclusive, as the #1 living philosopher Michael J. Sandel seems to suggest in *The Tyranny of Merit: What's Become of the Common Good* (2020), who uses the theological debate over heaven's entrance requirements between "deeds or grace" as the fulcrum of his argument. Is meritocracy simply "let the best rise?"

36  This is one area where Stanley Hauerwas and I agree. See his "To Be Made Human," *Image*, 60 (Winter 2008/09), 102–3: "I have never trusted the language of 'being human.' In *The Peaceable Kingdom* I even wrote a section entitled 'Why Being Christian is Not Equivalent to Being Human' in response to a Catholic moral theologian who had written that 'the fundamental ethical command imposed on the Christian is precisely to be what he or she is, "Be human."' He developed that claim by observing

that Christians have nothing to say about what it means to be human that moral philosophers have not already said. Such a view seemed quite strange to me given Jesus' command that we are to follow him—even to the cross. Yet I also believe, in the words of Herbert McCabe, who was also a Catholic moral theologian, that 'the claim that Jesus is perfectly human is the claim that his social world is co-extensive with humanity, that he is open to all men and moreover open to all that is in man.' McCabe, who had a way with words, even suggests that Jesus, not Adam, is the first human being. Jesus is so not as some ideal, but rather he is what we were created to be. . . . Christ's resurrection makes the future our present."

## PART ONE: BECOMING A JESUS HUMAN

1. Patrick Kavanagh, Twitter (@KavanaghWeekly) https://twitter.com/KavanaghWeekly/status/775043002330910720. Accessed 17 August 2023.

2. Wittgenstein wrote this in a 1931 letter to his friend and fellow philosopher, Rush Rhees. It is part of a collection of letters that was published posthumously in 1969.

3. Joni Mitchell, "Big Yellow Taxi," http://jonimitchell.com/musician/song.cfm?id=BibYellowTaxi. Accessed 10 June 2007. Original lyrics ©1966–1969, Siquomb Publishing.

4. Vidal also sees American society correctly, as an oligarchy. For Vidal's misguided argument against monotheism and pimping for paganism, see his *Live from Golgotha* (1992).

5. Gore Vidal, *Myra Breckinridge* (1968), 142.

6. The great proof of this is Philip Zimbardo's *Understanding How Good People Turn Evil* (2007).

7. Thomas à Kempis, *Imitation of Christ*, trans. John Rooney (1980), 26. He is quoting from Lucius Annaeus Seneca, *Ad Lucilium Epistulae Morales*, trans. Richard M. Gummere (1917), 1:31. "I come home more greedy, more ambitious, more voluptuous, and even more cruel and inhuman, because I have been among human beings."

8. Graham Greene, *Heart of the Matter* (1948), 32.

9. Abraham H. Maslow, "The Creative Attitude," *Structuralist* 3 (1963): 4–5; reprinted in his *The Farther Reaches of Human Nature* (1971), 58–59.

10. Romans 1:20

JESUS HUMAN

11  Matthew 6:28, KJV

12  John Henry Newman, *Lead, Kindly Light* (1834), public domain.

13  "An endless array of mind-boggling, implausible, and extraordinary truth . . . centered around a body of explicitly extraordinary and often fantastical truth claims . . . their members sincerely believe the manifestly unbelievable. . . . It is my fellow human beings' very honest, sincere, and proud acceptance of unbelievable, fantastical and unreasonable claims that makes religion a compelling topic for penetrating analysis and inquiry. Understanding why and how people can believe the manifestly unbelievable is the very reason why I got into this discipline." Phil Zuckerman, *Invitation to the Sociology of Religion* (2003), 123.

14  David Whyte, *What to Remember When Waking: The Disciplines of an Everyday Life* (2010).

15  Walter Benjamin, *The Arcades Project* (1999), translated by Howard Eiland and Kevin McLaughlin, 462. The original was written between 1929 and 1940, and originally published in 1982. The quote is followed by a Benjamin citation to Jules Michelet, who wrote in 1839: "Each epoch dreams the one to follow, creates it in dreaming."

16  Luke 1:34, NIV

17  Robert Lowell, "Waking Early Sunday Morning," in his *Near the Ocean* (1967), 15.

18  See Gandhi's book *All Men Are Brothers: The Life and Sayings of Mahatma Gandhi* (1949), 224.

19  Jonathan Sacks, Great Britain's Chief Rabbi, *The Dignity of Difference: How to Avoid the Clash of Civilizations* (2002), 45. 63.

20  Jonathan Sacks' broadcast on BBC Radio 4's "Thought for the Day," 23 November 2012, as found on https://www.rabbisacks.org/archive/we-need-side-by-side-dialogue-not-just-face-to-face/. Accessed 17 August 2023. See also Jonathan Sacks, *To Heal a Fractured World: The Ethics of Responsibility* (2005).

21  See Robert Mangabeira Unger's little book *Governing the World Without World Government* (2022).

22  This quote is part of a "Declaration Toward a Global Ethic" Küng proposed as a foundational approach at the historic interreligious gathering, the 1993 Parliament of the World's Religions in Chicago. The full quote is as follows: "No peace among the nations without peace among the religions. No peace among the religions without dialogue

between the religions. No dialogue between the religions without global ethical standards. No survival of our globe without a global ethic." To hear Küng himself talking about this, see https://www.facebook.com/watch/?v=777792743396903. Accessed 17 August 2023.

23  A trusted resource on Vatican II is by Shaun Blanchard and Stephen Bullivant, *Vatican II: A Very Short Introduction* (2023).

24  Among the Christians were twenty-seven different church bodies, including Greek, Russian, Georgian, Romanian, Bulgarian, Czechoslovakian, and Finnish Orthodox; Old Catholics, Anglicans, Lutherans, Reformed Churches, Methodists, Baptists, Disciples of Christ, Mennonites, Quakers, World Council of Churches, YWCA, YMCA, Unitarians, etc.

25  Fr. Pierre-Francois de Bethune, "After Assisi–Dialogue is New," *Aide Inter Monasteres*, 28 (February 1987), 11. Fr. Pierre is Novice Master at St. Andre in Beltium and Chair of D.I.M. (Intermonastic Dialogue in Europe) and liaison between A.I.M. (Aide Inter Monasteres) and the Vatican Secretariat for the Church's relations with non-Christians.

26  "World Religions: Together to Pray," *Origins*, 16 (1986–87), 367–71.

27  "World Religions: Together to Pray," *Origins*, 16 (1986–87), 368.

28  "World Religions: Together to Pray," *Origins*, 16 (1986–87), 369.

29  2 Timothy 2:19, NIV

30  "World Religions: Together to Pray," *Origins*, 16 (1986–87), 369.

31  "World Religions: Together to Pray," *Origins*, 16 (1986–87), 369.

32  From his encyclical letter *Dominum et Vivificantem* (No.65).

33  Pope John Paul II, "The Challenge and Possibility of Peace," *Origins*, 16 (1986–87), 370.

34  Pope John Paul II, "The Challenge and Possibility of Peace," *Origins*, 16 (1986–87), 371.

35  As quoted in Paul A. Crow, Jr., "Assisi and a Day of Prayer for True Peace," *MidStream: An Ecumenical Journal*, 26 (1987), 253–56.

36  Arnulf Camps, "The Prayers for Peace at Assisi," 27 October 1986, "What Was Shared?" in *On Sharing Religious Experience: Possibilities of Interfaith Mutuality*, eds. Jerald D. Gort, Hendrik M. Vroom, Rein Fernhout, and Anton Wessels (1992), 258.

37  "Responses to the *Lineamenta*," *East Asian Pastoral Review* (Manila), 35, (no. 1, 1998), 89, 55–129.

JESUS HUMAN

38  Most likely a fauxtation, although this quote was put in the *Congressional Record* (26 April 2006) by Nancy Pelosi as an original St. Francis quote.

39  Matthew 11:12, NRSV

40  Matthew 5:48; Luke 6:36, NIV

41  For more on this see Len Sweet and Len Wilson's, *Telos: The Hope of Heaven Today* (2022).

42  Mario Vargas Llosa, The Temptation of the Impossible: Victor Hugo and "Les Miserables," trans. John King (2007), 173.

43  Evangelii Nuntiandi: "Apostolic Exortation of His Holiness Pope Paul VI To the Episcopate, To the Clergy and To All the Faithful of the Entire World," 8 December 1975, section 21. http://www.vatican.va/holy father/paul_vi/apost_exhortations/documents/hf_p-vi_exh_19751208_evangelii-nuntiandi_en.html. Accessed 19 March 2018.

44  I borrow this phrase from Jacques Derrida in his discussion of unconditional forgiveness. See his *On Cosmopolitanism and Forgiveness* (2001), 45.

45  Genesis 1:4, 10, 12, 18, 21, 25, KJV

46  Genesis 1:31, NIV

47  Psalms 8:5

48  G. K. Chesterton, *The Everlasting Man* (1925), 89.

49  Abraham Joshua Heschel, Moral Grandeur and Spiritual Audacity: Essays (1997), 85, 86.

50  Almost always, St. Anthony Abbott is depicted with a trademark pig at his feet. One wonders why.

51  Nietzsche announced the death of God in 1882 in a book with the English title "*The Gay Science*" (*Die fröhliche Wissenschaft*).

52  As referenced in Peter Conrad, *Creation: Artists, Gods & Origins* (2007), 163.

53  Psalm 51:10, NASB

54  John Thompson and Randy Scruggs, "Sanctuary," ©1982, in *The Faith We Sing* (2000), 2164.

55  Marc Woodworth, ed., *Solo: Women Singer-Songwriters in Their Own Words* (1998), 219.

56  John 17

# NOTES

57 John 1:4, NIV

58 Wolfgang Pannenberg, "Towards a Theology of the History of Religions," in *Basic Questions in Theology, Volume 2*, (1971), 65–118.

59 Steve Brusatte, *The Rise and Reign of the Mammals* (2022).

60 Romans 12:3, NIV

61 Hebrews 2:7, KJV

62 Hebrews 2:9–10, NIV

63 Nikolaas Sintobin, SJ, "The Two Standards and Ignatian Leadership," *The Way*, 57 (October 2018), 119–128.

64 For more on this see Lynne A. Isbell's, *The Fruit, the Tree, and the Serpent: Why We See So Well* (2009).

65 Gorillas, baboons, African elephants, humans younger than 18 months . . . all fail the "mark test."

66 Psalm 8:5, NRSV

67 See *Mama's Last Hug: Animal Emotions and What They Tell Us about Ourselves* by Frans de Waal (2020).

68 Cathy O'Neil, *The Shame Machine: Who Profits in the New Age of Humiliation* (2022).

69 Harold Bloom, *Fallen Angels* (2007), 13. "I am increasingly reluctant to distinguish between good and bad angels, and I am not sure that the distinction is even tenable. The most interesting angels are those who are neither good nor bad, but who are both at once. These are the angels who are closest to us, who share our desires and our fears, and who help us to understand the complexity of the human condition."

70 Someone else who makes this argument is Rabbi Adin Steinsaltz, "What is the Right Way to Make a Cake?" *Parabola*, 31 (Spring 2006), 32–35.

71 See Leonard Sweet, *So Beautiful: Divine Design for Life and the Church* (2009).

72 Augustine, *The City of God*, trans. Marcus Dods (New York: Modern Library, 1950), 292. [bk.9, ch.13].

73 Rodney Stark, *The Rise of Christianity* (1997), 209–15.

74 James Allen, *As a Man Thinketh* (1957), 61.

75 "I am going to come to you in a dense cloud, so that the people will

hear me speaking with you and will always put their trust in you." (Exodus 19:9 TNIV).

76 Yeats' collection of poems *Responsibilities* (1914), which has an epigraph "In dreams begins responsibility," was attributed to an "Old play."

77 I borrow the definition of art as "wakeful dreams" (also "embodied meaning") from art critic Arthur C. Danto (d. 2013), who in turn borrowed it from the seventeenth century philosopher Thomas Hobbes, who invented the phrase.

78 Ephesians 2:10, NIV

79 See his book *The Unquiet Grave: A Word Cycle by Palinurus* (1945), 11. The larger quote is worth citing in its entirety: "The artist, the saint, the lover, the joker. Them and only them the capitalist cannot buy, the nationalist inflame, or the snob deflate. They are the only ones who can break through the barriers of class, nationality, and social status. They are the only ones who can speak to the universal human experience. They are the only ones who can change the world."

80 Ephesians 2:10, NLT. The communal dimension of this phrase "in Christ" cannot be overemphasized. In the words of James W. Thompson, "the body of Christ is an extension of 'in Christ.'" See *The Church According to Paul: Rediscovering the Community Conformed to Christ* (2014), 52.

81 See his book *The Unquiet Grave: A Word Cycle by Palinurus* (1945), 11. The larger quote is worth citing in its entirety: "The artist, the saint, the lover, the joker. Them and only them the capitalist cannot buy, the nationalist inflame, or the snob deflate. They are the only ones who can break through the barriers of class, nationality, and social status. They are the only ones who can speak to the universal human experience. They are the only ones who can change the world."

82 A quote from Martin Heidegger found in Jack Kerouac's journals: *Beitrage Zur Philosophie* (1989), as quoted in *Parabola*, Spring 2011, 19.

## PART TWO: YOU NEED THE DIVINE TO BE HUMAN

1 Quoted by Rowan Williams, *A Ray of Darkness* (1995), 151.

2 Albert Nolan, *Jesus Before Christianity: The Gospel of Liberation* (1976), 168. Thanks to Landrum Leavell III for finding this resource.

3 See Hume's Gifford Lectures on Natural Theology in Aberdeen University in 1963–64, 64–65, which became *The Spiritual Nature of Man* (1979).

# NOTES

For a more recent updating, see David Hay, *Something There: The Biology of the Human Spirit* (2006).

4   "What is highly valued by humans is detested by God" (Luke 16:15, NRSV).

5   The full quote is found on page 91 of *Gilead*: "I have come to believe that all lives can shine like transfiguration. You don't have to bring a thing to it except a little willingness to see."

6   In previous books, I have highlighted this paradox of "humbleconfidence" as the essence of a "right spirit" for humans. See *SoulTsunami: Sink or Swim in New Millennium Culture* (1999): "Humble confidence is not about being weak or insecure; it is about being strong enough to admit our weaknesses and still move forward" (186). See *Jesus Manifesto*, where we wrote: "Jesus was the ultimate example of humble confidence. He knew who he was and what he was called to do, but he also knew that he was dependent on God. He was not arrogant or prideful; he was humble and servant-minded" (10). See *A Is for Abductive: The Language of The Emerging Church* (2003): "Humility is not the opposite of confidence; it is the foundation of confidence. When we are humble, we are open to learning from others and to being changed by God. When we are confident, we are able to take risks and to act on our faith. When we combine these two qualities, we are able to live a life that is both meaningful and impactful" (13). Finally, see *The Three Hardest Words to Get Right* (2010): "The paradox of confidence and humility is that they are not opposites. They are two sides of the same coin. Confidence is the ability to believe in yourself and your abilities. Humility is the ability to recognize your limitations and to be open to the wisdom of others. When we combine these two qualities, we can achieve great things" (11).

7   Matthew 23:12; Luke 14:11, NIV

8   Genesis 1:26, NRSV

9   Season 8, Episode 6, 19 May 2019, the 73rd and final episode overall of *The Game of Thrones*, "The Iron Throne."

10  Paul explicitly depicts Christ as "The Last Adam" in 1 Corinthians 15:45. The Unification Church believes that Jesus, as Second Adam, also failed. They claim Rev Moon is the Third Adam, sent for completion. Because Jesus succeeded not failed in his mission, any child of the First Adam can become a child of the Second Adam, which sets you on the path of becoming a Third Adam.

11  Andy Johnson, "Gospel Themes as 'Glue' for Pauline Ecclesiological

Images," in Richard P. Thompson, ed., *Listening Again to the Text: New Testament Studies in Honor of George Lyons* (2020), 84–85.

12   Denis Minns O.P., "In his Image and Likeness," Torch, 21 March 2004. https://www.english.op.org/torch/in-his-image-and-likeness/. Accessed 17 August 2023.

13   Charles Wesley, "Hark! The Herald Angels Sing," in his *Sacred Poetry*, ed. by a lay Member of the Protestant Episcopal Church (1864), 361–62.

14   Quoted in Richard Harries, *Seeing God: The Christian Faith in 30 Images* (2020), 62.

15   Romans 12:21, NIV

16   2 Corinthians 1:20

17   See Adam Potkay's illustrated book *The Story of Joy: From the Bible to Late Romanticism* (2007) for why we live in a joy-less world.

18   2 Corinthians 1:20

19   E. Stanley Jones, *The Divine Yes* (1975). See also Ilion T. Jones' sermon in *God's Everlasting 'Yes'* (1969).

20   Genesis 2:9,7

21   Proverbs 20:27. James A. Fowler makes this connection to Proverbs, which I had heretofore missed, in *Derivative Man: Man as God Intended* (2017), 31.

22   Proverbs 20:27. James A. Fowler makes this connection to Proverbs, which I had heretofore missed, in *Derivative Man: Man as God Intended* (2017), 31.

23   Colossians 1:12, NIV

24   2 Peter 1:3–4, NRSV

25   The NRSV reads: "He said, 'Do not fear, greatly beloved, you are safe. Be strong and courageous!' When he spoke to me, I was strengthened and said, 'Let my lord speak, for you have strengthened me.'"

26   With thanks to Dr. Jim Allen for helping me see the accurate translation of this passage.

27   Colossians 1:10

28   2 Peter 1:4, NASB

29   This was John Wesley's journal entry for 24 May 1738. See John Wesley's *Journal*, edited by Albert C. Outler, vol. 2 (1980), p. 199.

# NOTES

30   2 Corinthians 5:17, NRSV: "Therefore, if anyone is in Christ, the new creation has come: The old has gone, the new is here!"

31   Ephesians 2:6, NIV

32   This quote "Make humanity your way and you shall arrive at God" is attributed to Saint Augustine. But it is not found in any of his writings so far. It is likely a paraphrase of the most famous quote from his *Confessions*: "Thou hast made us for thyself, O Lord, and our hearts are restless until they find their rest in thee."

33   Douglas John Hall, *Professing the Faith: Christian Theology in a North American Context* (1993), 233.

34   *De Incarnatione*, 54, or *On the Incarnation*, 54.

35   This phrase was later repeated by St. Athanasius. *De Incarnatione* 54.

36   *Against Heresies*, 3, 191:4, 33,4.

37   *On the Lord's Prayer*, 90877a.

38   *Opusculum*, 57.1–4.

39   *In Joannem*, 15:2.1.

40   *Interior Castle*, 7.2.

41   *The Living Flame of Love*, 3.5–8.

42   For more see Jacob Holsinger Sherman, "Becoming-Night, Becoming-Divine," *Modern Theology*, 2008, 12.

43   Aaron Riches, "After Chalcedon: The Oneness of Christ and the Dyothelite Mediation of His Theandric Unity," *Modern Theology*, 24 (April 2008), 202.

44   Douglas John Hall, *The Cross in Our Context: Jesus and The Suffering World* (2003).

45   Michael Christensen and Jeffery A. Wittung, eds., *Partakers of the Divine Nature: The History and Development of Deification in the Christian Traditions* (2008). See also Christensen's chapter on "Theosis in the Theology of T. F. Torrance" in *Theosis: Deification in Christian Theology*, edited by Stephen Finlan and Vladimir Kharlamov (2006), 145–66.

46   Patristic notions of deification are explored in Norman Russell *The Doctrine of Deification in the Greek Patristic Tradition* (2004). A broad and useful overview of the ecumenical importance of deification is found in Michael J. Christensen and Jeffery A. Wittung's, *Partakers of the Divine Nature: The History and Development of Deification in the Christian*

*Tradition* (2008). See also Stephen Finlan and Vladimir Kharlamov, eds., *Theosis: Deification in Christian Theology* (2006); Veli-Matti Karkainen's, *One with God: Salvation as Deification and Justification* (2004). On deification in Aquinas, see A. N. Williams', *The Ground of Union: Deification in Aquinas and Palamas* (1999). For recent works defending the importance of deification in Luther, Calvin, and Wesley, see J. Todd Billings', *Calvin, Participation, and the Gift: The Activity of Believers in Union with Christ* (2007); Carl E. Braaten and Robert W. Jenson's, *Union with Christ: The New Finnish Interpretation of Luther* (1998); S. T. Kimbrough's, *Orthodox and Wesleyan Spirituality* (2002).

47  As quoted in Michael J. Christensen, "The Problem, Promise, and Process of Theosis," in *Partakers of the Divine Nature: The History and Development of Deification in the Christian Traditions*, ed. Michael J. Christensen and Jeffery A. Wittung (2007), 28.

48  Psalm 82:6, NASB as quoted in John 10:34–35.

49  Psalm 82:4, TNIV. For the relationality behind the Wesleyan doctrine of Christian perfection, see Thomas J. Oord and Michael E. Lodahl's, *Relational Holiness: Responding to the Call of Love* (2005).

50  Psalm 8:5–6, NRSV. Notice how in Genesis 1:28, NRSV "dominion" theology" immediately follows the "image of God" verse. In other words, "dominion" is another way of talking about "tending and tilling" the garden in Genesis 2.

51  Michel Quoist, *Prayers of Life* (1963; first published in French in 1954), 8. The full quote is: "We are not God. We are simply the image of God. We are not the creator of the world, but we are created in the image of the creator. We have within us the potential to reflect God's love, compassion, and goodness in the world. Our task is gradually to discover that image and set it free. We do this by surrendering our lives to God and letting go of our own control. When we surrender, we open ourselves up to the power of the Holy Spirit, who can help us to grow in holiness and love."

52  In this sense Charles Darwin's *Descent of Man* (1871) got it half right.

53  A true kind of human is not a "be-all-you-can-be" kind of human. Everything I do to be a better kind of person is as useless as doing CPR on a dead body. Because of my baptism into the one who is The Way, The Truth, The Life, I now have the privilege of living Jesus' resurrection life in the world, and dreaming God's dream for the world. A true kind of human is not constructing better dreams through his or her own efforts. A true kind of human is not dreaming a better future for himself, or her family, or her church or his community. A true kind of human is

# NOTES

collaborating with God's inbreaking Advent. The ultimate dream come true is a gift that we receive and enter, not create and control. Dreams go wild precisely when we try to control them and create them.

54   Revelation 19:16, NIV

55   For disciplines of breathing, see my *The Greatest Story Never Told: Revive Us Again* (2012), 46ff. For other breathing rituals and exercises, see also my *Quantum Spirituality: A Postmodern Apologetic* (1991), 119ff.

56   With thanks to John Stackhouse for his understanding of the church as "new humanity." Contra Philip Yancey, Stackhouse argues that the worst *and best* argument for Christianity is the church. John G. Stackhouse, "What's 'Old, Old'? Our Ancient Christian Muission—and Our Even Older Human One," lecture at Regent College Pastors' Conference: "The Old, Old Story in a New, New Era: Evangelism for Today and Tomorrow," 09 May 2007. Portions of this lecture will appear in his upcoming book with the tentative title: *Making the Best of It: Christian Discipleship in the Real World* (2008).

57   Ephesians 4:24, NIV

58   Hebrews 4:15, NIV

59   Mark 4:37–38

60   Mark 14:33–34

61   Mark 8:2

62   Luke 19:41–42, NIV

63   John 11:35–37

64   Luke 7:11–17, NIV

65   Mark 10:46–52

66   Conversion is a strange concept in Islam, since you really can't convert to Islam. In Muslim theology everyone is a Muslim. It's just a question of when you embrace it, when you become what you already are, and are made to be.

67   2 Chronicles 7:14, NIV

68   From Rupert Shortt's *Does Religion Do more Harm Than Good* (2019). The best introduction to Islam is Shahab Ahmed, *What is Islam? The Importance of Being Islamic* (2015) and Toby Matthiesen's, *The Caliph and the Imam: The Making of Sunnism and Shiism* (2023).

69   John Paul II, "To the Bishops of Europe: Address of Pope John Paul II on

499

Fidelity to Vatican II by Bishops Participating in the Sixth Symposium of the Council of European Episcopal Conferences (October 11, 1985)," *The Pope Speaks #30* (1985): 343.

70   Galatians 5:22

71   Quoted in Michael Casey, *The Undivided Heart* (1994), 67.

72   Significant exceptions being Daniel and Ezekiel.

73   British priest Joseph O'Hanlon, author of *Jesus Who Was/Jesus Who is* (Columba Press), as found in "Questions, Questions," *The Tablet*, 22–29 December 2012, 29.

74   For this "double meaning" see David Lawrence Edwards, *Yes: A Positive Faith* (2006), 47.

75   John 15:9, NIV

76   John 20:21; 17:18, ESV

**PART THREE: WE DREAM, AND SOME DREAMS ARE INHUMANE**

1   Here is one website for the lyrics: https://genius.com/Switchfoot-new-way-to-be-human-lyrics. Accessed 18 August 2023.

2   No matter that Haley's non-fiction saga, where he travels to the Gambian village of Juffure to be reunited in spirit with Kunta Kinte, should be better classified as fiction. In 1978 Haley paid $650,000 to Harold Courlander along with the admission that large passages of *Roots* were copied from his book, *The African*. For a full account of this, and the allegation that the Kunta Kinte genealogy was "coached," see Philip Nobile, "Uncovering Roots," *Village Voice*, 23 February 1993, 31–38.

3   "Memory is a complicated business." So states the Afterword in Stephan Lebert's, *My Father's Keeper: Children of Nazi Leaders: An Intimate History of Damage and Denial* (2001), 244. Tim Kirk, in a review of *My Father's Keeper*, noted "priests, doctors, psychologists, and psychiatrists report an 'astonishing' absence of psychological problems related to guilt or shame in Germany after the war." Tim Kirk, "History," *TLS: Times Literary Supplement*, 16 November 2001, 30.

4   Daniel J. Miller, "Listening to the Wind in the Wheat," *Spirituality*, 9 (March–April 2003): 87.

5   *Souls on Fire* (1973), 58.

6   See Lev Grossman, "Times Person of the Year: You," https://

# NOTES

time.com/6258607/you-time-person-of-the-year-2006/. Accessed 18 August 2023.

7   Rhonda Byrne, *The Secret* (2006).

8   This is biophysicist Gregory Stock's word for a cyborgian "superorganism" consisting of the born and the made, humanity plus technology. See his *Metaman: The Merging of Humans and Machines Into a Global Superorganism* (1993), 20: "'Metaman,' meaning 'beyond, and transcending, humans.' This name both acknowledges humanity's key role in the entity's formation and stresses that, though human centered, it is more than just humanity. Metaman is also the crops, livestock, machines, buildings, communications transmissions, and other non-human elements and structures that are part of the human enterprise."

9   Mark 7:9–13

10  Vis a vis food, divorce, retribution (Matthew 5:21–48; Mark 7:15, 19).

11  This is the thesis of Adam Phillips and Barbara Taylor, *On Kindness* (2009).

12  "But the fruit of the Spirit is love, joy, peace, forbearance, kindness, goodness, faithfulness, gentleness and self-control. Against such things there is no law." Galatians 5:22–23, NIV.

13  Philip Larkin, "The Mower," in his *Collected Poems*, ed. Anthony Thwaite (1989), 214.

14  The first time I ever heard this phrase "Dream Society," was as the title of a Rolf Jensen book, *The Dream Society: How the Coming Shift from Information to Imagination Will Transform Your Business* (1999), I immediately thought: what a great translation of "the kingdom of God."

15  Jeremiah 23:26–32, NIV

16  1 Chronicles 29:11, 14, NIV

17  Timothy Morton, *Hyperobjects: Philosophy and Ecology After the End of the World* (2013), 14.

18  Roger Luckhurst, *Gothic: An Illustrated History* (2022).

19  In 2022, Netflix's most watched non-English-language series was the South Korean show about face-chewing zombies, "*All of Us are Dead.*"

20  Susan Sontag, *Illness as Metaphor* (1978).

21  As quoted by Chris Chivers in "A Preacher the World Needs," *The Tablet*, 20/27 August 2022, 22.

22  John Hayes, ed., *Maurice O'Connor Drury: On Wittgenstein, Philosophy, Religion and Psychiatry* (2018).

23  Martin Amis, *The Second Plane: September 11: 2001–2007* (2008), 12. What precedes the quote is just as harsh: "Religion is the great engine of human misery. It has been responsible for more wars, more oppression, more cruelty, more death, than any other single force in history. It has divided families, communities, and nations. It has been used to justify slavery, genocide, and torture. It has been used to deny women their rights, to suppress dissent, and to stifle free thought."

In *The Paris Review* (2000), Adam Begley conducted a 72-page-long interview with Martin Amis, where he revealed his father's helpful critique of his writing in a 1973 letter. It is the 151st interview in the series.

24  Paraphrase of a passage from *I and Thou* (1923; 1958 edition), in which Buber writes: "The religious community does not know God. It only knows its own faith in God, and it knows this faith only as its own activity" (55).

25  See Leonard Sweet with Mark Chironna, *Rings of Fire: Walking in Faith through a Volcanic Future* (2019), 189–94.

26  For more on this see Chris Arnade, *Dignity: Seeking Respect in Back Row America* (2019).

27  https://chatkjv.vzy.io/#chatkjv-helps-you-deepen-your-spiritual-journey—2. Accessed 18 August 2023.

28  See his *Rationality: What It is, Why It Seems Scarce, Why It Matters* (2021).

29  This is Rorty's shorthand way of saying what he wrote in *Contingency, Irony, and Solidarity* (1989), where he argues that truth is not a fixed or objective thing, but rather a product of conversation and negotiation. "Truth is not out there, waiting to be discovered. It is made by us, in the course of conversation and negotiation" (113).

30  Humans boast the largest brain-to-body mass of all species, with the six-layered cortex called the neocortex comprising 80 percent of the organ. The neocortex is responsible for the brain's higher functions, such as language, sensory perception, emotion, and cognition.

31  In 2018, the Programme for International Student Assessment (PISA) reported that 50 percent of the students across twenty-four countries were not proficient in math. The pandemic shut-downs have only made things worse. See Sal Khan, "The Lessons of Learning Loss," *The World Ahead 2023: The Economist* (11 November 2022), 78.

NOTES

32  See Iain McGilchrist, *The Master and His Emissary: The Divided Brain and the Making of the Western World* (2019).

33  As quoted in Alex Christofl, *Dostoevsky in Love* (2021), and quoted in *The Tablet*, 23 January 2021, 20. The exact quote appears on page 252 of Penguin Books' 1990 edition of *The Brothers Karamazov*: "But do you know what will be the very end of it all? It will end in the triumph of some '*ism*,' and what's more, the triumph of the most stupid *ism* that has ever existed on earth, and from which humanity can expect nothing but fresh disasters, incalculable disasters."

34  Fyodor Dostoevsky, *Notes from the Underground* (1864; 1993 Penguin edition), 16.

35  T. E. Lawrence, *Seven Pillars of Wisdom* (1926; Penguin Classics edition), 288.

36  Hebrews 11:1, KJV

37  David Woolley, ed., *The Letters of Jonathan Swift* (1999), Volume 1, 249–250.

38  Karl Rahner *Faith in a Wintry Season: Conversation and Interviews with Karl Rahner in the Last Years of His Life* (1990), 160. From an interview with Giancarlo Zizola in Rome, 1982. Cited by Bernard McGinn "The Future of the Past Spiritual Traditions," *Spiritus*, Spring 2015, 93.

39  Colossians 1:26–28. This is what Catholics talk about when they refer to the "paschal mystery" which is at work in us.

40  Since the publication of his Black Notebooks in 2014, it is getting harder to quote Heidegger at all or at least without apologies for his antisemitism and attraction to Nazism. See Richard Wolin, *Heidegger in Ruins: Between Philosophy and Ideology* (2023). Or Guillaume Payen, *Martin Heidegger's Changing Destinies: Catholicism, Revolution, Nazism* (2023), translated by Jane Marie Todd and Steven Rendall.

41  Galatians 2:20, NIV

42  "And Moses took with him the bones of Joseph, who had exacted an oath from the children of Israel, saying, 'God will be sure to take notice of you: then you shall carry up my bones from here with you'" (Exodus 13:19).

43  Sarah Brubeck, "A Man and His Horses: Jason Rutledge's Traditional Farming Methods," *The Conservation Voice* (2019). This is the Holmes County Soil and Water Conservation District's newsletter. See his Ted Talk, "Forest of Dreams," Jason Rutledge at TedXFloyd, https://www.youtube.com/watch?v=-QVdbj1i8gA. Accessed 18 August 2023.

JESUS HUMAN

44  John 15:7

45  Robert D. Kaplan, *The Coming Anarchy: Shattering the Dreams of the Post-Cold War* (2000).

46  Johan Verstraeten, "Economics with a Human Face," *The Tablet*, 25 February 2012, 12.

47  As quoted in *The Human Race: A Search for the Common Ground* (1974), 109, by John B. Cobb, Jr. and Charles Birch.

48  See the section on the inhumanity of bureaucratic structures in my *Rings of Fire* (2019), 243ff.

49  Nicholas A. Christakis, *Blueprint: The Evolutionary Origins of a Good Society* (2019).

50  Fred D'Aguiar's book of poetry *British Subjects (1994)* opens with this poem.

51  *Unions Renewed: Building Power in an Age of Finance* (2020) by Alice Martin and Annie Quick: "Rent-seeking activities—extracting wealth without producing it—have grown from 3 percent of the US economy in 1985 to 17 percent in 2015, a nearly 500 percent rise."

52  See the work of Jennifer M. Miller and Yiming V. Wang, "Ostrich eggshell beads reveal 50,000-year-old social network in Africa," *Nature* (2022): 601, 234–239. https://doi.org/10.1038/s41586-021-04227-2. Accessed 18 August 2023.

53  Matthew 13:45–46

54  "Defender of the Faith," *The Economist*, 10 December 2022, 28.

55  John 17:21

56  David Lloyd Dusenbury, *I Judge No One: A Political Life of Jesus* (2023).

57  Mattthew 5:23–24, NIV

58  As reported in Sanjay Gupta's *Keep Sharp: Build a Better Brain at Any Age* (2021).

59  Niccolo Machiavelli, *The Prince* (1513), Book III, Chapter 1.

60  @DavidAFrench tweet (24 November 2022).

61  *The Journals of Father Alexander Schmemann* (2002), 166.

62  USAmerica's historic fear of "standing armies" now only a distant memory, the US now has 750 military bases in 80 countries. It could be

# NOTES

that a civil religion or a global market that works is more dangerous than ones that don't if they're competing for our soul.

63  The biblical passage Proverbs 29:18, KJV; for G. K. Chesterton's quote see his essay, "Philosophy of Sightseeing," in his *Alarms and Discources* (1911), 93.

64  "Whatever You Did Unto One of the Least, You Did Unto Me," Mother Teresa MC in Michael Collopy, *Works of Love Are Works of Peace* (1996), 191–96.

65  H. J. Jackson, *Those Who Write for Immortality: Romantic Reputations and the Dream of Lasting Fame* (2015).

66  I often hear Hollywood as Hollyweird, but think of it as Hollywindow—a window to the worst and best of humanity.

67  This quote is the introductory statement that sets the theme and trajectory for James Truslow Adams' exploration of what he first called the "American Dream" in *The Epic of America* (1931).

68  G. K. Chesterton, *The Innocence of Father Brown* (1975), 153.

69  Genesis 11:4

70  See also Sam Quinones' groundbreaking book *Dreamland: The True Tale of American's Opiate Epidemic* (2015).

71  See Michael Shellenberger's *San Francisco* (2021).

72  As quoted in Bob Harris' *Gambling in Britain in the Long Eighteenth Century* (2023), 14.

73  The quote is found on page 12. Here is the full quote: "Life is a crazy, out of order, inside out, salt mixed with sugar place where the drowned can be walking on dry land. I know this because I have seen it with my own eyes. I have seen the dead rise up and walk among the living. I have seen the sun shine through the rain. I have seen the moon rise in the middle of the day. I have seen the stars fall from the sky. I have seen the impossible happen. And I have learned that nothing is ever as it seems."

74  John Semley, "High Stakes," *Wired*, Issue 30.09, 78–85.

75  See David Healy's, *Mania: A Short History of Bipolar Disorder* (2011). For the quote see *The Creation of Psychopharmacology* (2002), 135.

76  Robert Putnam originally said this in his book *Bowling Alone: The Collapse and Revival of American Community* (2000), 65.

77  For example, Richard K. Morgan, Greg Egan, Neal Stephenson, Philip K. Dick, William Gibson.

## JESUS HUMAN

78   Bernard Marr, "The 10 Scariest Future Tech Trends Everyone Must Know About Right Now," *Forbes*, 16 January 2023.

79   Teilhard de Chardin, *The Phenomenon of Man* (1955), chapter entitled "The Noosphere."

80   See Yuval Noah Harari's 2020 Commencement Speech, "Rebellion of the Hackable Animals," as published in *The Wall Street Journal*, 01 May 2020.

81   *Trends Journal*, 21 March 2023, 35.

82   See John Cornwell, *Church, Interrupted: Havoc and Hope: The Tender Revolt of Pope Francis* (2020).

83   See my collection of essays "Communication and Change" in *American Religious History* (1993).

84   See Josef Steiff and Tristan D. Tamplin, eds., *Battlestar Galactica and Philosophy* (2009).

85   The Four Horsemen: global warming, the global demographics time-bomb, endemic poverty, and pandemic diseases.

86   Jaron Lanier coined the term "virtual reality" and founded the first virtual reality company. But Lanier warned that we are "on the verge of abandoning the human realm altogether" as science no longer aims to better the human, but to probe the outer reaches of its own power and what it can do without regard for the human. In Lanier's words, "it grows harder to imagine human beings remaining at the center of the process of science. Instead, science appears to be in charge of its own process, probing, and changing people in order to further its own course, independent of human agency." Van Wishard, "Sleepwalking through the Apocalypse: The 9/11 Memorial Address," The Jung Page, https://jungpage.org/learn/articles/analytical-psychology/505-sleepwalking-through-the-apocalypse. Accessed 18 August 2023. Here is my #1 test for whether a technological advance is advantageous or apocalyptic: Does this technology promote human suffering, or healing? Or in the words of one technologist: "Do I want to live in a world where this technology is available, not only to myself, but to everyone?" See "When, If Ever, Should Technologies be Illegal?" in *Red Herring: The Business of Technology*, 19 September 2002, 35. [note: articles not signed] Jason Postin was the editor during this period.

87   Quoted by Matthew B. Crawford in *Why We Drive: Toward a Philosophy of the Open Road* (2021), 12.

88   As early as 2005, three forward-thinking authors—Dr. James Hughes (*Citizen Cyborg: Why Democratic Societies Must Respond to the Redesigned*

# NOTES

*Human of the Future*), Ramez Naam (*More Than Human: Embracing the Promise of Biological Enhancement*), and journalist Joel Garreau (*Radical Evolution: The Promise and Peril of Enhancing Our Minds, Our Bodies—And What It Means To Be Human*)—sat down with Jamais Cascio for a collective interview to discuss ideas about what human augmentation of the future might entail.

89  Julian Huxley coined the phrase "transhumanism" in the 1951 essay "New Bottles for New Wine." The essay was published in the journal *The Saturday Review of Literature*, on page 105. Here is how he defined it: "'Transhumanism' means the belief that man is not at the end of his evolution but only at the beginning, and that evolution is still going on, and that man can now take control of his own evolution and shape it towards his own ends." For more see Harry Parker, *Hybrid Humans: Dispatches from the Frontier of Man and Machine* (2022).

90  Regina Rini, *The Ethics of Microaggression* (2021).

91  "Transhumanism: The World's Most Dangerous Idea?" *Foreign Policy*, September/October 2004, 24.

92  Adam Rutherford, *Control: The Dark History and Troubling Present of Eugenics* (2022).

93  A lot of funding for transhumanism comes from In-Q-Tel, CIA's venture capital arm.

94  See also Bill McKibben, *Enough: Staying Human in an Engineered Age* (2003).

95  Tolkien made this distinction in a letter to his friend C. S. Lewis dated April 10, 1958. In the letter, Tolkien discusses the difference between true immortality, which he defines as "the state in which death is swallowed up in victory," and limitless serial longevity, which he defines as "the power of endless repetition." Tolkien argues that true immortality is a gift from God, while limitless serial longevity is a curse. See *The Letters of J.R.R. Tolkien and C.S. Lewis: Volume III: 1956–1963* (2008), edited by Humphrey Carpenter.

96  Wendell Berry, *The Selected Poems of Wendell Berry* (1998), 111.

97  Some of the major contenders are Beijing, China; Bangalore, India; Berlin, Germany; Boston, Massachusetts; Cambridge, Massachusetts; Dallas, Texas, Dublin, Ireland, Hyderabad, India; Melbourne, Australia; Montreal, Canada; Osaka, Japan; Paris, France; Palo Alto, California; Seoul, South Korea; Stockholm, Sweden; Tel Aviv, Israel; Tokyo, Japan; Vancouver, Canada; Warsaw, Poland; and Sydney, Australia.

## JESUS HUMAN

98  Eleanor Clayton, Barbara Hepworth: *Art and Life* (2021).

99  See my *So Beautiful* (2009) book, where I outline the original Operating System (OS) of the church.

100  Paul Ginsborg, *The Politics of Everyday Life: Making Choices, Changing Lives* (2005), 53–54.

101  On the Web, this saying has been attributed to Anonymous, Ursula le Guin (not verified), Madeline L'Engle (not verified), a pediatrician, an uncle, an old saying, etc.

102  Madeleine Albright with Bill Woodward, *The Mighty and the Almighty: Reflections on America, God, and World Affairs* (2006), 73; where Albright writes: "When I appeared on a panel with the Jewish writer and thinker Elie Wiesel, a survivor of the Holocaust, he recalled how a group of scholars had once been asked to name the unhappiest character in the Bible. Some said Job, because of the trials he endured. Some said Moses, because he was denied entry to the promised land. Some said the Virgin Mary, because she witnessed the death of her son. The best answer, Wiesel suggested, might in fact be God, because of the sorrow caused by people fighting, killing, and abusing each other in His name."

103  Some degrowth people just don't like human beings. Others believe the Earth already has too many humans. Pulitzer Prize winning poet and environmentalist Gary Snyder proposed a reduction of 90 percent of human life in his 1990 book, *The Practice of the Wild*, page 146.

104  Paul Auster quotes the historian in *Bloodbath Nation* (2023), 137.

105  Virginia Woolf, *A Room of One's Own* (1929), 53.

### PART FOUR: ABCEDARY OF A GLOBAL JESUS HUMANITY

1  Romans 10:20, NIV

2  As quoted by Jude Rogers, *The Sound of Being Human: How Music Shapes Our Lives* (2022).

3  See James Bridle's, *Ways of Being* (2022).

4  As quoted by the Former President of the People's Republic of China, Hu Jintao, "Friendship Between Our Two Nations," *Vital Speeches*, LXXII (May 2006), 424.

5  Leila Slimani, *Sex and Lies* (2020).

6  Selina O'Grady, *In the Name of God: A History of Christian and Muslim Intolerance* (2020).

NOTES

7   The story is told in Lance Morrow's *The Noise of Typewriters: Remembering Journalism* (2023), 167–170. The dinner took place in 1990, to celebrate the fiftieth anniversary of the media company Time-Life, Inc.

8   See Adam Tooze's, *Shutdown: How COVID Shook the World's Economy* (2022), where he explores the world's inability to muster "moments of collective agency."

9   See Pope Benedict XVI's 30 March 2006 address to the members of the European People's Party titled "To the Participants of the Congress Promoted by the European People's Party on the Occasion of the Study Days on Europe" available at https://www.vatican.va/content/benedict-xvi/en/speeches/2006/march/documents/hf_ben-xvi_spe_20060330_eu-parliamentarians.html. Accessed 18 August 2023.

10  The actual program for the coronation begins with a note on page 3: "Then, for the first time at a Coronation, The King prays publicly for grace to be 'a blessing to all' . . . of every faith and belief; and to serve after the pattern of Christ." Here is the particular and universal in action: the universality of "a blessing to all" and the particularity of "after the pattern of Christ." Although one hopes that this is not the "first time" monarchs prayed for all the peoples of their kingdom.

11  Based on a metaphor from thirteenth century Sufi poet Rumi. Also see Lillian Eichler Watson, ed., *Light from Many Lamps* (1951).

12  Thanks to Dr. Timothy Valentino for this reminder about Ecclesiastes.

13  Ivan Turgenev, "Christ," in his *Dream Tales and Prose Poems*, trans. Constance Garnett (1913), 303–304.

**ABECEDARIUM OF A JESUS HUMAN**

1   William Shakespeare, *Julius Caesar*, Act I, sc. 2.

2   *Abu Hayyan Al-Tawhidi and Abu Ali Miskawayh*: Translated by Sophia Vassalou and James E. Montgomery (2021).

3   Philippians 4:11

4   1 Corinthians 8:1, ESV

5   Sergio Del Molino, *Skin* (2022).

6   Cornelius Ernst (1924–77), Dominican theologian of the English Province, *The Theology of Grace* (Fides, 1974).

7   See his Sermon #36, "The Acquiring of Knowledge" in "*On the Song of Songs II.*"

8   "A Friend, A Booke and a Garden shall for the future perfectly circumscribe my utmost designes," wrote John Evelyn, born in 1620, in his early thirties. See Margaret Willes, *The Curious World of Samuel Pepys and John Evelyn* (2018); also see John Dixon Hunt, *John Evelyn: A Life of Domesticity* (2017).

9   Joseph D. Ban, Paul R. Dekar, eds., *In the Great Tradition: In Honor of Winthrop S. Hudson: Essays on Pluralism, Voluntarism, and Revivalism* (1982). See my contribution entitled "'A Nation Born Again:' The Union Prayer Meeting Revival and Cultural Revitalization," 193–213.

10  For humility and hospitality as "Two Conditions Necessary for the Possibility of Civility," see Geneva College President Calvin L. Troup's essay in the collection *Humility and Hospitality: Changing the Christian Conversation on Civility*, eds. Naaman Wood and Sean Connable (2022), 19–29.

11  Plato, *The Republic*, in Book VI, 493a.

12  P. M. Forni, *The Civility Solution: What to Do When People are Rude* (2008).

13  James 1:8, KJV: "A doubleminded man is unstable in all his ways."

14  Tarif Khalidi, "Adab Hand at Work," *TLS: Times Literary Supplement*, 31 March 2000, 8.

15  Philippians 4:8

16  The hadith is found in a number of hadith collections, including *Sahih al-Bukhari* and *Sahih Muslim*.

17  Byung-Chul Han, *The Disappearance of Rituals: A Typology of the Present* (2019), pp. 17–18.

18  John 17:18; 20:21, NIV

19  For more on "adversarial collaboration," see Kahneman's *Thinking, Fast and Slow* (2011), his lecture "Adversarial Collaboration: An EDGE Lecture" (23 February 2023), as found in https://www.psychologicalscience.org/news/adversarial-collaboration-an-edge-lecture-by-daniel-kahneman.html (Accessed 18 August 2023); and the website of the Adversarial Collaboration Project at the University of Pennsylvania: https://web.sas.upenn.edu/adcollabproject/ (Accessed 14 June 2023).

20  Source: The Threshold Society and the Mevlevi Order. http://www.sufism.org.

21  Robert Irwin, "From Persia to Casablanca: The Culinary Traditions of the

Middle East," http://www3.estart.com/iran/food/persia.html. Accessed 28 December 2021.

22  As found in *The Dimension of the Present and Other Essays* by Miroslav Holub, translated by Ian Milner (1984).

23  *Luther's Works, Volume 37: Word and Sacrament III*, edited by Robert H. Fischer (1976), 371.

24  St. Basil, *De Spiritu Sancto* (363), as quoted in Frederick J. Flo, "'Breaking Ground:' A look at the Impact of the Cappadocian Fathers on the Establishment of the Doctrine of the Holy Spirit During the Transition Between the Council of Nigeria (325) and the Council of Constantinople (381)," 7 *Verbum*, December 2009, Article 11.

25  Rick Warren, *The Purpose Driven Life* (2002), 252. The full quote is: "We don't have to see eye-to-eye on every issue to walk hand-in-hand in the same direction. We can disagree without being disagreeable. We can love without compromising. We can unite without uniformity. We can work together without compromising our convictions."

26  Roland Bainton, the great Reformation scholar of another era, said that the crusader spirit had four premises: 1) the cause is holy; 2) the crusaders are godly and the enemy is ungodly; 3) God fights for the crusaders and against their opponents; 4) the war is prosecuted unsparingly with a take-no-prisoners mentality.

27  We might want to consider this as a principle of how to handle bad reviews or critical comments by those who don't want discussion, only execration. Whatever you do or think, you are going to get criticized. On the evil side, some of terrorist Abu Musab al-Zarqawi's followers reproached him for cutting throats too fast . . . and not lingering enough for the blood to flow more freely so everyone watching could see the head detach more clearly. On the good side, even the Pope has been hit with a "dubium" by four cardinals accusing him of going against church teaching in five areas and asking for clarifications or face possible charges of heresy. If even the pope is accused of dubium, you will not be exempt from being hit by dubium whether dreamed up or drummed up.

28  1 Corinthians 16:13

29  2 Corinthians 1:20

30  The Rule "Life is not Fair" can be called "Rule 174.465" after Patent 174,465. It was issued on 07 March 1876 to Alexander Graham Bell, and may be the most profitable patent in history. But there is strong evidence

that a rival inventor, Elisha Gray of Western Electric, got his patent registered before Bell or at least was the true inventor of the telephone.

31  2 Chronicles 20:15, NIV

32  Nehemiah 4:20, ESV

33  Ephesians 3:20, NIV

34  Soren Kierkegaard, *The Journals*, quoted as the epigram of Hans Urs von Balthasar's *Theo-Drama*, V (1998).

35  In the sometimes arcane language of semiotics, Jesus came to incarnate "agapasm" (Charles Sanders Pierce's phrase), or again in semiotic language, "agapastic" evolution which is life that evolves by love: agapastic thought, agapastic living, agapastic vision, culminating in agapastic humans.

36  John 13:34, NIV

37  John 13:1, NIV

38  John 15:3

39  Romans 5:8

40  John 1:9

41  1 Corinthians 13:4

42  1 Corinthians 8:1, NIV

43  Here is the medieval monk Bernard of Clairvaux (1090–1153) exploring our mixed motives for learning. See his Sermon #36, "The Acquiring of Knowledge" in *"On the Song of Songs II."*

For there are some who long to know for the sole purpose of knowing, and that is shameful curiosity; others who long to know in order to become known, and that is shameful vanity. . . . There are others still who long for knowledge in order to sell its fruits for money or honors, and this is shameful profiteering. Others again who long to know in order to be of service, and this is charity. Finally there are those who long to know in order to benefit themselves, and this is wisdom. Of all these categories, only the last two avoid the abuse of knowledge, because they desire to know for the purpose of doing good."

44  1 Corinthians 13:2

45  In *The Rise and Fall of Adam and Eve* (2017), Stephen Greenblatt thinks the Fall is totally irrelevant to the modern world. Adam Baruch Seligman in *Modernity's Wager* (2000) thinks differently and makes it of utmost relevance.

# NOTES

46 Augustine, *The City of God* (426).

47 John Milton, *Paradise Lost* (1667), Book IX, lines 886–989.

48 "*Melius enim iudicavit de malis benefacere, quam mala nulla esse permittere.*" (For God judged it better to bring good out of evil than not to permit any evil to exist.)

49 Leibniz was a philosopher who was enamored of the doctrine of felix culpa.

50 John 15:13

51 For the suggesting of adventurer as a new name for a follower of Jesus, based on the living of daily ventures in advent, see Leonard Sweet and Michael Beck's, *Contextual Intelligence* (2020).

52 Although this quote is widely attributed to Augustine, I have not been able to find it in Augustine's writings (though I'm sure I have missed some). Father Raphael Simon's book *Formation of the Priest* (1964) has this quote on p. 125: "Now to fall in love with Jesus requires faith. We have to know the story of Jesus, of His coming into the world, of His teaching and deeds and fellowship in this world, of His passing to the Father, of His coming back in life after death to talk with His disciples and continue His fellowship with them, of His going to the Father and sending into our hearts the Holy Spirit and His love. This is the greatest story in the world, the greatest romance, and we are called to the greatest adventure."

53 Arthur William Edgar O'Shaughnessy, "Ode," in *Music and Moonlight: Poems of Arthur O'Shaughnessy*, sel, and ed. William Alexander Perry (1923), 39.

54 For a scholarly study of infant abandonment, see Paul A. Gilje's "Infant Abandonment in Early Nineteenth-Century New York City: Three Cases," *Signs, 8* (Spring, 1983), 580–590.

55 In 2005 Justin McRoberts released his *Grace Must Wound* album on which this song "Safe" is found.

56 The whole limbic system, and the temporal lobes in particular, are involved with sex.

57 Peter L. Bernstein, *Against the Gods: The Remarkable Story of Risk* (1996), 8.

58 Sam Kean, *The Tale of the Dueling Neurosurgeons* (2017), 209.

59 Malcolm Muggeridge, *The End of Christendom* (1980), 40.

60  1 Corinthians 13:4–7, MNT

61  Thomas Small, "Sinewy Strength," *TLS: Times Literary Supplement*, 11 January 2019, 11.

62  With this quote war surgeon David Nott ends his incredible memoir, *War Doctor: Surgery on the Front Line* (2019).

63  1 Kings 19:10–18

64  Jeremiah 38:1–6

65  Nehemiah 4

66  Frontispiece to the hymnbook *United Christian Ashrams Sing!*

67  Julia Ward Howe, "Battle Hymn of the Republic" (1861). The last line that Martin Luther King, Jr. ever spoke in public came from this song.

68  Mark 6:31

69  Librettist Ronald Duncan (1914–1982), in *Working with Britten: A Personal Memoir* (1981).

70  Mark 6:31–34, NIV

71  Gerard Manley Hopkins, "God's Grandeur," (1917), as first published in the collection edited by Robert Bridges *Poems of Gerard Manley Hopkins* (1918).

72  John Dixon Hunt, *Genius Loci: An Essay on the Meanings of Place* (2023).

73  Proxemics is a term coined by anthropologist Edward T. Hall in 1963. See his books *The Hidden Dimension* (1966) and *Beyond Culture* (1976). The best book on relating proxemics to faith is Joseph R. Myers, *The Search to Belong: Rethinking Intimacy, Community, and Small Groups* (2003).

74  As quoted in "A Man in Full: Leonard Bernstein at 100," *The Economist*, 20 January 2018, 77.

75  Nicholas Berdyaev, *The Destiny of Man* (1935), 247.

76  1 Kings 19:11–13, KJV

77  Ocean Vuong, *Time is a Mother* (2022).

78  Review.org survey on USAmericans cell phone use.

79  For what I call SAD, see Johann Hari, *Stolen Focus: Why You Can't Pay Attention* (2021).

80  See the powerful jeremiad by David George Haskell entitled *Sounds Wild and Broken: Sonic Marvels, Evolution's Creativity and the Crisis of Sensory Extinction* (2023).

# NOTES

81 The quote is from a lecture published in a collection of his essays. The lecture is titled "The Difficulty of Loving," and it can be found on page 25 of *The Dehumanization of Art and Other Essays* (1925). He argues that love is not a feeling that simply happens to us, but rather something that we actively create through our attention. The exact quote is "Falling in love is a phenomenon of attention. It is not that we fall in love because we find the other person lovable; rather, we find the other person lovable because we fall in love with them."

82 See the Netflix documentary on Steinway pianos called "Note by Note: The Making of Steinway L1037" (2007) on Tubi.

83 The obituary writer for *The Economist*, Ann Wroe, is also one of the best artists of the craft of writing in the world today.

84 Ann Wroe, obituaries editor of *The Economist* since 2003, "Frank Mohr," obituary in *The Economist*, 07 May 2022, 82.

85 William Ralph Inge, *The Cynic's Lexicon* (1929), 99.

86 Todd Longstaffe-Gowan, *English Garden Eccentrics: Three Hundred Years of Extraordinary Groves, Burrowings, Mountains and Menageries* (2022).

87 Todd Longstaffe-Gowan, *English Garden Eccentrics: Three Hundred Years of Extraordinary Groves, Burrowings, Mountains and Menageries* (2022).

88 Or in its original German, *Die Pathologie der Normalität: Zur Wissenschaft vom Menschen* (1953). See also my *Jesus Drives Me Crazy* (2003).

89 This is from her 2018 book *Creation and the Cross: The Mercy of God for a Planet in Peril*.

90 St. John of Damascus. "Among those who are sanctified," states Clement of Alexandria (c. 150–215), "even the seed is holy." *The Stromata, or Miscellanies/Book IV*, 2:6. The Stromata (Greek: Στρώματα, "Patchwork", i.e., Miscellanies), attributed to Clement of Alexandria (d. 215) is the third of a trilogy of works regarding the Christian life. The oldest extant manuscripts date to the eleventh century.

91 John Polkinghorne, *The God of Hope and the End of the World* (2002), 113.

92 *The Tablet*, 21 March 2008.

93 Genesis 1:26

94 Philippians 2:7

95 Daniel O'Leary, "Wisdom of the Ages," *The Tablet*, 19 October 2009, 15.

96 See Leonard Sweet and Michael Beck's, *Contextual Intelligence* (2020).

97  See John Drysdale's *Stoics Without Pillows: A Way Forward for the Somalilands* (2000).

98  The spelling "Dao" rather than "Tao" comes from the current Pinyin system which is the official system for translating Chinese script into the Latin alphabet in China. In his classic and prescient, *The Abolition of Man* (1943), C. S. Lewis borrows this non-Christian word recognized by people of all backgrounds to name the universal nature of all things: Tao. Tao is the Living Law, the set of absolutes about all things that usher us through generations of becoming.

99  Matthew 2:1–12, ESV. With thanks to Judge Jesse Caldwell III for helping me see this.

100 Mark 8:34–37

101 Isaiah 30:21. See also Isaiah 35:1–2, 7, 8, 9–10, NIV

102 In the old Scottish song "Loch Lomond,"

"O ye'll tak' the high road, and I'll tak' the low road,
And I'll be in Scotland afore ye."

103 Genesis 46:4, ESV

104 Ronald Blythe, *The Circling Year: Perspectives from a Country Parish* (2001), 123.

105 From a sermon by Nicholas of Cusa, Epiphany, 1456

106 Luke 22:19–20, NIV

107 Luke 22:24, KJV

108 With thanks to Andrew Purves for help in developing this insight.

109 For more see Leonard Sweet, *From Tablet to Table: Where Community Is Found and Identity Is Formed* (2019).

110 Luke 14:12–13

111 Luke 14:13–14

112 Sean Sinek wrote a best-selling business book entitled *Leaders Eat Last* (2017) based on the US Marine Corps custom of having senior officers serve up meals to junior members of the unit.

113 Acts 2:46

114 Acts 2:42, NIV

115 Romans 12:1, NIV

# NOTES

116 See Markus Barth, *Rediscovering the Lord's Supper* (1988), 13–16.

117 Brennan Manning, *Abba's Child: The Cry of the Heart for Intimate Belonging* (1994), 102.

118 See interview in *The Futurist*, July–August 2008, 50.

119 For an opposing view, see Rutger Bregman's New York Times best-seller *HumanKind: A Hopeful History* (2021). The son of a Dutch Protestant minister, Bregman discredits humanity's badness. He doesn't believe "sin" is innate, but that people are naturally inclined to good and hard-wired for cooperation.

120 Throughout *The Spiritual Exercises of St. Ignatius of Loyola* (1522–1524), Ignatius defines the devil as "the enemy of human nature."

121 Romans 3:23, NIV

122 Isaiah 53:6–7, KJV

123 1 John 1:8, NIV

124 Romans 7:19. See Robert Mulholland, Jr., *The Deeper Journey: The Spirituality of Discovering Your True Self* (2006), 24.

125 In Hebrew sin is "*hata*" and in Greek sin is "*hamartia*."

126 So argues David Konstan in *The Origin of Sin: Greece and Rome, Early Judaism and Christianity* (2023).

127 For original sin as a "moral taint" see Calvin University's Gregory Mellema, *Sin* (2023), which nevertheless has excellent sections on "collective sin" and "collective guilt."

128 Matthew 9:13

129 Geoffrey Robertson, in his book *Bad People: And How to Be Rid of Them: A Plan B for Human Rights* (2021) calls some people "the train drivers to Auschwitz" and further defines them as "those who did not and do not face justice as frequently as they ought."

130 Lucretius (99–55 BC) in his poem *De Rerum Natura* (*On the Nature of Things*) (54 BC), Book 3, line 1090.

131 Genesis 3:5

132 Genesis 2:17, ESV

133 Deuteronomy 30:19, NIV

134 W. H. Auden, *For the Time Being* (1944), 116.

135 Eric Lewis Cartoon, ID: 52809, Published in *The New Yorker*

October 14, 2002, https://www.art.com/products/p15063286736-sa-i6845345/eric-lewis-i-m-afraid-you-have-humans-new-yorker-cartoon.htm. Accessed 18 August 2023

136   This is the major critique of socialism as a philosophy: Are humans ever good enough for socialism? Is any form of socialism ever good enough to make us better humans?

137   Dietrich Bonhoeffer, *Creation and Fall* (1933), "Conclusion," 142–52.

138   Michael Foley, "Is the Age of Individualism Coming to an End?" *Philosophy Now* (2017).

139   Jude Rogers, *The Sound of Being Human: How Music Shapes Our Lives* (2023).

140   Brian Eno in the UK *Observer* (2003) discussing the Iraq war.

141   Edith Stein: *Essential Writings*, ed. John Sullivan (2002).

142   In Jonathan Edwards' *Miscellany*, 293, he argues that beauty is not simply a matter of physical appearance, but is also a matter of spiritual and moral excellence. He writes that "the beauty of the soul is the beauty of God in the soul." As found in *The Yale Edition of the Works of Jonathan Edwards*, Volume 13 (1994), 383–384.

143   For imagination as a muscle that gets stronger and better the more exercise it gets, see Alfred Read, *The Imagination Muscle: Where Good Ideas Come From (And How to Have More of Them)* (2023). Read is the managing editor of Conde Nast Britain.

144   Ephesians 5:19

145   Hans Urs von Balthasar, *Truth is Symphonic* (1987), 15.

146   The quote is originally from the character of the Earl of Kent in Shakespeare's play *King Lear*, Act 1, Scene 4, when Kent is trying to teach Lear's daughter Goneril about the difference between flattery and truth. Wittgenstein considered using the quote as an epigraph for his book *Philosophical Investigations* (1953), and wrote to his friend Norman Malcolm (29 October 1948): "I was thinking of using as a motto for my book a quotation from King Lear: 'I'll teach you differences'. This is what I mean: I want to show that things which look the same are really different, and vice versa." See Norman Malcolm, *Ludwig Wittgenstein: A Memoir* (1958), 55.

147   I talk about kopi luwak coffee in Chapter 7 ("The Experiential Church") of *The Gospel According to Starbucks* (2007).

# NOTES

148 I borrow this phrase from Darlene Cohen, a priest at the San Francisco Zen Center.

149 Dietrich Bonhoeffer, *Life Together*, chapter 1 "Community," (1939; Eng. Publication 1954). Thx! to colleague Tim Valentino for finding this quote.

150 *Redemptor Hominis* para.10.

151 For one such attempt, see Alan Jacobs, *The Year of Our Lord 1943: Christian Humanism in an Age of Crisis* (2018), 50; and more recently, the atheist humanist agenda of Sarah Bakewell, *Humanly Possible* (2023).

152 For a humanism that was pro-religion in public life, see Jacques Maritain, *Integral Humanism* (1938).

153 For more on false endings, see Leonard Sweet and Len Wilson's, *Telos: The Hope of Heaven Today* (2022).

154 See Ronald Wright, *A Short History of Progress* (2005), 33.

155 One of the most famous of Gandhi's quotes, but unable to verify if it is truly his.

156 George Newlands, *Christ and Human Rights: The Transformative Engagement* (2017).

157 See Tom Holland's *Dominion: How the Christian Revolution Remade the World* (2019); Glen Scrivener, *The Air We Breathe: How We All Came to Believe in Freedom, Kindness, Progress, and Equality* (2022).

158 Stephan Zweig called humanist optimism a "beautiful error" in his 1942 book *The World of Yesterday* where he attributes the rise of fascism and Nazism in Europe to the failure of humanist optimism.

159 The Christian Criticism of Life (1941), 273.

160 Here is French Catholic philosopher Jacques Maritain (1882–1973) defining *True Humanism* (1938), xii: "Leaving all these points of discussion open, let us say that humanism (and such a definition can itself be developed along very divergent lines) essentially tends to render man more truly human and to make his original greatness manifest by causing him to participate in all that can enrich him in nature and in history … It at once demands that man make use of all the potentialities he holds within him, his creative powers and the life of reason, and labor to make the powers of the physical world the instruments of his freedom."

161 *The Complete Prose of T. S. Eliot: The Critical Edition, Volume 3: Literature, Politics, Belief, 1927–1929* (2021), 614–622.

162 David Halberstam, *The Coldest Winter: America and the Korean War* (2008), 355.

163 Héctor García and Francesc Miralles, *Ikigai: The Japanese Secret to a Long and Happy Life* (2017).

164 Colossians 3:11

165 Iain McGilchrist, *The Matter With Things: Our Brains, Our Delusions and the Unmaking of the World* (2021).

166 Romans 1:18–20

167 As quoted in *The Economist*, 31 July 2021, 69.

168 Paul Klee, *Creative Credo* (1920). You can also find this saying in his diaries, which were published posthumously in 1957, and in a number of essays and lectures that he gave throughout his career.

169 Mark Miodownik, *Stuff Matters: Exploring the Marvelous Materials That Shape Our Man-Made World* (2015).

170 As revealed by Stanley Bill in his marvelous study of Czeslaw Milosz's *Faith in the Flesh: Body, Belief, and Human Identity* (2022).

171 Pico Iyer argues that "Anime is the natural expression of a culture steeped in animism" in "Relative Values," *TLS: Times Literary Supplement*, 22 November 2019, 37.

172 Makoto Fujimura, *Art + Faith: A Theology of Making* (2021). See also the excellent review by Katie Kresser in her "Art + Faith: A Theology of Making—A Review" in *Christian Scholar's Review*, LI (Summer 2022), 377.

173 The quote is not found in her book *The Montessori Method* (1912), but it is the key tenet of Maria Montessori's educational philosophy. The exact quote attributed to her is "The hand is the instrument of the mind."

174 See Leonard Sweet and Len Wilson's, *Telos: The Hope of Heaven Today* (2022).

175 See Leviticus chapter 8, especially Leviticus 8:23–24.

176 As formulated by Taro Gold, *Living Wabi Sabi: The True Beauty of Your Life* (2004).

177 Hemingway's macho persona, of course, did not use the word "trash."

178 Leviticus 23 lists these seven feasts in order of their seasonal observance: Passover, Unleavened Bread, First Fruits, Pentecost, Trumpets, Day of Atonement, and Booths or Tabernacles.

# NOTES

179 With thanks to Dr. Tim Valentino for pointing this out to me.

180 I have been greatly influenced in my understanding of Sabbath by Paul D. Patton, Robert H. Woods, Jr., *Everyday Sabbath: How to Lead Your Dance with Media and Technology in Mindful and Sacred Ways* (2021) and A. J. Swoboda, *Subversive Sabbath: The Surprising Power of Rest in a Nonstop World* (2018); Dan Allender, *Sabbath: The Ancient Practices* (2010); and Judith Shulevitz, *The Sabbath World: Glimpses of a Different Order of Time* (2011).

181 Leviticus 25: 8–10, ESV

182 The first convert in heaven was a convict given the name of "Dismas" in the Gospel of Nicodemus, portions of which may be dated to the fourth century. The name "Dismas" was adapted from a Greek word meaning "sunset" or "death." The other thief's name is given as "Gestas."

183 Acts 10:34–43: "Healing all who are oppressed by the devil" in Peter's words.

184 Luke 10:9,11; cf. Matthew 10:7; Luke 9:2, 60, NIV

185 Evolution is least successful in combining the other feature with which God imbued creation: telos. For more see Leonard Sweet and Len Wilson's *Telos: The Hope of Heaven Now* (2022).

186 John 12:32

187 Gerald O'Collins, *Jesus: A Portrait* (2008), 153.

188 See the William Wordsworth poem, "*The Prelude Book XI*" (1850).

189 Irenaeus of Lyons, *Against Heresies*, 4.20.7; see also 3.20.2. The translation is taken from John Behr's *Irenaeus of Lyons: Identifying Christianity* (2015).

190 For example, Jeremiah 3, Ezekiel 16, Hosea 2.

191 For example, Deuteronomy 32:6; Isaiah 63:16; Jeremiah 3:19. God as Father is rare: only twenty times is God named (or addressed) as 'Father' in the whole of the Old Testament.

192 Except for Matthew 5:35, which echoes Psalm 47:10.

193 Gerald O'Collins, *Jesus: A Portrait* (2008), 28.

194 See his *In Matt.* 24:7; on Matthew 18:23).

195 *Adversus Haereses* 4.20.7, written in c.180.

196 As quoted by Timothy Radcliffe's, *Alive in God* (2019).

197 With thanks to Dr. Sachie Noguchi, Japanese Studies Librarian,

C. V. Starr East Asian Library, Columbia University, for helping me track down the original meaning of *juten*.

198 See the website www.juut.com which has salonspas in Minnesota, Arizona and California. David Wagner is the artist/entrepreneur/owner/founder of Juut Salonspa and the author of the best-selling *Life as a Daymaker: How to Change the World by Simply Making Someone's Day* (2001).

199 As devised by philosopher Thomas Donaldson. It must be noted that the very notion of "human rights" is a secularization of Christian concepts of dignity, charity, and being created in God's image. See Thomas Donaldson's classic *The Ethics of International Business* (1989).

200 Josef Pieper, *A Brief Reader on the Virtues of the Human Heart*, trans. Paul C. Duggat (1991), 37–38.

201 Rhidian Brook, *Godbothering: Thoughts, 2000–2020* (2020), 6.

202 As referenced in *TLS: Times Literary Supplement*, 03 March 2023, 6.

203 Psalm 91 and 23

204 1 Corinthians 9:26, ESV

205 Isaiah 51:16, NIV

206 Michael Nylan, *The Chinese Pleasure Book* (2018),

207 David Bentley Hart's remarks at "The Future of Christian Thinking," 27–30 April 2022 at St. Patrick's Pontifical University, Maynooth.

208 Mark 4:38

209 1 Peter 5:7

210 As found in "Afterthoughts: Our Debt to Pleasure," *TLS: Times Literary Supplement*, 14 January 2022, 27.

211 Nicholas Ostler, *Passwords to Paradise: How Languages Have Re-invented World Religions* (2016), 72–73.

212 David Bentley Hart, *The New Testament: A Translation* (2017).

213 Revelation 22:16, KJV

214 See also my *So Beautiful: Divine Design for Life and the Church* (2009).

215 MAAMA made 1.4 trillion in 2022, 7 percent higher than 2021. Technology firms are no longer a separate category, since MAAMA-verse includes pharmaceuticals, video streaming, phones, etc.

216 *Messages From the Superior State: Communicated by John Murray, Through John M. Spear* (1853).

# NOTES

217 For more on this see Edward Brooke-Hitching's, *The Madman's Library: The Strangest Books, Manuscripts and Other Literary Curiosities from History* (2020), 187ff. There is still a small cult of true believers that believe this Metal Messiah is still out there, in seclusion, until it reaches sufficient strength and stature to reveal itself in its true state: the second coming of Christ.

218 The fact that Apple appears at times as much a cult as a company with employees better described as devout disciples did not escape the eye of Jobs' biographer, Walter Isaacson: "The absolutism, the ecclesiastical bearing, the sense of his relationship with the sacred, really works." Walter Isaacson, *Steve Jobs* (2011).

219 This phrase "mirrorworld" was first popularized by Yale computer scientist David Gelerner.

220 As quoted in *TLS: Times Literary Supplement*, 08 March 2019, 25.

221 Alduous Huxley, *Brave New World* (1932). George Orwell of 1984 fame had a French teacher who happened to be Aldous Huxley.

222 As quoted by Kevin Kelly, "History Will Be a Verb," *Wired*, March 2019.

223 The essay where this appears is in *The Revolt of the Elites and the Betrayal of Democracy* (1995), 17.

224 Francis Fukuyama in *Identity: Contemporary identity Politics and the Struggle for Recognition* (2019).

225 This is not to gainsay the beneficial effects of AI technology. At Massachusetts General Hospital, AI experiments have demonstrated that electrical stimulation controlled by AI can normalize brain activities in persons with mental illness.

226 These remarks were made at Shaw's 1988 commencement address at Westminster Choir College of Rider University.

227 Louis I. Kahn, as quoted in George S. Heyer, *Signs of Our Times* (1980), 69.

228 Timothy Leary, *The Seven Tongues of God* (1962).

229 See http://www.nanodic.com/molecular/Contelligence.htm. Accessed 18 August 2023.

230 Isaiah 11:1, KJV

231 See Isaiah 4:2, 11:1; Zechariah 3:8, 6:12; Jeremiah 23:5

232 Exodus 25:31–40; cf. Genesis 2:9. G. J. Wenham, *Genesis 1–15 (Vol. 1)*, (1987), 62.

233 Cf. 1 Kings 6:18, 29, 32, 35; 7:18–20.

234 Aurelie A. Hagstrom, "The Symbol of the Mandorla in Christian Art: Recovery of a Feminine Archetype," *ARTS*, vol. 10, no. 2 (1998).

235 Presently there are only thirty-four Doctors of the Church, and only three besides Hildegard are women (Catherine of Siena, Teresa of Ávila, and Thérèse of Lisieux). Over eight centuries after her death, Hildegard was finally canonized in May, 2012.

236 *Alexis de Tocqueville, Democracy in America (1835–40)*, Book I, Chapter 11. The exact translation: "In democratic societies, each man is forever thrown back on himself alone, and there is danger that he may be shut up in the solitude of his own heart. There, he may nurse his melancholy fancies and brood over his sorrows; and if he be not careful, he may lose all taste for life and fear death less than nothingness."

237 J. R. Briggs, *The Sacred Overlap: Learning to Live Faithfully in the Space Between* (2020).

238 A couple of good books on paradox are Jen Pollock Michel, *Surprised by Paradox: The Promise of And in an Either-Or World* (2019) and Jason Moore's, *Both/And: Maximizing Hybrid Worship Experiences for In-Person and Online Engagement* (2023). For my explorations of paradox and a "surround-sound" or "double-ring" faith, see my *AquaChurch: Essential Leadership Arts for Piloting Your Church in Today's Fluid Culture* (1999); *Postmodern Pilgrims: First Century Journeys for the 21st Century* (2001); *Quantum Spirituality: A Postmodern Apologetic* (1991); *Soul Tsunami: Sink of Swim in New Millennium Culture* (1991). See also my "From Sharp to Fuzzy" chapter 7 in my book *Carpe Mañana: Is Your Church Ready to Seize Tomorrow?* (2001).

239 Elijah's saying is explored by Kristen H. Lindbeck in her *Elijah and the Rabbis: Story and Theology* (2010), 120.

240 *The Revolt of the Elites and the Betrayal of Democracy* (1940), 285–94.

241 Mark 9:38–41

242 Matthew 12:30

243 God is One and God is Three. Overemphasize one or the other and it's heresy. Modalism overemphasizes God's oneness and subordinationism overemphasizes God's three-ness.

244 Matthew 23:12, NASB

245 Matthew 7:15–20

# NOTES

246 Hebrews 11:22, ESV: "By faith, Joseph, at the end of his life, made mention of the exodus of the Israelites and gave directions concerning his bones."

247 Genesis 50:24–26

248 Exodus 13:19, KJV

249 Joshua 24:32, NIV. "And Joseph's bones, which the Israelites had brought up from Egypt, were buried at Shechem in the tract of land that Jacob bought for a hundred pieces of silver."

250 Alicia Britt Chole, *Anonymous* (2006), 172.

251 "Sinifying Shangri-La," *The Economist*, 08 October 2022, 45.

252 See William MacAskill's best-seller, *What We Owe the Future* (2022).

253 This is partly the critique of the political left, as seen in philosopher Emile P. Torres, who denounces "longtermism" as "quite possibly the most dangerous secular belief system in the world today." See his "Against Longtermism," *Aeon*, 19 October 2021.

254 One of the most gutsy, and gusty, public intellectuals and literary critics of our era was Harold Bloom. At 89, he was busy teaching at Yale on October 10 of this year (2023). He died 14 October 2023. He lived by the mantra taught by his hero from the first century, Rabbi Tarfon of the School of Schammai: "You do not need to complete the work, but neither are you free to desist from it."

255 The Rule of Three goes all the down to soil microbiology. The rhizosphere is the zone of interaction between plants, roots, and microbes. Scientists studying the rhizosphere have learned that they can't just take a soil microbe from the rhizosphere and study it. That soil microbe is embedded in a network of relationships where they all interact and they all need each other. Scientists need to study at least three species of bacterial phyla if they want to learn about the rhizosphere: it's called THOR (The Hitchhikers of the Rhizosphere):
   1) pseudomonas koreensis
   2) Flavobacterium johsoniac
   3) Bacillus cereus

You can't study organisms in isolation or even in pairs of microbes. The magic threshold of three is how we once turned willows into aspirin, poppies into morphine, and foxglove into digitalis.

256 Adam Gopnik, *The Table Comes First: Family, France, and the Meaning of Food* (2012), 188.

257 "You have to say, Please forgive me, again and again" is most likely a paraphrase of something that Ignatius of Loyola said about the exercise called "Examination of Conscience" in his *Spiritual Exercises* (1548).

258 The quote can be found in Valerie Steele's "The Culture of Japanese Fashion" (2005).

259 As quoted by Meghan O'Gieblyn, "Dear Cloud Support," in *Wired*, 30.10, 025.

260 Even though written in 1917, it was only in 1965 that 'Art as Device' was read in the West thanks to the English translation by Lee T. Lemon and Marion J. Reis. See Alexandra Berlina, "Make it Strange, Make it Stony: Viktor Shklovsky and the Horror Behind Ostranenie," *TLS: Times Literary Supplement*, 11 March 2016, 14–16. As Shklovsky writes in *Art as Device*, "This method of seeing things outside of their context led Tolstoy to the ostranenie of rites and dogmas in his late works, replacing the habitual religious terms with usual words—the result was strange monstrous."

261 In the words of Kerri NI Dochartaigh, *Thin Places* (2021).

262 See the special double issue of *Poetics Today* (2005–2006).

263 See his *Other People* (1981).

264 "Tell all the Truth but tell it slant" is poem number 1129 of 1775 in Emily Dickinson's *The Complete Poems of Emily Dickinson* (1955). "Tell all the Truth but tell it slant —/Success in Circuit lies/Too bright for our infirm Delight/The Truth's superb surprise." This poem wasn't published until after her death in 1886.

265 "The War Prayer" was first published in *Harper's Magazine*, November 1916.

266 Jonathan Smith, *Gulliver's Travels* (1726), Part IV, Chapter V.

267 "On Memory as a Key to the Phenomena of Heredity," *Working Men's College*, London, 02 December 1882.

268 Simon Critchley, *Bald: 35 Philosophical Short Cuts* (2021), 10.

269 Originally published in *Wishful Thinking: A Seeker's ABC* (1993) and later in *Beyond Words: Daily Readings in the ABC's of Faith* (2004).

270 David James Duncan wrote this in his 2004 book *My Story as Told by Water*. The quote appears in the chapter "The River Why."

271 8 October 1833, as quoted in Maurice York and Rick Spaulding, *Ralph Waldo Emerson: The Infinitude of the Private Man* (2008).

272 See Croisé Jacques' novel *Europe et Valerius* (1949).

# NOTES

273 Concentration camps did not evolve from the mass incarceration of Prisoners of War during the First World War, but from the mass incarcerations by the British of Boer women and children, as well as Black Africans, during the Second Boer War (1899–1902) in squalid camps that had a 20 percent death rate. For more see Elsabe Brits, *Rebel Englishwoman: The Remarkable Life of Emily Hobhouse* (2019).

274 Frederic Raphael, *Going Up: To Cambridge and Beyond—A Writer's Memoir* (2015), 220.

275 Of course, the competition with the Soviets propelled the US there.

276 2 Corinthians 10:3–5, ESV

277 This is not unique to the church. "The counterculture—the heavenly alternative to the conformist world of the establishment—could create as much discrimination and abuse as the society it was meant to replace" according to Peter Doggeett, *Growing Up: Sex in the Sixties* (2022).

278 For the ways in which our war language shapes our war thinking, see my *The Lion's Pride: America and the Peaceable Community* (1987).

279 See the political commentator Dan Carlin's military podcast on Hiroshima in "Hardcore History–59, (BLITZ) The Destroyer of Worlds". https://www.dancarlin.com/product/hardcore-history-59-the-destroyer-of-worlds/. Accessed 18 August 2023.

280 Richard Hays, *The Moral Vision of the New Testament: Community, Cross, New Creation, A Contemporary Introduction to New Testament Ethics* (1996), 105.

281 A favorite of Francis Schaefer in his apologetics for the Christian worldview.

282 But most likely a misattribution. No one has ever been able to find this quote in Gandhi's writings.

283 Christopher Blattman, *Why We Fight* (2022).

284 Augustine, *De Trinitate*, IX, 2.

285 The earliest known source of this quote is a nineteenth-century biography of St. Francis, where most likely the quote was simply made up by the biographer to reflect Francis' sentiments.

286 This is my favorite translation of Ephesians 2:10, JET. The NIV has it like this: "We are His poem, crafted in the heart of Christ Jesus, to live a vibrant expression of His purpose on the Earth, that will serve to establish His kingdom."

287 I want to thank Kitty Heidelbaugh for pointing me to this word.

288 Les Murray, "Poetry and Religion", in *Collected Poems* (1998), 267.

289 See Dominic Johnson's, *God is Watching: How the Fear of God Makes us Human* (2016).

290 Proverbs 9:10, KJV

291 Ecclesiastes 12:13

292 Revelation 20:12, NIV

293 Matthew 25

294 David Bentley Hart, *That All Shall Be Saved: Heaven, Hell, and Universal Salvation* (2021).

295 Romans 1:18–20, KJV

296 *The Sayings of the Desert Fathers*, trans. Benedicta Ward (1984), 204.

297 Nadya Tolokonnikova, *Read and Riot: A Pussy Riot Guide to Activism* (2019), 23.

298 "Blessed are the pure in heart, for they will see God" (Matthew 5:8, ESV).

299 Psalm 51:10, NIV

300 1 John 3:2, NIV

301 Paul Ricoeur introduces this idea in *The Symbolism of Evil* (1960) and expands upon it in *The Rule of Metaphor: Multi-disciplinary Studies of the Creation of Meaning in Language* (1975).

302 As quoted in Andrew Nugent, *The Slow-Release Miracle* (2006), 27.

303 Evagrius Ponticus said this in his treatise *Ad Monachos* ("To the Monks"), Chapter 10. Most likely *Ad Monachos* was written in the late fourth century AD, during Evagrius's time at the monastery of Nitria in Egypt and reflects his own experiences as a monk.

304 As quoted in his *Christian Century* staff obituary, "Richard Niebuhr, theologian and teacher, dies at age 90," *Christian Century*, 29 March 2017.

305 1 Corinthians 2:12, NIV

306 Exodus 33:17, NIV; Isaiah 49:16, ESV

307 Dom Paul Delatte (1848–1937), *From The Spirit of Solesmes*, ed. Mary David Totah (2016), 50.

308 Lockdowns may have reduced deaths, but perhaps not as much as they

# NOTES

induced immense stress and anxiety. The toll these lockdowns had on children, as well as mental and physical health, will take decades to reveal.

309 Eric Hoffer, *The Ordeal of Change* (1952).

310 2 Timothy 1:6–14

311 2 Peter 3:1

312 Hebrews 10:24

313 The power of the small, the knife's edge, is showcased in this one quote: "The slim Republican house majority is owed to 6670 votes out of 107m cast, according to 'Inside Elections,' a nonpartisan publication. Elections have become so unpredictable, and policymaking so volatile, because profound outcomes result from slight shifts: a change of less than 1% of votes would have switched control of the White House in 2016 and 2020, and of the Senate in 2020." *The Economist*, 07 January 2023, 20.

314 Iain MacKintosh, *Architecture, Actor & Audience* (1993), 159.

315 Named after Stanford University computer scientist Roy Amara.

316 See Michael Dine's, *This Way to the Universe: A Journey Into Physics* (2022).

317 These words were spoken at a Templeton Prize event in 2012, as reported in Dom Christopher Jamison OSB, *Finding the Language of Grace: Rediscovering Transcendence* (2022), 32.

318 Feynman first said this in the Messenger Lecture Series at Cornell University in 1964. He put the seven lectures together under the title The Character of Physical Law (1965), 129. The full quote appears in the lecture "Probability and Uncertainty—The Quantum Mechanical View of Nature" and is as follows: "I think I can safely say that nobody understands quantum mechanics. Do not take the next few remarks too seriously. I am not trying to convey the impression that I understand quantum mechanics; I don't."

319 Galatians 2:20, NIV

320 *The Economist*, 15 August 2020, 69.

321 Other ressourcement theologians include Henri de Lubac, Jean Daniélou, Yves Congar.

322 Matthew 13:52

323 See the masterful Alexandra Walsham's, *Generations: Age, Ancestry, and Memory in the English Reformation* (2023).

JESUS HUMAN

324 I steal this from the book title *That Was Now, This is Then* by Vijahj Seshadri (2021).

325 The process of using a kedging anchor was described in a Royal Navy seamanship manual from 1904. https://www.leevalley.com/en-ca/shop/tools/books-and-dvds/48555-manual-of-seamanship-forboys-and-seamen-of-the-royal-navy-1904?item=49L8078. Accessed 18 August 2023.

Kedging is described as a means for maneuvering large engineless ships in and out of tight harbors and tidal river entrances. "Strapping young lads would take to the longboats and row out one of the ship's smaller anchors in the direction they wanted to move the ship. They would then drop anchor when they ran out of cable, return to the ship and take up on the capstan to pull the ship up to the anchor, usually 600 feet or so at a time. It was a slow, hard process."

326 Hebrews 6:19ff. See my exegesis of this metaphor in *AquaChurch 2.0: Piloting Your Church in Today's Fluid Culture* (1999).

327 Sam Willetts, *New Light for the Old Dark* (2011), 10.

328 The two texts called the Doctrine of the Mean (chap. 20) and Mencius (7a:16) have been grouped together with the Analects plus the Great Learning to form the four Confucian classics.

329 Two great books on resilience are *The Resilience Factor: 7 Keys to Finding Your Inner Strength and Overcoming Life's Hurdles* by Karen Reivich and Andrew Shatte (2002) and *Rising Strong: How the Ability to Reset Transforms the Way We Live, Love, Parent, and Lead* (2015) by Brené Brown.

330 An excellent exploration of resilience in practice is Dustin Benac's *Adaptive Church: Collaboration and Community in a Changing World* (2022), which tells the story of what is possible when communities of faith partner with one another in places where they occupy marginal social positions. The book is based on extended fieldwork in the Pacific Northwest.

331 Sometimes those "new adaptations" are a return to older traditions. Joseph Ratzinger participated in Vatican II which set aside the Tridentine Mass. As a young priest and a theological expert, he attended Vatican II as an advisor to Cardinal Joseph Frings of Cologne, helped to shape the council's document on the liturgy, *Sacrosanctum Concilium* (1963), which turned priests around to face the people and to speak to them in the vernacular. He advocated the council's call for a greater openness to the world and a more dialogue-oriented approach to inter-faith relationships.

# NOTES

Four decades later, as Pope Benedict XVI, he initiated efforts to restore the old liturgy as an alternative to the more contemporary one, and to about-face the priests to face the altar.

332  Consilience was the term Harvard University biologist Edward O. Wilson used in 1998 to describe the "unity of knowledge," the quest to "to create a common groundwork of explanation" to explain the universe.

333  *Nassim Nicholas Taleb, Antifragile: Things That Gain from Disorder* (2012), 28. Here is the full quote: "Antifragility is beyond resilience or robustness. The resilient resists shocks and stays the same; the antifragile gets better, thrives, adapts, evolves, and grows when exposed to stressors, shocks, volatility, randomness, disorder, and chaos. Antifragility leverages disorder and volatility to extract value from them."

334  Ludwig Wittgenstein, *Philosophical Investigations*, trans. G. E. M. Anscombe (1958), 8e.

335  I learned this phrase from career coach Pamela Slim who encourages everyone to start a "side hustle" no matter what job you're in. See her *Escape from Cubicle Nation* (2010).

336  See Hermione Lee, *Virginia Woolf* (1999), where she writes: "There are two ways of reading a book, I think, which I call vertical and horizontal reading. Vertical reading is going down into the book, following the thread of the argument or the story, and seeing how it develops. Horizontal reading is moving across the book, from one idea to another, from one image to another, making connections and seeing patterns. Both kinds of reading are necessary, but I think horizontal reading is often neglected. It is the kind of reading that allows us to see the book as a whole, to appreciate its artistry and its complexity." See "The Waves" chapter, page 499.

337  Søren Kierkegard, *Either/Or: A Fragment of Life*, (1992), 233–34.

338  Marcel Proust, *In Search of Lost Time (written 1909–22)*, 204. Scott Moncrieff translation.

339  See Francis Spufford's defense of Christianity, *Unapologetic: Why, Despite Everything, Christianity Can Still Make Surprising Emotional Sense* (2012).

340  As quoted in Nick Cohen, *What's Left?* (2007), 261.

341  In the Jewish faith, the Halakhah is the legal side of Judaism. The Aggadah is the imaginative side of Judaism. The Kaskalah movement began the quest for a rational faith, while the Hasidim denied there was any such thing as a rational faith and gloried in religious ecstasy.

342 This is actually known as the "reducing valve" theory of consciousness proposed by Aldous Huxley, William James and Henri Bergson, among others.

343 As quoted in Frederick Christian Bauerschmidt, *The Love that Is God: An Invitation to Christian Faith* (2021), 115.

344 For my critique of seeing Christianity is as a "belief system" see my *Out of the Question . . . Into the Mystery: Getting Lost in the GodLife Relationship* (2004).

345 Song of Songs 4:9

346 Naomi Booth in her book called *Swoon: A Poetics of Passing Out* (2002) argues that in the courtly tradition, it was men by far who fainted.

347 For more on what Francis Fukuyama calls this "cognitive wasteland," which is found in both the Populist Right and the Critical Left, see *Political Order and Political Decay: From the Industrial Revolution to the Globalization of Democracy* (2014).

348 The late Joan Didion is sometimes quoted for saying something similar.

349 These words were spoken upon winning an award for his prison drama "Time" (2021) As quoted in *The Tablet*, 25 June 2022, 29.

350 For more see Leonard Sweet and Michael Beck's, *Contextual Intelligence* (2019).

351 Isaiah 61:1

352 See the extensive research of cognitive scientists and psychologists like George Lakoff, Mark Johnson, Eleanor Rosch, Elizabeth Bates, and other scholars in the field of psycho- and neuro-linguistics.

353 Narraphor is a conjunction of narrative + metaphor. For more on narraphoric preaching see my *Giving Blood: A Fresh Paradigm for Preaching* (2014).

354 Tita Chico, *The Experimental Imagination: Literary Knowledge and Science in the British Enlightenment* (2022).

355 Richard Feynman, *The Character of Physical Law* (1965), 127.

356 For the destructive power of storytelling, see Peter Brooks, *Seduced by Story: the Use and Abuse of Narrative* (2023).

357 *The Power of Ethics: How To Make Good Choices in a Complicated World* (2022).

358 Albert Einstein essay "The World As I See It" (1931) in Phillip Lopate,

# NOTES

ed., *the Glorious American Essay: One Hundred Essays From Colonial Times to the Present* (2020). https://history.aip.org/exhibits/einstein/essay.htm. Accessed 17 June 2023.

359 Dorothy L. Sayers, *The Greatest Drama Ever Staged* (1938), 125. The chapter is entitled "The Man Who Was Hanged."

360 This quote is the popularized translation that circulates online. The literal translation is "Bad times! Troublesome times! This men are saying. Let our lives be good; and the times are good. We make our times; such as we are, such are the times." Augustine, Sermon #30 on the New Testament, Section 8. Translated by R.G. MacMullen. *From Nicene and Post-Nicene Fathers, First Series*, Vol. 6. Edited by Philip Schaff. (1888.) Revised and edited for *New Advent* by Kevin Knight.

361 Deuteronomy 14:2; 26:18. The reference here is, I think, to 1 Peter 2.9, which I've been pondering for a month or so. The Greek word underneath the AV's "peculiar" is *peripoieo*. My mind immediately recognizes *poieo* ("to make or fashion" and sometimes "to do") as the core verb, with the preposition *peri* serving as some form of modifier (often intensifying the meaning of the word it modifies). *A Greek-English Lexicon*, compiled by Henry George Liddell and Robert Scott suggest *peripoieo* can be translated as "to cause to remain over and above, keep safe, preserve" and other translations, but I want to explore this further. I think there is "new human/true human" implications in this verb.

362 Have you seen that they are now debating whether or not to remove St. George as the country's "patron saint." For some Anglicans St. George is "offensive to Muslims" and "too militaristic." The suggested alternative is St. Alban, and the proposal is to replace St. George's cross on the Union Jack with St. Alban's cross, which would be diagonal thin yellow bands. Christopher Morgan, "St. Alban is Holier than St. George," *The Sunday Times*, 2 July 2006.

363 "Anything but Ordinary Lyrics–Avril Lavigne," http://www.elyrics.net/read/a/avril-lavigne-lyrics/anything-but-ordinary-lyrics.html. Accessed 18 August 2023.

364 O. F. Snelling, *Rare Books and Rarer People: Some Personal Reminiscences of "The Trade"* (1982).

365 One of Martin Luther's favorite Latin phrases and highest compliments was "*rara avis*" or "rare bird." See for example "O what a rare bird will a lord and ruler be in heaven," in Luther's "An Open Letter to the Christian Nobility of the German Nation Concerning the Reform of the Christian Estate," in *Works of Martin Luther* (1930), 2: 163, and "You must know

that from the beginning of the world a wise prince is a rare bird indeed," in "Secular Authority: To What Extent It Should Be Obeyed," in *Works of Martin Luther*, 3: 258.

366 At least they had them with them when they left the Last Supper. See David L. Edwards', *Yes: A Positive Faith* (2006), 60, 88.

367 Note how each wave is a one-of-a-kind original embodiment of and expression of the ocean.

368 Andrew Nugent, *The Slow-Release Miracle: A Spirituality for a Lifetime* (2006), 56.

369 Fyodor Dostoevsky, The Brothers Karamazov, trans. David Magarshack (1958), 1:339.

370 Genesis 2:23

371 Matthew 25:40

372 Isaiah 2:4

373 King's actual words were, "With this faith we will be able to hew out of the mountain of despair a stone of hope." Martin Luther King Jr., "I Have a Dream" [delivered at the March on Washington for Jobs & Freedom, 28 August 1963,] in his *I Have a Dream: Writings and Speeches that Changed the World* (1992), 105.

374 *Sententia Super Metaphysician*, XII, 9. 2566 (Marietti's Latin edition [Turin, 1934], 1071), 599.

375 Eduardo Galeano, *The Book of Embraces: Images and Text*, trans. Cedric Belfrage and Mark Schafer (1991), 121.

376 See Laura Rendón's *Sentipensante (Sensing/Thinking) Pedagogy: Educating for Wholeness, Social Justice and Liberation* (2009).

377 Or in the words of Jesus, "The good person out of the good treasure of the heart produces good, and the evil person out of evil treasure produces evil; for it is out of the abundance of the heart that the mouth speaks" (Luke 6:45, NRSV). And again, "For it is from within, from the human heart, that evil intentions come" (Mark 7:21, NRSV).

378 Henri Nouwen, *The Inner Voice of Love: A Journey through Anguish to Freedom* (1996), 109–10.

379 For our ability to achieve high-order intentionality, as far as "fifth-order intentionality," see Robin Dunbar's, *The Human Story: A New History of Mankind's Evolution* (2005), 75–76, 191–92.

380 I first encountered this definition of Christianity as an anti-religion in a

book by Aiden Mathews: "Christianity is not primarily a religion of the Book, as Islam and the evangelical fundamentalists understand it, or even of the Jewish Law . . . Strictly speaking, it isn't a religion at all insofar as it tends to identity all official cult as mere cultural product. In many crucial and excruciating ways, it is an anti-religion, a critique of all the human forms of faith from a prophetic perspective which recognizes that religions generally decay into religiosity, that icons deteriorate into idols, and that aesthetic ritual degenerates into ritual anaesthesia. It urges agile vigilance against all human gods, especially the gods of reputation and status." *Fasting and Feasting: Radio Reflections on Christmas and Easter* (2016), 57.

381 At least in John 19:30. See also Matthew 27:46 and 50 KJV

382 *The Spiritual Life* (1962), 158. The quote appears in the chapter titled "Love and Justice." The full quote is worth the citation: "Love for one fellow human being always includes love for OTHER human beings and, in the last analysis, love for ALL human beings. Love is a universal principle and cannot be limited to one person or group of people. If I truly love one person, I must also love all people, because all people are interconnected and we are all part of the same human family. If I do not love all people, then my love for one person is not true love. It is only a selfish love, a love that is based on my own needs and desires. True love is always selfless, and it always seeks the good of the other person."

383 "And hast thy head erected to heaven, . . . that yet only thy heart of all others, points downwards . . . ." John Donne, *Essays in Divinity*, ed. Evelyn M. Simpson (1952), 30.

384 "This fact alone ought to be proof of God," writes PBS correspondent/poet Judy Valente, "The Mystic Eye," in Judy Valente and Charles Reynard, *Twenty Poems to Nourish Your Soul* (2006), 178.

385 Gregory of Nyssa, Homily Five, 119 (158, 17–19). Gregory writes this in Homily Five of *Homilies on the Song of Songs, as* translated with an Introduction and Notes by Richard A. Norris Jr, *Society of Biblical Literature*, Number 13 (2012).

386 See the work of my doctoral student, Dwight J. Friesen, in his works *Thy Kingdom Connected: What the Church Can Learn from Facebook, the Internet, and Other Networks* (2009); and see his contribution to Brian A. Ross, ed., *Signs of the Times: Pastoral Translations of Ministry & Culture in Honor of Leonard I. Sweet* (2016).

387 Teilhard de Chardin, *The Phenomenon of Man* (1955) or *The Divine Milieu* (1957).

## JESUS HUMAN

388 My translation of Romans 8:28.

389 Psalm 34:14, ESV

390 Geoffrey Hill said this in an interview with the *Paris Review* in 2000. The interview was published in the magazine's winter issue that year. Here is a link to the Paris Review interview with Geoffrey Hill: https://www.theparisreview.org/interviews/730/the-art-of-poetry-no-80-geoffrey-hill. Accessed 18 August 2023.

391 See Matthew 14:14–21; Mark 1:41; Mark 6:34–42; Luke 7:13; Matthew 15:32; Mark 8:2; John 6:5–13.

392 Exodus 34:6, NIV

393 Luke 17:11–19

394 Isaiah 33:5, NIV

395 The easiest tree to graft is an almond tree.

396 For a similar thesis, check out Stuart Murray's *Representing Autism: Culture, Narrative, Fascination* (2008). Murray's youngest son was diagnosed with "classical autism" in 2002. Also see the work an Amanda Baggs, who created a YouTube video entitled "In My Language" that looks at the world through her eyes.

397 Tony Jones, "A Conversation with Jurgen Moltmann," *Spectrum Magazine* 43, (September/October 2009), 24–31.

398 Pope Francis, General Audience, 13 April 2013, as quoted in "The Living Spirit," *The Tablet*, 13 May 2023, 15.

399 Wendell Berry, "Preserving Wildness" in *Home Economics* (1987), 139.

400 For more see Suzanne Simard's, *Finding the Mother Tree: Discovering the Wisdom of the Forest* (2021).

401 Paul Cheshire, *William Gilbert and Esoteric Romanticism* (2018), as referenced by Michael Caines in his review of the book in *TLS: Times Literary Supplement*, 07 December 2018, 14.

402 After Michael Rosen spent forty-seven days in intensive care and six weeks on a ventilator in an induced coma in a hospital in London, he wrote these words:

I didn't cancel death.
It just didn't happen right then.
And it is what we all do.
Life is postponing death.

# NOTES

See his *Many Different Kinds of Love: A Story of Life, Death, and the NHS* (2021).

403  Philippians 4:7

404  Sermon preached at Trinity College Chapel, Cambridge, 23 October 1983, as cited in Michael Mayne, *The Enduring Melody* (2006), 87.

405  Thanks to Robert C. Shannon for this metaphor.

406  Philippians 1:21

407  Wolfgang Vondey, *People of Bread: Rediscovering Ecclesiology* (2008).

408  With thanks to Mark Morrow for pointing me to this passage.

409  Acts 20:11–12

410  Matthew 26:26–30; Mark 14:22–26; Luke 22:17–20

411  Horowitz leaves the question unanswered as to whether Jewish faith is centered in sacred texts, or kashrus practices. Roger Horowitz, *Kosher USA: How Coke Became Kosher and Other Tales of Modern Food* (2016).

412  See Bretherton's chapter 10 called "Mundane Holiness: The Theology and Spirituality of Everyday Life" in the collection of essays, *Remembering Our Future*, but the quotes are from 234, 236–37, 246–47.

413  David Brooks, *The Second Mountain* (2019), 61.

414  France's obesity rate is well below that in USAmerica (40 percent), Mexico (33 percent) and Britain (26 percent). But it is now on the rise. See "Obesity in France," *The Economist*, 28 January 2023, 49.

415  This is found in her 1896 collection of food columns entitled "A Guide for the Greedy by a Greedy Woman," and quoted by University of Bonn medieval literature professor Irina Dumitrescu in "The Need For Greed," *TLS: Times Literary Supplement*, 02 December 2022, 35.

416  Exodus 15:26

417  Hugh of St. Victor, *De Sacramentis: On the Sacraments of the Christian Faith* (1134) as published in *On the Sacraments of the Christian Faith* (2016), 142.

418  See my *Health and Medicine in the Evangelical Tradition* (1994).

419  Matthew 9:20–22

420  Luke 8:43–48, NIV

421 See the Arthur C. Clarke's short story "Security Check" (1957), first published in the June 1957 issue of *The Magazine of Fantasy and Science Fiction*. It has since been reprinted in a number of collections, including the *The Collected Stories of Arthur C. Clarke* (2001).

422 Didascalicon, Book 1, Chapter 10. *The Didascalicon of Hugh of Saint Victor: A Guide to the Arts*, Jerome Taylor translation (1991), 42.

423 "Jesus Saves" by Priscilla J. Owens, public domain

424 *The Shattering of Loneliness* (2018). Dom Erik Varden is Abbot of Mount Saint Bernard Abbey in Leicestershire. Before entering religious life, he was a Fellow of St. John's College, Cambridge.

425 Luke 4:18–19

426 See Mark 10:50; John 5:6, CEB

427 There are forty-one references to healing in the four gospels.

428 American art historian Thomas F. Matthew, *The Clash of Gods: A Reinterpretation of Early Christian Art* (rev. and expanded edition; 1999), 92.

429 The story is found in all four Gospels. Though Malchus is specifically named only in John 18:10–11, he is also found in Mark 14:45–49, Matthew 26:50–54, and in Luke 22:49–53 as the "servant of the high priest."

430 John 18:13–14

431 Matthew 26:1–4; 14–16; 47–49

432 Wesley, Charles. "O for a Thousand Tongues," 1739. https://hymnary.org/text/o_for_a_thousand_tongues_to_sing_my. Accessed 18 August 2023.

433 Matthew 25:33–46

434 In the UK, the College of Policing has issued national guidelines that allow priests to access crime scenes to administer spiritual healing and last rites.

435 Ira Byock, *The Best Care Possible: A Physician's Quest to Transform Care Through the End of Life* (2013), 254–255.

436 Robert Pogue Harrison says this on the first page of his *The Dominion of the Dead* (2003), 1. Here is the full quote: "To be human means, above all, to bury. This is not simply a statement of fact, but a recognition of the fundamental role that burial plays in human culture. Burial is not just a way of disposing of the dead; it is also a way of acknowledging our mortality and creating a space for the dead to continue to be part of our

# NOTES

lives. In burying the dead, we are not simply saying goodbye; we are also saying hello to the future. Burial is a way of creating a bridge between the living and the dead, and it is through this bridge that we are able to pass on our stories and our traditions to future generations."

437 One cannot technically cite this as a direct quote because there is no verifiable primary source or recorded documentation of him saying those specific words, only oral recollections and references.

438 George Bernard Shaw, *The Devil's Disciple: A Melodrama by Bernard Shaw* (1900; play first produced in London in 1897), Act II, quote on p. 82.

439 Carlos Fuentes, *This I Believe: An A to Z of a Life* (2005), 70.

440 "Insight: Perspective on the World" Interview with Elie Wiesel in *The Arizona Republic*, 26 October 1986, Page C6, Column 1.

441 It's nice to know that, no matter what the mission, God always gives us something sweet.

442 The Bedouin dined on the "delicacies" of hedgehogs, lizards, and locusts.

443 This lone sentence is the entire content of chapter 19, "Orville Wright," in Gordon MacKenzie, *Orbiting the Giant Hairball: A Corporate Fool's Guide to Surviving with Grace* (1996), 191.

444 Paul Murray, *The New Wine of Dominican Spirituality* (2006), 170. Murray quotes Aquinas: "The vice opposed to drunkenness is unnamed; and yet if a man were knowingly to abstain from wine to the extent of molesting nature grievously, he would not be free from sin." *The Summa Theologica of St. Thomas Aquinas*, literally trans. by the Fathers of the English Dominican Province (1932), 13:92.

445 Ronald A. Knox, *Enthusiasm: A Chapter in the History of Religion with Special Reference to the XVII and XVIII Centuries* (1962), 591.

446 Ronald A. Knox, *Enthusiasm: A Chapter in the History of Religion with Special Reference to the XVII and XVIII Centuries* (1962), 591.

447 Claude Atcho, *Reading Black Books* (2022), chapter 7.

448 Matthew 11:29, NIV

449 Dallas Willard, *The Divine Conspiracy: Rediscovering Our Hidden Life in God* (1998).

450 John Scotus Eriugena, *Periphyseon* (867), 184.

451 Genesis 3:11, NIV

452 See Leonard Sweet and Michael Beck's, *Contextual Intelligence* (2019).

## JESUS HUMAN

453  Hebrews 12:1b

454  Psalm 16:8

455  Philippians 3:14, ESV

456  With thanks to friend Tom Bolton for these quotes.

457  Commenting on 2 Corinthians 2:15–17 in Zoom chat.

458  Floor Speeches, August 26, 1996: Christopher Reeve Speaks at the Democratic National Convention, http://www.pbs.org/newshour/convention96/floor_speeches/reeve.html (Accessed 11 January 2018).

459  Carl G. Jung, *Collected Works of C.G. Jung, Volume 6: Psychological Types* (1923), 518–19.

460  Ashley Ward, *Sensational: A New Story of Our Senses* (2023).

461  Anne Lamott calls intuition our "broccoli." See her *Bird by Bird: Some Instructions on Writing and Life* (1995), 110.

462  Luke 13:29; Matthew 8:5-13, DAR.

463  Personal conversation.

464  For more on Christian timekeeping, see Simon Goldhill, *The Christian Invention of Time: Temporality and the Literature of Late Antiquity* (2023).

465  Exodus 15:21, KJV.

466  Quoted in Fred R. Anderson, "Three New Voices: Singing God's Song," *Theology Today*, XLVII (October 1990), 261.

467  "The Miracle of Writing," *The Economist*, 02 July 2022, 79.

468  2 Timothy 3:15, NIV.

469  W. B. Stanford, *Enemies of Poetry* (1980), in a note to chapter six. Also see Plutarch, "On the Fortune of Alexander," 304a.

470  For Augustine see Christopher Jamison OSB, *Finding the Language of Grace: Rediscovering Transcendence* (2022), 97.

471  For more on vibration becoming vision, see my *Summoned to Lead* (2004).

472  Lenn E. Goodman and Richard McGregor, editors and translators of the 10th century classic of medieval Islamic learning called *Epistles of the Brethren of Purity: The Case of the Animals Versus Man Before the King of the Jinn: An English Translation of Epistle 22* (2012).

473  With thanks to Teri Hyrkas for this.

# NOTES

474 Luke 1:34, NKJV.

475 From verse 3 of the hymn "Praise to the Lord, the Almighty, the King of Creation."

476 See my *We and Me: God's New Social Gospel* (2014).

477 Hebrews 12:1, ESV

478 Oliver Clement, *On Human Being: A Spiritual Anthropology* (2000), 44.

479 Masaru Emoto, *The Miracle of Water* (2007), ix.

480 Masaru Emoto, *The Miracle of Water* (2007).

481 John 17:21

482 For more on this see my *Mother Tongue: How Our Heritage Shapes our Story* (2017).

483 2 Timothy 2:14–15, ESV

484 For "the dance of the MRI God's 'Go,' God's 'Yes,' and God's 'No'," see my *So Beautiful* (2009), 50.

485 Soren Kierkegaard, *The Concept of Anxiety* (1844) as reproduced in *The Concept of Anxiety*, trans. Reidar Thomte (1980), 42.

486 All outdoor uses of three main neonicotinoids are banned in Europe, but they are still widely used as treatments for pets. "The dose recommended for a medium-sized dog each month is enough to kill sixty million honeybees." See Dave Goulson, *Silent Earth: Averting the Insect Apocalypse* (2022).

487 Seirian Sumne, *Endless Forms: The Secret World of Wasps* (2022).

488 1 Corinthians 15:45; 47–49, NIV

489 This quote is from Will Bulsiewicz in "Fiber Fueled" (2020), 2–3.

490 Dan Saladino, *Eating to Extinction: The World's Rarest Foods and Why We Need to Save Them* (2022).

491 1 Corinthians 8:1b, ESV

492 John 2:24

493 John 1:48

494 John 4:30

495 Caryll Houselander, *The Passion of the Infant Christ* (1949).

496 Matthew 11:29, NIV

497 "This is My Father's World" by Maltbie D. Babcock (1901), public domain

498 As quoted in *TLS: Times Literary Supplement*, 25 January 1985, 93.

499 Donald Rumsfeld coined the phrase "known unknowns" during a 12 February 2002, news conference as he was responding to a question about the intelligence community's assessment of Iraq's weapons of mass destruction (WMD) program.

500 United States v. Jewell, 532 F.2d 697 (9th Cir. 1976).

501 1 Corinthians 2:2, NIV

502 Philippians 3:13–14

503 John Steinbeck, *East of Eden* (1952), 448.

504 Deuteronomy 29:29

505 Jeremiah 33:3. Or in the NLT translation: "Ask me and I will tell you remarkable secrets you do not know about things to come."

506 Luke 8:17

507 John 15:5, ESV

508 Mark 13:11, ESV

509 With thanks to Facebook friend Tom Bolton.

510 See Stephen B. Bevans' classic study *Models of Contextual Theology* (1992). He makes this declaration in his opening chapter.

511 1 Corinthians 14:10–11, ESV

512 This is a playful allusion to Paul in prison writing "I have learned in whatsoever state I am, therewith to be content" (Philippians 4:11, KJV).

513 C. S. Lewis, *The Screwtape Letters* (1942).

514 Lewis wrote a new preface for the 1961 paperback edition in which he addressed some of the questions which had been raised by readers where he offered this definition of hell. C. S. Lewis, *The Screwtape Letters* (1980), vii–viii.

## CONCLUSION

1  G. K. Chesterton, *Orthodoxy* (1908; Penguin edition, ed. D. J. Conroy, 2009), 168.

2  Paul Evdokimov, *Woman and the Salvation of the World: A Christian Anthropology on the Charisms of Women* (1994).

# NOTES

3 As told in *Global Values 101: A Short Course*, ed. Kate Holbrook, Ann S. Kim, Brian Palmer, and Anna Portnoy (2006), 186–87.

**INTERACTIVES**

1 As quoted in Michael Mayne's, *This Sunrise of Wonder: Letters from the Journey* (1995), 87.

2 sisu–finnish. http://www.bbc.com/capital/story/20180502-sisu-the-finnish-art-of-inner-strength . Accessed 18 August 2023.

3 For more see Ann C. Holm, "Meditation and the Christmas Tree Brain," blog dated 10 December 2011. https://www.annholm.net/2011/12/meditation-and-the-christmas-tree-brain/. Accessed 17 June 2023.

4 Mark Chironna, Twitter, 13 April 2023. https://twitter.com/markchironna/status/1646599690035646470. Accessed 18 August 2023.

5 Founder of Focolare movement Chiara Lubich (1920–2008), *Essential Writings* (2007).

6 Augustine of Hippo, *Confessions of St. Augustine* (397–400) X, xxvii, 38.

7 Rory Steward, "Take Off The Mask: Why Habits of Truth are Vital for Governing," *TLS: Times Literary Supplement*, 20 August 2021, 8–9, 9.

8 Rupert Shortt, *The Hardest Problem: God, Evil and Suffering* (2023). Stephen Hawking calls humans "no more than chemical scum hurtling through the void on a piece of rock" in his 2010 book *The Grand Design* on page 143.

9 C. H. Spurgeon warned against "ministerialism" in his "The Preacher's Private Prayer" in the book *The Metropolitan Tabernacle Pulpit* (1861), 19.

10 Henri de Lubac, *The Drama of Atheist Humanism*, from the chapter titled "The Christian and the Present Age" (1944; English translation 1963), 112.

11 "Skin in the game" is my friend Jarrod Hunt's favorite image for incarnation.

12 Richard Mouw, "The Challenge of Convicted Civility," *Christian Century* (2017), 28. Mouw first introduced the concept in *Uncommon Decency: Christian Civility in an Uncivil World* (1992). See also https://www.faithward.org/richard-mouw-on-disagreeing-with-convicted-civility/. Accessed 18 August 2023.

13 Kate Hennessy, *Dorothy Day: The World Will be Saved by Beauty—An*

*Intimate Portrait of My Grandmother* (2023). For the quote see Kate Hennessy, "Fail Gloriously," *The Tablet*, 08 July 2023, 12.

14  https://soundcloud.com/bloomsbury-1/ruth-moriarty. Accessed 18 August 2023.

15  His is parents came from Kenya, his paternal grandfather from Pakistan, he is Indian.

16  The publication in 29 November 2022 of the British census from the Office for National Statistics revealed that, for the first time in history, less than half the population of England and Wales consider themselves Christian. The number who clicked the "no religion" box soared by 57 percent. The number of Muslims rose by 42 percent. For more, see "Few on Pews," *The Economist*, 03 December 2022, 51.

17  Within a few decades, if present trends continue. Sixty-three percent of USAmericans identify themselves as Christians as of 2022. For the steep decline in Christianity, see the Pew Study: https://www.npr.org/2022/09/17/1123508069/religion-christianity-muslim-atheist-agnostic-church-lds-pew. Accessed 18 August 2023.

18  NRSV reads: "He said, 'Do not fear, greatly beloved, you are safe. Be strong and courageous!' When he spoke to me, I was strengthened and said, 'Let my lord speak, for you have strengthened me.'"

19  With thanks to Dr. Jim Allen for helping me see the accurate translation of this passage.

www.ingramcontent.com/pod-product-compliance
Lightning Source LLC
Chambersburg PA
CBHW072142070526
44585CB00015B/983